Gender, Sexuality and Mothering in Africa

GENDER, SEXUALITY 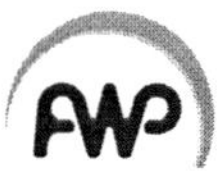 AND MOTHERING IN AFRICA

Edited by

Toyin Falola

and

Bessie House-Soremekun

AFRICA WORLD PRESS

Trenton | London | Cape Town | Nairobi | Addis Ababa | Asmara | Ibadan | New Delhi

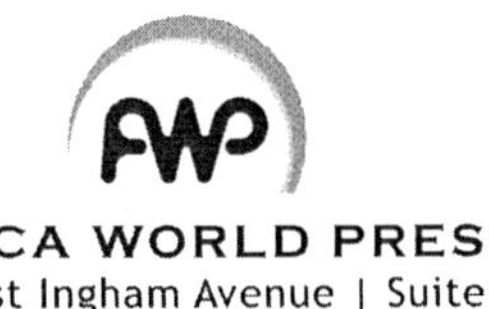

AFRICA WORLD PRESS
541 West Ingham Avenue | Suite B
Trenton, New Jersey 08638

Book and cover design: Saverance Publishing Services

Library of Congress Cataloging-in-Publication Data

Gender, sexuality and mothering in Africa / edited by Toyin Falola and Bessie House-Soremekun.
    p. cm.
  Includes bibliographical references and index.
  ISBN 1-59221-861-X (hbk.) -- ISBN 1-59221-862-8 (pbk.) 1. Women--Africa--Social conditions. 2. Sex role--Africa. 3. Motherhood--Africa. I. Falola, Toyin. II. House-Soremekun, Bessie, 1956-
  HQ1787.G445 2011
  306.874'30967--dc23
                          2011018917

This book is dedicated to our extraordinary mothers,
Mrs. Jo Frances House
and the late Mrs. Nihinlola Grace Falola.

Thanks for your tremendous love and encouragement
through the years. We are grateful.

_______________________________TABLE OF CONTENTS

List of Tables and Figures

Toyin Falola and Bessie House-Soremekun

Serious studies of gender as an analytical and social construct in African societies have steadily increased over the past few decades as more Africanist feminist scholars in particular have produced important analyses to illuminate more clearly the multifarious roles and status of African women across cultures. These studies have confirmed that women were important actors in the social, cultural, political, and economic realms of their respective societies. Social constructivist theorists also formulated arguments which emphasized that gender roles are not biologically or physiologically determined, but are rather the result of numerous complex social inventions which are outgrowths of cultural values, norms, and traditions in which activities deemed to be socially appropriate for women have been gendered "female" while those appropriate for men have been gendered "male." As Judith Lorber has so eloquently articulated,

> As a social institution, gender is a process of creating distinguishable social statuses for the assignment of rights and responsibilities. As part of a stratification system that ranks these statuses unequally, gender is a major building block in the social structures built on these unequal statuses. As a process, gender creates the social differences that define "woman" and "man".... As a social institution, gender is one of the major ways that human beings organize their lives...Gender and sex are not equivalent, and gender as a social construction does not flow automatically from genitalia and reproductive organs, the main

> physiological differences of females and males… Social
> statuses are carefully constructed through prescribed pro-
> cesses of teaching, learning, emulation, and enforcement.[1]

Several noteworthy studies have focused critical attention on the issues of gender and sexuality in African societies in recent years. For example, In *Re-thinking Sexualities in Africa*, edited by Signe Arnfred, the main focus of the book was to reconceptualize gender identities and sexuality in Africa with the end goal of determining to what extent African women have attained agency in their everyday lives with regard to both the attenuation and strengthening of patriarchy on one hand, versus the instances in which women have been able to effectively challenge it, on the other hand. The contributors also openly discuss issues centering on male and female sexual desire, a topic that has long been considered to be taboo in some African societies. The contribu-tors to the volume challenge many stereotypes about African sexuality, especially with regard to the controversial issue of whether same-sex relationships existed. According to Arnfred, conventional wisdom on this topic tended to support the idea that same-sex relationships were somehow "imposed on Africa from the outside." Some scholars and political leaders even espoused the view that terms such as "les-bianism and homosexuality" were non-existent in the various African languages. Arnfred presents compelling data which demonstrates that African men and women expressed their sexuality in various ways and in "remarkable quantity."[2] Moreover, while some of the same-sex rela-tionships were established at particular periods of time in the life cycles of the participants, in other instances, these relationships occurred at the same time that the individuals were simultaneously involved in heterosexual activities. Arnfred also confirmed that 'thigh'-sex existed in some African cultures and that it occurred between men and boys as well as between boys and girls. Also, female same-sex relationships existed in which females would also have female lovers that sometimes "had the status of a family friend."[3] She points out, however, that sexual activities that were primarily for pleasure were distinct from those that occurred in order to fulfill the need for biological reproduction. The volume provides convincing data that unearths various complex dimensions and modalities in which African sexuality was expressed in African societies across time and space.

In "Changing Gender Roles and Male Disempowerment in Rural and Urban East Africa, " Margrethe Silbeerschmidt situates her analysis within the broader umbrella of numerous challenges taking place with regard to the sexuality and sexual practices exhibited by men and women in African societies as a result of the Aids epidemic. According to Silberschmidt, "With deteriorating sexual and reproductive health, particularly in Sub-Saharan Africa, and more women than men now being HIV infected (often by their own husband), male involvement, men as responsible partners, and not the least male sexuality and sexual behavior have become increasingly unavoidable issues on the sexual and reproductive health agenda."[4] Because of these realities and numerous socio-economic shifts that have taken place during the 20th century, it has become imperative that scholars reconceptualize issues of sexuality with regard to African men and women. The main argument of her paper is that socio-economic changes have affected African men more deeply than the women. She believes that because of a number of factors which include changes in traditional structures, as well as constantly evolving social roles and values systems, lifestyles and identifies of men have been challenged while those of the women have been enhanced. According to Silberschmidt, one of the major reasons for men's diminishing status is the loss of income-generating opportunities they have experienced which has forced them to occupy a subordinate economic position in comparison to some of the women. Data from the research found that a strong relationship exists between masculinity and sexuality and men's ability to be the major breadwinners in their respective family units.[5]

Two important books that focus on the topic of mothering are *Breast Feeding and Sexuality: Behavior, Beliefs and Taboos among the Gogo Mothers in Tanzania* and *The Politics of (M)othering: Womanhood, Identity,* and *Resistance in African Literature.* In the first of these, *Breast Feeding and Sexuality,* Mara Mabilia presents the findings of her anthropological research that was performed to examine how elements of culture and social organization affect the methods used to feed infants in Dodoma which is located in Tanzania. Mabilia argues that international organizations through the implementation of their various public health initiatives in Africa tend to define women "always and only as mothers."This has important implications on women's behavior because little attention is given by international health care givers to the multitude of social, cultural, and even economic factors which may diminish the overall benefits of breastfeeding, most particularly in countries in which very high infant mortality rates already exist and breast milk is given to infants for significant periods of time. Mabilia stresses the need for the development of a more nuanced analysis of the health needs of African women who because of high fertility rates, often move through various pregnancies while simultaneously occupying various roles in the society which range from collecting water, getting the firewood, taking care and nurturing their children and families, as well as dealing with issues of poverty and violence which exert a tremendous impact on women who are sometimes dealing with malnutrition.[6]

In *The Politics of (M)othering: Womanhood, Identity, and Resistance in African Literature*, edited by Obioma Nnaemeka, conscious efforts were made to examine the role and place of gender in African literature, most particularly literature written by African female writers, by explicating how issues such as sisterhood, victimhood, agency, and others, are often reformulated and rearticulated so that important discourses can take place centering on African women's roles in their respective societies. While challenging the juxtaposition and placement of African women into various binary oppositional categories through the years such as powerful/powerless, and passive/active, they argue that these categories are not mutually exclusive of each other and that in some instances, victims are also agents who can change their lives and affect others in radical ways.[7] Some of the chapters in the volume force us to reexamine the important relationship between "women's politics" and "nationalist politics." According to Nnaemeka, "....the truth of the matter is that most of the time (on the African continent, for example), nationalist politics depoliticizes women's politics, forcing the repoliticization of women's politics back on the national agenda only as an aftermath of nationalist struggles."[8]

One of the most interesting chapters of this volume, "Mother Tongues and Childless Women: The Construction of "Kenyan" Womanhood" by Celeste Fraser Delgado, provides an interesting analysis of the use of the term "motherhood" both as a metaphor and in practice with regard to Kenyan society in an effort to understand the concept as it has evolved and been influenced by various tenets of feminist theory and discourse, international development organizations, and by anti-colonial activities. Delgado skillfully uncovers several inherent contradictions with regard to official government policy announced by the Kenyan government in the 1970s with regard to its' efforts to control population growth and female fertility rates on one hand, and the concrete reality, on the other hand, which was that in spite of the governmental efforts, Kenya continued to have one of the highest population growth rates in the world.[9] Delgado describes it thusly: "Many women have difficulty convincing male partners to use condoms because fertility is expected, even demanded, of a viable relationship...Denying a man children risks a number of things, among them, that he will stop supporting her and find another woman. A conflict exists between cultural expectations of fertility, the alternating political promotion of fertility or family planning, and individual desires for fertility control whether motivated economically or otherwise."[10] Thus, the Kenyan government's preoccupation with the utilization of various population control technologies during the administrations of Presidents Jomo Kenyatta and Daniel Arap Moi severely constrained women's reproductive capabilities that were linked to the image of the "Motherland.[11]

Female Circumcision and the Politics of Knowledge: African Women in Imperialist Discourses, also edited by Obioma Nnaemeka, provides an interdisciplinary examination of the controversial practice of female circumcision by problematizing the internationalization of publicity regarding this practice by individuals and entities that further the goals of western imperialist discourses. According to Nnaemeka, the unsolicited work of the two feminists, Alice Walker and Pratibha Parmar, may have done more harm than good in the process of promoting global debates and awareness regarding issues of female sexuality through their promulgation of books and candid discussions about female circumcision. Nnaemeka argues quite cogently that a big part of the problem is that women of color in the United States and Asia who are involved in the popularization of African women's causes are often imbued with the "imperial arrogance of white explorers, imperialists, and colonizers, which is at the heart of imperial and colonial discourses."[12] Within this context, the voices and participation of the genuine victims of imperialism who are colonized women often go unheard. According to Nnaemeka, the resistance exhibited thus far by some African women in global issues on the subject of female circumcision emanate not so much from the abhorrence that many have for the practice itself, but rather from the fact that they feel that they have been dehumanized in the global discourses centering on this topic and have not been accorded appropriate respect and dignity. Part of this disrespect is linked to the display of African women's female bodily parts on a global scale.[13]

In *Unravelling Taboos: Gender and Sexuality in Namibia*, edited by Suzanne LaFont and Dianne Hubbard, contributors discuss a number of cogent forces which influenced gender and sexuality during the pre-colonial era which included various local belief systems and ideologies, as well as teachings of Christianity. One of the chapters written by Philippe Talavera examines three generations of participants from northern Namibia to learn more about the types of sexual attitudes and belief systems that were prevalent when the participants were fairly young. The author discovered that within some of the ethnic groups in the country, children were given freedom to experiment with or explore their own sexuality with minimal involvement from their parents. He noted that although childhood sexual games were in place with regard to the San, Kavango, Caprivians, Himba, and Herero ethnic groups, forms of sexual experimentation that might culminate in pregnancy, were not allowed to continue once the youth reached the stage of adolescence. Talavera also found that because men were the operational head of their households, they exercised important decision-making capabilities relating to the sexual and reproductive issues of their respective family units. Women did not have the power to withhold sex from their husbands for fear of receiving physical punishment from their mates. Although men were given the right to marry multiple spouses, women were supposed to be faithful to their spouses within the context of monogamous unions.[14] Other salient topics addressed in the book include analyses of gender equity and legal reforms, sexuality issues among youth, sexuality and HIV/AIDS, as well as same-sex relationships.

Few studies published over the past few decades have interrogated the interrelationship between gender, sexuality, and the phenomenon of mothering in African societies. It is in this important area that our present volume, *Gender, Sexuality and Mothering in Africa* makes an important contribution. The genesis for our interdisciplinary volume was the culmination of academic scholarship presented at the Africa Conference held at the University of Texas at Austin in March 2010. The theme of the conference was 'Women, Gender, and Sexualities in Africa."Thus, the fourteen chapters of our book interrogate the interrelationship between gender, sexuality, and the phenomenon of mothering in African societies. This book has several major objectives: (1) to examine the social construction of mothering, marriage, and widowhood in African societies in the past and contemporary time periods; (2) to analyze the process of mothering and the critical role of language in the revival of African culture; (3)) to interrogate the ways in which African marriages were contested and negotiated during the Hausa Diaspora (5) to describe the recent phenomenon of increasing teenage pregnancies and the use of non-formal educational strategies to enhance the status of unwed mothers; (6) to discuss the multiple ways in which gendered violence impacts women in peace-time as well as in war-torn economies in Sub-Saharan Africa; (7) to explore the manifestation of violence in African women's lives as examined in the literary works and dramas of some of Africa's most prolific authors and play rights; (8) to explicate the increasingly important role of the legal sphere in mediating the outcomes of African women in the context of marital and inheritance laws, as well as recent legal reforms which have been enacted to ameliorate their status; and (8) to discuss the symbiotic relationship between sexuality, religion, and politics as they impinge on the lives of African women.

Part I of this volume focuses on motherhood, womanhood, and widowhood. Here, we examine the attainment of an important aspect of the lives of African women which is womanhood as well as the important roles that African women play with regard to having children and nurturing their families. While motherhood, an important rite of passage in the context of African cultural values, connotes high status and feelings of positive self-esteem for African women, the attainment of widowhood often results in a diminution of their status and roles. Nevertheless, the institution of marriage still maintains its importance in the contemporary period as various kinship groups on the continent continue to emphasize that individuals are deemed to be whole when they participate in the institution of marriage and develop their own households.[15] Within these households, men and women have particular roles to play pursuant to the existent sexual division of labor. As Toyin Falola has clarified,

> Within households, even if gender roles are complemen-
> tary, men are regarded as the heads of households while
> a woman has relevance as a mother and wife. She keeps

traditions and kinship alive by bearing children and socializing them. As a bearer of children, she acquires respect within the household; as bearers of male children, she acquires prestige and ensures the stability of her marriage and the continuity of kinship and its traditions. Culture affirms the power that is available to women.[16]

In chapter one, Iniobong Uko discusses the impacts of widowhood on African women. He argues that the status of widowhood brings with it a number of negative realities which include the stipulation that widows participate in mourning rituals which often are denigratory in nature and that the relatives of the deceased husbands in many cases divest the widows of their husband's properties. Moreover, he emphasizes that children of widows are sometimes taken away from their homes and that widows are often inherited by their husband's relatives through the cultural tradition of leviration. While acknowledging that some variation exists from one country to another with regard to the treatment of widows, overall, he portrays widowhood as "oppressive and dehumanizing" and emphasizes that a number of novels written by Mariama Ba, Zulu Sofola and Tess Onwueme all point out that widowhood "constitutes a type of violence against women." In the Western Cameroon, widows typically mourn their deceased husbands' anywhere from a few weeks to three months, are forced to have their hair shaven off, and are compelled by their relatives to sit on the floor in isolation from others throughout the mourning period. In the Sudan, widows have to mourn their husbands for four months and ten days. Mourning periods can last anywhere from three to six months in some of the non-Islamic areas of Western Nigeria and during this time period, the heads of the widows are shaven and male relatives of the deceased husband are allowed by tradition to remarry the widowed wife. According to African tradition, this remarriage allows the widowed wife to receive protection, authority, as well as access to her children within the familial context. Uko subsumes his analysis of widowhood within the umbrella of a close reading and interpretation of *The Trial and Other Stories* by Ifeoma Okoye.

Alexander Kure analyzes Bilqisu Abubakar's compelling novel, *To Live Again,* in chapter two within the much broader context of discussions on mothering and sexuality in African societies. Paramount to his discussion is an examination of some of the important questions that Abubakar's work poses for serious analysis in this area, including how sexuality is formulated with regard to African women, how the women are viewed and treated within the broader society as a whole, how women incorporate maternity and the important role of mothering into their everyday lives, and strategies that they utilize to enhance their own survival. According to Kure, *To Live Again* demonstrates that the conditions that African women experience are attributable both to forces inside of women and those that are external to them. Kure's chapter is generally supportive of the perspective advanced by Abubakar in the novel by illuminating the various possibilities that women have to alleviate challenges that are the result of discriminatory actions against women which exist in Nigerian society.

In chapter three, Cecilia A. Olarewaju presents the findings of her compelling analysis of the food consumption patterns of lactating mothers in Ondo West Local Government region of Nigeria. The purpose of the chapter is to discuss the nutrient intake of the 180 lactating mothers in her study, as well as to provide an assessment of the quality of life of the mothers and their babies. One key avenue through which women are able to provide appropriate nutrition for their offspring after their babies are born is through the important process of breastfeeding, which according to many medical studies, is considered to be healthier than the use of milk formula. These studies have also found that children who were breastfed achieved higher cognitive development levels than those who received milk formula. Breastfeeding is also an important part of the process of mothering because it allows for the development of emotional bonding between mother and child. Key facts that emerged from the analysis included statistical and demographic data which could be useful to governmental officials and political leaders, as well as women's organizations about the current nutritional status of the lactating mothers, as well as an identification of key variables that affect their dietary and food consumption patterns. Olarewaju found that 52.2 percent of the mothers earned less than N 10,0000 each month which was not enough for them to consume a balanced diet. Many of the mothers had also attained fairly low levels of educational training. Hence, education and class impacted the nutritional intake of the lactating mothers. The author recommends that a series of workshops, seminars, and lectures be provided through the use of mass media to educate lactating mothers about the number of kilocalories they need to consume daily to have the appropriate production of milk and the level of nutrients that are vital for their dietary needs.

In chapter four, Bola Dauda examines the processes of mothering and parenting as important aspects of African culture, as well as the role of language as an enabling tool to help citizens to control their environment. While drawing upon his experiences while coaching twenty British teenage mothers in the United Kingdom, he analyzes how their own personal experiences can offer important insights that can be used for the revival of African cultural values and identity. He reminds us that the primary source for socialization in African societies is the family unit and that the primary agent for this process is the mother under the auspices of the parenting process. He identifies several core aspects and stages for the process of parenting, which includes the nurturing and rearing of children until they reach the age of adulthood; the provision of spiritual training to help them to become humane citizens of the world; and rearing children to not only respect themselves, but also to respect others as well. He emphasizes that language is important for cultural survival and that mothers and parents are vital for helping children to develop a mastery of their language which is a critical ingredient in the survival of African cultural value systems.

Part II of this volume focuses on marriage, sexuality, work, and violence. Interspersed throughout this section of the volume are discussions surrounding the complex constellation of factors which impact on women's sexuality within the context of marital relationships, their work environments, educational systems, and war-torn economies. One thread that is interwoven throughout the chapters is the multitudinous ways in which various manifestations of violence—i.e, rape, physical abuse, vagina-sewing, female genital mutilations, and psychological forms of violence—permeate the lives of many African women. The chapters also discuss the various ways in which women's sexuality is often controlled by their male partners, husbands, and the dictates of African cultural traditions and norms. While in some cases, women are able to utilize strategies to ameliorate their situations, in other instances, women experience hopelessness, psychological paralysis, and despair.

In chapter 5, Harmony O'Rourke presents the rather interesting findings of her research on the Hausa Diaspora in which she deconstructs historical data to explicate the multitudinous roles that Hausa women played in the settlement of the frontier as well as in the activities that were subsumed under everyday activities of the Hausa people. Her research challenges older, more conventional analyses of the Hausa in which women were rendered largely invisible. The few studies in which women were included, stressed their involvement in the arena of goods and services, i.e., as "trade behind the purdah" or as courtesanship." According to O'Rourke, one major barrier to the development of more studies which provide a correct depiction of the important role of Hausa women was the fact that male researchers' did not have adequate entre to collect data from women who were secluded and consequently, their conclusions were based to a disproportionate degree on the collection of oral histories from adult men. This chapter highlights the various ways in which marriage, female enslavement, bigamy, and devotion to Islam, constituted the basis for hierarchies of power and inequality between Hausa men and women. She also demonstrates that for some members of the Hausa ethnic group, marriage as an institution provided important linkages between their homeland and the frontier and that "marital ties seem to have taken on greater significance with regard to how a woman's status was determined in Hausa Diaspora settlements."[17] Her research thus fills an important lacunae in the literature by explicating the nature of marital and power relationships among Hausa men and women, as well as the various ways in which power and authority were constantly reproduced and negotiated in the household and in the broader society at large.

Oluyemisi and Oladunni Obilade shift the analysis in chapter 6 to discuss the interrelationship between teenage sexuality, pregnancy, and the high drop- out rates experienced by school girls at the secondary level in Nigeria. The authors base their analysis on a study they performed on 150 teenage girls who attend six secondary schools in Osun State of Nigeria. They acknowledge that a host of factors have exerted impacts on women's lack of educational training in African societies. These include, among others, cultural beliefs, taboos, traditions, and the institutionalization of patriarchal norms and value systems which continue to devalue the status of women. They emphasize that the reluctance of the formal educational systems in Nigeria to "incorporate sexuality and sexual-education" into the curriculum has also had dire consequences for the girls as they often experience sexual harassment in the form of unwanted sexual advances by individuals in positions of power, including teachers. Sometimes, the school girls are also victims of rape, which is an act of uncontrolled violence. According to international data, more than 80% of the school drop-outs in the world are female and live in countries located in Sub-Saharan Africa. Sub-Saharan Africa and Asia also have the highest number of girls who become mothers by the time they reach the age of 16. Moreover, 75% of the children in Nigeria who do not attend school are also female. Added to the above challenges is the reality that teenage pregnancies also militate against the attainment of educational training for African teenage girls, which is the major focus of the chapter. Focus group discussions held by the authors indicated that teenage girls were not knowledgeable about pregnancy and sexually transmitted illnesses. Moreover, relatively few were aware of the existence or importance of female condoms and emergency contraceptive techniques. The authors stress the need for teenage girls to be given the appropriate information about sexuality issues, contraception, and other matters that can enhance their ability to avoid unwanted pregnancies and stay in school. They also point to the need to modify the schools' curriculums, teaching methodologies, and training methods to more effectively deal with critical issues that girls encounter in Nigeria.

Zahrah Nesbitt-Ahmed continues the discourse on issues of gender and sexuality by examining how they affect the work environment and conditions of female live-in domestic workers in Nigeria. In chapter 7, she examines the various strategies that employers use to control the sexuality of the domestic workers. Her study is based on research that she collected on male and female domestic workers in Nigeria. She reminds us that domestic workers are responsible for the performance of many types of jobs that include washing clothes, taking care of the children and elderly members of the families in which they reside, preparing meals, and cleaning the homes of their employers. Although the encounters which take place between domestic workers, their employers, and their families take place in decidedly private quarters and encompass the development of "direct personal relationships," issues of sexuality in this particular context and environment have not received a great deal of attention from the scholarly community. She argues that the working conditions of domestic workers are largely exploitative in nature and that the workers are consequently unable to make good decisions regarding quality of life issues, which makes them susceptible to abusive situations. Individuals who enter domestic work usually have low educational attainment and few alternative sources of employment. Their wages are very small and there is no "clear division between work and private time as working days may run from 5:00 a.m. until 1:00 a.m. and they [are] rarely allowed time off."[18] They are often not allowed to have guests or to leave the home of their employers and have intimate relationships with others. Female domestic workers also experience intimidation, rape, sexual harassment, and have little control over their own sexuality. If the domestic workers become pregnant by their employers or males in the household in which they work, they often have to make a critical decision between keeping the pregnancy or maintaining their jobs.

Ameh Dennis Akoh in chapter 8 examines gendered violence and the development of power relationships as interpreted through the drama of Tracie Utoh-Ezeajugh. One major argument put forward by Akoh is that men are not the only individuals who wield power and perpetrate violent acts against women. On the contrary, he posits that powerful women also instrumentalize violence against other women and men. In some cases, these power plays are formulated by women in order to enable them to acquire, expand, or maintain power. Although Akoh acknowledges that "all violence is gendered" and that the vast majority of sexualized gendered violent acts are perpetrated by men against women, he argues that women also regularly perpetrate violence against other women as well. Akoh stresses that the plays of Tracie Utoh-Uzeajugh emphasize the power plays and power differentials which sometimes exist between women as they exercise both political and physical forms of power. In this context, characters in the plays often assume "masculine" roles or those usually associated with men.

In chapter 9, Peter Dumbuya contextualizes the issues of gender, violence, and reconstruction efforts in Sierra Leone by focusing on the brutal and often inhumane treatment experienced by women and girls during the Sierra Leonean war which was fought from 1991-2002. According to Dumbuya, the Revolutionary United Front (RUF) started the conflict and referred to it as "Operation to Liberate the Motherland" which presented a false view to the world that the goal of the conflict was to save a loving nation from the corrupt hands of unscrupulous politicians. Rather than saving the nation, the RUP and other warring groups perpetrated numerous acts of violence in the country in which women and girls were specifically targeted. These acts included sexual abuse, rapes, and in some instances, sexual slavery. Ironically, in spite of the extreme physical abuses, mental anguish, and various psychological forms of stress experienced by the victims of these horrendous acts, data indicates that they were often rejected and discriminated against by their own relatives, friends, as well as members of their various communities. Data compiled by Amnesty International has confirmed that in excess of 250,000 women and girls experienced these inhumane treatments at the hands of the men. Dumbuya stresses that "a culture of silence" permeated the country in which the warring factions that perpetrated the violence against the women did so without being fearful that they would be held accountable for their actions. Finally, the chapter points out that various remedies that have been proposed or put in place to end violence that specifically targets female sexuality should be seen as part of an overall comprehensive strategy to empower women and girls by providing them access to education, economic opportunity, jobs, and health care.

Eliza Mary Johannes provides an examination in chapter 10 of Maurice Amutabi's *Because of Honor* in an effort to interrogate religion, gender relations, power, and social status. Johannes maintains that the female characters in *Because of* Honor are presented as being essentially powerless and marginalized in a society which is overwhelmingly influenced by cultural and religious patriarchies. Moreover, because of their constant marginalization and seeming victimization in the society, women must participate in constant negotiations with their male counterparts. Johannes' chapter examines the metaphor of honor in an effort to elucidate how it has been used to condone the perpetuation of violent acts against women in African societies. She draws upon various characters in the book such as Amina, Bela, Chiku and Tirudi to clearly explicate how each of their roles connect with issues such as sexuality, patriarchy, gender and class within the confines of their everyday lives. She posits that the women who challenge societal norms or defy them usually experience negative consequences which include death. These women are often secluded and considered to be social pariahs in their respective societies. Moreover, in the action of the novel, women's sexuality is usually curtailed and controlled under the aegis of various practices that are supported by tradition which include vagina-sewing, female circumcision, and forced marriages. Women's movements are also seriously constrained in some instances and within Islamic societies, women participate in purdah and accept the veiling system.

Part III of this volume examines Gender, Law, Sexuality, and Religion. Chapters in this section explore the manner in which legal systems, African cultural norms and traditions, as well as religious belief systems have affected African women's sexuality. As the chapter by Celemusa Zungu demonstrates, the legal system has constrained women's participation in society under the ambit of African customary laws. Alternatively, in the contemporary period as a result of constitutional and various types of legal reforms that have been put in place, the legal system has also facilitated an expansion in opportunities for women to participate in various areas of their respective societies. Data from chapter 12 by J.M. Ayuba also convincingly demonstrates the manner in which the political order has also reinforced religious values. In chapter 11, Celumusa Zungu discusses gender equality and customary law in South Africa. Zungu emphasizes the tremendous degree of change which has occurred in the lives of South African women within the legal sphere in the country since constitutional negotiations and reforms took place during the post-1994 time period. According to Zungu, prior to the enactment of constitutional reforms, women were subjected to the rules of customary law in which they were accorded few contractual capabilities. Moreover, they were not allowed to own or inherit property or to be appointed as chiefs. These practices were inconsistent with the national agenda articulated by the government which affirmed its intention to create a society that was both non-racist and non-sexist. It is encouraging that South Africa is the signatory to several international instruments that support the attainment of gender equity and also supports the Convention on the Elimination of All Forms of Discrimination Against Women. South Africa also supports the African Charter on the Rights of Women in Africa, a document which affirms the importance of eradicating various types of cultural norms and practices which continue to diminish the avenues for meaningful participation by South African women in the overall society.

J.M. Ayuba presents an interesting expose of politics and sexuality in Northern Nigeria during the second half of the twentieth century in chapter twelve by examining the impacts of the reintroduction of *shar'ia law* in various parts of the northern region. The chapter skillfully probes the important interplay between gender and sexuality by focusing on the activities of the '*Yan dauda*' who are Hausa homosexuals referred to by conservative religious and political leaders as "purveyors of sexual immorality." The major thesis of the chapter is that *shar'ia law* has exerted deleterious effects on homosexuals who reside in the region. The chapter also highlights the various problems and issues that homosexuals must contend with under the religious laws which exist in the region. Ayuba points out that prostitutes as well as homosexuals became obvious targets once *shar'ia law* was implemented as they were accused of being responsible for the various problems being experienced in Northern Nigeria because of sinful activities that they participated in. Ayuba notes that politicians in the region used their political power to affect not only various condemnations and statements made by politicians, but also that religious beliefs have also impacted on how homosexuals are viewed and treated in the legal system. Federal laws were passed in the country which defined homosexuality as an illegal act which is punishable by serving fourteen years in prison. When *shar'ia* law was reintroduced in some areas of Northern Nigeria, homosexuals were punished by being stoned to death.

Chapters 13 and 14 written by A.A. Lawal and Adepeju Olufemi Johnson-Bashua respectively examine the impacts of religion on women's status and sexuality. With regard to the impacts of Christianity in particular, Signe Arnfred has argued:

> Obviously the Christian influence on the ways in which sexuality in Africa has been/is seen is decisive. Furthermore, as has been the case for something like a century now, in many parts of Africa, Christianity is no longer just determining the ways in which gender relations are perceived from the outside, Christianity is also influencing the ways people see themselves, their past and present. [19]

In chapter 13, Lawal focuses on the various ways in which African traditional religions, Islam, and Christianity all prevented African women from attaining gender equality with their male counterparts. Lawal argues that sexuality encompasses many aspects of human behavior such as monogamy, polygamy, and polyandry, as well as various types of sexual identities which include heterosexuals, homosexuals, bi-sexuals, transsexuals, as well as issues relating to one's sexual relations and sexual desires. Lawal notes that tenets of Christianity that were brought to Africa by the Europeans supported male control over women and the diminution of women's status and roles in African communities. Within the teachings of Islam, Lawal emphasizes that women are considered to be under the control of their husbands. Women are also to be the object of sexual pleasure. With regard to exercising control over women's sexuality, according to Lawal, it is mandatory for women to keep their private areas covered in predominantly Islamic countries and to cover themselves when they are in public. Last, in chapter 14, Adepeju Olufemi Johnson-Bashua discusses African religion and various ways in which women are still subjected to various types of sexual exploitation in Nigerian society. Johnson-Bashua argues that although a number of people have criticized religion as a negative force on African women, African religions have also exerted positive impacts as well in a variety of ways, including the provision of opportunities for women to assume various spiritual leadership positions, as well as more recent efforts made by religious institutions in Nigeria to try to ameliorate the sexual exploitation experienced by women and girls.

In combination with each other, the chapters in this volume provide insightful information on a variety of factors that have occurred both in the past and contemporary time periods that have affected the interplay between gender, sexuality and various forms of mothering in Africa.

Notes

1. Judith Lorber, "Night to His Day: The Social Construction of Gender," 56, 60, accessed from http://www.csus.edu/indiv/s/shawg/courses/033/readings/social_constructions.pdf.

2. Signe Arnfred, *Re-Thinking Sexualities in Africa* (Uppsala, Sweden: Almqvist and Wiksell Tryckeri), AB.

3. Ibid.

4. Margrethe Silberschmidt, "Changing Gender Roles and Male Disempowerment in Rural and Urban East Africa: A Neglected Dimension in the Study of Sexual and Reproductive Behaviour in East Africa," Paper prepared for the XXIV IUSSP General Population Conference, Salvador, Brazil, 18-24 August 2001, 2.

5. Ibid., 1-6.

6. Mara Mabilia, *Breast Feeding and Sexuality: Behaviour, Beliefs and Taboos among the Gogo Mothers in Tanzania* (New York: Berghahn Books, 2005), 1-3.

7.   Obioma Nnaemeka, ed., *The Politics of (M)othering: Womanhood, Identity, and Resistance in African Literature* (London: Routledge, 1997), 1-3.

8.   Ibid., 2.

9.   Celeste Fraser Delgado, "Mother Tongues and Childless Women: The Construction of "Kenyan" "Womanhood" in *The Politics of (M)othering: Womanhood, Identity, and Resistance in African Literature* (London: Routledge, 1997), 130-134.

10.   Ibid., 133-134.

11.   Ibid., 130.

12.   Obioma Nnaemeka, ed., *Female Circumcision and the Politics of Knowledge: African Women in Imperialist Discourses* (Westport, Connecticut: Praeger, 2005), 5.

13.   Ibid., 26-30.

14.   Suzanne LaFont, "Overview: Gender and Sexuality in Namibia," in *Unravelling Taboos: Gender and Sexuality in* Namibia, Gender Research and Advocacy Project: Legal Assistance Centre, Windhoek: Namibia, 2007, 1-16; See also Philippe Talavera, "The Myth of the Asexual Child in Namibia," in *Unravelling Taboos: Gender and Sexuality in Namibia, 39-56*.

15.   Austin Ahonatu, "Kinship and Marriage in Modern Africa," in *Africa: Volume 5: Contemporary Africa,* edited by Toyin Falola (Durham, North Carolina: Carolina Academic Press, 2003), 534.

16.   Toyin Falola, *The Power of African Cultures* (Rochester, New York: University of Rochester Press, 2003), 251-52.

17.   Chapter 5 of the edited volume.

18.   Chapter 7 of the edited volume.

19.   Arnfred, *Re-Thinking Sexualities in Africa,* 14.

Bibliography

Ahanotu, Austin. "Kinship and Marriage in Modern Africa "in *Africa: Volume 5, Contemporary Africa* edited by Toyin Falola. Durham, North Carolina: Carolina Academic Press, 2003.

Amadiume, Ifi. *Reinventing Africa: Matriarchy, Religion and Culture.* London: Zed Books. Ltd, 1997.

Arnfred, Signe, ed. *Rethinking Sexualities in Africa.* (Uppsala, Sweden: Almqvist and Wiksell Tryckeri, 2005.

Falola, Toyin. *The Power of African Cultures.* Rochester, New York: University of Rochester Press, 2003.

LaFont, Suzanne and Dianne Hubbard, eds. *Unraveling Taboos: Gender and Sexuality in Namibia.* Windhoek, Namibia: Gender, Research, and Advocacy Project, Legal Assistance Center, 2007.

Lorber, Judith. *Paradoxes of Gender.* Yale University Press, 1994.

Mabilia, Mara. *Breast Feeding and Sexuality: Behaviour, Beliefs and Taboos among the Gogo Mothers in Tanzania.* New York: Berghahn Books, 2005.

Nnaemeka, Obioma. ed. *Female Circumcision and the Politics of Knowledge: African Women in Imperialist Discourses.* Westport, Connecticut: Praeger, 2005.

______. *The Politics of (M)othering: Womanhood, Identity, and Resistance in African Literature.* London: Routledge, 1997.

Silberschmidt, Margrethe. "Changing Gender Roles and Male Disempowerment in Rural and Urban East Africa: A Neglected Dimension in the Study of Sexual and Reproductive Behaviour in East Africa," Paper Prepared for the XXIV IUSSP General Population Conference, Salvador, Brazil 18-24 August 2001.

Part One

MOTHERHOOD, WOMANHOOD, AND WIDOWHOOD

AFRICAN WIDOWHOOD AND VISIBILITY

Iniobong I. Uko

> The death of a married man is a real disaster in every home,
> and when that disaster strikes... then begins the desert
> period. As a desert period, widowhood is a period of wilder-
> ness full of wastes. It is a barren period, infertile, unproduc-
> tive, sterile, unfruitful, desolate, bleak and inhospitable.[1]

The above quote provides a context within which to situate the concept of widowhood and the experiences of the widow in Africa. Widowhood in Africa is a concept that generates diverse responses and reactions from both men and women from the families of the deceased and the widow. It also raises several disturbing questions regarding the disparity that exists in the way that the society regards and treats the widow on the one hand, and the widower, on the other hand. Unlike the different categories that women belong to and the different roles that they perform, the only one that they hardly aspire or work towards attaining is widowhood.

Widowhood in Africa often portends evil. Not only is the widow subjected to rigorous, oppressive and humiliating mourning rites as stipulated by tradition, but her husband's relatives often strip her of the family's properties. In many cases, the children she had with her deceased husband are taken from her and she is expected to get inherited by her deceased husband's male relative in the tradition of leviration. These and other such other practices constitute the challenges that confront the widow in Africa. The practices are portrayed in several literary works in Africa. In this chapter, I argue that there are possible agendas that can be evolved in the contemporary African societies to protect and ensure the welfare of widows and to empower them to surmount the ubiquitous crosses and crises of their reality. This chapter situates the discourse within the framework of Ifeoma Okoye's *The Trial and Other Stories*.

Widowhood practice "… is the most flagrant tradition prevalent in many parts of Nigeria, which demeans and dehumanizes women. This occurs, upon the death of a spouse (husband) and the … wife is subjected to a number of mourning rites which are overwhelmingly oppressive and dehumanizing."[2] It is often preferable that the woman leaves an unpleasant marriage rather than being in a situation in which her husband dies and leaves her in the marriage. In the former case, she would be despised by the society and considered to be a failure regardless of whether she was the cause of the problem. In the latter case, she would be subjected to agonizing and inhumane treatment as a widow. Obviously, African societies do not make provision for the woman to operate with dignity as a widow. Nor is she evaluated on the basis of her self-worth. These issues have preoccupied a number of African literary writers, such as Zulu Sofola in *Wedlock of the Gods* (1972), Mariama Ba in *So Long a Letter* (1981), Tess Onwueme in *The Reign of Wazobia* (1988) as well as Ifeome Okoye in *The Trial and Other Stories* (2005). Regardless of the genre chosen to explore the concept of widowhood in Africa, Mariama Ba, Zulu Sofola and Tess Onwueme seemed to have paved the way for Ifeoma Okoye. They all demonstrate that widowhood practices constitute a type of violence against women. Eugene T. Aliegbe contends that those practices emanate from "societies which have little regard for the role and place of the women [sic] when the husband dies … The widow is deprived of all family property immediately after her husband dies. In some societies, she is expected to mourn her husband through acts that inflict [on her] physical and psychological violence and torture."[3]

ISSUES ON WIDOWHOOD
IN AFRICA AND BEYOND

In many communities in Africa and beyond, the widow is subjected to diverse forms of dehumanizing treatment and conditions.

Pat Okoye's survey in *Widowhood: A Natural or Ctultural Tragedy* indicates that in Islamic cultures, the mourning period for the widow is four months and ten days. In India where Hinduism and Buddhism prevail alongside Islam, the mourning period previously lasted a whole year. It was reduced to thirteen days and is now about four days. In the Sudan where the society is largely Islamic, the widow is expected to mourn her husband for four months and ten days. She is often isolated, and made to stay unkempt.[4] In Western Cameroon, the period of mourning varies from a few weeks to three months. The intensity of the practice derives from the fact that the widow is often suspected as being the killer of her husband. The widow is usually forced to have her head clean-shaven, and then to sit on the floor in isolation from her friends and relatives throughout the period of mourning.[5]

However, there are some cultures in which oppressive widowhood practices no longer prevail. They include Ghana and Kenya and Pakistan. Women in those cultures are encouraged to get educated and take up paid jobs. There are agencies of government and non-governmental organizations that specifically attend to widows and their problems. In Pakistan, in addition to several non-governmental organizations that provide various forms of support to widows, the government set up a program called *Zakat Fund*. This requires each worker to pay two and a half percent of his/her annual income into the main treasury. In the situation of the death of a man or woman, the spouse benefits from the savings to cater for the family. In Ghana, widows' causes are supported by such bodies as the Committee on Minority and Women's Rights and the Association of Widows, etc.[6] These organizations work to ensure the welfare and protect the interests of widows. In many situations, widows are made to become skilled and set up to be self-reliant or employed. In Kenya, there is extensive enlightenment that has helped families to stop exploiting widows. In fact, members of the deceased's family condole with the widow and take full responsibility of the funeral to save the widow from more emotional burden. However, there are still several forms of oppression that widows suffer in some parts of Kenya. According to Okoye, widows in some parts of Kenya are still ostracized and deprived of rights to their deceased husbands' estates.[7]

In Nigeria, widowhood practices vary among the diverse cultures and religions among the people. In many areas in Northern Nigeria, widowhood rites vary between the Islamic and non-Islamic communities. Generally, the woman is kept in absolute seclusion to determine if she was pregnant before her husband's death. She is restricted to the use of specific apparel, and at the end of the mourning period, she has to participate in an outing ceremony. The outing ceremony is an occasion during which the widow along with a retinue of followers – mostly women of her family and her husband's family – is taken out around the village to demonstrate that she is innocent of her husband's death. It is usually an elaborate ceremony and the two families look forward eagerly to it. Among the Muslims, the period is four months and ten days; in the non-Islamic communities, it lasts between three weeks and one year. The widow wears sack cloths that are often tattered and her hair is cut off during the seclusion period.[8]

In many non-Islamic communities in Western Nigeria, mourning lasts from three months to six months, during which the widow's hair is shaven, and then a male relation of the deceased is selected by the family to re-marry her in the tradition of leviration. The levirate marriage is believed to provide protection and some authority to the widow and her children within the family and society. In the Islamic communities in Western Nigeria, the widow mourns in confinement for four months and ten days. Leviration is also practiced.[9]

In examining widowhood rites in Eastern Nigeria, here typified by the practice in Enugu, the widow has no right to the family's property; whatever she gets comes from her children, especially her sons who directly inherit the family's property. The widow is confined to a room for a period of time lasts somewhere between seven and nine native weeks. She may not be allowed to bathe during the mourning period and she does not enjoy a change of clothing. After the mourning period, older widows shave the new widow's hair and make her undergo cleansing. Often, leviration is observed.

THE PORTRAYAL OF WIDOWHOOD IN AFRICAN LITERARY WORKS

Generally, women dread the implications of widowhood far more than the loss of their husbands. Be they urban or rural, educated or uneducated, women can hardly escape the traditional stipulations for widows. Widowhood is considered a desolate tract: deserted, isolated, uninhabited, bleak, wild and extremely depressing. Many who get near the circumstance of being related to the widow have an easy option to abscond or flee from the scene because all around the widow is a heavy presence of sorrow and a gnawing vacuum. Indeed, there is an air of intense depression around the widow. She tends to be desecrated, damaged, defiled, vandalized, devastated, ravaged and even insulted. Since this particular desert period is full of wastes, there is plenty of misuse, abuse, exploitation, maltreatment and mishandling.[10] Mariama Ba's *So Long a Letter*, which has received much acclaim and critical response, depicts widowhood in Islamic cultures. After their marriage of thirty years, which produced twelve children, Modou Fall decides to abandon Ramatoulaye and marry young Binetou, who is their daughter's contemporary. While Ramatoulaye is a school teacher, Modou Fall is a technical adviser in the Ministry of Public Works. He dies without any savings because he had earlier terminated the joint savings account that he operated with his wife. He did that because he needed some financial autonomy so as to freely sustain his union with the young Binetou whom he influenced to drop out of school.

Ramatoulaye's travails as a widow begin as her in-laws strip her of all the money given to her as goodwill gestures from friends and sympathizers at Modou's funeral. Then she is subjected to mourning rites. She notes:

> Alone, I live in a monotony broken only by purifying baths, the changing of my mourning clothes every Monday and Friday, I hope to carry out my duties fully. My heart concurs with the demands of religion. Reared since childhood on their strict precepts, I expect not to fail. The walls that limit my horizon for four months and ten days do not bother me. I have enough memories in me to ruminate upon. And these are what I am afraid of, for they smack of bitterness.[11]

Ramatoulaye's bitter experiences are couched within, first, the ambience of Modou's deceit, betrayal and abandonment; second, the reality that "in loving someone else, Modou burned his past, both morally and materially ..." [12] However, at the completion of the mourning rites, the widow is expected to get married to her deceased husband's relative. This is what empowers Modou Fall's brother, Tamsir to declare to Ramatoulaye thus:

> When you have 'come out' [... of mourning], I shall marry
> you. You suit me as a wife, and further, you will continue
> to live here, just as if Modou were not dead .... You are my
> good luck, I shall marry you. I prefer you ... [13]

Unfortunately, the normally silent Ramatoulaye decides to respond. She rationalizes:

> ... Your strategy is to get in before any other suitor ... You
> forget that I have a heart, a mind, that I am not an object
> to be passed from hand to hand ...
>
> What of your wives, Tamsir? I shall never be the one
> to complete your collection ... Tamsir, purge yourself of
> your dreams of conquest ... I shall never be your wife. [14]

Ramatoulaye is unequivocal about her aversion to being levirate. In fact, she also refuses to marry Daouda Dieng, her former suitor, a well-built and decent high-profile politician. Ramatoulaye's mother urges her to accept Daouda Dieng, but she refuses because according to her, "abandoned yesterday because of a woman, I cannot lightly bring myself between you [Daouda] and your family." [15]

The unique feature in Ba's *So Long a Letter* is that it is set in the Islamic culture that permits polygyny and requires leviration for the widow, yet Ramatoulaye rejects both. Her rejection is based on her recognition of the oppressive and often dehumanizing consequences that both practices have on women. Ramatoulaye realizes that she has been silent throughout the thirty years of her marriage to Moudo Fall. This silence is synonymous with invisibility. To be heard and visible, Ramatoulaye resolves not to remarry. Even though she conforms to the trado-religious requirement of mourning her husband for four months and ten days, she is conscious of the enormous waste and dehumanization that it constitutes. She is aware of the contradiction that is involved in her mourning a man who had walked out on her and their twelve children, and then destroyed the joy and peace that she savored in a marriage of thirty years.

Zulu Sofola's *Wedlock of the Gods* reveals another perspective of the ordeal of widowhood. The play portrays Ogwoma who is forced by her parents to marry Adigwu, rather than Uloko, her lover. This is because Adigwu, not Uloko, can pay the high bride-wealth that the family needs for sacrifice for Ogwoma's brother, who is deathly ill. By implication, Ogwoma is condemned by her parents to a life of misery in a repulsive marriage. Three years into the marriage, Adigwu dies, and Ogwoma feels relieved to re-admit Uloko into her life, but tradition requires of her to be in mourning for her deceased husband for three months.

She becomes pregnant for Uloko a month after Adigwu's death, thus making it impossible for anyone to consider that she can be inherited by Okezie, her brother-in-law. By her act of defiance, Ogwoma challenges the validity of the notion expressed by her friend, Anwasia, that "...our people say that a man's daughter is a source of wealth to him. ...You should have been happy that your money saved the life of your own brother."[16] But Ogwoma's ideas are not only more advanced but also more profound than Anwasia's above. Ogwoma is much more vocal and pro-active than Ramatoulaye in Ba's *So Long a Letter*. She discloses to Anwasia her resolve to resist living her life to serve and please other people. She states:

> Let the moon turn into blood;
> Let the rain become fire;
> Ogwoma loves and
> Ogwoma will do it again.[17]

Indeed, Ogwoma is determined to fight anyone who stands between her and Uloko. She is convinced that she obtains fulfillment from her relationship with him:

> ... their plans will fail ... I will be buried alive before I
> become Okezie's wife. They will see fire from me .... God
> will continue to fight for me ... God is not asleep.[18]

Ogwoma's consciousness of the traditional practice of female exploitation, which she has already experienced, hardens her adequately to confront the triple-thronged conflict with her mother, Nneka, with Adigwu's mother, Odibei, and with Uloko's mother, Ogoli. Ogwoma is at the centre of the grievances of the three mothers. She is a source of shame to her mother, who finds it difficult to interact with people in the community. She is trying to drag Uloko to destruction, and her promiscuity led to Adigwu's death. Thus, for each of these mothers, Ogwoma is evil and an effective agent of destruction.

The portraiture of Ramatoulaye and Ogwoma above is significant because even though the former is educated and has an urban orientation, and the latter is traditional, uneducated and rural-based, both are confronted by the dehumanizing implications of widowhood. This means that the oppressive traditional practices that attend widowhood in Africa defy the widow's educational status.

In Tess Onwueme's *The Reign of Wazobia*, Wazobia, the King Regent, though a woman, is expected to inherit the three wives of the deceased King of Ilaa. For a widow to complete the funeral rites for the husband and be vindicated of responsibility for his death, she would have to shave her hair, stay in seclusion and in ashes and then dance nearly naked at the market square in the full glare of everyone. The Omu as "King" of all women in Ilaa states that a woman who dies mourning her husband is unclean and must be left to rot in the evil forest. Wazobia implores the widows that they should neither kneel in her presence as King, nor struggle to gain her attention. She rules that her "women will not dance naked in public to appease the eyes of a wrathful populace. This is no era for dancing to entertain lustful eyes."[19]

OKOYE'S PERSPECTIVES ON WIDOWHOOD

The stories by Ifeoma Okoye in *The Trial and Other Stories* examine much more dynamic and profound experiences of widows. They show the widow as a victim of the ubiquitous tradition as well as male tyranny. The underlying issue as articulated by Ifeoma Okoye is that in Africa:

> … where widows are subjugated, discriminated against and
> denied their fundamental human rights, the general belief
> is that women are inferior to men and under them, and
> that men should decide what is good or not for women.[20]

The above is true of each of the ten stories in Okoye's collection, in which concerns are as varied as they are real. The persecution of the widow finds authenticity within the patriarchal framework that guides the people. Even though the experiences of widows as captured in the stories are prevalent in many African communities, Ifeoma Okoye derives much of her data from the experiences of widows in her native Enugu culture in Eastern Nigeria.

It is common for the widow to be dispossessed of her children and properties by members of her deceased husband's family. This forms the thrust of some of the stories in Okoye's *The Trial and Other Stories*. In "Soul Healers," Somadi is dispossessed of her two children after the death of her husband. The family is unhappy with Somadi because she decided to find employment when her husband's business in Kano crumbled and the family was strained economically. The employment was a bank job in Lagos, which caused her to move with their two children to Lagos. According to her:

> ...work didn't mean earning money only. It also meant freedom, empowerment, self-fulfillment and self-esteem. It meant meeting people, gathering experience, building character and learning to live.[21]

Desiring to acquire the ideals listed above, Somadi defies her husband and takes up the bank job in Lagos. She fits into the context that Iniobong Uko develops for women, which she explains in the following way: "it is important that work outside the home ... gives a woman a feeling of personal fulfillment. It makes her feel she is contributing positively to the services of her wider society. It also gives her the opportunity to associate with other members of her society, thus making her a more rounded personality."[22]

Unfortunately, Somadi's husband has a stroke and dies. Her in-laws are hostile to her; they accuse her of the husband's death, they get the children from her, stop her from seeing the children, and warn the children's teachers never to allow her to visit the children at school. These actions provide the basis for Somadi to go surreptitiously to Owerri from Lagos to take back her children. Her plot succeeds largely because of her economic empowerment, which also engenders self-confidence.

In another story, "Second Chance," Ogoli's experience is similar to Somadi's. She married Chibuzo five months after she finished at the secondary school, and Chibuzo died three years later. Her salary as a clerk cannot sustain her and her two children since Chibuzo died. Considering re-marrying, she goes to inform Azu, Chibuzo's uncle and foster father, but he assures her that the family would take custody of the children (of ages five and three) if she should re-marry:

> The children are ours and I must make sure you don't take them along with you to your new husband. If it means taking the children from you by force, I'll not hesitate to do it. The children belong to our family under our customary laws and our customary courts uphold these laws. The laws are based on our tradition and customs. I don't think you'll let the matter reach the stage of going to court. If you do, I assure you, you'll lose the case.[23]

Obviously, the customs are wicked and discriminatory against widows and the children of widows. In this story, Ogoli's sense of freedom at the death of her husband is threatened by her brother-in-law's exposition above, thus confirming the notion by Ada Azodo and Maureen Eke that:

> [The woman's] ... pseudo-independence is debunked and proven to be a mere sham as soon as she is in the presence of her man, be he her father, brother, uncle or husband.[24]

Gerry, the widower, who wishes to marry Ogoli, already has three children. On hearing of Ogoli's dilemma, i.e., her willingness to marry him, but her unwillingness to relinquish her children to her in-laws, he resolves it by leaving Enugu for Ibadan on transfer. He also relocates Ogoli and her two children, gets them settled in Ibadan and they live happily as one family. By that act, both Gerry and Ogoli demonstrate that they are more concerned about their happiness than what people would say and the stipulations of tradition. They are convinced as Clenora Hudson-Weems is that it is always advantageous to have someone to talk to, someone who is concerned about one's needs, someone to give and receive positive feedback from and action, both on a personal and a professional basis.[25]

In yet another important story, "From Wife to Concubine," Fred, Arit's husband dies and Arit is subjected to diverse dehumanizing widowhood rites by the *Umuada,* Fred's patrilineal female relatives. She recounts:

> I was forced to sit on a mat on the hard floor throughout
> the burial ceremony. I was not allowed to take part in plan-
> ning for the burial, although I was asked to provide the
> money needed. ... I had every strand of my long beautiful
> hair completely cut off as soon as the burial was over.[26]

In spite of the trauma experienced by Arit, her brother-in-law, Paul, took custody of certain documents immediately after Fred's death. They were the documents on the block of flats which Arit built, but which were registered in Fred's name, as well as all the documents on the marriage between Arit and Fred. Paul argues that Arit has no proof of any marriage to Fred, and that indeed she was never married to Fred, and so she and her children are not qualified to make a claim of any property.[27] Paul's motive is to obliterate all evidence of Arit's marriage to Fred, so as to rule out her right to any property of the family.

Rather than resign and accept Paul's intimidation and cheating, Arit tells him that she knows everything about how Samuel, Fred's cousin died. She had earlier learnt from her husband that he, Samuel and Paul were on Samuel's farm to settle the dispute on the correct boundary between Samuel's and Paul's farm-lands. Then a shot suddenly killed Samuel, and Paul had a gun. However, the incident was kept a secret. What people generally heard was that Samuel accidentally shot himself. To help herself, she reneges on the promise that she made to her deceased husband to keep secret the true version of Samuel's death. By this act of re-visiting the circumstance of Samuel's death, Arit deliberately fights back. The disclosure weakens Paul and he quietly returns the documents to Arit, and no longer raises the issue of acquiring the block of flats.

The issue of leviration or widow-inheritance is examined in "A Strange Disease" in which Onumba pressurizes Enu to marry him after the death of Enu's husband. Onumba is Enu's brother-in-law who already has two wives:

> He was selfish, high handed and untrustworthy. She knew
> that he beat his wives for the flimsiest of reasons. She
> herself had had enough battering from her late husband;
> enough to last her for the rest of her life. Why then should
> she marry another wife beater?[28]

Thus, to put Onumba off, Enu informs him that she has a disease which she would not want to pass on to him. She makes bold to show him her naked body to prove to him the validity of her story, and adds that "the doctor says that any man who touches me gets the disease. And the disease is worse for men."[29] This strategy proves successful as it sends Onumba away from Enu.

The story, "The Trial," portrays the cruelty to which the widow is subjected in most African societies. Anayo is on trial before the *umu-okpo* or Daughters of the Lineage, for allegedly killing her husband. Anayo "had arrived in the village from Lagos only the evening before, bringing her husband's body with her. She had expected sympathy and understanding, not insensitivity from the women, more so as she was one of them."[30] Hudson-Weems explains Anayo's disappointment and disillusionment within the context that "it is often [the woman's]... female support system, or lack thereof, rendering or denying psychological and physical assistance, that either helps or hinders in bringing her immediate or life goals to fruition."[31] Anayo confronts the reality that widowhood is a terrible desert period and it is fraught with a myriad of extremely negative things like sorrows, indignations, reproach, and dishonor. Udoh, *Fruities*, 39. Eletty, the leader of the women's group, informs Anayo:

> Later today, before your husband's body is committed to
> our mother earth, you'll go through our traditional trial
> *by ordeal* to prove your innocence. If you refuse to do this,
> we'll ostracise you.[32] (My emphasis).

Anayo is accused by her brother-in-law, Ezeji, of having poisoned her husband, Zimuzo. Udoh argues that "in a society where one does not die a natural death most of the time, as a widow, you are the first suspect as the killer of your husband. Some people might even tell you directly while others might just fabricate vicious gossip around that ... line."[33] And Eseyin and Ohaeri observe that where a woman is suspected of having a hand in her husband's death, the only way to demonstrate her non-complicity in her husband's death is to drink the water with which her husband's corpse was washed.[34] In the story "The Trial", Anayo's mother and friends urge her to undergo the trial, but she is averse to the whole concept of the trial, which involves her drinking the water with which her late husband's body is washed.

However, Anayo's brother-in-law, Ezeji, washes the deceased and before giving the water to Anayo to drink, he dips his forefinger into the bowl. Anayo is alarmed and accuses Ezeji of poisoning the water. She demands of Ezeji to first drink the water as proof that the water is not poisoned, Ezeji refuses, and the women ask him to drink it. Anayo's mother accuses him: "You want to kill my daughter. Drink that water if you're sure you didn't drop poison into it ... [35] Ezeji's refusal to drink the water raises tremendous controversy and Ezeji walks out in disappointment and anger, promising Anayo that he will ensure that she does not inherit anything from her husband. And Anayo does not drink the water; she escapes the debilitating trial, and thus demonstrates that "... the changes associated with losing a life partner may trigger new strengths, even among women who had very good relationships, who miss the partner deeply, and who list loneliness as their biggest adjustment problem."[36]

In the story, "Between Women,"Ebuka is a widow who works as a house-keeper for Mr. and Mrs. Edet in Enugu. She wishes to take her only child, Amara, with her but Mrs. Edet disapproves of that, stating that Amara would "be in your way, and your job will suffer."[37] Ebuka is entitled to neither an annual leave nor a day off all year round. Of course, she is also neither educated nor skilled. Mrs. Edet exploits her. As she inadvertently gets an egg that she has burned while cooking, Mrs. Edet is so angry that she throws at her the serrated table knife at her, which injures Ebuka on the left eyebrow. Mrs. Edet's high propensity to violent utterances and actions makes Ebuka afraid of her. Ebuka learns of Amara's illness and hospitalization; she asks Mrs. Edet to be excused for a day to enable her to see her daughter and also give some money to her mother-in-law who takes care of Amara. But Mrs. Edet refuses to allow this, and consequently:

> At five-thirty in the morning and before the Edet family
> woke from sleep, Ebuka sneaked out of the compound
> with all her belongings tied up in a plastic shopping bag.[38]

She casts a final glance at the house where she has lived for two years; she heads for the motor-park to travel home to see her only child. There is a disturbing factor that seems to underlie many of the stories and indeed the lives of the widows. This is the reality of the conscious disempowerment of the widows, and it manifests itself in various forms.

Quite apart from the traditional stipulations that debase the widows which the men are usually delighted to implement, there are diverse situations of women persecuting the widows, women striving to strip the widows of their integrity, honor and power. There are few instances of the widows enjoying the cooperation of the local people, especially the women around them. The critical need for genuine sisterhood, which is essential for a positive society, cannot be over-emphasized here because it is important for women, the broader family to communicate, interact, and assist each other in their daily affairs.[39]

The role of the *umu-okpo* in the story "The Trial" reveals the hostility of fellow women to the widow. Accused of having killed her husband, the women summon Anayo for questioning. According to the omniscient narrator:

> As Anayo stepped into the Obi, the women's eyes hit her
> like a thousand arrows. They were hostile eyes staring
> out of grim faces. The silence that followed her entrance
> was so sharp it could have sliced a piece of yam. ... The
> women's group... was reputed to be ruthless and resolute
> in its decisions even in matters concerning its members.
> It was also notorious for applying rigidly the clan's tradi-
> tional laws and sanctions and for being easily offended.[40]

Standing before the women, Anayo feels that they have already condemned her. She feels weak and tense because of the reality of what she is made to undergo.

In the story "Between Women," Ebuka is cruelly treated by Mrs. Edet, her mistress. She is unhealthy and looks far older than her age because "each day including Saturdays and Sundays, she retired to her room in the domestic workers' quarters after eleven o'clock in the night. She didn't have any time off. She never visited anyone .... No one had visited her. But what worried her most was money. Her salary was small and often times she had lain awake at night wondering how to provide her daughter with all she needed."[41] In spite of these things, Mrs. Edet does not permit her to go home to see her daughter who is hospitalized. Ebuka's resolve to go and her actual departure from the Edets demonstrate her ability to surmount the "fear of the unknown that keeps us glued to a deplorable situation."[42]

THE POSSIBILITIES FOR THE MODERN WIDOWS

There are diverse possibilities for the widows in contemporary African society that would make them both visible as persons to be reckoned in spite of their status, and fulfilled as active, effectual and productive persons. In *The Trial and Other Stories*, Ifeoma Okoye has carefully illuminated the different situations, environments and backgrounds from which the widows emerge. The women are not just oppressed and down trodden; they also are struggling to widen their options. They play a part in maintaining the social context that limits their opportunities even as they struggle against them.[43] By implication, the widows may be educated, enlightened and urban-based, or uneducated, un-exposed and rural-based. The stories indicate that the widows are cruelly treated as a prelude to being disempowered. To be disempowered here means to be irrelevant, inconsequential and invisible, which means that widows do not enjoy certain rights nor is any provision made for their survival once their spouses pass away. Eseyin and Ohaeri contend that:

> Women's rights should be given due recognition and protection under our statuses as human rights and not as privileges. Women must be economically empowered by giving them equal access to economic resources, education ... to eliminate ... the high poverty level among women, the problem of economic dependence and ... their invisibility in public life participation.[44]

Generally, Okoye's message is that the modern widow must fight for herself. Indeed, while she weeps because of the death of her husband, she should keep her eyes open to spot the intrigues that are planned against her, the exploitation and oppression that are targeted at her, and the perpetual poverty that she and her children may have to subsequently live in. According to Ifi Amadiume:

> Women who recounted the indigenous mourning rituals said that women in mourning for their husbands went through hell-fire, *oku-nmuo*. When they cried and feared the death of a husband, it was not so much out of loss, but through dread of the punishment in store for them.[45]

Okoye insists that the modern widow must be conscious of the misogynist tendency of the men, especially the male relatives of her deceased husband. She must also be conscious of the women who have been conditioned by patriarchy to hate their fellow women – the widows. Okoye notes in "Letter to the Reader" that she wrote the stories

> ... to show that widows can do something by themselves to solve some of their problems. They may seek help only if and when they need it. Solving their problems by themselves, if they can, will increase their self-confidence and self-esteem and will help them maintain their dignity.[46]

The stories generate self-questioning among the people around the widow. The author states in her letter to the readers that if one does "something for someone who is a widow, the world of widows would be a less gloomy one."[47]

However, each story in the collection depicts a widow that has succeeded in surmounting the unjust, discriminatory, and repressive custom. This trend implies that in the modern society, the widow has transcended the complacence, voicelessness, and invisibility that characterized her counterpart in the past. She is determined to survive (along with her children) the hostilities that the society often visits on the widow. Some of the widows in the stories deploy unconventional strategies to attain freedom and sustain some degree of power to control some issues around them. By doing so, they destroy the myth of manhood/womanhood. According to Tesfa Gebremedin:

> Traditional cultural norms and practices, through the long and oppressive history of women sustain the stark contrast between the incalculable advantages of being born male and the all consuming burden of being born female. Cultural beliefs about the status of women can be distinguished into two categories: (1) those tending to overcome gender inequalities and (2) those entrenching gender inequalities further.[48]

Indeed, the male is positioned at the centre; he is supreme, he is the norm, while the female is in the periphery, is subordinate and different. Women are controlled by being told to behave like women, cry like women, walk like women, sit like women and that means do things differently from a man, less conspicuously or spontaneously.[49]

The more challenging reality that confronts the widow is not really what she experiences in the hands of the men, but her experiences in the hands of her fellow women. This calls to question the validity of the concept of sisterhood. Usually, the men who rationalize their actions as reifying African culture and tradition, use women to actualize their agenda of hostility on women. The *umuada* constitutes the machinery of intimidation and oppression of the widow. This confirms the observation that "the contours of the feminist literary landscape in Africa, in general, and Nigeria in particular, present a panorama of undulating topography, it is a house divided against itself and at present looks discomfortingly like the leaning tower of Pisa."[50]

In conclusion, Okoye's vision for the widow in modern societies is articulated by Tess Onwueme through Wazobia in *The Reign of Wazobia*:

> Why ... must widows be subjected to the torment of incessant funeral rites that men are free of under similar situations ...?[51]

Okoye envisions that the widow should look beyond her grief and devise means that will ensure her survival and sustenance in the society that is so hostile. Okoye's short stories depict an intense ambition to liberate women from the shackles of repressive and retrogressive tradition. Herein lies the relevance of D.I. Nwoga's assertion that "we must now review the belief system based on our current situation, and re-think our practices in such a way as to achieve continued social cohesion and discipline."[52] Okoye indicates that apart from widowhood, "the business of womanhood is a heavy burden. Aren't we the ones who bear children? And these days it is worse, with poverty ... on one side and the weight of womanhood on the other ..."[53] Okoye condemns all practices that cause and perpetuate female oppression and backwardness. Through her portraiture emerges the image of a widow that is positive, resolute, courageous, productive, and modern. She also addresses women who are happily married regarding the need to seek empowerment so that they would not be stranded should their husbands die at anytime.

Current realities reveal the need for women to be interested in and to participate directly or indirectly in the economic activities of their husbands. Whether educated or uneducated, the widow in modern societies must evolve ways of surmounting the prevalent challenges and attain visibility and relevance. She must not seek pity from her fellow women, but cooperation, so that together, they may address their common problems of oppressive and discriminatory treatment by their male counterparts. These will surely propel the woman and equip her to face the twenty-first century challenges in spite of the death of her husband.

Notes

1. Imelda I. L. Udoh, *Fruiting in the Desert of Widowhood*. (Uyo: Fruities' Publications Ltd., 2008), 40.

2. Mojisola Eseyin and Victoria Ohaeri, *Women's Rights in Nigeria: How Protected?* (Uyo: Lanaki Production, 2007), 21.

3. Eugene T. Aliegbe, "Violence Against Women: Its Nature and Manifestations", in *Perspectives on Violence Against Women in Nigeria* ed. Charity Angya. (Makurdi: Aboki Publishers, Nigeria, 2005), 116.

4. Pat U. Okoye, *Widowhood: A Natural or Cultural Tragedy* (Enugu, Nigeria: Nicik Publishers, 1995), 60.

5. Okoye, *Widowhood*, 82.

6. Ibid., 15.

7. Ibid., 72.

8. Aliegbe, "Violence Against Women," 95.

9. Eseyin and Ohaeri, *Women's Rights*, 95.

10. Udoh, *Fruiting in the Desert*, 40-41.

11. Mariama Ba, *So Long a Letter* (Oxford: Heinemann, 1981), 8.

12. Ibid., 12.

13. Ibid., 57.

14. Ibid., 58.

15. Ibid., 68.

16. Zulu Sofola, *Wedlock of the Gods* (London: Evans, 1972), 9.

17. Ibid., 10.

18. Ibid., 22.

19. Tess Onwueme, *The Reign of Wazobia* (Ibadan, Nigeria: Heinemann, 1988), 20.

20. Ifeoma Okoye, "Letter to the Reader" in *The Trial and Other Stories* (Lagos, Nigeria: African Heritage Press, 2005), 2.

21. Ibid., 12.

22. Iniobong I. Uko, *Gender and Identity in the Works of Osonye Tess Onwueme* (Trenton, N.J.: Africa World Press, 2004), 100.

23. Okoye, *The Trial*, 75.

24. Ada Azodo and Maureen Eke, "Introduction: Shifting Meanings, Erotic Choices" in *Gender & Sexuality in African Literature and Film*. Trenton, New Jersey: Africa World Press, 2007), 3.

25. Clenora Hudson-Weems, *Africana Womanist Literary Theory* (Trenton, New Jersey: Africa World Press, 2004), 66.

26. Okoye, *The Trial*, 68.

27. Ibid., 69.

28. Ibid., 31.

29. Ibid., 34.

30. Ibid., 46.

31. Hudson-Weems, *Africana Womanist*, 67.

32. Okoye, *The Trial*, 48.

33. Udoh, *Fruiting*, 41.

34. Eseyin and Ohaeri, *Women's Rights*, 77.

35. Okoye, *The Trial*, 53.

36. Hilary M. Lips, *A New Psychology of Women: Gender, Culture & Ethnicity*. 2nd ed., (New York: Mc Graw-Hill, 2003), 375.

37. Okoye, *The Trial*, 15.

38. Ibid., 25.

39. Hudson-Weems, *Africana Womanist*, 66.

40. Okoye, *The Trial*, 44-45.

41. Ibid., 22.

42. Ibid., 25.

43. Melinda Robins, *Intersecting Places, Emancipatory Spaces* (Trenton, New Jersey: Africa World Press, 2001), 155.

44. Eseyin amd Ohaeri, 109.

45. Ifi Amadiume, *Male Daughters, Female Husbands: Gender and Sex in an African Society* (London: Zed Books, 1995), 81-82.

46. Okoye, Letter, 2.

47.   Ibid., Letter, 3.

48.   Tesfa G. Gebremedin, Women, *Tradition and Development* (Asmara, Eritrea: The Red Sea Press, 2004), 64.

49.   Azodo and Eke, "Introduction: Shifting Meanings," 3.

50.   Charles E. Nnolim, *Issues in African Literature* (Yenagoa, Nigeria: Treasure Resource, 2009), 136.

51.   Onwueme, *The Reign*, 20.

52.   D. I. Nwoga, "Widowhood Practices: The Imo State Experience" in *Widowhood Practices in Imo State. Proceedings of the BLPFW Workshop* (Owerri, Nigeria: Government Printer, 1989), 37.

53.   Tsitsi Dangarembga, *Nervous Conditions* (London: The Women's Press, 1988), 16.

Bibliography

Aliegbe, Eugene T. "Violence Against Women: Its Nature and Manifestations." In *Perspectives on Violence Against Women in Nigeria,* ed. Charity Angya, 116. Makurdi: Aboki Publishers, Nigeria, 2005.

Amadiume, Ifi, *Male Daughters, Female Husbands: Gender and Sex in an African Society.* New Jersey: Zed Books, 1995.

Azodo, Ada and Maureen Eke, "Introduction: Shifting Meanings, Erotic Choices." In *Gender and Sexuality in African Literature and Film.* Trenton, New Jersey: Africa World Press, 2007.

Ba, Miriama. *So Long A Letter.* Oxford: Heinemann, 1981.

Dangarembga Tsitsi. *Nervous Conditions.* London: The Women's Press, 1988.

Eseyin, Mojisola and Victoria Ohaeri, *Women's Rights in Nigeria: How Protected?* Uyo: Lanaki Production, 2007.

Hudson-Weems, Clenora. *Africana Womanist Literary Theory.* Trenton: New Jersey: Africa World Press, 2004.

Lips, Hilary M. *A New Psychology of Women: Gender, Culture, and Ethnicity.* 2nd Edition. New York: McGraw-Hill, 2003.

Nnolim, Charles E. *Issues in African Literature.* Yenagoa, Nigeria: Treasure Resource, 2009.

Nwoga, D.I. "Widowhood Practices: The Imo State Experience" in *Widowhood Practices in Imo State.* Proceedings of the BLPFW Workshop. Owerri, Nigeria: Government Printer, 1989.

Okoye, Ifeoma, "Letter to the Reader." In *The Trial and Other Stories.* Lagos, Nigeria: African Heritage Press, 2005.

Okoye, Pat U. *Widowhood: A Natural or Cultural Tragedy.* Enugu, Nigeria: Nicik Publishers, 1995.

Robins, Melinda. *Intersecting Places, Emancipatory Species.* Trenton, New Jersey: Africa World Press, 2001.

Udoh, Imelda L. *Fruiting in the Desert of Widowhood.* Uyo: Fruities' Publications, Ltd. 2008.

Uko, Iniobong I. *Gender and Identity in the Works of Osonye Tess Onwueme.* Trenton, New Jersey: Africa World Press, 2004.

Zulu, Sofola. *Wedlock of the Gods.* London: Evans, 1972.

OVERWHELMING THE BURDEN OF WOMANHOOD IN *TO LIVE AGAIN* BY BILQISU ABUBAKAR

Alexander Kure

INTRODUCTION

Fictional narrative, especially one that is socially committed, is often connected to life experiences. Interestingly, literature written in Nigeria by some women and men has continuously focused on the condition of women. No wonder, Bilqisu Abubakar's maiden novel, *To live Again* (2007),[1] has made the condition of women, especially in the Hausa/Fulani-Islamic-Northern Nigerian region, its central concern. The novel interrogates the sources of this condition and shows that it emanates both from within women and outside of them. However, instead of the usual acceptance of the status quo of women as often reflected by some writers in Northern Nigeria like Zaynab Alkali, the author argues that women in particular and the society in general can influence both the overt and covert notions that women have been constructed socially, economically, politically, culturally, and religiously to remain perpetually subservient in whatever circumstance they find themselves.

Bilqisu Abubakar's *To Live Again* can well be situated within mainstream discourse on sexuality and mothering. This is because in the novel, she examines these issues by asking questions and finding answers regarding what constitutes sexuality in the woman; how the woman is viewed and treated in the society she lives in; how women integrate maternity into their sense of self; the mothers' struggles to balance themselves amid a set of polarities, tensions, and that of mothering situated within a phenomenological matrix of such tensions; developmental issues that include loss of self/expansion of self, omnipotence/liability, life-destroying/life-promoting behavior, maternal isolation/maternal community, cognitive strategies/intuitive responses, maternal desexualization/maternal sexualization and above all, an investigation into how mothers cope with these tensions in their efforts to survive their sexuality and mothering.

In light of the above, this chapter supports Bilqisu Abubakar's point of view by situating the analysis of the novel within the context of a discussion of constraints and possibilities that will shape opportunities for Northern Nigerian women to overcome problems that arise from discrimination or limit their ability to do so. The central argument here is that the burden imposed and shouldered by women in each society takes different forms, and that workable strategies need to be developed in different historical periods to understand more fully the factors that continue to contribute to the institutionalization of gender inequality.

Discrimination against women is defined by Article 1 of the United Nations Convention on the Elimination of Discrimination Against Women of 1979 (hereto referred to as the 1979 Convention) as "any distinction, exclusion or restriction made on the basis of sex which has the effect or purpose of impairing or nullifying the recognition, enjoyment or exercise by women, irrespective of their marital status, on a basis of equality of men and women, of human rights and fundamental freedoms in political, economic, social, cultural, civil or any other field."[2] In this context, discrimination then is symptomatic of situations where patterns of structural inequality are maintained by rules, norms and procedures which dictate a subordinate role for women in all spheres of societal existence. The forces calling for an end to all forms of discrimination against women emphasize the need for a radical re-definition of the process and content of economic, social and political development and stress the need for a holistic orientation which acknowledges the vital role of women in development planning and processes as equal partners with men.

In examining the burdens imposed on women, this chapter approaches questions concerning human rights and discrimination against women from a perspective that differs slightly from the predominant points of view in the human rights literature. The often-held view to this chapter's understanding has an intrinsic pro-western bias which holds the implicit assumption that international human rights have their origin from Western liberal ideologies. Contrary to this dominant perspective, and in line with the point of view expressed in Bilqisu Abubakar's novel, it is argued that all human societies have a conception of human rights based on their prevailing cultural circumstances. The chapter argues that the existence and defence of human rights against discrimination, in this case of Northern Nigerian women, must of necessity be located within the particular historical, social, political, economic, cultural, religious and other types of experiences that these women face.

Meanwhile, the problem of discrimination against women can correctly be conceptualised to involve the denial of self-determination to women. But while being wary of what may be termed "the obvious globalisation of discrimination against women," I argue that discrimination emanates from the erection, maintenance and perpetuation of structures of inequality against women as opposed to men. In this vein, I acknowledge that both individuals and groups play an instrumental role in the creation of the unequal structures and their maintenance. The development of alternative rules, norms, and procedures provides the avenue through which real structural transformation may be engineered. It is here noted that the process to engender transformation may involve both the violent or non-violent manipulation of rules, norms, and procedures as well as organisation of political action by women to protect what rights they have, enhance the quality of protection and increase the comprehensiveness of the rights to which they are entitled. In other words, the agent-structure concept can be useful for understanding the central role that structures play in constraining as well as enabling human agency; that is, a structure can limit or foster change but structures allow for the transformative interventions of human agents.[3]

The brief evaluation of discrimination against Hausa-Fulani-Muslim women in Northern Nigeria presented here also interrogates the level of success of all local, national, and international legislation that seeks to prevent discrimination against women. In addition, it demonstrates that although most of these laws seek to improve the condition of women in Northern Nigeria, they have not had any real positive impact on their lives.

It is pertinent to emphasize that since the aforementioned local, national and international legislative efforts outlined above have remained ineffective, it, therefore, impresses on Bilqisu Abubakar the very strong need to call for the reinforcement of their applications. She does this by narrating in story form what sexuality and mothering could literally mean in Northern Nigeria apparently as a contribution to the continuous discourse and efforts to overcome the burden of womanhood in Northern Nigeria.

EFFECTS OF STRUCTURES OF INEQUALITY ON WOMEN IN NORTHERN NIGERIA

It may be argued that pre-colonial Nigeria had a sexual division of labor. However, the nature and implication of such a sexual division of labor may be misinterpreted. While male dominance was wielded into the social system of most Nigerian ethnic groups, women played a significant and vital role in all aspects of the lives of their communities. That was due to the complementarities of male and female roles and functions. The effect of complementarities was to give women a great deal of autonomy in their own affairs to a degree that was unmatched in western societies. Women, however, are not a homogenous category and some differentiation did exit with regard to their status and roles. For example, some women became leaders in politics, religion, and the economy and experienced discrimination both on the basis of their class and their gender. Women who by virtue of their acquired or ascribed status became decision makers were by no means treated in the same way as other women in terms of their rights. Elements of structural inequality could be observed in regard to their unequal access to the means of production and control thereof, as well as inequality in the ability to control reproduction.[4]

In feminist literature, discrimination against women is taken to manifest itself in the forms of gender, class, and personal discrimination that arise from women being discriminated against as women. In some perspectives, discrimination is caused by structural factors. The most important structural sources of discrimination are social formations such as the family, which conditions its members to conform to socially acceptable norms in terms of male and female roles in the division of labor from childhood.[5] Although the general concept of the traditional division of labor in Nigeria was one in which distinctions existed between men's and women's work, social expectations on what constituted men's or women's work varied. To be specific, Catherine Coles and Beverly Mack say that in Northern Nigeria, men generally speaking, had a higher status than women within the family; hence women were only active in child-bearing and rearing. Issues that border on decision-making, full-time trading, and food processing were, and still are, partially the preserve of men since women were constrained by the purdah imposed on them.

In addition, elders were more privileged than the young and husbands more privileged vis-a-vis the wives. The significance of this state of affairs becomes obvious when one realizes that it is not only the men marrying the women that are their husbands. All the members of the patrilineage into which a woman marries, that is, both male and female, stand as husbands in relationship to her. Relationships such as these, however, are not sexual. These relationships cannot always be conceptualized in terms of gender.[6]

The ideological dimension of discrimination becomes evident when the positive contributions made by women remain unacknowledged while negative stereotypes on the role of women in pre-colonial society are stressed. An example of the negative portrayal of Northern Nigerian women and their role in society is that the existence of a sexual division of labor is often taken to mean that the majority of women were excluded from decision-making roles in society. Pieces of evidence existed of opportunities for women to participate in decision making as leaders of institutions paralleling those of men. Women within the family had to combine some productive work like selling fried groundnuts and the like through the use of small children but were able to take some advantage of help from the extended family, including the polygamous family unit, which reduced the burden of a double workload.[7]

The fact that women are known to take part in some commercial ventures is lucidly buttressed by findings as expressed by Catherine VerEecke in Bessie House-Midamba and Felix Ekechi's edited book when she states as follows:

> these and many other works show that a vast majority of married Hausa women from such cities as Kano, Katsina and Zaria and their rural environs often earn a stable living from petty or large-scale trade while participating in the Islamic institution of Purdah, in which they must remain secluded in the house. As a result of this work, the hidden trade has been viewed as a Hausa, a Nigerian, or perhaps a West African woman's institution that serves the dual function of enhancing both their prestige and modesty and of providing them with some remuneration for their household labor.[8]

However, without prejudice to the above, while it is very evident those women in the East and West of Nigeria enjoy a good measure of freedom to participate openly in commercial activities, this chapter argues that such kind of involvement by women in Northern Nigeria is the opposite. VerEecke agrees with Polly Hill when they describe such engagement by women from the North as "hidden trade."[9] Therefore, one wonders how the involvement of women in such "hidden" commercial activities where they are not physically present because of the constraints of purdah amount to the same autonomy enjoyed by their female counter-parts in other parts of Nigeria. The point being pursued is that it implies that supervision of such ventures remains in the hands of men. That being the case, one can safely conjecture that there is minimal change of status of women in the context of this discourse.

The polygamous system, which is often condemned as being disadvantageous to women, was an aspect of a social institution which could have enabled women to make concrete contributions to society since it provided more hands to handle the various functions in the home, thereby enabling the participation of the co-wives in other productive social and economic ventures. However, with the imposition of colonialism and the influx of Islam, there was a contraction of opportunities within which women could play meaningful leadership roles. The colonial government policies, for instance, did not encourage women to take up and exercise leadership functions like those of men. Due to the colonial policy of indirect rule in Northern Nigeria, traditional and cultural structures, especially as they affected women, were left intact and hence women were disadvantaged vis-a-vis the men. With regard to Islam, as quoted elsewhere in this chapter, neither the teachings of the prophet Mohammed nor the precepts of the Qur'an or the Hadith recommended polygamy as a matter of course. Conversely, there are responsibilities which accompany the decision to marry more than one wife just as there is a good argument for the privileging of males over females in Islam, in terms of education and equal opportunities. In addition, even though polygamous marriages are likewise not regulated even in contemporary times, some women choose to be part of that structure voluntarily and argue that the benefits outweigh the costs. [10]

Pre-colonial Nigerian societies were structured around the centrality of kinship as the determinant of the productive and reproductive role of the individual in society. Childbearing was considered central to the worth of a woman. Since children were regarded as economic assets, polygamy was encouraged and a childless woman was considered to be incomplete. As a general rule, the more children an individual had, the more power he/she had in their respective societies. With the introduction of colonialism, most elements of the kinship support system disappeared or were considered outdated. Discrimination against women who are childless continues in customary law in cases where a man claims the full dowry paid for a childless woman while deductions are allowed if a woman has children. The right of women to work was affected by both the social relations within the family as well as in the larger society. Women in general had access to land which they could cultivate. However, the right to dispose of land was vested in the male head of the patrilineage. Therefore, access to the means of production was open to both sexes, but control was usually vested in men.[11]

In Northern Nigeria, colonialism diminished more than it enhanced the position of women in society. Women lost a great deal of authority and the opportunity to participate in decision-making processes due to their exclusion from all levels of administration. They also lost the very little and inconsequential manoeuvrability and power which they had exercised during the pre-colonial era because the male-dominant elements of society were stressed above all others and applied in social, economic, and political life. Education was generally considered a boon to women, who were able to emancipate themselves from oppression as a result of Westernization. The libratory effects of Western education are overrated because the emphasis of the colonial government was to prepare women for domestic work rather than for leadership roles within society.[12] Concrete pieces of evidence exist about the effect of education, which became the most important requirement for upward mobility during colonial rule. Since fewer women than men were educated, there was consequently less opportunity for women to gain access to positions of authority than men. During the colonial period, it may be conjectured that women were not unwilling to use new legal provisions regarding the capacity to engage in litigation against their not having prior consent to their marriage arrangements before or after its occurrence. In turn, they could not gain the enhanced property rights instituted by statutory law in divorce due to their lack of exposure and the constraints imposed on them by tradition, culture, and religion. The effect of Islam in Northern Nigeria was that it curtailed the economic independence of women as farmers and traders and totally excluded the royal women, who had political offices and positions of power. This was a result of the introduction of seclusion, which did not prevent women from involvement in trade but did prevent them from overtly organizing for political action as early as in the Southern region of Nigeria. Colonialism protected Islam and permitted its expansion. However, even though Muslim women in Northern Nigeria were denied access to Western education and consequently had fewer opportunities to gain employment in the colonial administration than their Southern counterparts, many Muslim women were educated in Qur'anic schools and continued to be educated by their husbands after marriage but in Islamic education. Since this form of education depends on the husband's cooperation, it is not the norm, but is rather, an exception.[13]

From the foregoing analysis, the origins of the structures of inequality leading to discrimination against women are therefore to be found in pre-colonial societies with predominantly male-dominant social systems in the institutionalization of "Native Law and Customs" that occurred during the colonial imposition as well as in the imposition of colonial rule and a new legal structure. Customs such as child marriage and betrothal and widowhood rites have their origins in the pre-colonial era, as did genital operations. The imposition of colonialism involved the construction of a system where women had less opportunity to participate in administration. In addition, an economic system was instituted where men had more opportunities than women for meaningful participation. A legal system was introduced wherein women lost some of the benefits open to them in pre-colonial societies and a religious system was imposed which deprived women of their pre-colonial power and authority. More males than females attended school and the form of Islam which had attained the stature of orthodoxy in the North was protected despite its discrimination against women.[14]

While women in Nigeria have always been active economically, the extent and significance of their activism has always been rewarded by commensurate degrees of political power vis-a-vis men. The situation remains the same at present despite the willingness of women to exercise the rights that they have. Structural constraints from the pre-colonial, colonial, and postcolonial eras continue to prevent the elimination of discrimination against women. It is possible to distinguish between two major positions espoused by organized women's groups within Nigeria, the one stressing the importance of more visibility in prominent positions for women as part of the decision-making apparatus and the other calling for radical changes and structural transformation so that providing rights for all women will have a continuing relevance. The first position constitutes the top-down approach held by the National Council of Women's Societies (NCWS) and the second, the more comprehensive and broadly-based approach of Women in Nigeria (WIN). Both organizations have made attempts to generate academic and other interest in the elimination of discrimination against women as they define it. Thus far, the position of the NCWS has received support by the successive Nigerian governments. The approach is usually taken to correct discrimination by appointing a few token women into positions where they have high visibility. However, this in no way helps the majority of women.[15]

Discrimination affects women's political and civil rights. The enfranchisement of women in Northern Nigeria was one of the political demands made by women's organizations in both the East and West of Nigeria after their own enfranchisement but the right to vote was only granted to women in the North of Nigeria in 1976. In the East, it had been granted in 1954 and in the West in 1958. Some have argued that the exercise of this right may be problematic even where it is guaranteed because of social constraints on the movement of women in purdah. Jadesola Akande suggests that women who are secluded in purdah may be unable to vote as a result of the electoral rules which end the voting day at 6 pm while women in purdah cannot go out until after sundown.[16] However, Oruene Joel, quoted in Patrick K. Uchendu's book states that it is common knowledge that women in purdah turned out in such large numbers to vote in the 1976 local government elections (which was the first in which they could participate on an equal footing with men) that the voting day was extended by those who exercised their rights as well as organized collective action within political interest and pressure groups toward the struggle for the enhancement of women's rights in society.[17]

There are still fewer women contesting for elections as compared to men, a situation that is also found in the United States and most democracies. The implication of Nigerian citizenship differed for men and women until this discrepancy in the status of women as compared to men was corrected by Nigeria's 1999 Constitution. Nonetheless, the attainment of some rights may still be outside the grasp of women due to continuing social and administrative challenges.[18] According to the Nigerian Constitution of 1999, discrimination on the basis of sex is prohibited. With reference to political and civil rights, all women and men have a right to vote once they have reached the age of 18. No expressed customary prohibitions prevent women's participation in politics but women have not contested for political positions on a level matching their male counterparts. The hesitancy of women to be involved in politics also dates back to the period of decolonization when politics was characterized by gross abuse and physical violence. Jadesola Akande contends that Nigerian women do not have full legal capacity insofar as they are unable to "independently enter into contracts ... acquire and own property ... enter into other legal transactions, sue or be sued."[19] The extent of practical freedom that a woman has also varies with class, level of education, and type of marriage. Within monogamous marriages, women may have more freedom than within polygamous marriages because there is a presumption of legal unity in the latter form of marriage which gives the man the advantage in terms of the capacity to marry, the right of consent and the requirements of dowry payment. Within this context, women's right to independent decision making may be curtailed.

Penal laws affect men and women differentially regardless of the fact that constitutionally, there are no legal distinctions between citizens in the protection of their property, freedom, reputation, and personal safety. The distinctions that exist are also attributed to prevailing social mores. Inadequacies exist with regard to access to health care, family planning facilities, social security programs, education, and in employment. Child betrothal and the marriage of individuals who are considered to be minors are carry-overs from the pre-colonial era which continue today in Northern Nigeria. In terms of the social systems that were operative then, individuals were deemed competent to be married at puberty. This violates contemporary provisions for the protection of women against discrimination but considering community standards at that time, the act did not constitute discrimination insofar as it applied to both sexes. However, it may be considered a denial of the right to self-determination to both males and females because the consent of the individuals getting married was not a prerequisite. Discrimination enters into the question when one of the partners was older than the other and was thus more competent to take such an important step and when marriage was imposed on unwilling parties.[20]

Another source of discrimination concerns the inability of women to control their own reproduction since social mores dictate the desirable number of children and their spacing. Childlessness was a stigma for both men and women but was often considered to be caused by the woman. Similarly, the institutionalization of the man as the primary and final decision maker and the head of the family after the codification of customary law during the colonial era curtailed the rights of women significantly. The effect of such institutionalized male dominance was in some cases, to endanger the health and life of a woman or curtail her right to vote and her freedom of movement, the denial of equality within a family to women, inequality in childrearing and decision making processes concerning child care and in the right to inherit and own property. In Northern Nigeria, keeping concubines is another pre-colonial holdover that is still prevalent and places women in a situation where they have absolutely no rights but exist wholly at the mercy of their male patrons.[21] Bilqisu Abubakar captures this last issue in the novel when Ahmad's mother reminiscences thus:

She took a deep breath, and pondered over her younger days. She recalled vividly how she insisted that her husband took another wife after the death of one of her co-wives… She had never imagined how life would be like with a woman living in a large house all by herself without a co-wife who would serve also as friend and companion.[22]

Other pre-colonial institutions became subject to abuse as well. The requirement for the payment of the bride price in some societies was accompanied in pre-colonial times with compulsory performance of bride-service, a clearly enunciated rule of behaviour that was proper for all parties to a marriage. However, the payment of the bride price has become institutionalized in a negative manner that is tantamount, in some cases, to a drastic reduction in the personal freedom of women and a gross reduction in their capacity for independent action.[23]

The above problems arose from ideological and structural sources; in the first place, from the manner in which indigenous social structures were institutionalized during colonial rule. Consequently, Bolanle Awe confirms that men's and women's rights differed and led to their inequality in the family, lineage, and political affairs. Secondly, from both the practice of Islam and Christianity came a prescription of a purely domestic role for women. Third, colonial rule provided an elaboration of the differences between the sexes and the creation of substantial legal, social, and material inequalities between men and women. For instance, men were more educated, owned business concerns because they could go out, could gain white collar jobs, and were financially more disposed to acquire other materials of life. The post-colonial government in Nigeria merely maintained policies responsible for material inequality. This is both for concrete gain by men vis-a-vis women and for the ideological maintenance of the superiority of men as opposed to women.[24]

In the post second republic era, specifically under the leadership of Gen. Ibrahim B. Babangida, Nigeria underwent the implementation of a Structural Adjustment Program (SAP), which combined policies of economic contraction due to the austerity experienced in the country along with the devaluation of the country's currency, drastic cutbacks in government spending and a significant economic contraction due to the privatization of government-owned businesses. It was common knowledge that those very salient actions affected the condition of all Nigerians, but particularly the situation of women. Women's economic rights were affected most directly since there were fewer employment opportunities and more competition for those that existed in the rural and urban areas. In this vein, Jane Parpart notes that whereas development schemes had traditionally hindered rather than helped women and technology and training benefited men and marginalized women, the situation was more gruelling under conditions of structural adjustment. This was because of a contraction of social spending and also to less money being available from international sources for development projects. The provision of basic infrastructure while inadequate in the past has become even more so in the present. In addition, health care, education, training, access to appropriate technology and to necessities of life such as potable water, have become even more inaccessible, both to rural and urban women.[25] This is the background against which the existing discrimination against women in Nigerian society should be viewed.

SOME PERCEPTIONS OF THE BURDEN IN *TO LIVE AGAIN*

Bilqisu Abubakar was born into the male dominated, Islamic Hausa-Fulani ethnic group in Northern Nigeria. *To Live Again* (abbreviated as TLA), Abubakar's first novel, made only the long list in Nigeria's popular and prestigious Liquefied Natural Gas Award for Literature in 2008. For Abubakar, the manner in which women are burdened by discriminatory social, economic, and religious structures, as well as possible remedies to these constraints, is of primary importance. In the context of the above and having taken a critical assessment of all the methods hitherto applied in order to find possible and lasting solutions to these constraints, Abubakar has decided on finding other ways to ensure that the women, starting from the point of their sexuality up to their period of mothering, are able to overwhelm the burden society in general has placed on them. TLA is a flash-back that narrates the very simple love-marriage/voyage into uncertainty of the divorced protagonist, Uwani, with her erstwhile adorable Ahmad which was based on innocence, love, and respect. In the course of recounting her experiences after just eleven years of marriage to Ahmad, she pours out her feelings of irritation, shock, rancour, and frustration at her husband's desertion of her for other wives. She expresses her confusion in her attempts to unravel the mind-set of Ahmad, in particular, and men in general, who marry out of love only to dump the wife for another without any feeling for the woman that is so dumped. The novel shows that it is only after Uwani decides to rebuild her life and find fulfilment that she learns to rely on her own efforts.

The burden placed on Uwani, the representative of women in this novel, comes from internal and external sources. The novel shows that women have internalized a socially constructed sense of self that makes them accept, either consciously or unconsciously, the role of a second fiddle in society. Commenting on this behaviour, Ashley Montagu says "women have been so long conditioned in the environment of masculine dominance that they have come to expect the male to be dominant and the female to be subservient."[26] In Northern Nigerian society where the novel is set, there is no gain-saying that women are always treated as second-rate or non-humans. They are seldom consulted on general family matters in spite of the existence of such a requirement in the Holy Qur'an and the Hadith. This is even more so before a husband makes the decision to marry an additional wife (s). For example, Ahmad marries Khadija, his immediate near juvenile ex-student, best friend to his oldest daughter, and Uwani's (his first wife's) hair stylist. He marries Khadija on claims of love, but in reality, it is an act meant to please his mother and to show that he is a man. The bottom line, however, is that the act is planed and executed without discussing the issue with Uwani, his first wife. Subsequently, in such related issues, the opinions of his wives do not matter with regard to their marriage or on subsequent marriages.[27]

Is it conceivable that a man's planned marriage to a second wife could be concealed and announced to the fist wife as if nothing unreasonable is going to happen. That is how Uwani is treated by Ahmad. This same treatment repeats itself when Ahmad eventually takes a third and fourth wife. Unfortunately, such treatment is meted out to women who serve their husband dutifully. While Uwani is yet to fully recover from the grave shock of the divorce that also separates her from her two children, her father encourages her to get married immediately. He says: "I have been fair to you; in fact I have been called names by a number of people all because of you." She tries to speak but he cuts her off. "That I allowed you acquire western education is not a license for you to do what you please."... "If you fail to bring a man soon enough I will have to arrange for one myself. I don't have anything more to say to you."[28] Uwani's mother also contributes thus: "You have to settle down Uwani. Being single is not and will never be a (sic) a part of our tradition and cultural heritage... The society can never see anything good in you. You do not command any respect, neither do you have any honour if you remain single."[29] The above quote exposes the position of the woman in Northern Nigeria. Uwani our stereotype in this case is reduced to the status of a voiceless personality. In addition, the statement implies that she is also placed in a position where she must help save herself and members of her family from the condemnation that emanates from the insensitivity of society that desires a woman to obey its rules of existence without providing any sympathy for the negative effect that these actions would have on her personality. Not only does Uwani politely decline the piece of advice but she begins to chart a way for her survival and self fulfilment. This male (or is it societal) perception of a woman as a possession to be carried away by the highest bidder is reinforced in the novel when a man's money and not his moral qualities is all that matters to families. Uwani's father, for example, is piqued because Uwani does not see the reason to marry a man like Alhaji Abdulkadir. While her father foresees the fruit of such a union in material terms, also bearing in mind his very poor and uncolorful background, Uwani looks at it from the moral and emotional perspectives. Hence the author records it thus in the novel:

> Girls of about 14 years were married off immediately; men came from the big cities and towns, in different cars in search of young girls to take home as wives. The parents always preferred such men over those from their community; they felt that the men were capable and had the wherewithal to cater for their daughters and members of her extended family. One of such men was Alhaji Abdulkadir.
>
> Uwani's father had been captivated by the man's wealthy background.
>
> "Alhaji will guarantee you all the happiness you deserve; you won't have to worry about anything whatsoever should you marry him;" he said to Uwani in all sincerity. Her mother who was seated close by nodded in approval.

"All a woman needs is a man capable of giving her all she desires, as for love, it grows with time," she added.

If there was anything Uwani dreaded so much, it was divorce. With three sisters below the age of twenty-one who were already divorcees, she felt that perhaps arranged marriages was the reason why their marriages failed.

She had confided in her mother why she wanted so much to be married to Ahmad and wanted her mother to understand her reasoning:.

"I would not want to be a victim of failed marriage, I believe in marriage and want it to work for me," she said trying to convince her mother who snapped back almost immediately.

"Listen Uwani, what will be will be. Even marriages built on love do collapse. That your sister's marriages broke up is not anybody's making, it is simply an act of fate."

With rumour agog in their small community that Uwani was contemplating marrying Ahmad instead of the wealthy businessman, her mother's patience ran out. She began to lose sleep and would occasionally be caught talking to herself. Uwani who had encountered her on one such occasion asked in total surprise.

"Are you alright mother?"

With a frown on her face she retorted, "I could be better if only you stop reasoning like a child."

Holding on to her wrapper and wiping the sweat from her forehead she turned to Uwani.

"Just what kind of life you want beside the one Alhaji is willing and desperately wants to give you?" she asked rather calmly.

The last thing on Uwani's mind was a second thought about her choice of man. She vowed never to have anything to do with anyone beside Ahmad.

"I love him so much, he means so much to me and I know that I will find lasting peace with him," Uwani said trying to reassure her mother who would not want to hear anything positive about her choice.

"You can only be happy when you have a wealthy man to take care of all your needs. Forget about the tales of love Ahmad preaches to you, besides that is all he has to offer."

"Oh no mother, please don't talk like that!"

Uwani cuts in, but her mother would not stop at that.

"A man who only preaches love is not worth his salt. A real man shows the depth of his love for his woman by showering her with money and the good things of life," she said looking towards another direction avoiding Uwani's reaction.

"But what about time and affection with one another? She managed to ask.

"Only lazy men spend time at home with their wives under the pretext of love and affection," she replied.

Uwani went through a series of counselling from friends and family members while some just watched events unfold before their eyes. Some felt that she was being foolish by not agreeing to marry Ahmad while some felt indifferent and believed that what will be will be.

Habiba her sister would always console her saying, "Do not worry Uwani, if it is the will of Allah that you become Ahmad's wife, nobody including Baba can stop that."

But not so for Zainabu, who was about the same age with Uwani. She would scornfully say to her, "Since when did it become a pride to dishonour one's parent? Or are we more knowledgeable than them?"

"The last people I could ever dishonour are our parents, I may have rejected their choice of man, but that does not mean that I have chosen Ahmad over them."

"Why don't you accept their choice then if they mean so much to you like you claim?"

"It's not as easy as you think, my heart simply belongs to someone else," replied Uwani.

Zainabu tried to make her feel guilty most of the time; she was unlike Uwani who was more of an introvert, and on the reserved side. Her life ambition was to live a life of affluence.

"I would not hesitate in marrying a man like Alhaji if I find one, what can be as nice as having someone to take care of all your bills?"

"What about love and affection Zainabu?" Uwani asked. "Love is all-encompassing, what is love when you are denied the basic things of life?"

She was Uwani's step-sister; they shared the same father and were of the same age with the difference of a few months. Uwani's mother had no choice but to submit to her husband's wish. The same could not be said of Zain-abu's mother who had an obsession for worldly things. Most young men in their village stayed away from any of her daughters.

"Forget about love, it only breeds unhappiness when it goes sour, but with a lot of money, you will always find happiness," was her usual admonition.

Uwani's father had gradually lost his patience. In anger and desperation, a few days later, he entered her mother's room without saying the usual, *Assalamu Alaikum*. It was just before the Magrib prayers and mother and daughter were both seated on the mat spread across the floor in the not too spacious room.

"Thank God you are both here," he said looking very angry and disappointed.

"Anything the matter?" her mother managed to ask.

"Oh sure, everything is the matter, you have failed me as a wife," he said as he shook his head in disappointment pointing towards Uwani's direction.

"All I ask of you Uwani is to marry Alhaji but you refuse. What have I not done for you as a father?" he roared.

Uwani began to sob with her head bent downwards, in an emotion-laden voice she pleaded with him.

"I have never loved Alhaji. Even if I accept to be his wife now, I would still come out of the marriage later. I don't want to start what I cannot finish."

"At least you would have honoured me," he said. As he made for the door, she called out to him gently.

"Father, please I ask for your forgiveness, I learnt that Alhaji is proposing to marry Luba now and she has accepted.

"Who wouldn't?" her father retorted. "A man like Alhaji can get any kind of woman that pleases him," he commented.

Alhaji's choice was Uwani but he opted out when he discovered that she had someone else in mind. His new bride, Luba, was a beautiful fifteen-year old girl, a cohort of Uwani. Her parents had given her out as sadaka to him.

In no time, wedding arrangements were made and it was the event that everyone looked forward to. Princes, Islamic scholars, and title-holders were in attendance as they graced the wedding. Praise-singers were not left out. The Ango made a grand entrance. He had an unusual size. He was dark-skinned with a big round stomach and one could easily perceive the fragrance of expensive perfume he wore, complemented with the heavily embroiled Bab-barriga and turban. The Almajirai could not have wished for more than they got that day. They had more than enough to eat and take away.

The bride's parents, apart from a promised journey to the Holy Land, had their old home renovated, with a constant supply of foodstuff in sacks enough to go round the large family. They became the envy of most parents.

The bride's portmanteau had so much of every-thing including expensive perfumes, gold necklaces, and bangles of mostly Saudi Arabian design. The sets of boxes contained expensive fabrics and the Atampa were of high quality just like the shadda and voiles. There were geles of different colours and designs. The wedding was the talk of the town for a long time. They became members of Alhaji's already large household and their upkeep and well-being became his sole responsibility. The union between the duo was a welcome development to some of his friends and associates. All his wives were well taken care of and he kept watchful eyes over them. None of them were allowed to leave the vicinity of their home without his consent and they were hardly ever granted the right to go out.

Most of the women he divorced were replaced almost immediately. He never hesitated in divorcing any woman who craved for independence. Not known for half mea-sures, he lavished good money on his wives and in-laws.

"Only the best is good enough for me," he said when-ever he was being complimented on his choice of women. "Oh? Do you expect me to spend so much money on something that is not worthy of it?" he asked his associates rhetorically.

And they would round up with a hearty laughter. He had the last say and his words were important. He was always surrounded by Jama'a and he was a man of the people as his alias suggests Alhaji Abdulkadir mai Jama'a. The not well-educated man was always in the know of what happened within and outside the country as a widely travelled man.[30]

It might have been a non-issue a century ago for women to accept the concept of polygamy, but it is certainly an important issue now in the twenty-first century. Polygamy, to some women, symbolises denigration, exploitation, and domination in Northern Nigeria. Literally, the 'home' or 'family' unit is symptomatic of a place where one is both at ease and at peace with him/herself, regardless of whether that family is made up of one or more women. On the contrary, data available even to the layman on marital issues indicate that the polygamous home is akin to a market with a cacophony of voices and tempers. The co-wives, children, and the husband are always under immense tension that is continuously engendered by envy, intrigues, and all other sorts of overt and covert manipulations of passions. It is imperative to state that although the Islamic religion sanctions polygamy, in the same vein, it provides a very serious and thought-provoking proviso when the Qur'an says:

> Marry women of your choice,
> Two, or three, or four;
> But if ye fear that ye shall not
> Be able to deal justly (with them)
> Then only one.[31]

But in the context of this discourse, the real practice, it has been impossible for men to treat more than one woman equally. Real life pieces of evidence as enunciated by the novelist show that the newest wife (meaning last or youngest wife) at each point in time in the marital chess board is usually favored by the husband even when the Qur'an stipulates, requests, and insists on fair treatment for all of the wives. After just a few years of marriage when the embers of love are deemed to still be hot, Ahmad decides to marry a second and third wife in successive turns and for very untenable reasons. As it were, materially and morally, each last wife enjoys his immense pampering to the disadvantage of the wife or wives before them. Uwani is virtually abandoned in all respects as soon as the second wife steps in and the same situation exists for her and the subsequent wives. In spite of that, Uwani is still prepared to love her husband according to the Islamic and cultural injunctions and expectations. But the unreasonable behaviour of Ahmad when he decides to serve her with a divorce letter instead of sympathizing with her plight makes her think deeply.

Issuing from the above, one notes that either wittingly or unwittingly, religious beliefs, in this case, Islamic religion, coincide very often with cultural practices to keep women in perpetual subjection. Interestingly, before the advent of Islam, polygamy had been the mainstay of marital relationships in Northern Nigeria; however, institutionalized polygamy as laid down in the Qur'an gives its adherents a justification for the practice which cannot stand rational interpretations in the twenty-first century. The Qur'an enjoins men to marry more than one wife so long as they can love them equally. Since this cannot be quantified, it simply offers men the mischievous opportunity to marry as many women as they can. Meanwhile, that misinterpreted injunction gives men the right to see themselves as superior as compared to women. Sadly, religion exerts such a powerful influence on the women so much that they willingly accept its precepts unquestionably even when such are arbitrary. Hence, Uwani is expected to accept Ahmad's misbehaviour as sacrosanct. This is more so when justification for self-serving actions against women are most times anchored in the Islamic belief that whatever happens is God's will. One example of this is when Ahmad struggles to justify his second and subsequent marriages and the achievements of Uwani after her divorce. Ahmad's mother prepares ground for this when she says "Marriage has been ordained by God Almighty, whosoever tries to obstruct a marriage is not only bad but evil." [32] Therefore, Ahmad supports his action when he also says "Life is all about change. Nothing in life is constant."[33]

Uwani's divorce reopens the wounds inflicted on her all through her marriage of servitude and makes her reflect on marriage in general in Northern Nigeria. Her state of mind can be fathomed from the opening passage in the novel:

> She sat hurdled in a corner of the room, her grief almost tangible but not concealing her innate beauty.
>
> "So this is it?" Uwani thought.
>
> Eleven years of marriage and all she had to show for it was a bruised heart, a remorseless husband and an unknown future...
>
> Trying to dwell on the positive side of the past but it was all back like it was just yesterday. She was barely sixteen when she married Ahmad, she never met any

> other man, never loved any other; he was her first and only
> love. The courtship had lasted less than three months..."[34]

The above situation only underscores the pain, frustration, disappointment, and anger experienced by a woman who does not expect to be treated so unkindly by a man she had loved and served so devotedly. The situation is compounded for Ahmad's second wife, Khadija, Uwani's co-wife when Ahmad marries a third wife (Zulai). Having enjoyed a good measure of patronage at the expense of Uwani, the first wife, Khadija is traumatised beyond expected limits when it becomes her turn to play second fiddle to a third wife. As stated earlier, she becomes completely traumatised to the extent that she engages in using unconventional methods to win back her husband's love; this includes the use of voodoo! Her actions in this regard are hinged on the very common societal belief that the new wife, Hajara, who is far older and more exposed in worldly ways, has used a local charm to lure Ahmad to marry her. Meanwhile, based on the story in the novel, it is clear that other than invoking the provisions of the Islamic religion to support his actions, Ahmad's rising status in society engendered the desire to marry and relate with only those that are at his level even when they are deemed older than him as in the case of the third wife. The fourth wife is well travelled, educated, wealthy, and has entrepreneurial, political, economic, and social connections. These are attributes that none of the other wives possessed and could boast of and that are dear in Ahmad's heart because of his desire to move in relevant circles.

Though the novel does not dwell principally on the relationship between wives, in-laws, and other women, tangential aspects of such relationships are still explored somewhat. The author shows how the role and influence of the in-laws is yet another burden for the married woman. In the Northern Nigerian society portrayed in the novel, the woman does not talk back to her in-laws. Nor can her husband refuse to do the bidding of his parents even when it is against his immediate desire. This is the source of the initial clash that occurs in the course of Uwani and Ahmad's marriage. No sooner that it becomes clear that Uwani is unable to give birth after having borne two children, her mother-in-law requests her son to consider marrying another wife to enable her to have more grand-children before her death. The old woman plots her actions in a clever and crafty manner as shown in the following quotations of her discussions with her son:

> *Assalamu Alaikum,* Ahmad said to announce his presence
> "Dan Gayu" she called out. She had just finished her sup-
> plication when Ahmad went to see her, (sic) she had been
> thinking of him and he appeared just in time.
>
> "Thank God you are here my son."
>
> "Is everything ok Gwaggo?"
>
> "Everything is ok, except that as you can see, I am old
> and tired."... "Haba Gwaggo."
>
> "No, you don't get it my child."
>
> "Get what, Gwaggo?"...
>
> "You have given me enough to eat, I have good shelter
> and I have never lacked what to wear."
>
> "Then what is the problem mother, remember you tell
> me almost everything," Ahmad said trying to convince her
> to speak out.
>
> "It's Uwani." She began to speak.
>
> "What about her?"
>
> "Can't you see, two children are not enough, I need
> more grand-children from you, I am getting old."
>
> "So this is your problem?" he asked with a frail smile.
>
> "Oh yes child that's all I ask of you," she replied.
>
> "Do you anyone in mind? he asked.
>
> "Oh yes, have you taken a good look at Wasila
> lately?"[35]

Having sown her mischievous seed in the mind of Ahmad to consider marrying her friend's fourteen year old daughter or any other girl
at that, in Uwani's dream, while asleep on their way back to the city
after the fateful visit to the village, Ahmad's mother convenes an emergency meeting of all her daughter's-in-laws for the final kill:

> Tossing and turning she heard Nana asking Gwaggo:
>
> "Just why have you decided to assemble us all here?
> referring to the nine wives of some of her children includ-
> ing Uwani.
>
> Gwaggo had instructed that all wives gather for an
> urgent issue to be discussed.
>
> "Just when will she realize that like her own children,
> we are also human and stop this idea of meddling into our
> affairs?" one of them pondered....
>
> "As you are all aware, I am old and tired."...

> "I have gathered you all here in appreciation of your good deeds since you became my children's wives over these years."...
>
> "Marriage has been ordained by God Almighty, whoever tries to obstruct a marriage is not only bad but evil" she stressed...
>
> "As for you, Uwani you have been a wonderful wife to your husband only God can reward you for your humility and kindness"....
>
> "You need to show gratitude to your husband for sticking to you alone over these years. The trend is not only unusual among us, I also find it strange."
>
> She took a deep breath, and pondered over her younger days. She recalled vividly how she insisted that her husband took another wife after the death of one of her co-wives... She had never imagined how life would be like with a woman living in a large house all by herself without a co-wife who would serve also as a friend and companion.
>
> "I learnt that your house in the city is big enough to accommodate another wife?" She quizzed Uwani.
>
> "Well then, since all you have given him is a boy and girl, allow him marry another wife".
>
> "It is true, I have only been able to give him Yasmin and Faisal, but I have never deprived him of taking another wife, his decision to remain monogamous is entirely his," Uwani said in all sincerity.
>
> "And why have you as a virtuous woman not encouraged him to take another wife?" she fired back...
>
> "The best among you is one whose Imam is strong enough not only to embrace her co-wife as her own flesh and blood but to also withstand her presence in the home" she concluded. [36]

Additionally, in some instances in the novel such as when the family prepares to welcome Ahmad back from school, Uwani's mother-in-law acts as though she should have more rights over her son than Uwani and her children. And because Ahmad's station in life is improving at a fast rate, the Matron in his school devises ways and means to enable her young daughter, Khadija, to marry Ahmad and thus become the second wife. This is in the Matron's bid to improve her societal status.

Unfortunately, this divisive effort undermines any of the negative effect the Matron's action is expected to have on the other woman, Uwani, the first wife in the house. This untoward attitude not only turns the woman into a near worthless piece of cloth without dignity and claim to her individuality, but it also shows her as someone whose only goal in life is to procreate. It also shows that women are also the root cause of the travails of other women.

Further, whether literate, if the woman succeeds in acquiring an education before a marriage as in the case of Khadija (Uwani's co-wife), or is illiterate, as in the case of Uwani who only succeeds to acquire the education that comes to her eventual rescue, the women in monoga-mous/polygamous families bear the burden of being wives, mothers, house/peace-keepers and child-bearers. As a primary teacher, Khadija is expected to perform the double responsibility of being a worker and a married woman. Uwani, a full-time house-wife, performs her functions too. The woman remains the workforce of the house in this situation. She organises, supervises, and performs most of the domestic functions in the home. Women's labor is symbolic of the enormous unappreciated responsibility that they shoulder. Apart from performing physical chores, a mother's mental capacity is taxed to the fullest while trying to sustain the family sometimes using very lean resources (and even when the resources are fat, there is the issue of the absence of satisfaction), settling quarrels between rival wives and children, offering guidance and counselling to children, and when the children misbehave or something goes wrong, getting the blame for it. For example, interspersed with so many acts of indignities on his various wives, instead of pacifying them, Ahmad lashes out angrily at Uwani. Ahmad calls his three wives for a meeting (see pages 89-94) apparently to tell them he has taken another wife. He seems to take too much time to pass on this information. Suspecting an inner confusion that makes him unable to find his bearing, as usual, Uwani comes to his aid by asking if he intends to take another wife again. It is at this point Ahmad finds a away out, precipitating the crisis that earns Uwani the final divorce.

Abubakar also shows that the burdens borne by women often have their origins in traditional practices, beliefs, and prejudices that are often linked or confused with religious practices. They thrive partly because of the ignorance about the role and ability of the woman in a society and a deliberate desire to subordinate them. Female subservience is not biologically produced but is culturally imposed. No wonder, other than the sections of the novel already referred to, pieces of evidence abound in the novel where parents, friends, and relatives keep emphasizing the place of culture/tradition in marital relationships. To them, the woman is expected to be subservient, passive, and accepting at all times even when the men or the society that governs them act in ways inimical to the survival of the woman even in these modern times. In the novel, Uwani's parents and sisters drum this message into Uwani before and after her failed marriage.

TOWARDS OVERWHELMING THE BURDENS

In the context of the foregoing flux in respect of the burdens of the women in Northern Nigeria, Abubakar's novel raises incisive and fundamental interpretations of the situation and strategizes on how those can be overcome by the women. The crucial aspects of these are unmindful but a challenge to the existing points of view and plethora of efforts being marshalled by the Nigerian government and various agencies towards overcoming the discussed burdens. A few of those are briefly elaborated below. Pointedly, unlike often taunted perceptions on the forces that engender discriminations against women especially in Northern Nigeria, Abubakar insists that neither the Qur'an, which signifies the Islamic religion, nor tradition/culture create the basis to pillory women with burdens. As contextualized in the novel, Ahmad's actions are predicated principally on a flagrant and intentional misinterpretation of the dicta in the Qur'an and tradition/culture by the society in general and men in particular to ensure that women are perpetually kept in servitude. Using Ahmad and Abdulkadir (husband to Asmau, Uwani's childhood friend) as examples, their continuous exploitative tendencies against their wives are a manifestation of the innate evil nature of man. Man exploits all those societal strictures placed on the path of women for his own personal self-aggrandizement. Additionally, the author also shows how, in the twenty-first century with all its developments that should ensure cordial human co-existence, women just like men, sometimes fan the embers of the fire that both creates and facilitates the placing of various burdens on women. For how does one explain the roles played by Khadija's mother that ensures that Ahmad marries her daughter as the second wife; Gwaggo, Uwani's mother-in-law that sows the seed that enables the marriage of Khadija and the co-wife of Asmau, Uwani's childhood friend? The cumulative conclusion of these actions by the women indicates that women also work against women. In addition, the lack of economic, political, and educational power by the women continues to keep them in a position of disadvantage relative to men and keeps them perpetually tied to the whims and caprices of men. The combinations of these forces also subject all the women in the novel except "Hajara, the latest wife, to such perennial servitude. She was a trained nurse from a wealthy family"[37] and Nana, Uwani's home-teacher and mentor, to be at the receiving end of the brutal actions of men.

In light of the issues raised above, Abubakar proffers some modest strategies to solve the problems. First, is the need for women to believe in themselves and their capacities, like the existentialists, to ensure that they know that their destinies lie in their hands and that things will be better! She bemoans and debunks the erroneous assumption that oftentimes women do not believe in this ability to move beyond the proverbial letter 'C' (ala George Orwell's *Animal Farm*) unless assisted by men and contrasts the development of Uwani with those of Khadija, Asmau, Gwaggo and Uwani's mother. The cardinal example in the novel is Uwani's unwavering decision to denounce all social, religious, economic, political, and cultural strictures to embrace education as a panacea to her predicament. In the context of this realization, though in pains by all the onuses that bestrode her life before the long awaited divorce, she eventually believes that she has the capacity to achieve long life fulfilment if only she strives to achieve. This means surmounting all of the barriers placed in her way by all the aforementioned forces to plunge herself into uncertainty by proceeding to acquire an education, the seed of which was sown by the Ghanaian widow, Nana.

In the first place, her decision to marry Ahmad has been confirmed, in the context of the story, to be akin to a voyage to uncertainty; so her desire to acquire further education is a continuous journey to come face to face with that uncertainty, except that this voyage is worth the effort. Nana and all her female friends that she interacts with at the University and the Law school make her aware that educating a woman, apart from providing her with a profession which translates into economic, social, and political independence, makes her eventually self-reliant, giving her self-confidence and self-fulfilment. She gets married but after eleven years of that marriage, she realises that a woman that depends on a husband or on lovers for her livelihood is doomed to suffer perpetually. So, after eleven years of marriage, she does not only proceed to complete her university education by earning the Bachelors of Law degree, but also proceeds to study for and passes the Law School examination to practice as a Barrister. At this point, because of her ugly past experience, she is sceptical of the love overtures of Umar even when he means well.

CONCLUSION

To conclude, it is safe to say that the summary of Abubakar's point of view in the novel is that she feels strongly that in order for women to be perpetually free from constant domination by men, there is the need for society in general and women/men in particular to have a change of heart which translates to a change in attitude. This confirms the postulation by Awa Thiam when she says "to truly liberate (the) woman, a change of mentality is indispensable." [38] Man is encouraged to discard his pervasive habits of seeing a woman "as a means of satisfying his excessive sexual propensity or a necessary complement to his social and economic functions."[39] Among many other postulations as extrapolated before now, the author insists that the relationship between men and women is complementary. To the author, masculinity in men and femininity in women are not qualities that indicate superiority or inferiority. It is only in the spirit of providing equality between the man and woman, working together, especially in the twenty-first century, that we can hope to ensure that the final death knells are applied to eradicate the numerous problems placed on the shoulders of women in Northern Nigeria.

Notes

1. Bilqisu Abubakar, *To Live Again* (Kaduna: Zakara Communications Ltd, 2007).

2. Consideration of Reports Submitted by States Parties under Article 18 of the Convention: Initial Reports of States Parties, Nigeria-Geneva Committee on the Elimination of Discrimination Against Women (11 May, 1987) 1-5.

3. These views are explored and shared in Andrew Colin Bymes, *The "Other" Human Rights Treaty Body: The Work of the Committee on the Elimination of all Forms of Discrimination Against Women* (Unpublished), Columbia University Thesis, 1988; Nina Emma Mba, *Nigerian Women Mobilized: Women's Political Activity in Southern Nigeria, 1900-1965* (Berkeley, California: Research Series / University of California, Berkeley Institute of International Studies, 1982); Claude E. Welch and Ronald Meltzer (eds), *Human Rights and Development in Africa* (Albany, New York: State University of New York Press, 1984).

4. Bolanle Awe, *Nigerian Women in Historical Perspective* (Lagos: Sankore / Bookcraft, 1992), 62-65; Catherine Cole and Beverly Mack, *Hausa Women in the Twentieth Century* (Madison: University of Wisconsin, 1991), 17.

5. Ifi Amadiume, *Male Daughters, Female Husbands: Gender and Sex in an African Society* (London: Zed Books, 1987), 72; Amina Wadud, "Rights and Roles of Women," *in Islam in Transition: Muslim Perspectives, ed. John J. Donohue and John L. Esposito* (New York and Oxford: Oxford University Press, 2007) 157 and 169.

6. Catherine Cole and Beverly Mack, *Hausa Women in the Twentieth Century* (Madison: University of Wisconsin, 1991) 16-17; Amina Wadud, "Rights and Roles of Women' in *Islam in Transition: Muslim Perspectives,* eds., John J. Donohue and John L. Esposito (New York and Oxford: Oxford University Press, 2007), 157 and 169.

7. Ramatu Abdullahi, *Self-Concept and Cultural Change Among the Hausa* (Ibadan: Ibadan University Press, 1986), 62-64.

8. Catherine VerEecke, "Muslim Women Traders of Northern Nigeria: Perspectives from the City of Yola" in, *African Market Women and Economic Power: The Role of Women in African Economic Development,* eds, Bessie House-Midamba and Felix K. Ekechi (Westport: Greenwood Press), 59.

9. Ibid., 59.

10. The opinions expressed by the notable Northern Nigerian prose-stylist Zaynab Alkali bear this argument out as the ideas are explored in her novels *The Stillborn* (London: Longman, (1986), *The Virtuous Woman* (London: Longman, 2005), *The Descendants* (Zaria: Tamaza); Mansur Ibrahim Said, "The Influence of Culture and Tradition in Divorce: Implications for Marital Stability" in *The Rights of Widows and Divorcees in Hausa-Fulani Society,* eds. Ibrahim A. Malumfashi and Salisu Yakasa (Sokoto: Garkuwa Media Services, 2002), 70-72; Bilkisu Yususf, "Hausa-Fulani Women: The State of the Struggle" in *Hausa Women in the Twentieth Century,* eds., Catherine Cole and Beverly Mack (Madison:

University of Wisconsin, 1991), 80-81; and Bilkisu Yusuf, "Sexuality and the Marriage Institution in Islam: An Appraisal", Understanding Human Sexuality Seminar Series 4 (Lagos: Africa Regional Sexuality Resource Centre, 2005), 6-8.

11. Ramatu Abdullahi, *Self-Concept and Cultural Change among the Hausa* (Ibadan: Ibadan University Press, 1986), 67-68.

12. Peter Kazenga Tibendarana, 'The beginning of Girls Education in the Native Administration Schools in Northern Nigeria, 1930-1945," in *The Journal of African History*, 26, 1985, 93-94 and in Jean Trevor, "Education of Moslem Hausa Women from Sokoto", *MSS. Afr. S.* 1755 (79A) (Oxford: Rhodes House), 56.

13. Hafsatu I. Kaita, "Women's Education in the States of Nigeria 1950-1972" in Jean Trevor, *MSS. l Afr. S.* 1755 (79A) (Oxford: Rhodes House) 12; *Eastern Region of Nigeria Gazette*, 26/8 (Enugu: Eastern Region of Nigeria Gazette, 37:8), 258-9.

14. Ayesha Imam, Ruth Pittin and Harriet Omole, *Women and the Family: Edited Proceedings of the Second Annual Women in Nigeria Conference* (Dakar: Codesria, 1985), 5-7; Catherine Dinnick-Parr, MSS. Afr. S., " Education of Moslem Hausa Women from Sokoto" in *MSS. Afr. S.* (1889) (Oxford: Rhodes House), 105-108.

15. Ayesha Imam, Ruth Pittin and Harriet Omole, Women and the Family: Edited Proceedings of the Second Annual Women in Nigeria Conference (Dakar: Codesria, 1985), 5-7.

16. Jadesola O.Akande, *Laws and Customs Affecting Women in Nigeria* (Lagos: International Federation of Women Lawyers, 1979), 72.

17. Patrick Kenechukwu Uchendu, *The Role of Nigerian Women in Politics: Past and Present* (Enugu: Fourth Dimension Publishers, 1993), 85.

18. Chapter Four of the *Constitution of the Federal Republic of Nigeria* Promulgated in the 1999 Decree No. 24 explains in greater details these various freedoms.

19. Akande, *Laws and Customs Affecting Women in Nigeria*, 80.

20. Ibid., 81.

21. Bolanle Awe, *Nigerian Women in Historical Perspective* (Lagos: Sankore / Bookcraft, 1992).

22. Abubakar, *To Live Again*, 59.

23. Catherine Cole and Beverly Mack, *Hausa Women in the Twentieth Century* (Madison: University of Wisconsin, 1991), 97-8.

24. Abubakar, *To Live Again*, 59.

25. Jane Parpart, *Women and Development in Africa: Comparative Perspectives, Dalhousie African Studies Series 7* (Lanham, Maryland: University Press of America, 1989), 69.

26. Ashley Montagu, *The Natural Superiority of Women* (London: Collier Macmillan, 1974), 26.

27. Abubakar, *To Live Again*, 62-65.

28. Ibid., 160.

29. Ibid., 161-3.

30. Ibid., 5-14.

31. Yusuf Ali, *The Holy Qur'an, Translation and Commentary* (Cairo: Islamic Publication Bureau, 2009), 100.

32. Op cit, 58.

33. Ibid., 65.

34. Ibid., 1.

35. Ibid., 50-53.

36. Ibid., 57-60.

37. Ibid., 94.

38. Awa Thiam, *La Parole aux Négresses* (Paris: Denoë, 1978) 191.

39. Thomas Melone, Mongo Béti: l'homme et le destin (Paris: Présence Africaine, 1971), 191.

Bibliography

Abdullahi, Ramatu, *Self-concept and Cultural Change among the Hausa.* Ibadan: Ibadan University Press, 1986.

Abubakar, Bilqisu, *To Live Again.* Kaduna: Zakara Communications Ltd, 2007.

Alkali, Zaynab, *The Stillborn.* London: Longman, 1984.

______, *The Virtuous Woman.* London: Longman, 1986.

______, *The Descendants.* Zaria: Tamaza, 2005.

Ali, Yusuf, *The Holy Qur'an, Translation and Comment.ary.* Cairo: Islamic Publication Bureau, 2009.

Akande, Jadesola O., *Laws and Customs Affecting Women in Nigeria.* Lagos: International Federation of Women Lawyers, 1979.

Amadiume, Ifi, *Male Daughters, Female Husbands: Gender and Sex in an African Society.* London: Zed Books, 1987.

Awe, Bolanle, *Nigerian Women in Historical Perspective.* Lagos: Sankore / Bookcraft, 1992.

Bymes, Andrew Colins, *The "Other" Human Rights Treaty Body: The Work of the Committee on the Elimination of all Forms of Discrimination Against Women*. Unpublished, Columbia University Thesis, 1988.

Cole, Catherine and Beverley Mack, *Hausa Women in the Twentieth Century*. Madison: University of Wisconsin, 1991.

Consideration of Reports Submitted by States Parties under Article 18 of the Convention: Initial Reports of States Parties, Nigeria-Geneva Committee on the Elimination of Discrimination Against Women. 11 May, 1987.

Dinnick-Parr, Catherine, "Education of Moslem Hausa Women from Sokoto". In *MSS. Afr. S..* 1889. Oxford: Rhodes House, 1954. *Eastern Region of Nigeria Gazette*, 26:8. Enugu: Eastern Region of Nigeria Gazette, 1958.

Imam, Ayesha, Pittin, Ruth, and Omole, Harriet, *Women and the Family: Edited Proceedings of the Second Annual Women in Nigeria Conference*. Dakar: Codesria, 1985.

Kaita, Hafsatu Isah, "Women's Education in the States of Nigeria 1950-1972". In Trevor, Jean, *MSS. Afr. S. 1755. 79A*. Oxford: Rhodes House, 1954

Mahdi, Hauwa, *Gender and Citizenship: Hausa Women's Political Identity from the Caliphate to the Protectorate*. Germany: Gothenburg Press, 2006.

Mba, Nina Emma, *Nigerian Women Mobilized: Women's Political Activity in Southern Nigeria, 1900-1965*. Berkeley, California: Research Series / University of California, Berkeley Institute of International Studies, 1982.

Melone, Thomas, *Mongo Béti: l'homme et le destin*. Paris: Présence Africaine, 1971.

Montagu, Ashley, *The Natural Superiority of Women*. London: Collier Macmillan, 1974.

Parpart, Jane,. ed, *Women and Development in Africa: Comparative Perspectives, Dalhousie African Studies Series 7*. Lanham, Maryland: University Press of America, 1989.

Said, Mansur Ibrahim, "The Influence of Culture and Tradition in Divorce: Implications for Marital Stability" In, *The Rights of Widows and Divorcees in Hausa-Fulani Society*, eds. Ibrahim A. Malumfashi and Salisu Yakasai. Sokoto: Garkuwa Media Services, 2002.

The Constitution of the Federal Republic of Nigeria Promulgated in the 1999 Decree No. 24.

Tibendarana, Peter Kazenga, 'The Beginning of Girls Education in the Native Administration

Schools in Northern Nigeria, 1930-1945", in *The Journal of African History*, 26,. 1985 Trevor, Jean *Education of Moslem Hausa Women from Sokoto, MSS. Afr. S. 1755. 79A.* Oxford: Rhodes House, 1954.

Thiam, Awa, *La Parole aux Négresses*. Paris: Denoë, 1978.

Uchendu, Patrick Kenechukwu, *The Role of Nigerian Women in Politics: Past and Present*. Enugu: Fourth Dimension Publishers, 1993.

VerEecke, Catherine, "Muslim Women Traders of Northern Nigeria: Perspectives from the City of Yola" in *African Market Women and Economic Power: The Role of Women in African Economic Development*, eds, Bessie House-Midamba and Felix K. Ekechi. Westport: Greenwood Press.

Wadud, Amina, "Rights and Roles of Women' in *Islam in Transition: Muslim Perspectives*, eds. Johan J. Donohue and John L. Esposito. New York and Oxford: Oxford University Press, 2007

Welch, Claude E. and Meltzer, Ronald eds, *Human Rights and Development in Africa*. Albany, New York: State University of New York Press, 1984.

Yusuf, Bilkisu, "Sexuality and the Marriage Institution in Islam: An Appraisal", Understanding Human Sexuality Seminar Series 4. Lagos: Africa Regional Sexuality Resource Centre, 2005.

______, "Hausa-Fulani Women: The State of the Struggle". In Catherine Cole and Beverly Mack. eds, *Hausa Women in the Twentieth Century*. Madison: University of Wisconsin, 1991.

FOOD CONSUMPTION PATTERN OF LACTATING MOTHERS IN ONDO WEST LOCAL GOVERNMENT AREA OF NIGERIA

Cecilia A. Olarewaju

INTRODUCTION

"Research and writings on the place of womanhood in African traditional societies," writes Miriam Nwoye, "figure prominently in African literary and social science literature."[1] African female novelists such as Flora Nwapa,[2] Miriama Ba,[3] Buchi Emecheta,[4] Bessie Head,[5] Rebecca Njau,[6] and Grace Ogot,[7] all write from an African feminist perspective and have dominated the field in this direction. Buchi Emecheta's [8] writings focused purely on the oppression of patriarchy in traditional African societies and protest against the cultural injustice on the female child in traditional societies. Her writings drew serious attention to the brutalities, subordination and other oppressive realities and manifestations of tradition on women in Africa.

Flora Nwapa's[9] works exposed the woman's situation within traditional and contemporary African societies, especially her role as wife and mother. She highlighted the importance attached to having children and stressed the detestable lot of childless or barren women within the community. She discussed the need for the attainment of economic independence through determination and hard work to achieve self-fulfillment and freedom for the African woman. She was of the opinion that African women can "lead a life of fulfillment within or outside marriage unfettered by men, provided they are economically independent."[10]

Writings by the authors referred to above have sensitized the conscience of the men folk towards focusing their attention on the education and welfare of girls in African societies.[11] They have shown "that what ever a man can do a woman can do it even better.[12] There is now "a new vision for a balanced education of the modern girl child in contemporary Africa."[13]

In spite of the positive contributions of the writings highlighted above, feminist studies in Africa, however, have some shortcomings. One of these is the lack of an adequate discussion about the effect of proper feeding during critical stages of womanhood (e.g., pregnancy and breast-feeding). Adequate feeding is important during these periods in order for mothers to have healthy children and provide them with adequate milk during their formative years.

According to the Free Online Medical Dictionary,[14] lactation is the medical term for yielding of milk by the mammary glands which leads to breastfeeding. "Human milk contains the ideal amount of nutrients for the infant, and provides important protection from diseases through the mothers' natural defenses."[15] Breastfeeding naturally follows pregnancy as the mother's body continues to nourish the infant. The mammary glands secrete milk for this purpose. They develop during puberty but remain fairly active until pregnancy. During pregnancy, hormones promote the growth and branching of a duct system in the breasts and the development of the milk-producing cells.[16] Breastfeeding is an important process of mothering as it provides an important way for infants or young children to receive breast milk directly from the female breast (i.e., via lactation, rather than from a baby bottle or other containers).[17] Babies have a suckling reflex that enables them to digest the milk. Most mothers can breastfeed for six months or more,[18] without the addition of infant formula or solid food. Breastfeeding is also important because numerous scholarly medical studies have indicated that breast milk is the healthiest form of milk for babies. There are a few exceptions, such as when the mother is taking certain drugs or is infected with tuberculosis or HIV.[19] These studies also have demonstrated that breastfeeding was associated with significantly higher scores for cognitive development than formula feeding. It is also associated with detectable increases in the cognitive ability and educational achievement of breastfed children. These effects are reflected in standardized tests, teacher ratings, and academic outcomes in high school.[20] The beneficial effects of breastfeeding in the New Zealand study were long-lived and extended throughout childhood into young adulthood. There was a tendency for the Bayley Mental Development Index to be higher among breast-fed infants than among bottle-fed ones. (The Bayley Scales of Infant Development (BSID) measure the mental and motor development and test the behavior of infants from one to 42 months of age).[21] They are also used to describe the current developmental functioning of infants and to assist in diagnosis and treatment planning for infants with developmental delays or disabilities. The test is intended to measure a child's level of development in three domains: cognitive, motor and behavioral.[22]

The process of mothering is an important one in Nigerian society because the more children that a woman has, the higher her status will be. In traditional Nigerian culture and in the modern period, the institution of marriage is interwoven with the process of biological reproduction.

The purpose of this chapter is to present the results of a study that I conducted on the food consumption patterns of lactating mothers in Ondo West Local Government Area of Nigeria in order to assess their nutrient intake, the quality of life experienced by the mothers and their infants. Specifically, the study was designed to gather data regarding the demographic distribution of lactating mothers in Ondo West Local Government Area and to identify key factors that had an impact on their dietary and food consumption patterns so that an information database could be developed that could be used in the future by mothers and government officials who may be interested in developing intervention programs to enhance the nutritional needs of the women.

MATERNAL ENERGY AND NUTRIENT NEEDS DURING LACTATION

According to Ellie Whitney and Sharon Rolfes,[23] the lactating mother must continue to eat foods rich in nutrients throughout the lactation process. She needs an adequate diet to support the stamina, patience and self-confidence that nursing an infant demands. A nursing mother produces about 25 ounces of milk per day.[24] This varies from one woman to another and from time to time in the same woman depending on the infant's demand for milk. To produce an adequate supply of milk, she needs almost 500 calories a day above her regular nutritional needs during the first six months of pregnancy. To meet this energy need, she can eat an extra 330 calories of food each day and allow the fat reserves she accumulated during pregnancy to provide the rest. "Most women need at least 1800 calories a day to receive all the nutrients required for successful lactation. Severe energy restriction may hinder milk production."[25]

ENERGY NUTRIENTS

Recommendations for protein and fatty acids intakes are about the same during lactation and pregnancy but they increase for carbohydrate and fibers. "Nursing mothers need additional carbohydrate to replace glucose used to make the lactose in breast milk."[26] Fiber recommendation is 1 gram higher.

VITAMINS AND MINERALS

Nutritional inadequacies reduce the quantity, not the quality of breast milk. "Women can produce milk with adequate protein, carbohydrates, fat and most minerals, even when their own supplies are limited."[27] For nutrients listed above and folate as well, milk quality is maintained at the expense of maternal stores. Dietary calcium has no effect on the calcium concentration of breast milk. Maternal bones lose some density during breast-feeding if calcium intakes are inadequate. Breastfeeding does not have long-term harmful effects on bones because bone density increases again when lactation ends. Nutrients in breast milk that are most likely to decline in response to prolonged inadequate intakes are the vitamins B6, B12, A and D.

WATER

"Despite misconceptions, a mother who drinks more fluid does not produce more breast milk."[28] To protect herself from dehydration, the

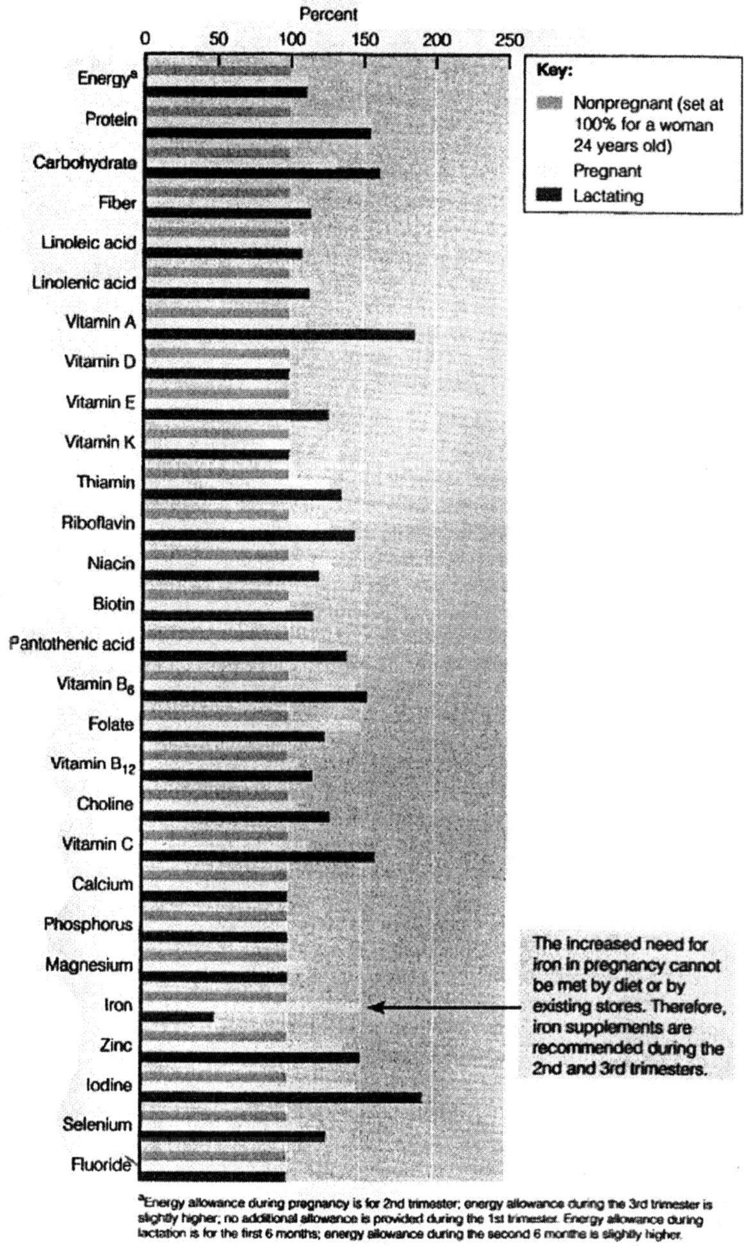

FIGURE 3.1: COMPARISON OF NUTRIENT RECOMMENDATIONS FOR NONPREGNANT, PREGNANT, AND LACTATING WOMEN
Source: Ellie Whitney and Sharon R. Rolfes, *Understanding Nutrition* (Belmont: Thomson Learning Inc., 208) 521.

lactating woman needs to drink plenty of fluids. She should drink a glass of milk, juice, or water at each meal and each time that the baby suckles.

NUTRIENT SUPPLEMENTS

Most lactating women can obtain all the nutrients they need from a well-balanced diet without taking vitamin or mineral supplements. Some may need iron supplements to refill their depleted iron stores (not to enhance the iron in their breast milk). The mother's iron levels decrease during pregnancy as she supplies the fetus with enough iron to last through the first four to six months of the baby's life. In addition, she might have lost some blood during childbirth. Therefore, lactating mothers may need iron supplements during breast feeding even though until menstruation resumes, her iron requirement is about half that of other non- pregnant women of her age.[29]

Diet in lactating mothers should be low in:

1. Simple carbohydrates: This breaks down quickly to produce glucose and milk that has higher levels of lactose. High levels of lactose can lead to indigestion (in baby) after feedings take place.
2. Alcohol: This goes through the breast milk and can affect the baby and interfere with a good supply of milk.
3. Preservatives, artificial flavors and colors: These may go through the milk and affect the baby.

The nutritional demands on the lactating mother are greater than when she was pregnant. There is a decrease in folate and iron needs and an increase in the need for energy, vitamins A, E, and C, riboflavin, copper, chromium, iodide, manganese, selenium, and zinc. A reasonable approach for a breast-feeding woman to use is for her to eat a balanced diet that supplies at least 1800 calories per day, which has a moderate fat content, and includes a variety of diary products, fruits, vegetables, and grains.[30] They should consume 1000 to 1300 mg. of foods that are rich in calcium. The National Institutes of Health of the United States Department of Health and Human Services puts it at 1,500 mg. per day.[31]

Water is the best beverage and should be drunk to satisfy thirst. Drinking to quench thirst encourages the ample production of milk (a total of 8 to 12 cups per day) and it is important to have enough milk on hand when sitting down to breastfeed. Until the baby reaches three months of age, lactating mothers should keep simple carbohydrates, i.e., fruits, alcohol, and anything from tin cans or packets containing sugars, to a minimum.[32]

A lactating mother should be properly exposed to direct sunlight to ensure the production of Vitamin D. Drinking four to six glasses of milk that is fortified in Vitamin D each day is also beneficial. Soy beverages that are low in fat are good nutritional supplements for feeding lactating mothers. Vitamin supplements will help to compensate for the nutritional deficiencies caused by the diet but it is always better to eat properly and avoid the intake of supplements. Nursing mothers should eat plenty of vegetables which are the sources of many essential micro-nutrients.[33]

In a study on weight loss that occurred during prolonged lactation in rural Bangladesh, Nihar Sakar and Richard Taylor[34] discovered that Bangladeshi women who breast-fed for up to 24 months were of lower weight than non-lactating mothers, most likely due to the effects of lactation. It was recommended that mothers consume additional foods that were rich in nutrients during the first 24 months of lactation. In another study of this topic performed by Reza Mahdavi and colleagues on fluids intake and beverage consumption patterns among lactating women in Tabriz, Iran,[35] the infants' weight was positively and significantly associated with the maternal weight and Body Mass Index (BMI). Mothers with higher values of BMI had better nourished children than those with lower values.

In his study of lactating women from different areas of Shiraz city, Islamic Republic of Iran by Seyyed Ayatollahi,[36] he discovered that the mothers' estimated average daily intake of carbohydrates was 2250 kcal. whereas protein and Vitamin C intake were significantly higher than United States Recommended Dietary Allowance (RDA) while iron and calcium intake were significantly lower. Protein intake was insufficient among 9% of women, calcium in 35.7%, iron in 18.8%, and Vitamin C in 15.00%.

In yet another study of nutritional intake of women in the Vaal triangle in South Africa performed by Hema Kesa and Wilna Oldewage-

Theron,[37] daily intakes (mean + SD) were 8511.94±2047KJ, 76.24±25g protein, 61.95±22.3g fat, 294.37±64.2g carbohydrate and 10.50 ±4.0 mg iron. Most of the women (98%) resided in towns and (79.3%) were unemployed. The diets of the subjects consisted primarily of plant-based foods. Animal foods were scarce except for milk and most of the items consumed were low in iron. In a study performed on the evaluation of Vitamin B12 status in Egypt on food consumption patterns among lactating mothers and their impact on the intake of the Vitamin by Sahar Aziz and Laila Husein,[38] the estimated Vitamin B12 intake averaged 4.17+0.74ug/d. Only 25.8% of the mothers had adequate Vitamin B12 intake. Three quarters of the studied population were consuming Vitamin B12<2.5ug/d. Out of those, 50% had estimated daily intake<2.0ug/d.

This confirms the additional burden on the lactating mothers to satisfy the daily Vitamin B12 requirement for their breast-fed babies. Socio-cultural factors such as religious beliefs, food preferences, gender discrimination, education, and women's employment all have a noticeable influence on food consumption patterns.[39]

STATEMENT OF THE PROBLEM

Many women think that the need for increased nutrient intake ends with delivery. This is not true. A breast-feeding mother requires quite a high quantity of vitamins, minerals and other nutrients. She needs to take in an additional 500 calories per day in order to make up for the energy that her body uses to produce milk. Of all the vitamins and minerals, five are most important as far as a lactating mother is concerned. These are calcium, zinc, magnesium, Vitamin B6, and folate. Vitamin D is extremely important for the well-being of the baby. The main source of this vitamin for a breast-fed baby is its mother's milk. The amount of this vitamin in breast milk is directly proportional to its intake through diet. An unhealthy or malnourished mother may still be able to produce milk, but such milk produced may be deficient in Vitamin A, D, B6 and B12. The quality of food that the lactating mother takes is of great importance since her diet will affect the nutritional quality of her breast milk, her health, and that of her baby. This study was designed to find out the food consumption pattern of the lactating mothers in Ondo West Local Government Area with the aim of determining their nutrient intake, their quality of life, and that of their infants.

RESEARCH DESIGN AND METHODOLOGY

Descriptive survey research design was used. This involves the study of a large population by selecting a representative sample to discover relative incidence distribution and interrelation of variables. It involves the collection, organization, analysis, and description of the variables as they exist in a natural setting without interference. The result of the representative sample can be inferred or generalized.

As stated earlier, this study was carried out in Ondo West Local Government Area of Ondo State in Nigeria. Ondo State is made up of three Senatorial Zones (Ondo North, Ondo Central and Ondo South). Ondo State consists of eighteen local government areas (six in each zone). Ondo West local government area is one of the six local government areas in Ondo Central Senatorial Zone of Ondo State. Ondo West local government area is made up of 12 wards, namely,[40]

- Enuowa/Obalalu
- Gbagenha/Gbongbo Ajagba Alafia
- Ifore/Odosida/Loro
- Ilunla/Bagbe/Odowo 1
- Ilunla/Bagbe/Odowo 2
- Litaye/Obunkekere/Igbindo
- Lodasa/Iparuku/Lijoka
- Odojomu/Erinketa/Legiri
- Okeagunla/OkerowoOkeuta
- Oke-Otunba/Okediba/Sokoti
- OkelisaOkedoko/Ogbodu
- Orisunmbare/Araromi

The population used for this study consisted of lactating mothers in Ondo West Local Government Area. Thirty six lactating mothers were randomly selected from each of the five postnatal clinics in this local government area (Surulere, Civic Centre, Iya Oba, Akinjagunla and the main market) to make a total of one hundred and eighty.

Copies of an open-ended questionnaire were used to collect data for the study. The questionnaire consisted of two sections. Section A included questions that asked information about the demographic and socioeconomic status of the respondents while section B consisted of items that determined the food consumption pattern of lactating mothers.

Two hundred copies of the questionnaire were administered through personal contact by the researcher. The questionnaire was filled out by the literate respondents, while the researcher filled the copies of the non-literate subjects. The questionnaire was validated by three experts in nutrition and childcare. The validation was necessary to ensure that the questionnaire was appropriate for the collection of the data, the measurement of the variables, and that ambiguous words were removed or changed in order not to confuse the respondents.

Test-retest was used to determine the stability and consistency of the instrument. A pilot study was conducted on twenty persons that were not included in the final sample within an interval of two weeks. Pearson product moment (r) was used to determine the correlation coefficient. 0.78 and 0.892 was obtained showing a high reliability of the instrument.

ANALYSIS OF DATA AND RESULTS

Data collected was analyzed using tables, frequency counts and percentages.

TABLE 3.1

(A) DEMOGRAPHIC CHARACTERISTICS OF THE POPULATION

AGE	NO OF RESPONDENTS	%	EDUCATION		
16-20	15	8.3	RESPONSES	NO OF	%
21-24	43	23.9	Primary Six	36	20
25-29	80	44.4	Grade Two	8	4.4
30-34	6	3.3	Senior Secondary School Certificate Examination (SSCE)	55	30.6
35-39	19	10.6	NCE(Nigeria Certificate of Education)	46	25.6
40-45	9	5.0	Graduate	**14**	**7.8**
Above 45	8	4.4	M.Sc/Ph.D	1	0.6
TOTAL	180	99.9	TOTAL	180	100

3.1 (B)

OCCUPATION	NO OF RESPONDENTS	%
Farming	24	13.3
Trading	85	47.2
Government Worker	57	31.7
Any Other	14	7.8
TOTAL	180	100

3.1 (C)

MONTHLY INCOME		
AMOUNT (₦)	NO OF RESPONDENTS	%
Below 10,000	103	57.2
Between 10,000 & 30,000	55	30.6
Between 30,000 & 50,000	13	7.2
About 50,000	9	5.0
Total	180	100

The distribution of respondents according to age shows that 44.4 percent of the total respondents were between the ages of 25-29; 23.9 percent between 21-24; 10.6 percent between 35-39; 5 percent were between the ages of 40-45; 3.3 percent between 30-34; and 4.4 percent were above 45 years of age. Table 3.1(a and b) indicates that most of the lactating women used as subjects in Ondo West Local Government (68.3 percent) were within the age range of 21-29 years. The data also shows that 47.2 percent of the women were traders; 31.7 percent were government workers; 13.3 percent were farmers and 7.8 percent did other work. The greater percentage of the respondents (47.2 percent) were traders followed by government workers (31.7 percent).

The respondents' distributions according to the amount they earn in a month as presented in table 3.1(c) were as follows: 57.2 percent of respondents earned below ₦10,000 per month; 30.6 percent earned between ₦10,000 and ₦30,000 monthly; 7.2 percent earned between ₦30, 000 and ₦50,000 monthly, while just 5 percent earned above ₦50,000 monthly. This shows that many of the lactating mothers (57.2 percent) earned below ₦10,000 monthly. As a result of this, there will not be enough money for lactating mothers to consume a balanced diet.

Table 3.1(a) shows that 30.6 percent of the total respondents has SSCE Certificate; 25.6 percent had NCE certificate; 20 percent had primary six certificates; and 7.8 percent were graduates, while 0.6 percent had M.Sc/Ph.Ds. This shows that 80.6 percent had NCE certificates and below and they may not be very knowledgeable about nutrition education.

TABLE 3.2. NUMBER OF BABIES BREASTFED NOW

RESPONSES	NO OF RESPONDENTS	%
Single	163	90.6
Twins	13	7.2
Triplets	4	2.2
TOTAL	180	100

Table 3.2 above shows that almost all (90.6 percent) of the respondents were breastfeeding single babies as at the time of the study.

TABLE 3.3. PERCENTAGE DISTRIBUTION OF RESPONDENTS ACCORDING TO VENUE OF MEALS

VENUE	RESPONDENTS	%
Canteen	22	12.2
Food Vendors	18	10
I Cook For Myself	140	77.7
TOTAL	180	100

Table 3.3 above shows that most of the respondents (78 percent) cook their food themselves; 12 percent eat in the canteen, while 10 percent buy food from the food vendors.

TABLE 3.4: PERCENTAGE DISTRIBUTION OF RESPONDENTS AS THEY CONSUME FRUITS

RESPONSES	NO OF PEOPLE	%
With meals	30	16.7
As Snacks	70	38.9
After Meals	80	44.4
TOTAL	180	100

As seen from the table 3.4 above, the greater percentage (44.4) consumed their fruits after meals. Fruits are supposed to be consumed with meals to aid digestion of food and stimulate appetite. They also contain ascorbic acid which helps in the absorption of iron.

TABLE 3.5: FOOD CONSUMPTION PATTERN AT BREAKFAST, LUNCH AND DINNER

CONSUMPTION PATTERN	RESPONDENTS	%
BREAKFAST		
Carbohydrate	127	70.6
Protein	50	27.8
Iron	3	1.7
TOTAL	180	100
LUNCH		
Carbohydrate	120	66.7
Protein	38	21.1
Iron	22	12.2
TOTAL	180	100
DINNER		
Carbohydrate	124	68.9
Protein	53	29.4
Iron	3	1.7
TOTAL	180	100

Table 3.5 above shows that 70.6, 66.7 and 68.9 percent of the respondents consumed carbohydrate foods for breakfast, lunch, and dinner respectively; 27.8, 21.1 and 29.4 percent consumed foods rich in protein for breakfast, lunch and dinner respectively; 1.7, 12.2 and 1.7 percent consumed foods containing iron for breakfast, lunch and dinner respectively.

TABLE 3.6: PERCENTAGE DISTRIBUTION OF RESPONDENTS THAT EAT IN BETWEEN MEALS

RESPONSES	NO OF RESPONDENTS	%
Yes	62	34.4
No	118	65.6
TOTAL	180	100

Table 3.6 shows that most (65.6 percent) of the respondents did not eat in between meals while 34.4 percent ate in between meals. The fact that most of the respondents did not eat in between meals reduces their chances of meeting the recommended dietary allowances for many or all nutrients needed by them. The more the number of times one eats, the more nutrients he or she consumes.

FINDINGS

Out of the total respondents examined in my study, table 3.1A shows that 68.3 percent were 21-29 years of age. Similarly, I discovered as is reported in table 3.5 that 70.6 percent, 66.7 percent, 68.9 percent of the respondents ate carbohydrate foods for breakfast, lunch and dinner respectively; and 27.8, 21.1 and 29.4 percent consumed protein foods for breakfast, lunch and dinner. In corroboration with this finding a study of lactating women from different areas of Shiraz city, Islamic republic of Iran,[41] indicated that the estimated average daily intake of the lactating mothers was 2250 kcal, and that the protein and vitamin C intake were significantly higher than the United States Recommended Dietary Allowances (RDA), while iron and calcium intake were significantly lower. Protein intake was insufficient among 9.0 percent of women, calcium in 35.7 percent, iron in 18.8 percent, and vitamin C in 15.0 percent.

In another study of nutritional intake of women in the Vaal Triangle, South Africa performed by Hema Kesa and Wilna Theron,[42] daily intakes (mean +SD) were 8511.94 ± 2047KJ, 76.24 ± 25g protein, 61.95 ± 22.3g fat, 294.37 ± 64.2g carbohydrate and 10.50 ± 40.mg iron. Most of the women (98 percent) resided in towns and 79.3 percent were unemployed. The diets of the subjects consisted primarily of plant-based foods. Animal foods were scarce except for milk. Most of the items consumed were low in iron.

CONCLUSION

The results of this study showed that similar to other studies carried out in other parts of Africa referred to above in the discussion, lactating mothers in Ondo West Local Government Area consumed more of carbohydrate foods than those that are rich in protein and iron. They are likely to meet the Recommended Dietary Allowances (RDA) for carbohydrates but may not meet the requirements for protein and iron. Many of the lactating mothers (57.2 percent) earned below ₦10,000 monthly. With the present economic situation of Nigeria, ₦10,000 will not be enough to meet family needs and allow the lactating mothers to consume the nutritious foods they need. Most of them (80.6 percent) had NCE certificates (Nigeria Certificate in Education) and below. Out of the 80.6 percent, only 25.6 percent had NCE certificate, 30.6 had SSCE (Secondary School Certificate Examination) and 20 percent had primary six certificates (the first six years of Nigerian educational system). Even more educated people believe that the pregnant women and not the lactating ones needed to eat for two. With their educational status, they may not be aware of the nutrients needed in the diet of lactating mothers. It is encouraging that 77.7 percent cook their meals themselves because when they become enlightened about foods rich in nutrients that they need, they will be able to include them in their diet. The fact that 44.4 percent of them consume fruits after meals will affect the absorption of iron (since ascorbic acid present in fruits helps them to absorb iron from their food). Fruits are supposed to be consumed with meals to aid the digestion of food and stimulate one's appetite. Most of the respondents (64.6 percent) did not eat in-between meals. Eating in-between meals increases the chances of meeting the recommended dietary allowances for many nutrients.

RECOMMENDATIONS

1. Lectures, seminars, workshops, and enlightenment programs through mass media should be organized to teach lactating mothers that they need an extra intake of 330 kilocaries per day during the first six months of lactation and 400 extra kilocaries during the second six months.[43] They should also be made aware that to ensure adequate milk production and avoid nutrient deficiencies, they should consume at least 1,800

kilocaries per day. They also need an additional 25 grams of protein over the non-pregnant RDA.[44] This means that they should increase their carbohydrate and protein intake as well as Vitamin A, E, and C, riboflavin, copper, chromium, iodine, manganese, selenium and zinc.[45] Their diet should have a moderate fat content and include a variety of dairy products, fruits, vegetables, and grains. They should also drink about 2 liters (1-8 cups) of water in a day and at least one cup of water each time they breast-feed their babies.[46]

2. They should be made aware of local foods that are rich in the nutrients they require.

3. They should be exposed to empowering skills like catering, fashion design, interior decoration, making of tie and dye fabrics and so on to augment their income for better nutritional status.

4. The government should give micro-credit loans to assist the trained mothers in setting up businesses.

5. Other interested researchers can carry out studies on consumption of other nutrients not covered by this study on lactating mothers in this Local Government and other Local Government Areas.

Notes

1. Miriam A. C. Nwoye, "Role of Women in Peace Building and Conflict Resolution in Africa Traditional Societies: A Selective Review" (2010). in www.afrikaworld.net/afred/chinwenwoye.htm.

2. Flora Nwapa, *One is Enough* (Enugu: Tana Press Ltd, 1981), www.afrikaworld.net/afred/chinwenwoye.htm.

3 Ba, Miriam. *So Long a Letter* (London: Heinemann, 1981), www.afrikaworld.net/afred/chinwenwoye.htm

4. Buchi Emecheta, *Destination Biafra* (London: Allison and Busby Ltd. 1982), www.afrikaworld.net/afred/chinwenwoye.htm

5. Bessie Head, *When Rain Clouds Gather* (London:Victor Gollanez Ltd, 1968), www.afrikaworld.net/afred/chinwenwoye.htm

6. Rebecca Njau, *Ripples in the Pool* (London: Heinemann, 1978), www.afrikaworld.net/afred/chinwenwoye.htm

7. Grace Ogot, *The Island of Tears* (Nairobi: Uzima Press Ltd, 1980), www.afrikaworld.net/afred/chinwenwoye.htm

8. Buchi Emecheta, *Destination Biafra* (London: Allison and Busby Ltd, 1982), www.afrikaworld.net/afred/chinwenwoye.htm

9. Flora Nwapa, *One is Enough* (Enugu:Tana Press Ltd, 1981), www.afrika-world.net/afred/chinwenwoye.htm

10. Ibid.

11. Miriam A. C.. Nwoye "Role of Women in Peace Building and Conflict Resolution in Africa Traditional Societies: A Selective Review," (Accessed December 10, 2010) htm.

12. Ibid.

13. Ibid.

14. Lactation-definition of lactation in the Medical dictionary-by the Free Online Medical Dictionary, Thesauraus and Encyclopeda http://medical-dictionary.thefreedictionary.com/lactation

15. Ibid.

16. Ellie Whitney and Sharon.R.Rolfes, *Understanding Nutrition* (Belmont: Thomson Learning Incorporation, 2008), 533.

17. Mary Frances Picciano "Nutrient Composition of Human Milk," *Pediatric Clinics of North America*, 48, (2001): 53-67.

18. Ibid.

19. Mary Frances Picciano "Nutrient Composition of Human Milk," *Pediatric Clinics of North America*, 48, (2001): 53-67.

20. James W Anderson: Bryan M Johnstone: Daniel T. Remley, "Breast Feeding and Cognitive Development: a Meta-analysis," *American Journal of Clinical Nutrition* 70 (1999); 525-535.

21. Bayley Scales of Infant Development-Definition, Purpose, Description 2004 www.healthofchildren.com/B/Bayley-Scales-of-Infant-Development.html

22. Walter, J. Rogan. and B. C. Gladen, "Breast-feeding and Cognitive Development". *Early Human Development* 31(1993):181-93.

23. Ellie Whitney and Sharon Rolfes, *Understanding Nutrition*, 534.

24. Ibid.

25. Ibid, 535.

26. Ibid.

27. Ellie Whitney and Sharon Rolfes, *Understanding Nutrition*, 535.

28. Ibid.

29. Ellie Whitney and Sharon Rolfes, *Understanding Nutrition*, 536

30. Gordon. M. Wardlaw, Jeffrey. S. Hampl, and Robert. A. Disilvetro, *Perspectives in Nutrition* (New York: McGraw Hill Higher Education, 2004), 588-600.

31. Pregnancy information-nutrition for pregnant women http://womens-health.health-cares.net/pregnancy-nutriton.php

32. PDF Appendix. FOR BREASTFEEDING MOTHERS http://www.patricia hatherly.com.published-articles/appendix.PDF Accessed Feb 7 2011

33. Ibid.

34. Nihar Sakar and Richard Taylor, "Weight Loss during prolonged lactation in Rural Bangladshi Mothers," *The Journal of Health, Population and Nutrition* 23 (2005):177-183.

35. Reza Mahdavi, Leila Nikniaz and Seyedrafie Arefhosseini "Energy, Fluids Intake and Beverages Consumption Pattern among Lactating women in Tabriz, Iran" *Pattern Journal of Nutrition* 8 (2009): 69-73.

36. Seyyed Ayatollahi "Nutritional Assessment of Lactating Women in Shiraz in relation to recommended dietary allowances," *Eastern Mediterranean Health Journal* 10 (2004): 822-827.

37. Hema Kesa and Wilna Oldewage-Theron, "Anthropometrics indications and nutritional intake of women in the Vaal Triangle South African," *Public Health* 119 (2005): 294-300.

38. Sahar A. Aziz and Laila. Husein "Evaluation of Vitamin B12 Status in Egypt IV: Food Consumption Patterns among lactating Mothers and their impact on the intake of the Vitamin," *International Journal of Food Sciences and Nutrition,* 56 (2005): 455-462.

39. Abdulrahman.Musaiger "Socio Cultural and Economic Factors Affecting Food Consumption Patterns in the Arab Countries," *The Journal of the Royal Society for Promotion of Health,* 113 (1993): 68-74.

40. Ondo West Local Government Area National Population Office 2011.

41. Reza Mahdavi, Leila Nikniaz, and Seyedrafie Arefhosseni, "Energy, Fluids Intake and Beverages Consumption pattern among Lactating Women in Tabriz, Iran," *Pakistan Journal of Nutrition,* 8 (2009): 69-73.

42. Hema Kesa and Wilna Oldewage-Theron, "Anthropometrics Indications and Nutritional Intake of Women in the Vaal Triangle South Africa" *Public Health* 119 (2005): 294-300.

43. Paul Insel, Elaine Turner, and Don Ross, Nutrition, (Surbury: Jones and Bartlett Publishers, 2007), 663-666.

44. Ibid.

45. Gordon. M. Wardlaw, Jeffrey. S. Hampl, and Robert. A. Disilvetro, *Perspectives in Nutrition,* 588-600.

46. Paul Insel, Elaine Turner, and Don Ross *Nutrition*: 663-666.

Bibliography

Anderson James, W. Johnstone, M. Bryan, and Daniel T. Remley. "Breast Feeding and Cognitive Development: A Meta-Analysis." *American Journal of Clinical Nutrition*, (1999): 525-535.

Ayatollahi Seyyed, M.T. "Nutritional assessment of lactating women in Shiraz in relation to recommended dietary allowances." *Eastern Mediterranean Health Journal*. 10: 6 (2004): 822- 827.http://www.emro.who.int/ publications /Emhi/1006/Nutritional.hpm.

Aziz, Sahar A. and Hussein, Laila, "Evaluation of Vitamin B12 status in Egypt IV:food consumption pattern among lactating mothers and their Impact on the intake of the Vitamin," *International Journal of Food Sciences and Nutrition*, Issue 7 (2005): 455-462.

Ba, Miriam. *So Long a Letter.* London: Heinemann, 1981.

Bayley Scales of Infant Development, Definition, Purpose, Description, 2004 www.healthofchildren.com/B/Bayley-Scales-of-Infant-Development. html

Emecheta, Buchi. *Destination Biafra.* London: Allison and BusbyLtd., 1982.

Head, Bessie. *When Rain Clouds Gather*, London: Victor Gollanez Ltd, 1968.

Insel Paul, Turner R. Elaine, and Ross Don Nutrition, (Sudbury: Jones and Bartlett Publishers, 2007), 663-666.

Kesa, Hema and Oldewage-Theron Wilna. "Anthropometrics indications and nutritional intake of women in the Vaal Triangle South African," *Public Health* 119 (2005): 294-300.

Lactation-definition of lactation in the Medical dictionary-by the Free Online Medical

Dictionary, Thesauraus and Encyclopedia http://medical-dictionary.

Mahdavi, Reza; Nikniaz, Leila and Arefhosseni Seyedrafie. "Energy, Fluids Intake and Beverages Consumption pattern among Lactating Women in Tabriz, Iran. *Pakistan Journal of Nutrition* 8 (2009): 69-73

Musaiger, Abdulrahman. O. "Socio Cultural and Economic Factors Affecting Food Consumption Patterns in the Arab Countries. *The Journal of the Royal Society for Promotion of Health*, (113) 2,(1993): 68-74

Njau, Rebecca. *Ripples in the Pool.* London: Heinemann, 1978.

Nwapa, Flora. *One is Enough* Enugu: Tana Press Ltd, 1981.

Nwoye, Miriam A. C., "Role of Women in Peace Building and Conflict Resolution in Africa Traditional Societies: A Selective Review" (2010) in www. afrikaworld.net/afred/chinwenwoye.htm.

Ogot, Grace. *The Island of Tears.* Nairobi: Uzima Press Ltd., 1980.

Ondo West Local Government Area National Population Office, 2011.

Piacciano, Mary F. "Nutrient composition of human milk," *Pediatric clinical North America,* Vol. 48 no 1 (2001): 53-67.www.ncbi.nim.nil.gov/pubed/111236733

Pregnancy information-nutrition for pregnant women http://womens-health.health-cares.net/pregnancy-nutriton

Rogan Walter. J., and Gladen B. C., "Breast-feeding and Cognitive Development," *Early Human Development* 31(1993):181-93.

Sarkar, Nihar Ranjan and Richard Taylor. "Weight Loss during prolonged lactation in Rural Bangladeshi Mothers. "*The Journal of Health, Population and Nutrition,* 2: 2 (2005): 177-183.

Wardlaw, Gordon M; Hampl, Jeffrey. S and DiSilvetro, Robert. A *Perspective in Nutrition.* New York: McGraw Hill Higher Education, 2004.

Whitney, Ellie and Rolfes, Sharon. *Understanding Nutrition.* Belmont: Thomson Learning Incorporation, 2008.

A MOTIVATIONAL TREATISE ON PARENTING

Bola Dauda

INTRODUCTION

In order to provide a reexamination for a new developmental approach or strategy for Africa, this chapter highlights mothering in particular and parenting in general, and the critical role of language in the ability of any individual to master his or her environment. The world does not come with explanatory notes, after all. In perceiving and experiencing things, we have to frame them in particular ways to give them meaning. I write as a parent and elder, using experience, teaching and research, to offer some suggestions. I adopt a conversational, rather than an academic, framework. I start with the language we use to communicate, and end with some of the contents in our communication that affect parenting.

LANGUAGE: THE SOFTWARE OF CULTURE

The framing of human thoughts, feelings, actions, and cultural norms of what constitutes 'good and bad' (values and beliefs) is done with language. Culture is the sum total of the way of life of a people. It is the essence of one's identity. The child's primary source or institution of socialization into the culture is the home. The most important agent is the mother; the process is through parenting; and the means is language.

Language is critical not only for the survival of any culture but also for its revival. Language is the software for the storage, retrieval, processing, and use of culture. Any threat or danger to language spells doom to a culture and consequently to the essence and identity of a people. The French know the power of language. In the colonial era, learning and speaking perfect French was enough to become French. Once you spoke French, you were accepted or "assimilated" into the French society. Today, France ensures that all official business is conducted in French, even when the French officials speak the language of their counterparts in business. For the British, colonization and civilization meant some replacement of African beliefs, language, and culture with the Christian faith and English language. There is no scientific evidence to support how much the return of Mahatma Gandhi back to his cultural roots, contributed to his subsequent success in mobilizing Indians to fight for independence from the British, but there is no doubt that the emergence of India as a world power can be linked to Mahatma Gandhi's development of a socio-economic policy of self-reliance, and his legacy for Indians to show pride in their language, clothes, and food. He made Indians proud to be Indian.[1]

Today, in our global village in which an average Dutch or Italian also speaks English, French, German, and Spanish, Africans are bringing up their children not only without a second language, but without the mastery of any African language. I cannot assess French speakers, but any high school teacher or university professor in Africa will admit that the new generation of monolingual Africans does not command enough mastery of the English language to communicate effectively with the outside world or indeed to express themselves. They lack the basic skills needed for the everyday civil conversations and communications. They are aggressive and violent in expressing themselves because they have no language. They consider every challenge as an attack on their person. How can we be democratic without the use of language to exchange ideas and opinions, and to express objections and dissent?

This trend of rearing Africans who have not mastered their indigenous ethnic languages is not only a denigration of African culture, but it is also a serious concern to academics and citizens alike. After all, without being proud to be African, we are paradoxically condemned to be second class citizens at home and abroad. And how can we develop our economy when we are not proud of our skin, language, food, clothes, and any homemade goods? How can we promote decency in our relationships, be it in politics or in business, in the rule of law and fair trade, without a good mastery of language? How can we eradicate air and water borne diseases, superstition, ignorance and poverty without a language to promote public enlightenment? Language is critical to the future of the African culture and, without being sexist or attempting to be pretentious, mothering and parenting play critical roles in the child's language development and consequently in inculcating African culture and identity.

ROOTS AND WINGS: LESSONS FROM TEENAGE MOTHERS IN THE UNITED KINGDOM

This chapter evolved from my experiences of coaching twenty British teenage mothers. While the teenage mothers were only twenty, it is important to note that they represented the British population as this small number included an Asian, a Chinese, and an African Caribbean. My encounter with the British teenage mothers started me to think about how the experiences of this small group could be representative of the wider African society in particular, and the global village in general. How they became pregnant is less significant than why and what contributions their parents made to their life, and more importantly, what lessons their pregnancies offered them and their nation-state. My encounter with the British teenage mothers was in the United Kingdom. Two factors inspired me to write this chapter regarding lessons that can be used for the revival of African culture and identity. The first factor is the British government's recognition of teenage pregnancies as an important social issue and its support for the teenager mothers to take guided responsibilities for their pregnancies. The second factor is the positive mental attitude exhibited by the teenagers to confront their condition and to consider their pregnancies as a minor setbacks and challenges in their lives.

The teenage mothers were separated from the mainstream schools. In order to help them to continue their education until they reached the age of sixteen, the Local Authority and the Central Government established an educational and social welfare center for them. The government also took care of them during the period of their pregnancies and subsequently also cared for them and their babies. Some were provided with foster parents. They bonded with, and breastfed, their babies during their coffee breaks. Both the British government and the teenage mothers considered these pregnancies to be unwholesome! (The story is different in Africa as some parents for various reasons give away their teenage daughters at the sign of first menstruation). At the end of their academic-year party, the retiring manager for the center recalled how much things had changed since the center was established in 1978/79. At such a party in 1979, the teenage mothers were kept in a separate room and screened-off the audience. But that was a great improvement over the old practices of 'sectioning' and ostracizing pregnant teenagers, and at the point of birth (right from the labor room), the babies were taken away from them for a compulsory adoption.

I asked the twenty teenage mothers if they would like to be grandmothers when they are thirty and they all stated that they would not. Today, with a lifespan of about 45 years, Africans who are under thirty years of age constitute over eighty percent of all Africans, and they were born into an independent Africa. How long shall we wait to become as resolved and determined as the teenage mothers to change our colonial heritage and mentality and take on our African identity?

Teenage mothers have demonstrated the critical role of mothering and parenting for the success of their children. They have shown that we could no longer live in the twenty-first century's global village in the same way and with the same beliefs and values of our ancestors who lived in decades gone by. Times have changed, and we too need to change. They also demonstrated that success is about discipline and determination to follow through and implement decisions that have been made and that the most successful people are not always the most brilliant ones, but rather, those that are able to complete their tasks. They are decisive, disciplined, and determined. They finish the projects that they have begun, and are receptive to new ideas. They are able to work with others to make things happen. What most successful people lacked in skills, they made up in the quality of their efforts. Teenage mothers have demonstrated that parenting and in particular, mothering, are critical in giving our children roots and wings, i.e., their culture and self-identity.

Anyone who has had the privilege of working with children and young people would agree with Johann Wolfgang von Goethe that "If children grew according to early indications, we should have nothing but geniuses."[2] My heart bleeds when I think about how children who started life with all indications of being geniuses became infested with what I call social leprosy. But we do not need to be overwhelmed by the enormous job of saving the whole world. Because of the power of compounding efforts, we can do a great job making a difference to one child or two. It would be great if we could influence and make a difference for ten. Mother Teresa used to emphasize that, to help one person is more than enough, and she viewed a homeless person living in cardboard box anywhere in the world as one too many.

IS PARENTING THE MOST DIFFICULT JOB IN THE WORLD?

That is the most difficult job in the world, remarked the cashier as I paid for Richard Templar's book, *The Rules of Parenting*.[3] I had just purchased four books that I didn't plan to buy. I simply agreed with the cashier because I didn't want to hold up the line and, more importantly, I was too preoccupied with compulsive spending and money issues. Regrettably, I missed the opportunity to learn why she thought parenting is the most difficult job in the world. Parenting comes with mixed feelings and challenges of joy and pain. Parenting is like eating a wild walnut and drinking water thereafter—sweet while eating it and with drinking after, it tastes bitter. Parenting is unique and special because there is nothing more rewarding than seeing a child growing up. Yet, nothing is more challenging than raising a child because nothing could prepare a parent for this important work. Manuals are like statistics. They deal with principles and the general matters. I agree with Professor Stephen Covey, the famous author of *The 7 Habits of Highly Effective People*, who said, "While practices are situationally specific, principles are deep, fundamental truths that have universal application. They apply to individuals, to marriages, to families, to private and public organizations of every kind. When these truths are internalized into habits, they empower people to create a wide variety of practices to deal with different situations."[4]

There are no manuals on parenting that could tell accurately and specifically how each child would respond to social training and upbringing. Nothing tests human character more than parenting and letting go of the children after years of bringing them up. Each child is different and each responds differently to the same parents and situation or circumstance. We (my wife and I) have twins and they are as different from each other as if they were born to different parents.

As a "lifer," I know that parenting is a life sentence. In parenting, life means life. You never get out of it alive. There is no parole for good behavior. So how do you make the best of a situation that has no end in sight? How do you enjoy a journey that has no destination? The mere thought of the fact that there is no exit clause in parenting and no end to parenting is enough to make it a difficult job for both parties—the parents and the children. A close friend of mine who is sixty-three years old and already retired shared with me how her ninety-three year-old mother orders her around as if she is a toddler. As far as her mother is concerned, my pensioner friend is her baby.

THREE PRIMARY JOBS AND AIMS OF PARENTING

There are three aspects and stages for the job of parenting. The primary job of parenting and probably the easiest and most natural is nurturing and rearing children until they are old enough to take care of themselves. I consider this to be the easy and natural way because all animals do it. Chickens, goats, and cows raise their chicks, kids, and calves respectively in a similar fashion.

The second job and the more challenging one, which often times reveals the stuff of our character and commitment to parenting, is to give our children spiritual training that would make them become human and humane; to make them cultured with a socially approved self-image or self-identity and self-esteem. For us to give our children a purpose and meaning of life requires that we lead a life of purpose and we ourselves have a meaningful life. We need to know what life is about, as well.

Respect is one of the core features of African culture and identity. This includes self-respect and respect for guests, strangers, and elders. To bring up our children to respect themselves, and to have respect for others, means that we must show them respect. We also must demonstrate respect for them as our children; for the partners in our parenting relationship; for ourselves as individuals; and for others in our life, including animals, plants, and property. This aspect is so critical and crucial that failure in this area means a total failure in parenting. It is so important that I would counsel that if we haven't got it to give our children, we must utilize the help of our relatives, friends, and the state to support us.

An African child is a child of the community. The Yoruba say that "It's only a pregnancy we cannot help to carry, everyone helps to carry a baby." Everyone considers it as a duty to help look after the children. Fortunately, what children require is a safe environment to consistently experience and feel the security, love, and care of adults. Unfortunately however, children's needs cannot wait. It has to be met as and when due. It is like a scheduled flight. It doesn't wait for passengers. If you miss it, it is a serious problem. Failure to take care of a child's needs at the appropriate time creates a lot of complications and most of them are irreparable.

This second aspect of parenting is about leading our children. It is about showing them how to share with others. It is about demonstrating to them the way to give and receive love and trust. It's about leading them on how to make choices and decisions, both simple and difficult ones. It is about being a living example to them of how to respond to and accept the inevitable events in life. And more importantly, it is about guiding them on how to freely and responsibly express their individuality while respecting and contributing to the collective good and community life. The essence of this chapter is this second aspect of parenting.

The third duty of parenting is that of preparing our children to earn a living, i.e., giving and creating options and choices for our children. We must help our children to know what they want, and create and enhance their chances and opportunities to be able to choose careers and have a livelihood by exposing them to many sports, hobbies, and friends. Children learn through play. Creating a simple, rich, and safe environment for children to explore, to experiment, and to play is the best way to get children to learn how to grow, to be discerning of what works and what doesn't, to learn how to take risks, to learn how to cope with mess and untidiness, and many other important transferable life skills. Schools, homes, and the rest of the society have a shared responsibility in this area of child rearing and social training.

Some parents think that this third aspect of child rearing is the role of schools and government. Parents must be in the driving seat to coordinate the efforts and contributions of all other agents and institutions. They have a leading role to play not only because children spend more time with them, but also because it is in the self-interests of parents to help their children to successfully make the transition from childhood through adolescent to adulthood. Failure to negotiate the passage correctly means that children would remain a life burden to their parents and the state. But the pain is more for parents than the faceless state bureaucracies of probation, social service, hospitals, and prison services. Parents pay for the rest of their lives. What else can we do to making parenting an interesting, exciting, and enjoyable experience for children and ourselves as adults? I want to offer a few suggestions.

ADJUSTING PARENTING ROLES AS CHILDREN GET OLDER

Parenting can both be an art and a science! We could all learn the techniques of doing any trade—we can learn the craft and science side of any trade. What about the art of parenting? The art of a trade is different. The distinction of an artist from an artisan is in the painstaking mastery of the strokes. The genius, the mastery, and the control of the strokes of an artist are obvious, but incredibly due to the creativity, imagination, intuition, and the vision of the artist. Most people learned the art of parenting from their childhood experiences of how to or not to be a parent. And their children teach them how to be a parent.

The Yoruba say, "It's only a rogue who could trace and identify the footprints of a rogue on a rock." I had been a clever child and it is easy for me to know when children are trying to play games with me. However, I respect and love them as well. They respond warmly to me. We (my wife and I) still adjust how we deal with our children as they grow older. We change our job prescription. When they were in diapers, we treated them as diapers' wearers. When they were toddlers, we took away all the electronic wires and removed all things they could pull down or that could fall on them and hurt them. We made the floor or room safe for them to explore rather than shouting at them.

When they're in the impressive age of five to seven and were unable to distinguish between real and fictional horrors, we kept them away from violent programs that could impact on their psyche, and give them nightmares. And as teenagers, we treated our children with respect to the degree most adults would consider as spoiling them. We let them know that they have rights and we respect their rights. But they know they could not play clever with us. And to the young adults, we give them all the respect we would give adults. We treat them as friends and equals, and as our consultants. We provided our children with the support and the environment for them to grow up well, and we challenged them to do something worthwhile with their life.

A SAFE ENVIRONMENT AND THOUGHTFULNESS

In parenting, looking means and implies loving and appreciating; and to love and appreciate we need to pay attention to details. We need to be thoughtful and responsive. Parenting involves the hard work of reading children as if they were books or listening to them as if they were music, or appreciating them as if they were paintings and the works of art. The real message in a book is the unwritten one, hiding between the lines. The melody of music is in the silence between the notes, between the sounds of music. The beauty of painting is in the shadows and spaces between the shades. Parenting is exactly the same. It is about reading, interpreting, and decoding the hidden and noisy messages in the silences of our children, and the monosyllable responses from our adolescents. I found out that parenting can be simple science. All it requires is trust and creating a safe environment for children to grow and to show thanks and gratitude. But do adults provide children with a safe and secured environment to show their gratitude and appreciation? They hardly get a safe space for it.

Trust is the key to relating with children. Adults need to demonstrate to children that they can be impartial, non-critical, non-judgmental, and trusted. But it has to be mutual. Adults need to feel confident and able to trust children. And adults cannot fake trust. Children know whether adults are sincere or not. Children know when adults are patronizing them and they do not respond positively to this situation. They would rebel and do exactly the opposite of what adults want them to do. Children respect honesty and fair play more than adults could believe.

LEADERSHIP-BY-EXAMPLE

What sort of examples and role models are you to your children? One of the most difficult things for adults to do is to admit fault and to say I am sorry. Insurance companies advise their clients not to admit faults, because they know that there are loopholes in the law. In parent-child relationships, there are no loopholes. You get what you give.

Adults want children to say thank you and to say they are sorry. It is unclear if they realize that having a child to wait for five minutes can seem like an eternity to them. A child left alone for five minutes interprets the experience as not just an abandonment, but death. An apology and an explanation given to the child for the lateness mean a lot to a child. You have planted seeds of respect, honesty, and assurance for your child. Consistently being punctual to pick your child at school is more than an ordinary habit. It is worth more than all the luxurious toys in the world. A seed of justice and fair play is planted when you found out who started a fight instead of wrongly blaming the older child. A seed of love is planted when parents show respect to one another in front of their children. A civil behavior before your children is worth more than one thousand lectures on civics and citizenship.

Leading by example is all that a parent needs to do to bring out the best in their children. If you haven't got it, get your children to relate with the extended family of uncles, aunts, cousins, and of course godparents. You may want to register them for leadership youth training and clubs. Expose them to leadership and quality character role models, not only of the famous and the champions, but also of the successful ordinary people doing extraordinary things in all walks of life. I asked a child in my neighborhood why he looked miserable. I told him that the way he looked made me unhappy. Since then, each time I see him on the street, he always heartily assured me that he is happy. This is done because he doesn't want to make me unhappy. Children are vulnerable and their self-esteem and identity are often in jeopardy because they tend to think they are the cause and responsible for the way adults in their lives feel. They think they are the cause of divorce, disputes or disharmony between their parents.

Our children are facing a greater challenge than we would want to admit. They are growing up in a world that is changing rapidly, and I believe we owe it a duty to prepare them for the change. Although our Children have more resources today and are exposed to more advanced technology than we were at their age. Yes, they are more aware than we were at their age, but they face a different type of challenge, and their need of support is no less than ours. They need our guidance and support to cope with the fast changing global village. Change in technology means that lifestyle is changing as well.

My generation had choices of jobs when we left university in the 1970s and now there is graduate unemployment. Children need our leadership to fit into a world that is more open, more liberal, more spiritual, and less religious and dogmatic; is more discerning about what is right and wrong, and more interdependent. In my childhood time as an African, adults ruled the world and their words were final. Children did as they were told. Yes, our children challenge adults today, but they still need adult leadership to exercise their freedom with responsibility.

TRAINING AND PREPARING THE FUTURE LEADERS

Parenting is about preparing our children to fit into the world they were born into and also for the future. The whole purpose of social and spiritual training is to get children to fit into their present and future society. We could only do that successfully when we are aware of the changes in our world. We could only be aware when we are truly engaged in the affairs of our world. We need study, effort, training, and commitment. We need open minds to receive and review information and to apply knowledge of the known to predict and interpret the unknown.

The essence of culture is that as a human race, we have records of the past. We have the natural endowments of imagination, creativity, and intuition to help us to project into the future. We are endowed with the ability to think about what we are doing. We have the capacity to be aware that we are alive. We can be the scene and the scenery. We can think of our thoughts. We can learn how to learn and can also unlearn information. We can learn to remember. And more importantly, we can teach our children how to learn, how to remember, and how to be aware of their thoughts, and the effects of their actions and inactions on themselves and on others. All of these activities constitute the human culture. And we imbibe and transmit them with language.

I would like to think that parenting is more than rearing children until they could be on their own. It is about creating a world better than we were born into. It is also about preparing our children to take over the running of that world in a cultured way—in a more loving and effective way that would make us feel proud. The failure of newly independent countries is an example of failure of our parenting and leadership. Building the character of our children begins with what values and beliefs we expose them to. Our ability to make hard decisions and to draw the line between what is acceptable, and what is not, would be the test of our character, civility, and culture. Failure to stand up and be counted in small matters has a grave implication for the big ones.

SETTING BOUNDARIES: HUMAN AND HUMANE CHILDREN

African culture and identity are about interdependence and interconnectedness of the community and parenting is about making our children know that Africans are communal without being communist. The Yoruba say, "A farmland doesn't belong to father and son without a demarcation or boundary between them." Parenting is about making our children realize that there is John Smith and Jane Adams behind every financial institution. There is a family behind the person who is laid off. There are human souls behind the statistics and figures. Yes, we prepare children for a career. Yes, we provide opportunities for them to have choices and options. But the bottom line for all jobs and careers is to produce services and products that would add value to ours and other people's lives. Making our children realize that we are all interconnected and that our most important task in life is to be humane to others. Hence, parenting is about training our children, not to behave naturally, but to become humane. Animals do natural things. Human beings do things unnaturally. Human beings have a right way, a right time, and a right place to do things. In any civilized human culture, the end does not justify the means, and in human behavior, ninety-nine percent is not a passing mark. One percent of unacceptable behavior wipes out the ninety-nine percent credit. Being aware of these simple truths about humanity is what makes parenting both challenging and exciting.

DO BETTER WHEN YOU KNOW BETTER

Lest I have painted a misleading picture that I am a perfect parent and godfather, nothing could be further from the truth. I have made many mistakes. Our children were brought up to focus on academic pursuits. Even though that was the consciousness of our time, I would be the first to admit that I think we went too much to the extreme. For example, it did not cross our minds that learning to drive is important. One of our twins learned to drive at the age of thirty-four. His twin brother got his driving license at the age of thirty-two. But how did we do with their siblings? We recognized that it is easier to learn to drive when you are young and we made sure that their siblings learned and got their licenses before they were eighteen. Because I know the value of keyboard skills, I provided typewriters for our children to learn to type.

We now know that children could speak as many languages as they are exposed to and while we made the mistake of not encouraging our third son to keep speaking Yoruba when we arrived in Britain, we however brought up our daughter who was born in Britain to speak and study Yoruba. She did well in both Yoruba and English at the school certificate level. While studying engineering in the university, she chose to learn Spanish. Both our twins who read science subjects in the university are fluent in French and English. I wouldn't want to list how many other mistakes we made. Some we were able to correct, and many others we could not. But the point is that we kept on learning and adjusting as we went along. Regrets, self-pity, and wallowing in guilt are a waste of time. The important principle is to do better when you know better.

BELIEFS AND VALUES

Culture is about values and beliefs and life is a perpetual exchange of love and joy and, sometimes unfortunately, life is an exchange of misery and hardships. It is not only time and bad conditions that do not favor beauty. Bad beliefs and values destroy beauty. Our beliefs and values are the fountain sources for our feelings, thoughts, words, and actions. Beautiful feelings, thoughts, words, and thoughtful acts of kindness flow out from beautiful springs of beliefs and values that are in harmony with the organic body and universal purpose of life. We are as beautiful as our values and beliefs. We are as rich, wealthy, and healthy as our values and beliefs will allow us to be. We are as connected with life as our value and belief systems.

Belief systems are the blueprints of the mind and culture. They provide the basis upon which the structure of thought rests, and directly influences behavior. Building blocks of belief systems involve things like principles, ideas, code of ethics, and constructs that define our world. Social influences such as culture, religion, education, family, and the person's own individual experience model the constructs and the frame of reference we use to interpret and give meanings to events in our life.

The reassuring fact and purpose of this chapter is to demonstrate that belief systems are learned and imbibed. The child is not born with them. We can learn to change them or we can consciously and deliberately plan to unlearn them. The gratifying news is that we now have enough knowledge about the relationships of our language, our internal dialogues, our physiology, our emotions, and our state and status in life. We can alter the patterns of our feelings and thoughts simply by changing our language, our internal dialogues, and our physiology. We can now instantly change our emotions by being aware of the mindset that produced the emotions. Our beliefs and values influence our language and our internal dialogues determine our emotions.

Change your thoughts and internal dialogues and you change your motion. How we carry our body influences our feelings. Consequently, our motions create our emotions. We can also change our habits when we change the behavioral conditioning and association that created the habits and attitudes in the first place. Change our habits and we change our character. And when we change our character, we change our destiny in life. African political economy can be transformed and changed once we understand the dynamics of language and cultural identity.

The quality of our life is a function of our problem-solving capacity, our constructive and creative imagination, and our productive and positive mental attitudes to care and add value to ourselves and others. No one wants to know what you think and who you are until you show how much you care. It would be nice to be important but it is more important to be nice. Please be nice and add value to, and care for yourself, and others. Our place, status, and condition in life are in direct proportion to how much we care and the value we add everyday to ourselves and others. Our faith not our fate determines our success in life. We are as rich and wealthy as we are able and willing to care and add value to and improve ourselves and others. Boldly begin to live a life of integrity because, **"*The gods are not to blame*".** Colonialism and imperialism may no longer be enough and valid excuse for the state of African political economy.

LIFE AS A THEATER

Culture and identity are about role play and many Africans have accepted "the poor me" and "the colonial and imperialist victim mentality and identity." Many African leaders have adopted "the slave owners and colonizers" culture and identity. It's very easy to point an accusing finger and explain the conditions in Africa with slavery, trade in human beings, colonial heritage, and how Europe exploited and underdeveloped Africa. Today, more than eighty percent of Africans were born after independence and most of the African heads of states grew up in republican African nation-states. So, for how long will Africans accept and take on "the poor me" and "the victim" identity? This is even more problematic given the level of corruption and kleptomania that exists. How long will it take for African leaders to drop "the slave owners and colonizers" identity? I know with a new form of parenting, Africans can revive and transform African culture and identity.

Life is a drama, a long play with many plots and subplots. William Shakespeare, a dramatist, who knew more about drama than anyone who ever lived on our planet earth, once remarked this world is a stage.[5] We are all actors entering and exiting the stage to play different roles and parts in the drama of life. As actors in the game and play of life, sometimes we are born into a role as members of a dynasty or royal family; sometimes we have the role assigned and thrust upon us as parents or fortuitously or serendipitously as in when we happened to be at the right place and at the right time; and sometimes we worked for, carved out and achieved, or accomplished the role we play in life because we have a say and a choice in it.

The judge of the outcome of our performance in the role we play in life often depends on how we came to play the role in the first instance. When we are born into a role, we run the script and we derive our authority to play from our royal position and status in the pecking order of the dynasty or kingdom. When the role is thrust upon us, we run the script and derive our authority from our charisma and the grace we commanded from the fortuitous situation that gave us the power to play the role. When we work to carve out a role for ourselves, we end becoming the playwright and the judge of our performances, and whether or not we believed, thought, and felt we have succeeded would depend on how much our expectation matched our reality.

THE SCRIPTS WE PLAY: PERSONALITY ARCHETYPES

Between the infant age of total dependency and the official age of adulthood, children experience a spectrum of events. They also respond by picking up skills, knowledge, and attitudes for survival. A balanced and an ideal process will produce an adult who is mature and able, in the words of Caroline Myss, "to see beyond the physical aspects of life to find symbolic meaning in ... actions, from political activism and social idealism to love and spiritual exploration."[6]

Around the age of twenty-eight it is expected that the young adult naturally transitions into the next cycle of life as an interconnected, responsible adult. The lucky ideal ones rarely need a coach or a therapist. However, not everyone is lucky and consequently they need therapist and coaches to help with issues relating to variants from the ideal.

There is huge literature on personality archetypes. For the purpose of this chapter, I am applying the wisdom of two authorities on the subject. I chose and adopted the two authorities because I found their categorizations the simplest and easiest to digest. They are James Redfield[7] and Caroline Myss.[8] Redfield in his classic book, *The Celestine Prophecy,* examined the importance of energy in our every day life and how we exchange energy when we interact with others. Because life is energy, we are alive to play the game or drama of giving and receiving energy. He identified four personality archetypes, i.e., *personas* (the way we behave when we are with other people or in a particular situation which gives people an idea about our character) or control dramas or games we play to give and receive energy: intimidator, interrogator, aloof, and poor me. He noted that there is a tendency to see these dramas in others, but to think that we ourselves are free from such devices. Each of us must transcend this illusion before we can go on.

Almost all of us tend to be stuck, at least some of the time, in a drama and we have to step back and look at ourselves long enough to discover what it is. The first step in the process of getting clear, for each of us, is to bring our particular control drama into full consciousness. Nothing can proceed until we really look at ourselves and discover what we are doing to gain energy.

Caroline Myss in her book: *Sacred Contracts: Awakening Your Divine Potential* (Bantam Books, 2002) came up with a personality typology of four archetypes: Child, Victim, Prostitute, and Saboteur.

Because not everyone has the ideal and balanced upbringing, the variants of the ideal process of growing up from infancy to adulthood are as follows: The never-grown up Child, the Victim, the Prostitute, and the Saboteur. Sometimes we all have a bit of each archetype in us, but often some aspects would be more dominant than others.

ARE YOU THE CHILD WHO NEVER GREW UP?

The Child archetype as the guardian of innocence establishes our perceptions of life, safety, nurturing, loyalty, and family. Its many aspects include the Wounded Child, the Abandoned or Orphan Child, the Dependent Child, the Innocent Child, the Nature Child, and the Divine Child. The core issue of all the Child archetype is dependency and responsibility: when to take responsibility, when to have healthy dependency, when to stand up to the group, and when to embrace communal life.

Myss noted that confronting the Child archetype within you awakens a new relationship with life, a fresh beginning. Regardless of which aspect of the Child you relate to most intimately, this archetypal pattern brings you into contact with the untapped resources connected to creative thought. This is the core of the Innocent Child—the sensation that anything and everything is possible.

As the guardian of your innocence, the Child helps heal, repair, and put a stop to the inner-directed abuse of the Wounded Child. If you are consumed with the Wounded, Neglected, Abandoned, or Orphan Child's psyche, you need to identify—or initiate—a new relationship or creative enterprise that makes you appreciate life. Ask your Child what it needs in order to heal or feel nurtured or cared for.

The Child often inspires you to act outside restrictive boundaries or explore an adventure without the burdensome weights of the adult mind.

Myss advised that you indulge some of these inspirations as a means of making contact with your inner Child. She however warned that you don't become over-attached to the wound; don't overindulge the Child so that it becomes an inner brat. But give it the support it needs to grow up.

ARE YOU THE PROSTITUTE WHO SELLS THE SOUL FOR SECURITY?

The Prostitute as the guardian of faith comes to play most clearly when our survival is threatened. Its core issue is how much you are willing to sell of yourself—morals, your integrity, your intellect, your word, your body, or your soul—for the sake of physical security.

The Prostitute archetype also dramatically embodied and tested the power of faith. Anytime you are in a crisis of faith, try to become mindful of your thoughts and fears. The Prostitute appears when you begin to believe that you could order your life if you just had the money to control the world around you—and to buy just a bit of everyone in it.

Caroline Myss concluded that, "If you have faith, no one can buy you. You know that you can take care of yourself and also that the Divine is looking out for you. Without faith however, you will eventually meet the price you cannot turn down. Think of the Prostitute as a guardian of faith and as an ally who puts you on an alert every time you contemplate shifting your faith from the Divine to the physical."

ARE YOU THE VICTIM WHO HAS NOT THE COURAGE AND SELF-ESTEEM TO LIVE?

The Victim archetype may manifest the first time you don't get what you want or need; are abused by a parent, playmate, sibling, or teacher; or accused of or punished for something you didn't do. You may suppress your outrage at the injustices if the victimizer is bigger and more powerful than you. But at a certain point, you discover a perverse advantage to being the Victim. You may be afraid to stand up for yourself, or you may enjoy getting sympathy. The core issue of the Victim is whether it's worth giving up your own sense of empowerment to avoid taking responsibility for your independence.

The Victim archetype as your guardian of self-esteem, self-respect, and social, professional, and personal power demands that you evaluate your relationship to power, particularly in your interactions with people with whom you have control issues and to construct personal boundaries.

You have contracts with people who are directly connected to the Victim archetype. Their primary role is to help you develop self-esteem through acts of honesty, integrity, courage, endurance, and self-respect. Those people will play, or have played, the leading roles in awakening in you an awareness of the value of these spiritual qualities and how essential they are to your well-being. Rather than reacting physically, emotionally, and mentally to them, you will need to take notice of them as the intuitive inner voice of "you're the Victim" guardian of self-esteem.

ARE YOU THE SABOTEUR WHO WOULD DO ANYTHING TO DISRUPT THINGS IN YOUR LIFE?

Like the Prostitute and the Victim, the Saboteur archetype is neutral energy within you. It usually makes itself known through disruption. It can sabotage your effort to be happy and successful if you are not aware of the patterns of behavior that it raises in you. It can cause you to resist opportunities.

The Saboteur is the mirror that reflects your fears of taking responsibility for yourself and for what you create. You can silence this archetype with acts of courage and by following your intuition. It serves you brilliantly as a gut instinct that directs you to take action based on hunches rather than on rational thought. Start with small choices, which may be life-transforming acts of will, disguised as harmless impulses.

The core issue for the Saboteur is fear of inviting change into your life, change that requires responding in a positive way to opportunities to shape and deepen your spirit. Yet it is impossible to stop the process of change. Deep in your tissue, you know that having power and using it necessitates change. And although many people want to have it all, they don't want to pay the price.

All choices you make do not necessarily have the same potential to transform the condition and the environment of your life. The choice to respond to intuition or the inner voice that directs you to pursue your spiritual life is obviously one that can rearrange your familiar world.

CONCLUSION

Africans are all evolving and growing spiritually and the dynamics of individual spiritual growth and evolution is that while there is a pattern of human commonality of endowments of choice, creativity, imagination, and intuition to addressing all our problems and challenges, sweeping generalization, categorizing, and stereotyping are in the least misleading and too simplistic. We Africans will need to write and rewrite our script, direct and redirect, and produce and reproduce the play of our life as we want it. We'll also need to be discerning and wise in discriminating between what we can; what we cannot; and the wisdom to know the difference. Parenting is something we can all do. Most animals do. And language is what will enable us to do better than animals.

The first law of life is self-preservation for survival. We could not redesign our lives until we know who we are; and we are ready to be who we are. African culture and identity define who we're within the human race. Language is the means to expressing who we are, and mothering or parenting is critical to the revival of African culture and identity.

Notes

1. Louis Fischer, *The Life of Mahatma Gandhi* (London: Harper Collins, 1997).

2. Quoted in Reader's Digest, *Quotable Wit and wisdom for all Occasions: Quote s from the World's Most Popular Magazine* (Westmount: The Reader's Digest, 1998).

3. Richard Templar, *The Rules of Parenting* (Edinburgh Gate: Pearson Education Ltd, 2008).

4. Stephen R. Covey, *The 7 Habits of the Highly Effective People* (London: Simon & Schuster, 1989).

5. Quoted in Reader's Digest, *Quotable Wit and Wisdom for all Occasions: Quotes from the World's Most Popular Magazine* (Westmount: The Reader's Digest, 1998).

6. Caroline Myss, *Sacred Contracts: Awakening Your Divine Potential* (London: Bantam Books, 2002).

7. James Redfield, *The Celestine Prophecy: An Adventure* (London: Bantam Books, 1994). (Redfield is a great writer with inspiring insights and understanding about human behaviors and desires for growth. I find all his books truly inspiring).

8. Caroline Myss, *Sacred Contracts: Awakening Your Divine Potential* (London: Bantam Books, 2002).

Bibliography

Achebe, Chinua. *Things Fall Apart.* London: Penguin Books, 1958. (Achebe is one of the founding fathers of African voice in contemporary African Literature. He is a great story teller).

Albom, Mitch. *Tuesdays with Morrie: An Old Man, a Young Man, and Life's Greatest Lesson.* London: Time Warner Paperbacks, 2003.

Axline, Virginia M. *Dibs in Search of Self.* London: Penguin, 1990. (This is an excellent book on child psychology and parenting).

Bennis, Warren. *On Becoming a Leader.* New York: Addison-Wesley Publishing Company, 1994.

Clason, George. *The Richest Man in Babylon*, 1926.

Coelho, Paulo. *The Alchemist.* London: HarperCollins Publishers, 1999. (Paulo Coelho is one of the greatest writers of our time. He is a genius motivational story writer, and he writes from his heart).

Covey, Stephen R. *The 7 Habits of the Highly Effective People.* London: Simon & Schuster, 1989.

______. *Principled-Centered Leadership.* London: Simon & Schuster, 1990.

______. *The 8th Habit: From Effectiveness to Greatness.* London: Simon & Schuster, 2004.

Covey, Stephen R. et al. *First Things First.* New York: Simon & Schuster, 1995.

De Bono, Edward. *Six Thinking Hats.* London: Penguin Books, 2000.

Emerson, Ralph Waldo. *The Art of Successful Living: A Collection of Essays (Love, Friendship, and Self-Reliance).* Slough: New Dawn Press, 2005.

Falola, Toyin. *A Mouth Sweeter than Salt: An African Memoir.* Ann Arbor: Michigan University Press, 2004.

Fischer, Louis. *The Life of Mahatma Gandhi.* London: HarperCollins, 1997.

Forster, E. M. *A Passage to India.* London: Penguin Books, 1924, 1979.

Frankl, Victor E. *Man's Search for Meaning: The Classic Tribute to Hope from the Holocaust.* London: Rider, 2004. (An excellent book on the power of human spirit to survive when there is a cause to live for).

Gladwell, Malcolm *Outliers: The Story of Success.* London: Penguin Books, 2009.

Goleman, Daniel. *Emotional Intelligence: Why It Can Matter more than I.Q.* London: Bloomsbury, 1996.

Koch, Richard. *The 80/20 Principle: The Secret of Achieving More with Less.* London: Nicholas Brealey Publishing, 2000.

Mandela, Nelson. *Long Walk to Freedom: The Autobiography of Nelson Mandela.* London: A Little, Brown Book, 1994.

Maybury (Uncle Eric), Richard J. *Whatever Happened to Justice?* Placerville, CA: Bluestocking Press, 1993.

McCormack, Mark H. *What They Don't Teach You at Harvard Business School.* London: Harper Collins Publishers, 1984.

Myss, Caroline. *Sacred Contracts: Awakening Your Divine Potential.* London: Bantam Books, 2002.

Redfield, James. *The Celestine Prophecy: An Adventure.* London: Bantam Books, 1994. (Redfield is a great writer with inspiring insights and understanding about human behaviors and desires for growth. All his books have moved me to action).

Ruddell, Tom. *The Mecca Factor: 5 Imperatives for a Successful Life*, 2nd Ed. Tampa, Florida: Capstar Corporation, 1997.

Russert, Tim. *Big Russ & Me: Father and Son: Lessons of Life.* New York: Hyperion, 2001.

Templar, Richard. *The Rules of Parenting.* Edinburgh Gate: Pearson Education Ltd, 2008.

Waitley, Denis. *Seeds of Greatness: The Ten Best-kept Secrets of Total Success.* New York: Pocket Books, 1983.

Part Two

Marriage, Sexuality, Work, and Violence

"I AM NOT HIS SLAVE:" CONTESTING MARRIAGE AMONG THE HAUSA ON A CAMEROONIAN FRONTIER, c. 1920-1955

Harmony O'Rourke

Studies on diasporas in Africa are few even though migration writ large often finds itself the subject of scholarship.[1] Oliver Bakewell suggests that the African continent is not home to many internal diasporas in part because socio-cultural identification in Africa has traditionally been fluid. "Perhaps," writes Bakewell, "the answer lies in the way that people have actually moved and been able to create new identities." However, Bakewell suggests that the case of the Hausa, like the Wangara and the Fulani pastoralist diaspora, diverges from this larger African pattern.[2] For more than forty years, scholarly works on the Hausa diaspora have defined it as a trading diaspora in which dispersed people had a distinct culture and relied on a shared ideology—in this case, Islam.[3] Indeed, for trading diasporas, cultural distinctiveness was central to the project of maintaining commercial networks that were spread across a vast geography. In the case of the Hausa, it has been argued that traders relied on a sense of ethnic solidarity vis-à-vis traders of other ethnic groups in order to maintain dominance over long-distance trades in particular markets, especially in livestock and kola-nuts.[4]

In his influential *Custom and Politics in Urban Africa: A Study of Hausa Migrants in Yoruba Towns*, Abner Cohen contended that it was Hausa diasporic customs—differentiated from Hausa culture in the homeland—that provided the "stable institutional set-up" necessary to facilitate the mobility of people and to establish further settlement in the name of Hausa trade. The most important Hausa customs that separated Hausa men from others along the frontier were, for Cohen, their sense of superiority, donning of white robes, Islamic beliefs and practices, 'Arabic' learning, and an overall, intense pride in these customs. Cohen argued that "Hausa trade and Hausa customs [went] hand in hand...in the dynamic process of the continual ramifying of the Hausa network."[5]

Such characterization of diasporic Hausa culture and society fits neatly into the parameters set by label of "commercial diaspora." Though the narrative this terminology provides in explaining Hausa expansion and settlement is useful in illustrating the general, structural patterns of Hausa diasporic history, studies have neglected women and gender in this history. When the role of women was acknowledged, women's contribution to community life was still perceived through the lens of the exchange of goods and services—either as "trade behind the purdah" or as courtesanship. Not only this, but analyses of Hausa identity reproduction on the frontier have taken for granted assumptions about Hausa masculinity, patriarchy, and forms of community leadership. In essence, the reliance on religion and long-distance trade in past historical narratives has overemphasized, or at minimum taken for granted, the role Hausa men had in establishing settlements and maintaining social networks. Male researchers' lack of access to secluded women limited them to collecting oral traditions almost exclusively from adult men. Such a gendered imbalance in sources has rendered androcentricism as the normative condition of Hausa itinerancy, settlement, and diasporic identity. Consequently, the category of "commercial diaspora" is colored with androcentric properties.

Such critiques may also be applied to historian Nehemia Levtzion's research on the intricate relations between Muslim strangers and local chiefs during the pre-colonial period in the Middle Volta Basin.[6] Muslim traders, including the Hausa, traveled to the basin primarily to acquire kola nuts by exchanging a variety of products from Hausaland including textiles, leather goods, jewelry, slaves, livestock, kola, dried onion leaves, and natron. In every caravan, there was at least one malam who kept the records, advised on auspicious days for travel, and "offered prayers for the success of the adventurous trip."[7] A recurring theme in the oral traditions that Levtzion collected suggests that these malams were the most instrumental in leaving traces of their religion along trade routes, sometimes leaving the caravan at the request of a local chief in order to offer religious services. The chief would give the malam a wife, often his own daughter, a conjugal act that traditionally represents the birth of new Muslim communities on the ever expanding frontier.

Malams, however, were not the only Muslim men to make such cultural inroads into local populations. Levtzion's sources revealed that chiefs in Dagomba State often gave their daughters in marriage to immigrant Muslims of various professions, Hausa and non-Hausa alike. Offering one's daughter was regarded as a "generous gift," but one that was accompanied by a chiefly motivation to "bind a Muslim" to his court.[8] Although Levtzion's descriptions of frontier marriages populate his exploration on the process of Islamization in the Middle Volta Basin, his interpretation of their historical significance is decidedly androcentric, in part because, like many of his contemporaries, Levtzion lacked access to secluded Muslim women, and also because of biases held by the men he interviewed who seemed to favor patrilineal narratives over matrilineal or bilateral ones. Local women married to Muslim foreigners figure as props in a grander tale about the relationships established between men from two different cultures. Muslim women who may have trekked across difficult terrain with their husbands or male guardians are left out of the story entirely. To provide evidence to the contrary, the Canadian missionary A.W. Banfield wrote in 1905 that the Hausa trader "...lives like a gypsy, and one often sees a Hausa man with his children and wives, each carrying a load, going from their country down to the coast to buy English goods...."[9] Other sources show that Hausa men migrating from Northern Nigeria to Accra in the nineteenth century took their women and children with them.[10]

While it certainly may be true that the majority of Hausas traveling outside of Hausaland during the nineteenth and twentieth centuries were men, the footsteps of many women were laid down on those paths as well. Some of these women hailed from Hausaland while others joined traders and their caravans either en route or in the process of settlement.[11] As such, this chapter explores the gendered ways that identity was transported, challenged, and reproduced in Hausa diasporic communities during the twentieth century by focusing on Hausa experiences in the Cameroon Grassfields.[12] Analyzing narratives of marriage and domestic slavery found in Islamic court records reveals the many contestations that took place among men and women over the means by which people could become incorporated members of Hausa diasporic society in the Grassfields. The central issue that this chapter seeks to address is how Hausas in the diaspora socially reproduced themselves and what role do contested narratives over kinship-based identity play in the ramification and reproduction of Hausa identity on the frontier.

More precisely, this chapter seeks to enhance our understanding of Hausa diasporic history by viewing it through the lens of marriage and the multiple negotiations that accompanied such intimate and often uneven relationships between men and women. Such scrutiny offers a nuanced view of the roles women played in settling the frontier and in the social reproduction of Hausa daily life. It illuminates the gendered principles upon which power and authority were reproduced at household and community levels. It also brings to light how conflicts among men and women, and between families, ultimately provoked debates about what cultural elements and social practices constituted Hausa identity and a sense of belonging in Hausa society. My research demonstrates that there were a number of ways in which men and women established and challenged various forms of power and authority in order to exert their understanding of Hausa ethnic identity in the diaspora.

Through the examination of an Islamic court case from the early 1950s, we find that marriage and the concomitant issues of female enslavement and bigamy formed the terrain upon which many men and women of the Hausa diaspora contended with hierarchies of power to control their own lives and the lives of others. Such debates elucidate the layers of legal and cultural ambiguity over what types of behavior, knowledge, beliefs, and social status constituted Hausa identity. These factors are especially significant when we consider that many first-generation Hausa women in the Grassfields were not born Hausa or Muslim but joined the diaspora through relationships of dependence, be they marriages, enslavement, adoption, or other forms of protection and servitude. Moreover, this chapter demonstrates that it was often imperative that women establish and maintain ties to Hausa diaspora communities through male guardianship, which often limited women's ability to define their roles within such relationships as well as the kind of treatment they could expect. We find that many of the men and women in these situations did their absolute best to manipulate patriarchal authority in their favor, which they were able to do because of geographical distance and anonymity, and because of the ambiguity that permeated Hausa and Islamic definitions of what constituted acceptable forms of female dependency and behavior.

As I contended above, marriage was a central point of contention among the Hausa. One reason for this was that marriage and adherence to Islam are considered as the normal conditions of adulthood and for full acceptance in Hausa society.[13] Secondly, the conceptual linkage between marriage and domestic slavery created a sense of ambiguity regarding which people were considered to be full-fledged members of Hausa society and which people were enslaved by its members. As many scholars have argued, historically, there was much ambiguity between female enslavement and wifehood among the Hausa. In the cultural lexicon of the Hausa, this vagueness is expressed in a variety of ways. For example, the Hausa term *baiwa* refers to a gift or the act of giving for a betrothal of a woman to a male suitor, and, with a slightly different tone, to a female slave.[14] Furthermore, studies have shown that the ambiguity involved in distinguishing a full wife from a concubine in colonial Northern Nigeria was in part responsible for British ambivalence on the matter of domestic slavery. The British system of indirect rule rested squarely on the shoulders of the Sokoto Caliphate's aristocratic and mercantile classes, a patriarchal society heavily interested in consolidating its power over women—free and unfree— and through them the caliphate's cultural reproduction. Paul Lovejoy attests that concubines were indeed slaves even though the British wanted to believe that there was no fundamental difference between concubinage and marriage. Lord Richard Lugard himself declared that concubinage was "a question of marriage rather than slavery."[15] Furthermore, according to the Maliki school of Islamic law, wives could inherit property and own land, two entitlements unavailable to concubines at least without consent from their masters. Concubines and female slaves were also not allowed to marry but were bound to their masters without recourse should their masters prove abusive. Wives, on the other hand, could seek divorce in such cases.[16]

Third and finally, marriage was essential to the process of settling the frontier and for the reproduction of Hausa daily life. In the context of the Hausa diaspora, Hausa men traveling to and settling the frontier used both marriage and enslavement as a means of incorporating female outsiders to assist in establishing and reproducing Hausa frontier communities. In fact, the word *abakwa*, which Hausa settlers used to name their frontier communities in Cameroon, implicitly marks the significance of women in creating and sustaining these communities. *Abakwan riga*, which literally means "novices of the robe or gown," refers to descendants of mixed marriages between Hausa men and local, mainly non-Muslim women.[17] *Abakwa* offers credence to the role that a multicultural group of women have played in sustaining Hausa cultural and social reproduction on the frontier. However, because the maternal heritage of Hausa in the diaspora has largely been non-Hausa, most people in the diaspora emphasize their patrilineal ancestry to claim their identity as Hausa. Historian Mahdi Adamu likewise observed in the 1970s that the *abakwan riga* of the Ivory Coast, Burkina Faso, Mali, and the middle belt of Nigeria, could claim—even if they did not speak Hausa fluently—an identity as Hausa "simply because of their family histories [showing] that they had Hausa paternal ancestors." Adamu also states that most of the *abakwan riga* in the Benue and Plateau States of Nigeria displayed great "tenacity... in claiming descent through the father."[18] Thus, patrilineality has been reinforced on the frontier in multiple Hausa communities throughout West Africa. However, one must note that *abakwa* is also contentious because it overlooks the variety of ways in which Hausa women originating from Hausaland participated in the diaspora.

For some Hausa, linkages between their homeland and the frontier were even sustained by marriage. During the process of migration, some of Hausaland's itinerant merchants and other traveling men deployed their marital bonds in a kind of "trading-post polygyny" where a man's wives or slave-wives would be stationed both at "home" in Hausaland and on the frontier. Merchants may have found slave-wives particularly ideal, because their kinless, rootless existence would have made it easier for them to place these women strategically along trade routes.

Many Hausa itinerant traders, Qur'anic teachers, butchers, and other men making their livelihoods on the Cameroon frontier in the Grassfields thus traveled side-by-side with wives and slave-wives originating from both Hausaland and sojourns along the way. Whether a woman was of Hausa birth or not, what seemed to be different for women participating in the dispersion of the diaspora—as opposed to the experience of many women in Hausaland—was the significance that marital bonds had in establishing their identity. First, marital ties seem to have taken on greater significance with regard to how a woman's status was determined in Hausa diaspora settlements. As the discussion on *abakwa* indicated, marriage and Islam were central to non-Hausa women becoming Hausa, central to women's sense of incorporation into the Hausa community, and central to their security in this patrilineal society.

Second, one pillar of stability that many divorced or widowed women in Hausaland could rely upon—whether these women were of Hausa or other ethnic origin—was simply not present for a good number of wives traveling in the diaspora. In Hausaland, after the termination of a marriage, women would generally return to their natal homes for a short period of time before remarrying.[19] On the frontier, however, should a husband's death, abandonment, or pronouncement of divorce leave a woman without a marriage, the sheer distance separating her from her consanguine relations was sometimes insurmountable and she could end up without members of her kin network close by. These realities underscore the complexity, contestedness, and potential insecurity of marriage in the Hausa diaspora. The story of a woman of the Hausa diaspora named Hadija and the contested narratives surrounding the manner in which she was incorporated into Hausa society on the frontier, serve as an excellent case with which to illustrate these points, as her identity came into question a few months after the death of her Hausa husband.

Hadija appeared in the archival record in October 1952 when she was accused in the Grassfields Alkali Islamic court of entering into a sacrilegious second marriage before she had completed her period of mourning after the death of her husband.[20] This period, known as *takaba*, lasts 130 days, during which time a widow must refrain from having sexual relations with other men for doing so would be considered sinful.[21] The man she illegally married was named Yusufu, an iterant merchant residing in the Grassfields. The marriage was short-lived, however – just lasting three days. In Yusufu's words, "Hadija said to me…she said she did not like me, then I buy 100 kola-nuts to make sacrifices for the sake [of] this marriage divorced."

The couple's brief marriage and divorce were not the controversial issues, however. Rather, a debate arose over the relationship between Hadija and her deceased husband, Alhaji Gashin Baki. Hadija's male guardian, who was an acquaintance of the deceased Alhaji, was present at the court with her that day. The Alkali asked the guardian whether Hadija was a "daughter or a slave"— whether the society of her origins claimed her as a daughter, as a member of their kin group, or whether she was sold as a slave to the Alhaji. To this question, Hadija's guardian replied that she was a slave. This meant that she was Alhaji Gashin Baki's slave-wife. Hadija rejected this slave status, however, asserting that she had been Alhaji's wife. For the Alkali presiding over the hearing, this question had to be answered because it had an important bearing on the outcome of the case. If Hadija were a slave, then she would not have had to observe *takaba*—or at least observe it completely—and then her marriage to Yusufu would not have been illegal. Her social status was also controversial because Hadija was not Hausa, nor was she from the Grassfields. Rather, she was brought there by the Alhaji from the region of Lere (either in Nigeria or Chad; the court records are ambiguous).

A couple months after the original court date in 1952, the litigants and the Alkali reconvened – together with a number of witnesses, who claimed to understand the nature of Hadija's social status. Hadija's guardian argued that the *alhaji* purchased Hadija from the Chief of Lere with "10 bags," presumably ten bags of cowry shells.[22] Hadija vehemently disagreed with this assertion, stating:

> It is not so…. [He] is not speaking the truth about the 10 bags. Yes, the chief of Léré received 10 bags from the late Alhaji Gashin Baki, my husband. But the 10 bags were paid to the chief of Lere before the chief took me and gave me to the late Alhaji. […] And [then] the late Alhaji married me and gave me this name, Hadija.

Hadija thus opposed her guardian's interpretation of the transaction that took place between the chief of Lere and her late husband. At the same time, however, Hadija implicitly informed the court that she was not Muslim prior to her marriage with Alhaji Gashin Baki, for her birth name had not been Hadija, a common namesake for Muslim women. There would be no other reason to change her name to Hadija if she had already been Muslim possessing a Muslim name. In this case then, and from Hadija's perspective, marriage, religious conversion, and naming operated in tandem and the groom exercised control and responsibility for the bride's religious indoctrination and inculcation into the cultural beliefs of the Hausa people. By extension, one may argue that Hadija's identity as an incorporated Muslim woman within the Hausa diaspora was linked in a unidirectional fashion to the beliefs, identity, and, ultimately, the fate of her husband. Hadija had nothing but her own recollection of past events to support her claim to a Hausa personhood, while both her supporters and naysayers could rely only on their personal understandings of the late Alhaji's intimations on what Hadija had meant to him.

Hadija's guardian, for example, continued his contestation producing additional information, which he believed proved Hadija's slave status. He claimed that Hadija was a slave because Alhaji Gashin Baki said that, if he died, Hadija should not inherit his wealth in the way a widow would. To complicate matters, an ongoing court battle was being waged over Alhaji Gashin Baki's inheritance at the very same time as Hadija's status was being debated, a battle in which British District Officers intervened. In a letter from the Wum District Officer to the Senior District Officer in Bamenda, we learn that Hadija, labeled as a slave wife in the colonial record, was apportioned the same amount in the estate distribution as Alhaji Gashin Baki's senior wife.[23] The Wum District Officer ordered a "suspension of the judgment," however, in part because, "According to...the District Officer Kano...no slave can inherit his or her master's property on the latter's death. In this distribution however, the Alkali gave the slave wife a share on the estate."

Just as Hadija's guardian was set on crystallizing Hadija's slave status through the court system, the Wum District Officer was determined to do likewise because of the colonial principle that viewed codified Islamic law as static and unchanging—and because of the view that women's roles in society should be understood only through their relationships to men. The district officer's stance on the matter also amplifies how the colonial edifice of power relied on keeping the patriarchal structures of the Hausa community intact even if that meant allowing the domestic enslavement of women, which the British officially outlawed in 1936 in Nigeria—sixteen years prior to Hadija's appearance in court.

But the Alkali was not convinced that Alhaji Gashin Baki's supposed neglect of Hadija in his oral will provided sufficient evidence to establish the veracity of her enslavement. The court went on to hear from a number of other witnesses, all with opposing testimonies. In the end, the judge was unable to find proof indicating whether Hadija was a slave and not a Muslim woman belonging in Hausa society. Though one of Alhaji Gashin Baki's sons, who traveled from Kano to the Grassfields to receive his inheritance, said that his father told him to "hold [Hadija] fine as [his] mother," such ambiguous declarations failed to help the Alkali make a decision.

After much debate, the court asked the male litigants if they would allow Hadija to swear to the truth on the Qur'an. After their approval, Hadija swore on the Qur'an, stating, "I ... swear on Muhammadan Kuran that the [deceased] have married me, I am not his slave." But the Alkali was left perplexed by Hadija's sinful actions during her period of mourning, asking her, "You know that you are not a slave then why [when] you make Takaba...you didn't make as God said?" Hadija offered an innocent admission which we witness for the first time in this protracted case, as she said, "I never know, and they didn't [inform] me [about] the months I will make Takaba." In the end, the court was able to determine culpability, and Hadija was fined 10 pounds for her illicit behavior.

The question of Hadija's marital status acts as a prism through which debates on Islamic and Hausa slavery, marriage, and other forms of relationships between men and women are refracted. Some of these debates center on the blurry lines paradigmatically separating market-based property exchange from bridewealth payments or the social contract that binds slaves to masters from that which binds Muslim women to men. Other aspects of this case, however, illuminate contestations associated with the means by which Hausa cultural knowledge and identity were spread and maintained in the diaspora, as well as on how hierarchies of power shaped the way people defined and debated membership in frontier communities.

As the story of Hadija's contested identity shows, marriage and the attendant issue of domestic slavery figure centrally as social institutions and as negotiated processes in the expansion and settlement of the Hausa frontier—even during the middle years of the twentieth century. In examining the contested narratives concerning Hadjia's role in Hausa society, we see how women and men tried to exploit or challenge that ambiguity to direct patriarchal authority in a manner that benefitted their strategies.

Though enslavement and marriage have shared theoretical and practical similarities in the lives of African women throughout history, individuals have also perceived differences between the two institutions and how they limit or broaden the scope of options one may use to enhance their daily lives. For instance, if indeed Hadija had been Alhaji Gashin Baki's slave wife, it is possible to view her situation in the diaspora and the decisions she made after her master's death in a slightly different light than had she been a free woman. While the widowed Hadija would have essentially been kinless regardless of whether she was free or not, she had no alternative methods by which to establish herself as free but to obstinately argue for it in the court of the Alkali. None of the witnesses in the case mentioned anything about a possible "death-bed manumission" on the part of the deceased husband, a common practice among Muslim slave owners. Hadija never bore Alhaji Gashin Baki a child, which in accordance with Islamic law could have theoretically secured her freedom upon his death regardless of whether he promised manumission or not. Perhaps Alhaji's use of the kinship idiom of motherhood was an indirect extension of an Islamic principle stating that an impregnated slave shall receive the name "mother of offspring" upon the birth of her master's child and be allowed enfranchisement owing to that newfound motherhood.[24] However, though it is clear that Alhaji Gashin Baki incorporated Hadija into his notion of family by instructing his children to "hold her fine as [their] mother," Alhaji did not unequivocally view Hadija as a full wife either, stating she should receive only fifty pounds upon his death, an amount less than half of what she would be legally entitled to as a free Muslim widow.

Given that such ambiguities are apparent even in the way Alhaji Gashin Baki and his children spoke of Hadija's role in the family, it is important to continue to tease out what Hadija's strategies were, both in the moment of her marriage to Yusufu and in the moment of her guilty admission in the court room. On one hand, if Hadija was indeed a wife and a member of her Lere kin group, the marriage between her and Alhaji Gashin Baki provides a perfect illustration of the many frontier marriages that characterize a significant aspect of the history of the Hausa diaspora. First, as Alhaji Gashin Baki had an adult son who traveled to Kano to claim his inheritance, it is highly plausible that Alhaji had been married to another woman or women before departing Kano, participating in the "trading-post polygyny" characterized earlier. Second, with the death of the Alhaji, the community's solution to Hadija's temporary kinlessness was to place her under the guardianship of one of his acquaintances. Taking this vulnerable social position into account, we can understand why Hadija found it necessary to hastily establish marital ties to another man of her choice, Yusufu, attempting to create through him a distinct linkage between herself and her adoptive society.

On the other hand, had Hadija been a slave before the court hearing, she could have used the distance she traveled and the anonymity that came with it to assert a new and better social status. Though claiming an identity based on wifehood and adherence to Islam came with an admission to sinful behavior and acceptance of criminal punishment for her marriage to Yusufu, for Hadija this risk outweighed the alternative which was to resign herself to enslavement. By exploiting the conceptual ambiguity that did little to distinguish wifehood from concubinage, Hadija was able to elevate her social status in the public forum offered by the Alkali's court, an institution of diasporic origins to which she had access as an adopted Hausa woman. Paying the fine and court fees associated with the guilty verdict can thus be viewed as an act symbolizing self-redemption. And through this redemption Hadija—officially recognized as a widow—could also claim a share of Alhaji Gashin Baki's estate, a total of 122 pounds. The ultimate outcome of the choice made by an unfree Hadija to confess her transgressions was thus to elevate and secure her status as a Muslim woman, establish her identity as a member of the Hausa diaspora, and claim a fair portion of her former master's wealth.

Earlier findings of functionalist anthropologists working in Hausaland pointed to the relative insignificance that marriage had on an individual's social status in part due to a "cultural cleavage" between men and women in Hausa society.[25] However, such conclusions reduce the cultural import of marriage in the lives of the men and women who participate in it. While investigating Hausa culture through the analytic yet functionalist lens of social status and hierarchy has its merits, it nevertheless neglects the cultural relevance of other institutions and beliefs that are just as central, if not more so, in the ways people imagine identity within their communities. In the spiritual realm, for example, scholars have shown that because women have less spiritual worth than do men in local conceptions of Islam, women depend greatly on their husbands in order to have access to Paradise in the afterlife. Using insights from the work of Guy Nicolas from the 1970s, historian Barbara Cooper explains that the Hausa in Maradi believe that women must have a marital tie before death, "a literal thread to a man who has the 'pull' to get them into heaven through prayer." Cooper has also shown that many Hausa women consider the institution of marriage to be central to their lives and find it easier to discuss than politics or history in the Western sense of these terms.[26]

Studies exploring the relationship between marriage and social status in Hausa society as a function of the nature of relations between men and women also appear to take for granted the free status of the individuals involved. In the widow Hadija's case, for example, proving the existence of her marriage itself became absolutely essential in establishing her social status as a free woman. Based on our understanding of the kind of regard a free Hausa woman could expect in the diaspora, it becomes clearer why a free Hadija made particular choices after the death of her husband. Just as the importance of establishing a protective kinship alliance and link to God may have led her into a hasty marriage with Yusufu, her potential awareness of the heightened degree of vulnerability that a concubine could experience at the hands of her master—as opposed to the expected rights of a full wife—spurred her to assert her free status despite the penalty that accompanied this admission. However, these very same reasons could have also prompted an enslaved Hadija into outright dishonesty. It is entirely possible that Hadija was misled on what the intentions of Alhaji Gashin Baki were for her status and identity as he brought her from her homeland to a new and distant location. The conceptual ambiguity separating marriage from slavery was thus potentially exploited by an unfree Hadija before the authority of the Alkali to claim an identity as a free woman.

The courtroom debate over Hadija's social status and her relationship to Alhaji Gashin Baki shows that the litigants and the Alkali together challenged and reinforced expected gender roles and behaviors in the diaspora. This case also demonstrated how the legal, moral, and patriarchal authority of the Alkali was strengthened, while a commoner could exploit the social ambiguities at play in determining the course of her life. Hadija was able to use distance and the anonymity that resulted from it, to maneuver her way into Hausa community membership. Hadija's evasion and ignorance of a fundamental Islamic principle did not jeopardize her claim to Hausa identity, which she secured through Qur'anic ritual under the watchful eye of household, community, religious, as well as colonial authorities. In the end, her recognition of the power that marriage wielded in defining her status in the diaspora outweighed her imperfect knowledge of Qur'anic laws in the formation and defense of her identity as Hausa.

The stories of Hadija, Alhaji Gashin Baki, and many other men and women who lived in the Hausa diaspora of the Cameroon Grassfields show the enormous significance of women and marriage in the creation and maintenance of diasporic communities in Africa and beyond. Diaspora, travel, merchants, country wives, and country marriages: these are the movements, activities, people, and negotiated processes that together have formed both the nucleus and fringes of many societies. Looking at marriage more closely can only bring us a more nuanced perspective of the multiple ways in which people participated in the making and marking of Diasporas and identity.

Notes

1. The research for this article was funded by the U.S. Department of Education Fulbright-Hays Doctoral Dissertation Research Award, the Harvard University Frederick K. Sheldon traveling fellowship, a Pitzer College Faculty Research Award, and a Pitzer College Mellon Junior Faculty Research grant. I would like to thank Emmanuel Akyeampong, Caroline Elkins, Elizabeth Moore, Robert Karl, Afsaneh Najmabadi, Judith Surkis, and the Harvard University Interdisciplinary Workshop on Gender and Sexuality for their critical feedback on earlier versions of this chapter.

2. Oliver Bakewell, "In Search of the Diasporas within Africa," *African Diaspora* 1 (2008): 18-19, 22.

3. The most prominent monographs that deal with the Hausa diaspora include: Edmund Abaka, *'Kola is God's Gift': Agricultural Production, Export Initiatives, and the Kola Industry of Asante and the Gold Coast,*

c.1820-1950 (Oxford: James Currey, 2005); Mahdi Adamu, *The Hausa Factor in West African History* (Zaria and Ibadan: Ahmadu Bello University Press, 1978); Abner Cohen, *Custom and Politics in Urban Africa: A Study of Hausa Migrants in Yoruba Towns* (Los Angeles: University of California, 1969); Nehemia Levtzion, *Muslims and Chiefs in West Africa: A study of Islam in the Middle Volta Basin in the Pre-colonial Period* (Oxford: Clarendon Press, 1968); Paul E. Lovejoy, *Caravans of Kola: The Hausa Kola Trade, 1700-1900* (Zaria, Nigeria: Ahmadu Bello University Press, 1980); John Works, *Pilgrims in a Strange Land: Hausa Communities in Chad* (New York: Columbia University Press, 1976). A notable exception to past studies that focused mainly on commercial and religious networks in the Hausa diaspora is the work of Deborah Pellow. See: Deborah Pellow, "From Accra to Kano: One Woman's Experience" in *Hausa Women in the Twentieth Century*, eds. Catherine Coles and Beverly Mack (Madison: University of Wisconsin Press, 1991); Deborah Pellow, *Landlords and Lodgers: Socio-Spatial Organization in an Accra Community* (Chicago: University of Chicago Press, 2002).

4. Cohen, *Custom and Politics*, 7-9.

5. Ibid., 8-9.

6. Levtzion, *Muslims and Chiefs in West Africa*, xxv, 160.

7. Ibid., 23.

8. Ibid., 110-111.

9. A.W. Banfield (1905) in Abaka, *'Kola is God's Gift,'* 71.

10. Cohen, *Custom and Politics*, 52. Cohen cites J. Rouch's 1956 study titled "Migration au Ghana" found in *Journal de la société des africanistes*.

11. Studies conducted by R.M. Prothero in the 1950s and 1960s indicate that most men migrated from Northern Nigeria alone without their families. During his research in the mid-1960s Abner Cohen also reported that among the individuals in the Hausa community of Sabo who were born elsewhere, "the number of women [was] nearly half of the number of men." Cohen's findings revealed that Sabo's "supply of women" came not from Hausa women born along the frontier, but those either born directly in Sabo or in Hausaland in the North. Though Cohen's study was thoroughly researched and incredibly detailed, it must be noted that he did not discuss the history of female enslavement in the settling of the diaspora, which may or may not have been the case in Sabo. Cohen, *Custom and Politics*, 52-3.

12. With the creation of the Sokoto Caliphate in the early nineteenth century, new communication and trade pathways were opened; and by the end of that century, Hausa traders became the primary agents

directly linking the Grassfields to Hausaland for the first time in the region's history. Like their auxiliary role in the economic expansion of the Sokoto Caliphate, at the turn of the twentieth century, British imperial forces relied on Hausa soldiers and police to conquer parts of Nigeria, while the Germans recruited many Hausa traders to act as their guides and spies in Cameroon, as well as their soldiers in military campaigns. Hausa participation in such projects of imperial expansion increased their numbers throughout Cameroon, including the Grassfields. During and after the First World War, the Grassfields experienced a further increase in Hausa settlement as the British took control over the region. Such historical processes account for the Hausa presence in the Grassfields and form the broader context for this chapter.

13. M.G. Smith, "The Hausa System of Social Status," *Africa* 29 (959): 246.

14. Barbara M. Cooper, *Marriage in Maradi: Gender and Culture in a Hausa Society in Niger, 1900-1989* (Portsmouth: Heinemann, 1997), 10.

15. Paul E. Lovejoy, "Concubinage and the Status of Women Slaves in Early Colonial Nigeria," *Journal of African History* 29 (1988): 248.

16. Ibid., 245-48. On the British misunderstanding or ambivalence regarding domestic slavery in Northern Nigeria, see also Ibrahim M. Jumare, "The Late Treatment of Slavery in Sokoto: Background and Consequences of the 1936 Proclamation," *International Journal of African Historical Studies* 27 (1994): 303-322.

17. R.C. Abraham, *Dictionary of the Hausa Language* (London: University of London Press, 1962 [1949]).

18. Adamu, *The Hausa Factor*, 3, 39, 43, 198.

19. Barbara J. Callaway, *Muslim Hausa Women in Nigeria: Tradition and Change* (Syracuse, NY: Syracuse University Press, 1987), 42.

20. North-West Alkali Court (NWAC), Ndop, North-West Province, Cameroon. "Alkali" (pl. alkalai) is the Hausa form of the Arabic "al-Qadi."

21. *Takaba* is a period of mourning lasting 130 days performed by a widow after the death of her husband, during which time she must refrain from sexual relations with other men. In the NWAC documents, *takaba* is referred to as God's punishment on the woman's head. *Takaba* may be considered as similar to, if not the same as, *idda*, which prescribes the same period of waiting but applies to women whose marriages were dissolved by either death or divorce. Completing *takaba* or *idda* enables a woman to contract a new marriage. It should be noted that among the Hausa, and according to M.G. Smith, "No linguistic distinction is made between divorcées and widows. The important distinctions are between unmarried girls [*budurwai*], married women [*amare, mata*],

and women previously, but not at present, married [*zawarawa*]." Hausa words were not included in the original text. M.G. Smith, "Introduction" in Mary F. Smith, *Baba of Karo: A Woman of the Muslim Hausa* (New Haven: Yale University Press, 1981 [1954]), 25.

22. According to historian Paul Lovejoy, in 1906, one bag of cowry shells contained 20,000 cowries. At this time in Northern Nigeria, 8 bags of cowries were enough to serve as the "redemption money" for a female slave. This is the earliest figure I have on exchange values of female slaves in the region. Presumably, the number of bags to purchase slaves changed considerably from 1906 to c.1950 when our story takes place. Lovejoy, "Concubinage and the Status of Women Slaves," 251.

23. North-West Provincial Archives (NWPA), Bamenda, Cameroon. According to Malikite norms, free women received half of the male share of estates. See Lovejoy, "Concubinage and the Status of Women Slaves," 247.

24. F.H. Ruxton, *Maliki Law: Being a Summary from French Translations of the Mukhtasar of Sidi Khalil* (Westport: Hyperion Press, Inc., 1980 [1916]), 100.

25. Smith, "The Hausa System of Social Status," 244-245; Jerome H. Barkow, "Hausa Women and Islam," *Canadian Journal of African Studies* 6 (1972): 328.

26. Cooper, *Marriage in Maradi*, xxiii-xxvi.

Bibliography

Primary Sources

North-West Alkali Court (NWAC), Ndop, North-West Province, Cameroon.

North-West Provincial Archives (NWPA), Bamenda, North-West Province, Cameroon.

Secondary Sources

Abaka, Edmund. *'Kola is God's Gift': Agricultural Production, Export Initiatives, and the Kola Industry of Asante and the Gold Coast, c.1820-1950.* Oxford: James Currey, 2005.

Abraham, R.C. *Dictionary of the Hausa Language.* London: University of London Press, 1962 [1949].

Adamu, Mahdi, *The Hausa Factor in West African History*. Zaria and Ibadan: Ahmadu Bello University Press, 1978.

Bakewell, Oliver. "In Search of the Diasporas within Africa." *African Diaspora* 1 (2008): 5-27.

Barkow, Jerome H. "Hausa Women and Islam," *Canadian Journal of African Studies* 6 (1972): 317-328.

Callaway, Barbara J. *Muslim Hausa Women in Nigeria: Tradition and Change.* Syracuse, NY: Syracuse University Press, 1987.

Cohen, Abner. *Custom and Politics in Urban Africa: A Study of Hausa Migrants in Yoruba Towns.* Los Angeles, CA: University of California, 1969.

Cooper, Barbara M. *Marriage in Maradi: Gender and Culture in a Hausa Society in Niger, 1900-1989.* Portsmouth: Heinemann, 1997.

Jumare, Ibrahim M. "The Late Treatment of Slavery in Sokoto: Background and Consequences of the 1936 Proclamation," *International Journal of African Historical Studies* 27 (1994): 303-322.

Levtzion, Nehemia. *Muslims and Chiefs in West Africa: A Study of Islam in the Middle Volta Basin in the Pre-colonial Period.* Oxford: Clarendon Press, 1968.

Lovejoy, Paul E. *Caravans of Kola: The Hausa Kola Trade, 1700-1900.* Zaria, Nigeria: Ahmadu Bello University Press, 1980.

Lovejoy, Paul E. "Concubinage and the Status of Women Slaves in Early Colonial Nigeria," *Journal of African History* 29 (1988): 245-266.

Pellow, Deborah. "From Accra to Kano: One Woman's Experience," In *Hausa Women in the Twentieth Century*, edited by Catherine Coles and Beverly Mack. Madison: University of Wisconsin Press, 1991.

Pellow, Deborah. *Landlords and Lodgers: Socio-Spatial Organization in an Accra Community.* Chicago: University of Chicago Press, 2002.

Ruxton, F.H. *Maliki Law: Being a Summary from French Translations of the Mukhtasar of Sidi Khalil.* Westport: Hyperion Press, Inc., 1980 [1916].

Smith, Mary F. *Baba of Karo: A Woman of the Muslim Hausa.* New Haven: Yale University Press, 1981 [1954].

Smith, M.G. "The Hausa System of Social Status," *Africa* 29 (1959): 244-245.

Works, John. *Pilgrims in a Strange Land: Hausa Communities in Chad.* New York: Columbia University Press, 1976.

COMBATING TEENAGE PREGNANCY AND EARLY MARRIAGE THROUGH NON-FORMAL EARLY EDUCATION

Oluyemisi O.Obilade and Oladunni O. Obilade

The purpose of this chapter is to examine the issue of teenage pregnancy, early marriage, and high dropout rates among secondary school girls in Nigeria. Our goal is to help to reduce the incidence of teenage pregnancy and early marriage through the provision of improved knowledge and the development of informed decision-making skills. Teenage girls in Nigeria, as in most African countries, have continually been victims of gender oppression as a result of the existing patriarchal culture which devalues women's lives and achievements. Gender discrimination has been so entrenched in the fabric of African social norms that it has made the girls become "puppets of society" and has ensured that their futures are determined by a host of traditions, culture, and taboos that have consistently penalized them because of their biological attributes and functions rather than on the basis of their abilities and potential. Unfortunately, these factors are usually outside of their control.[1] Culture and social values rooted in patriarchal ethos have often been used successfully in keeping young girls out of school, pushing them out if they "wander-in," and/or preventing them from actualizing their potential. Statistics demonstrate exactly how acute gender disparity is in the areas of enrollment, retention, and educational completion rates at all levels of the educational system. For instance, globally, of the 121 million out-of-school children, 65 million are girls[2] and over 80% of these girls live in Sub-Saharan Africa.[3] Statistical data from Nigeria collated in 2001 and 2003 also highlight the following facts: First, that girls access to basic education in Nigeria, especially in the northern states, remain low with as few as 20% of women either being illiterate or having ever attended school, and the proportion of girls to boys in school is as high as 1 to three in some geo-political areas;[4] Second, 75% of the 3.4 million children that currently do not attend school in Nigeria are girls and gender gaps in primary school enrollment which favor boys could sometimes be as high as 48% in some states;[5] Third, Oluyemisi Obilade when analyzing 2003-2005 data collated by the National Bureau of Statistics Nigeria, highlighted the fact that less than 30% of those enrolled at the tertiary level are females.[6]

Besides the gender gap in enrollment, the problem of retention is much more pronounced for girls in comparison to their male counterparts. There are myriad socio-economic pressures and harmful traditional practices that continue to act as obstacles to impede the educational progress of these girls. Prominent among these are teenage pregnancies which often result in the development of forced or early marriages and which lead to a high rate of dropout among this group. Global statistics show that about 16 million teenage girls give birth each year accounting for 10% of all births globally; 78% of these pregnancies are unintended with at least 2.5 million pregnancies ending in abortion; the highest rate of girls who become mothers by age 16 is found in Sub-Saharan Africa and Asia; and adolescent pregnancy is correlated with low educational levels for girls because about 83% of these teenagers who give birth are more likely to come from poor or low-income families which is typical of developing countries like Nigeria.[7] Pregnancy and childbirth would thus appear to seal the fate of these young women thus ensuring their (often permanent]) dropout from school and introducing a negative trajectory into their future. The situation is not helped by the cultural taboos and aversion to open discussions of sexuality, sexual education, and reproductive health among the people of Nigeria.

SEXUALITY, SEXUAL EDUCATION AND THE NIGERIAN TEENAGE GIRL

- On a daily basis, teenage girls in Nigeria experience their share of struggles that their counterparts go through in many other parts of the world. Teenage girls, especially those just attaining puberty, undergo a lot of changes and these affect their vulnerability. Puberty is a stage of maturity when the endocrine and gamete-producing functions of the gonads first develop to the point where reproduction is possible. Pubertal changes can be physical changes which include growth spurts, breast budding, and the development of pubic and axillary hair;
- Biological maturation which includes increased vaginal lubrication and menstruation;
- Psychological changes that may presage new concerns with ones' physical appearance and body image; and
- Social adjustment. [8]

Teenagers have to cope with the physical changes taking place in their bodies as well as the resultant emotional and social pressures brought about by these changes. People experience these changes at different rates and physical maturity may well be achieved in advance of psychological or social maturity. At the same time, young people are bombarded with so many conflicting messages from diverse sources, including the (media, their family members, peers, educational institutions, places of worship, the internet, and others). Unfortunately, they sometimes lack the necessary adult guidance to properly decode these messages in order to make appropriate and well-informed decisions.

This is because the society in which they live is both unable and/or unwilling to assist them because of prevalent patriarchal cultural inhibitions and taboos shrouding the issue of sexuality and sexual relationships. In Nigerian communities, as in most parts of Africa, 'relations of intimacy are informed by the same cultural prescriptions and notions of personhood that operate within the larger society'[9] such that the concept of sex and sexuality are usually not a part of public discourse. Rather, as Oluyemisi Obilade and Tinuade Adewale observed, these topics are mystified and interrogated with masculine ethos.[10] Thus, sex and sexuality are taboo subjects that are not to be discussed by 'good girls' and there is usually a conspiracy of silence around them. Consequently, a girl or woman who expresses interest in matters relating to sex and sexuality is labeled a freak and made to feel like a social outcast. The society chooses to pretend that these issues do not exist. However, this ostrich–head-in-the–sand approach tends to ignore the real and pressing needs of young teenage girls for guidance and direction during this difficult period of their lives. Thus, as Nike Esiet succinctly puts it, many young teenage girls in Nigeria, without guidance from responsible adults, make decisions daily about sexuality, relationships, and health issues which regrettably neither benefit from accurate information nor are based on clear, well- considered values. The result is that they often make the wrong decisions with catastrophic consequences for their future. [11]

STUDY RATIONALE

As we performed research for this study, we were aware that although a lot of work has been done to remove the external barriers to girls' schooling as part of global concerted efforts to redress gender imbalance in education, much more work needs to be done to identify and address the 'internal barriers' (barriers encountered during the course of schooling) that discourage girls who enter school from completing the course of their schooling and achieving their full potential.[12]

These realities led us to focus our attention on some of the key factors leading to school drop-out, i.e., sexuality/sexual relationships, teenage pregnancies, and child marriages. Our decision to undertake this study among secondary school teenage girls was influenced by the awareness of the realities of the Nigerian environment to the sexual health, sexual welfare, and educational opportunities of teenage girls in Nigeria. The Nigerian environment is very often hostile and unwholesome to the teenage girl and the media is overrun with stories which corroborate this. Elizabeth Abama and Chris Kwaja, when discussing the issue of violence against women and the achievement of the Millennium Development Goals (MDGs) in Nigeria, highlighted how the country's drive to attain its goals in the area of Universal Primary Education (a key component of the MDGs) is hindered by gender-based factors and cultural norms/practices (including violence against women and lack of security) that devalue the education of girls and prevents girls and young women from entering and completing school.

They observed that for some girls (often quite a sizeable number), the lack of safety in or around schools is the chief obstacle to getting an education.[13]

One major form of violence against school girls that keeps them out of school or ensures that they underachieve and/or drop-out, is sexual harassment. Nan Stein defines sexual harassment in schools as

> unwanted and unwelcome behavior of a sexual nature that interferes with the right to receive an equal education opportunity,…limits the student's (victim's) ability to participate in or benefit from an educational program or activity, or … create(s) a hostile or abusive educational environment.[14]

It is usually initiated by someone in a position of power relative to the person being harassed. Sexual harassment by a teacher of the student has been described as a breach of trust; "unprofessional, exploitative, lousy behavior"[15] capable of causing particularly serious and damaging (short and long time) consequences for the victim.

Sexual harassment is not a new phenomenon and is not restricted to developing countries like Nigeria. For instance, the American Association of University Women (AAUW) in a 2002 survey reported that 83% of American school girls in grades 8 through 11 had been sexually harassed.[16] The situation for the Nigerian school girl is made more serious because the society does not appear to be predisposed to viewing it as a major problem and there is less urgency to put policies and structures in place to curb the act and its rate of occurrence. One of the few public acknowledgements of sexual harassment as a major problem for Nigerian school girls occurred in 2007 during a meeting between a [then] Minister of Education, Dr. Obiageli Ezekwesili, and a group of 1,000 school children in grades 8 through 11 (JSS 1- JSS 3) in both public and private schools in Nigeria. At that meeting, all the girls reportedly told the Minister that their greatest problem in school was sexual harassment.[17] Although some fleeting media attention was given to this topic at the time, it all soon declined. As is usually the case of all sexual issues, patriarchal ethos held sway and a blanket of silence was later thrown over the whole issue. However, except for the Obafemi Awolowo University, Nigeria which is in the process of developing a sexual harassment policy for use in the university, no other attempt has been made since then, especially by the different levels of government, to produce a sexual harassment policy or introduce legislation that criminalizes the act. Many teachers therefore continue to see these girls as "fringe benefits."[18] Thus, as a consequence of the general negative societal attitude to the victim often-typified by disbelief, blame-shifting, and stigmatization, many victims fear to make reports because of the possible repercussions. Very often for the victims, "the outcome [of reporting] is usually worse than silence."[19] The Nigerian girl often lives in a social mine-field [as far as sexual relations are concerned], for which she needs high level skills and knowledge to navigate in order not to jeopardize her future.

Highlighted below are some of the stories, extracted from various Nigeria media, of teenage girls who have been forced, coerced, or lured into sexual relationships with disastrous consequences for their future.

Case 1 – A teenage girl who is encouraged and supported by her mother to conceive and have babies for childless couples in exchange for a fee, ranging between $1000 for a female baby and $1667 for a male child. At the time the story came out in the newspaper, she was carrying her third pregnancy in 20 months. Her greatest fear was for her younger sister who, she was afraid, might suffer the same fate. [20]

Case 2 – A 12 year old girl who was repeatedly raped and impregnated by the 56 year old husband of her guardian, with the full consent and in the presence of the wife. The rapist threatened to behead her if she reported the rape to the neighbors and the wife, on discovering the young girl was pregnant, gave her a mixture of salt and water to induce abortion.[21]

Case 3 – Teenage junior secondary school (9th grade) girls who were lured into prostitution by a syndicate organized by wealthier, much older men. The girls would sneak out of their school to have sexual intercourse with men old enough to be their fathers and grandfathers. Each girl was paid the equivalent of $3.50 per partner out of which the pimp took $2.50, leaving the girl with just $1.00.[22]

Case 4 – An 18 year old secondary school girl, who was stripped naked, raped, and tortured by political party thugs.[23]

Case 5 – A 29 year old woman raped by her pastor at 17 years of age. She subsequently had a psychiatric breakdown that left her homeless and roaming the streets for 12 years until she was found and rehabilitated by a non- governmental organization.[24]

Case 6 – Closely related to this was the case of a 17 year old girl who was raped by her Pastor when she went for special prayers to pass the University entrance examination.[25] Needless to say, she was too traumatized to sit for, talk less of passing the examinations.

Case 7 – 14 teenage school girls in a boarding school who tested HIV positive after being gang-raped on their way to the stream (river) to fetch water.[26]

Case 8 – Two young girls, aged 11 and 13 years, for which monetary gains were withdrawn from school by their parents and given out in marriage as wives number 3 and 4 to men older than their fathers. [27]

Case 9 – Similar to the case above was the story, carried by various news media outlets, of a former Northern State Governor and serving Senator in Nigeria who recently got married to a 13-year-old Egyptian girl (about the same age as some of his grand children). He had earlier divorced another minor, a 17-year-old girl, whom he had married two years earlier, in order to marry the new 13-year-old wife. Commenting on this, a father saw nothing wrong in the Senator's action and claimed that "if I have a 13-year-old, and she has reached puberty, I will give her out in marriage to whoever desires."[28]

Case 10 – A teenage Junior Secondary School (9th grade) boy who impregnated two teenage girls in 7th grade, raped a teenage girl in class 9, and was caught having sex with another teenage girl in class 8.[29]

Case 11 – An 11-year-old primary school pupil in Southern Nigeria who got pregnant, received no ante-natal care, had a prolonged labor lasting two weeks, had multiple internal ruptures, and subsequently had vesico vaginal fistula.[30]

Bearing in mind the culture of stigmatization and silence in Nigeria, it is estimated that less than 10% of such stories get to the media. The enormity of the problem can then be imagined.

The impact of the cases above on young girl's health and well being, as well as access to, retention, and completion of various forms/levels of education is better imagined than experienced. For instance, highlighting the link between early marriage, pregnancy, and childbirth, the *Nigerian Tribune* observed that in countries where early marriage is the norm, many girls [usually poor, uneducated, rural dwellers] become pregnant in their teens, are often predisposed to obstructed labor because of their under developed pelvis, usually lack access to adequate medical care, are most times attended to by unskilled birth attendants who simply cut through the vagina to create passage for the baby, and consequently become inflicted with vesico vagina fistula (VVF, a breakdown in the tissue between the vaginal wall and the bladder) or recto vagina fistula (RVF, a breakdown in the tissue between the vaginal wall and the rectum). RVF and VVF are particularly malodorous conditions which cause the sufferers to become outcasts in the society. They are usually condemned to a lonely existence and bleak future. Many may never bear a child, or have a husband again, and they cannot go back to school. [31]

In our research process, we decided to adopt the non-formal education mode and move the location of the research interactions outside of the formal school settings, for certain reasons. Nigerian schools, as representatives of their counterparts all over Africa, exhibit the same patriarchal characteristics as the larger society in which they exist. They are known to emphasize school cultures that encourage stereotypical masculine (dominant) and feminine (acquiescent) behaviors which make girls particularly vulnerable. They have also been identified as locations for high risk sexual practices [32] and sites for multiple-oppression for young girls. They were, therefore, not considered as 'safe spaces' for girls to express their opinions and seek information/assistance about their concerns on sexuality, sexual relationships, and reproductive health. Also, there appeared to be a reticence on the part of the formal school system to incorporate sexuality and sexual education into its curriculum due to the prevailing culture of silence and taboos around such matters. These were considered enough reasons to militate against our use of the formal school setting as sites for our research project.

The reticence of the formal school system to incorporate sexuality and sexual-education into its curriculum as well as the failure of the school-based guidance/counseling units as sites for accessing information and assistance, influenced our decision as researchers to focus on non-formal education as an important area of inquiry. In Nigerian schools, as Nike Esiet puts it, "until now, the teaching of comprehensive sexuality education has not happened." [33] Thus, our objective was to explore the possibilities inherent in the combined use of non- formal education and local resources as essential, affordable, and effective means of encouraging access to information and capacity-building for teenage girls in dealing with issues arising from their sexuality and reproductive health concerns. Furthermore, from our previous experiences in working with young adults, we have realized the need for the use of imaginative and participatory methodologies, not only to capture the interests of these youths, but also to bring them into sustainable partnerships such that they take ownership of the intervention outcomes and structures and ensure its continuity. Finally, the selection of teenage secondary school girls as the target group for our research analysis was premised on the realization that involving these teenage girls as participatory agents in identifying and addressing their strategic interests and concerns, will both encourage them to take ownership of the process and solutions, as well as enhance sustainability of the structures and programs put in place during the participatory intervention, especially the Girls Fora. This chapter is thus an attempt to bridge the gap between research and action in addressing the issue of teenage pregnancy, child marriages, and the resultant truncation of schooling for teenage girls in Nigerian Secondary schools.

RESEARCH OBJECTIVES

The objectives of the research are as stated below:

- To raise greater awareness of issues of teenage sexuality, pregnancy, child marriage and drop-out among secondary school girls.
- To develop and initiate a trial of a range of small scale strategic interventions to address gaps in knowledge and assist with confidence-building and effective communications with peers, parents, and health care providers.
- To build a core of peer educators to serve as sources of information, counseling, and support for their colleagues in the schools and ultimately help them to be in better control of their sexuality, sexual lives, and health.
- To encourage the 'ownership' of the process and solution to enhance sustainability of the intervention.
- To encourage provision of the necessary support structures for the peer- educators and counselors.

THEORETICAL UNDERPINNINGS
OF THE RESEARCH

The theoretical framework considered appropriate for this research is the Participatory Humanitarian theory. Participatory Humanitarian theory rests on the assumption that if intervention will be effective and sustainable, the recipients have to be involved to decide for themselves the extent of their need; the degree of their willingness to do something to meet these needs; and to organize, plan and execute their projects. It emphasizes the participation of the beneficiary population in the process of programs at various stages. J. M. Cohen and Norma Uphoff perceive participation as the involvement of a significant number of persons in situations or actions which enhance their well-being.[34] Expanding further on this, John J. MacDonald conceives of participatory method as a paradigm shift from the paternalistic attitude which hitherto dominated developmental intervention programs/projects whereby improvements were made for the local people, not by them.[35] It is an important prerequisite for successful implementation of effective delivery of human services.

The base line of these definitions is that in any developmental endeavor at the community or personal level, the beneficiary population should not be passive but be actively involved in the decision- making process at all stages of the program cycle starting from need identification, planning, implementation, and evaluation. This approach enables people to be actors and not just tools; it sensitizes people to wake up from their slumber to react strongly against their limiting state of being. It is in essence an instrument per excellence by help givers to assist a marginalized people in the society and take the initiative to shape their own future.

METHODOLOGY

In our research and analysis process, we adopted a multi-layered methodology combining both quantitative and qualitative methods and this was undertaken in five stages. The sample consisted of 150 teenage girls selected from six secondary schools in Osun State of Nigeria. Using a stratified random selection process, 2 schools each were selected from urban, semi-urban, and rural locations. Twenty-five students were then randomly selected from each of the six schools. The research then followed the five stages discussed below.

Stage 1: This was the stage of primary data collection and involved a series of interviews and focus group discussions (FDSs) with the selected students. The interview questions and FGDs sought to assess their entry knowledge of contraceptives, pregnancy, sexually transmitted infections (STIs) including HIV/AIDS; their sources of information about these; their level of previous sexual activity and/or pregnancy; the sources of social pressures and coercion, as well as their apprehensions and fears about their sexuality and sexual relations. The teenage girls were assured of strict confidentiality and encouraged to freely and openly express themselves. This stage provided the necessary preliminary data and information that paved the way for the first of the series of small-scale strategic interventions to address the issue.

Stage 2: This stage was the trial of the first level of strategic intervention. It consisted of a series of sensitization and awareness- raising exercises using playlets, jingles, book markers, and stickers, as well as talks by various people, volunteers from women and youth- focused NGOS, role models, young university undergraduates, etc. Another series of FGD was conducted after this to track emerging issues of concern and reactions of these teenage girls.

Stage 3: This stage included the implementation of the second level of strategic intervention. It enhanced the knowledge base of the participants, as well as building their skills and capacity as peer educators, counselors, and peer support groups. It involved intensive training workshops on gender relations and consciousness raising, sexuality, sexual relations, and reproductive health. Trainers included gender experts and volunteers from women and youth-focused NGOs; medical doctors, and other relevant health service providers; guidance counselors; traditional birth attendants (TBAs), as well as Faith- based Birth attendants (FBAs). The intensive training workshops were followed by visits to ante-natal clinics with observation of some of the procedures e.g., antenatal exercises like singing, dancing, health talks, blood pressure monitoring, urinalysis fetal heart rate and growth monitoring; as well as interactions with service providers and some of their clients.

Stage 4: Involved exhaustive FGDs to identify strategic needs, the way forward, and to identify persons to coordinate and drive the process of change.

Stage 5: Involved the inauguration of peer educators and counselors; the formation of Girls' Forums as a mechanism to organize and discuss issues, and the Girls-for Girls – a sisters' support group to mobilize support for girls under pressure for sexual relationships/early marriages; as well as to offer hands of friendships to any girl ostracized by her close friends as a result of her saying no to sexual pressure.

RESULTS AND OBSERVATIONS

Tables 6.1, 6.2, and 6.3 contain information about the data collected upon which the discussions are based.

Table 6.1 contains pre- and post-intervention data about the girls' knowledge of contraceptive use, pregnancy, STIs and HIV/AIDS.

TABLE 6.1: PRE-ENTRY AND POST-INTERVENTION KNOWLEDGE OF CONTRACEPTIVES, PREGNANCY, STI/ HIV/AIDS

ITEMS	LEVEL OF KNOWLEDGE (%)			
	PRE ENTRY		POST INTERVENTION	
	Passing knowledge	*Sound knowledge*	*Passing knowledge*	*Sound knowledge*
Male Condom	65	35	-	100
Female Condom	7	0	-	100
Natural Calendar Method	30	12	-	95
Withdrawal	45	17	-	92
Pills	38	15	-	100
Injectables	38	10	-	100
Emergency Contraception (Morning after pills)	15	5	-	100
Foams/Jelly	42	12	-	100
Others/Traditional methods)	18	0	18	0
Gonorrhea	55	25	-	92
Syphilis	55	23	-	92
Chlamydia	0	0	-	82
HIV/AIDS	100	58	-	100
Pregnancy	75	22	-	100
Childbirth	35	15	-	100

Passing knowledge: has heard/has little information about this.

Sound knowledge implies respondent can explain correctly the method of usage/mode of infection/processes and consequences.

As can be seen from the table, the pre-intervention sound knowledge base for most of the girls were very low ranging from 0% for three of the items to 25% for most of the other items assessed. The initial FGD also shows a frighteningly high level of ignorance about pregnancy and STIs. Many of the girls believed that a girl could not get pregnant if she was having sex for the first time; if she had sex only once a month; or if she was forced to have sex; they also believed that if a girl washes with soap and water immediately after sexual intercourse, she could protect herself from pregnancy and STIs.

Furthermore, although a significant proportion also had a passing knowledge on some contraceptive methods such as male condoms, only a few had passing knowledge on some such as the female condoms and emergency contraception. Data from the Population Reference Bureau (USA) showed the percent of single sexually active 15-19 year old females using modern contraception during the last time they had sexual intercourse to be <11% in Mozambique, Malawi, Niger, Haiti and Madagascar; 11-20 % in Tanzania, Liberia, Nigeria, Zambia, Paraguay, Burkina Faso, Mali, Côte d'Ivoire, Cameroon, Kenya, 21-40 % in Ghana, Togo, Peru, Zimbabwe, Botswana, Costa Rica and > 40 % in the Democratic Republic of the Congo and Brazil.[36]

However, after the strategic intervention, the sound knowledge base of the participating girls improved remarkably and ranged from 82% to 100% for the items assessed. Many of them also reassessed the previous myths in line with current information. This would tend to underscore the fact that with the right pro-active, innovative and participatory methodology, teenage girls could be equipped with accurate information not only to make informed decisions based on sound value judgments, but to pass on the same to their peers in assisting others in the decision- making process. Table 6. 2 presents the data on the preferred sources of information and counsel on issues of sexuality, sexual relations, contraceptives, pregnancy, reproductive health and STIs / HIV/AIDS.

TABLE 6.2: SOURCE OF INFORMATION AND COUNSEL

SOURCE	RATING (1-11)
Media (radio, TV., newspapers)	2
Internet	4
Friends	1
Brothers & Sisters	3
Health service providers	8
Teachers	9
Parents	10
Libraries (Books, Journals, Magazines)	5
Youth Centers	6
Religious Centers	11
Others	7

Rating scale of 1-11, with the highest, most common/usual source of information rated.

From the Table 6.2 above, it is clear that the most often preferred source of information and counsel are the peer groups (friends, brothers and sisters) with the parents and teachers falling into the least preferred categories. This would appear to portend a set back to efforts at institutionalizing sexual and reproductive health education within the formal school curricula and setting, using teachers and traditional modes of instruction.

The implications of this are multiple. There would appear to be an urgent need to equip teenage girls with the requisite capacity in information, knowledge, and skills to serve as reliable sources of information and counsel to others. This could be done through the training and inauguration of peer educators. Furthermore there is a necessity to overhaul the curricula, training modules, and teaching methods of the formal school system in other to adequately address the issues confronting these girls and attract/ retain their attention. Teacher counselors in the formal school system also need retraining in understanding youth culture and language as a way of breaking down barriers and getting their messages across. Table 6.3 presents information about participant's previous sexual activities, pregnancies, and childbirths.

TABLE 6.3: PREVIOUS SEXUAL ACTIVITY / PREGNANCY/ABORTION

ACTIVITY	RESPONSE	
	YES %	NO %
Previous sexual intercourse	45%	55%
Forced	60	
Co-erced	28	
Consensual	12	
Previous Abortion	25	75
Induced	100	
Spontaneous	0	
Previous Pregnancy/Childbirth	5	95
Still birth	60	
Live birth	40	
Previous Engagement in transactional Sex	25	75
Previous Consent to early marriage.	10	90

It was a clear pointer to the fact that regardless of societal attitude of silence and assumption of teenage chastity, young teenage girls in Nigeria are sexually active with many of them being engaged in transactional sex and abortions. In separate studies conducted in different parts of Nigeria, it was found that the mean age of initiation into sexual activity for young women was 15 years. Some of these studies were performed by A.O.U. Okpani and J.U.Okpani. [37] Many of the girls, lacking proper guidance from significant adults in their lives, end up making wrong decisions with catastrophic consequences for their futures. Statistics show that teenagers account for 80% of individuals having unsafe abortions in Nigeria.[38] It is imperative that a re-examination of societal reticence around issues of sexuality and sexual relationships be undertaken so that society can respond adequately to the real and current needs of teenage girls in this area.

FGDs: The FGDs also identified other issues regarding the underlying reasons for teenage girl's choices and options in decisions. Many of the girls confessed to non-consultation with parents and teachers as a result of the fear of recrimination and stigmatization (as a bad girl); the general indifference and sometimes hypocrisy of the adults;

while a few others spoke of apparent collusions and pressures from their parents, guardians, and teachers to succumb. A few of the girls confessed to getting encouraged by their parents/ teachers to engage in transactional sex for shared economic benefits while two of the girls spoke of parents collecting bride-prices from elderly suitors and arranging their marriages without their consent. They therefore saw their friends as the only 'trusted' sources for information and assistance on sexual matters.

However, the greatest reason expressed by most of the girls for engaging in pre-marital sex was the fear of ostracization/isolation by their friends in case of their refusal. The pressure to conform and be acceptable by their peers was a key factor in adolescent girls' initiation of and involvement in sexual activity. This informed the basis for the formation of the Girls-for-Girls support group to provide companionship and support for girls under such pressure. Many of the girls also mentioned economic considerations and lack of a trusted support structure in the school/community in cases of pressure from 'sugar daddies' (older men who wanted a transactional sexual relationship).

CONCLUSION

At the end of the research and strategic interventions in our research, a preliminary impact assessment was undertaken viz-a-viz the earlier stated objectives.

- It was discovered that many of the participants had developed the inner consciousness to be able to resist pressures for sexual intercourse, to be able to, as one of them puts it, "say no and mean no.
- The Girls Forum has been used to provide safe spaces to discuss issues and expand options for the girls and sensitize others to the issue.
- The teenage girls have taken ownership of the process; they have taken the initiative to introduce the process to other girls and are working to ensure sustainability of the intervention program/activities.
- Many of the school administrators and guidance-counselors in the selected schools have expressed satisfaction with the

conduct of their female students; the decrease in drop–out rates due to pregnancy and early marriage; and have expressed willingness to participate in future trainings organized for them. We believe that the Girls Fora has in no small way complemented and enhanced the efforts of other Non-Governmental Organizations and Development Partners working in the area of adolescence health and women's literacy. Furthermore, even though the Girls Education Project, a joint initiative of DFID and UNICEF targeted at young girls from Northern Nigeria, is not being implemented in the Southern States where this study is located, we nevertheless recognize the potentially beneficial flow-back effect of such a project on the outcomes of our study.

As a result of the findings above, it is suggested that Girls Fora be established in other school communities and strategic structures in the form of legislation, school, and community- based support groups be put in place to assist the teenage girls. Furthermore, bearing in mind the fact that girls enrollment in and completion of various levels/ forms of education is a critical component of individual and national developmental efforts, the researchers are of the opinion that policies and programs [by governments and non-governmental organizations] seeking to promote girl-child education as a means to individual and national development, should incorporate innovative and participatory methodologies to enhance success and sustainability.

In conclusion, the research results would appear to be a validation of the position that local people, using local resources and moving outside the 'conventional boxes' to address local problems and issues, have greater chances of achieving success that can be sustained over time. Greater attention should be given to forging partnerships with adolescents in all efforts to address the issue of their sexuality and sexual well-being. People who wear the shoes know where the thorns pinch them and have the greatest success not only in removing the thorns, but also in blocking future entry. All interventions must take cognizance of the fact that adolescents learn best when their views are listened to and respected, and when learning incorporates their previous experiences.[39]

Notes

1. Johnson Gachie, "The Girl Child and Education in Southern Sudan." *IPS-Inter Press Service* 2006. (accessed November 13, 2007).

2. UNICEF, *Information Sheet – Girls Education,* UNICEF Nigeria Country Office 2007. (accessed October 3, 2010).

3. Elizabeth Abama and Chris Kwaja, "Millenium Development Goals and the Challenges of Violence Against Women in Nigeria," *Adult Education in Nigeria* 6 (June 2008):19.

4. UNICEF, *Information Sheet – Girls Education,* UNICEF Nigeria Country Office 2007.

5. DFID/UNICEF, "Project Concept Note: Girls Education Plus, Nigeria,"MS CODE: 048-550-034 (Unpublished) 4.

6. Oluyemisi Obilade, "Opening Doors and Enhancing Opportunities for the Girl-Child Education Through Paternal Literacy in Northern Nigeria," *Adult Education in Nigeria* 16, (2007): 206.

7. United Nations Population Fund, *UNFPA Fact Sheet: Young People and Times of Change.* (accessed October 3, 2010).

8. Action Health Incorporated, *Comprehensive Sexuality Education - Trainers' Resource Manual.(* Lagos: Action Health Incorporated, 2003) 79-93.

9. Carolyn Baylies, "Perspectives on Gender and Aids in Africa," in Aids, *Sexuality, and Gender in Africa,* ed. Carolyn Baylies and Janet Bujra (London; Routledge,2000), 7.

10. Oluyemisi Obilade and Tinuade Adewale, "My Body, My Sexuality: Tracking Emerging Gender Relations in a Nigerian University." *Proceedings of the International Interdisciplinary Women's Studies Conference.* Sakarya: Sakarya University (March, 5-7 2009), 510.

11. Nike Essiet, "Foreword" *Comprehensive Sexuality Education - Trainers' Resource Manual. Lagos:* Action Health Incorporated (2003), 3.

12. Fiona Leach et. al., *An Iinvestigative Study of the Abuse of Girls in African Schools.* Sevenoaks; DFI (, 2003) vii – ix.

13. Elizabeth Abama and Chris Kwaja, "Millenium Development Goals and the Challenges of Violence against Women in Nigeria," *Adult Education in Nigeria, 19.*

14. Nan Stein, *Sexual Harassment in Schools.* Wellesley College Stone Center: National Violence Against Women Prevention Research Center, Wellesley Center for Women, www.musc.ed/vawprevention/research/sexharass.shtml.

15. Richard Klein, in Roger Kimball, *The Distinguished Professor – on Jane Gallop and Her Book, Feminist Accused of Sexual Harassment.* The New Criterion, April,1997. http://www.newcriterion.com/articles.cfm/The-distinguished-professor--3348 (accessed May 5, 2010).

16. American Association of University Women, *Hostile Hallways: The AAUW Survey on Sexual Harassment in American Schools,* Washington D.C. AAUW, 2002.

17. Katharine Houreld, "Lecturers Prey on Nigerian Women, Girls," *Associated Press Writer* Sunday March 25, 2007. http://www.nigeriavillagesquare.com/articles/nvs/lecturers-prey-on-nigerian-women-girls 13.html (accessed May 12, 2010).

18. Oluyemisi Obilade, in "Lecturers Prey on Nigerian Women, Girls," by Katharine Houreld, *Associated Press Writer,* Sunday March 25,2007. http://www.nigeriavillagesquare.com/articles/nvs/lecturers-prey-on-nigerian-women-girls 13.html (accessed March 25, 2010).

19. Naomi Wolf, "The Silent Treatment," *New York Magazine.* New York: (accessed May 7, 2010).

20. National Life. "Pregnancy Contract-Why I Agree to Conceive for Childless Couples," Lagos: *National Life* (Saturday August 8, 2009) 6.

21. Emmanuel Ojukwu,"12 year old girl raped, pregnant," Lagos: *Saturday Sun* (May, 17 2008): 8-9.

22. Olalere Adebayo and Ayodele Salawu, Bizarre – JSS Female Students Hawk Sex" Lagos; *National Life.* (July 24, 2009): 6 – 7.

23. Tunde Odesola, "How I was Raped, Tortured by Party Thugs – SSS student" Lagos: *Sunday Punch.* (September 23, 2007): 48-49.

24. John Okolo; Stories that Touch the Heart: This Lady was raped by her Pastor at 17 and that Made her Mad for 12 years. Ibadan: *Sunday Tribune* (November 2008): *2.*

25. Isaac Adelusi, *Holy Spirit Removed Her Pants, Sunday Tribune:* Ibadan; (May 2, 2010) 2.

26. Gold F.M. *Headlines Today,* Ilesha; Federal Radio Corporation of Nigeria (Gold F.M), 2008.

27. Gold F.M. *Headlines Today,* Ilesha; Federal Radio Corporation of Nigeria, (Gold F.M), 2009.

28. Sulaiman Aliyu, "I'll marry out my daughter @ 13 – Islamic Scholar," Lagos: *National Life* (Saturday May 8, 2010), 39.

29. Bojuri "Akekoo omo JSS 3 di obuko sileewe." *Bojuri,* Ile-Ife (10 October, 2008), 3.

30. Sunday Tribune (2010). 'Health Matters: Vesico Vagina Fistula,'*Sunday Tribune*, Ibadan 9 May, 2010, 17.

31. Ibid.

32. Leach, Fiona et. al., An Investigative Study of the Abuse of Girls in African Schools, Sevenoaks, DFID (2003) vii – ix.

33. Nike Essiet, Foreword to *Comprehensive Sexuality Education - Trainers' Resource.*

34. John Michael Cohen and Norman Thomas Uphoff, "Participation's Place in Rural Development: Seeking Clarity Through Specificity," *World Development* 8 (1980): 213-235.

35. John MacDonald, "An Historical and International Perspective," www.ncbi.nlm.nih.gov/pmc/articles/PMC2560359/pdf/(1)

36. Population Reference Bureau, *The World's Youth2000.* (Washington, MEASURE Communications, 2000) 10 -11. Accessed October 31, 2010.

37. Anthony Okpani, and Judith Okpani, Sexual activity and contraceptive use among female adolescents – A Report from Port Harcourt, Nigeria,' *African Journal of Reproductive Health* 4 [1] (2000):40-47.

38. Action Health Incorporated, *Comprehensive Sexuality Education - Trainers' Resource Manual,* (Lagos: Action Health Incorporated, 2003), 5.

39. Nike Essiet, "Foreword," *Comprehensive Sexuality Education - Trainers' Resource.*

Bibliography

Abama, Elizabeth and Kwaja, Chris. "Millenium Development Goals and the Challenges of Violence against Women in Nigeria," *Adult Education in Nigeria* l6 (June 2008):19.

Action Health Incorporated. *Comprehensive Sexuality Education - Trainers' Resource Manual.* Lagos: Action Health Incorporated, 2003. 79-93.

Adebayo, Olalere and Salawu,Ayodele. "Bizarre – JSS Female Students Hawk Sex," Lagos: *National Life.* July 24, 2009: 6 – 7.

Adelusi, Isaac. "Holy Spirit Removed Her Pants," *Sunday Tribune.* Ibadan; May 2, 2010, 2.

Aliyu, Sulaiman. "I'll marry out my Daughter @ 13 – Islamic Scholar," Lagos: *National Life.* Saturday May 8, 2010: 39.

American Association of University Women. *Hostile Hallways: The AAUW Survey on Sexual Harassment in American Schools.* Washington D.C. AAUW. 2002.

Baylies, Carolyn. "Perspectives on Gender and Aids in Africa. In *Aids, Sexuality, and Gender in Africa,* edited by Carolyn Baylies and Janet Bujra (London: Routledge, 2000).

Bojuri, "Akekoo omo JSS 3 di obuko sileewe," *Bojuri:* Ile-Ife. 10 October, 2008: 3.

Cohen, John Michael and Norman Thomas Uphoff. "Participation's Place in Rural Development: Seeking Clarity Through Specificity," *World Development* 8(1980): 213-235.

DFID/UNICEF. Project Concept Note: Girls Education Plus, Nigeria.MS CODE: 048-550-034 (Unpublished), 4.

Essiet, Nike. "Foreword," *Comprehensive Sexuality Education - Trainers' Resource Manual. Lagos:* Action Health Incorporated, 2003, 3.

Gachie, Johnson. "The Girl Child and Education in Southern Sudan," *IPS-Inter Press Service,* 2006. Accessed November 13, 2007.

Gold, F.M. *Headlines Today.* Ilesha: Federal Radio Corporation of Nigeria. Gold F.M: 2008.

______. *Headlines Today.* Ilesha: Federal Radio Corporation of Nigeria, Gold F.M: 2009.

Houreld, Katharine. "Lecturers Prey on Nigerian Women, Girls," *Associated Press Writer,* Sunday March 25, 2007. http://www.nigeriavillagesquare. com/articles/nvs/lecturers-prey-on-nigerian-women-girls   13.html   . Accessed May 12, 2010.

Klein, Richard in Roger Kimball, *The Distinguished Professor – on Jane Gallop and Her Book, Feminist Accused of Sexual Harassment.* The New Criterion: April, 1997. http://www.newcriterion.com/articles.cfm/The-distinguished-professor--3348 Accessed May 5, 2010.

Leach, Fiona et. al. *An Investigative Study of the Abuse of Girls in African Schools.* Sevenoaks: DFID, 2003, vii – ix.

MacDonald, John. "An Historical and International Perspective," www.ncbi. nlm.nih.gov/pmc/articles/PMC2560359/pdf/(1).

National Life. "Pregnancy Contract-Why I Agree to Conceive for Childless Couples," Lagos: *National Life.* Saturday, August 8, 2009, 6.

Obilade, Oluyemisi and Tinuade Adewale."My Body, My Sexuality: Tracking Emerging Gender Relations in a Nigerian University," *Proceedings of the International Interdisciplinary Women's Studies Conference.* Sakarya: Sakarya University March, 5-7 2009, 510.

Obilade, Oluyemisi. "Opening Doors and Enhancing Opportunities for the Girl-Child Education through Paternal Literacy in Northern Nigeria," *Adult Education in Nigeria* 16 (2007): 206.

Obilade, Oluyemisi. In Katharine Houreld, "Lecturers Prey on Nigerian Women, Girls," *Associated Press Writer*. Sunday March 25, 2007. http://www.nigeriavillagesquare.com/articles/nvs/lecturers-prey-on-nigerian-women-girls-13.html .Accessed March 25, 2010.

Odesola, Tunde. "How I was Raped, Tortured by Party Thugs – SSS student," Lagos: *Sunday Punch*. September 23, 2009; 48-49.

Ojukwu, Emmanuel."12 year old girl raped, pregnant," Lagos: *Saturday Sun*. (May, 17 2008) 8-9.

Okolo, John. Stories that Touch the Heart: This Lady was raped by her pastor at 17 and that made her mad for 12 years. Ibadan: *Sunday Tribune* .November 2008: 2.

Okpani, Anthony and Okpani, Judith. (2000). "Sexual Activity and Contraceptive use Among Female Adolescents – A Report from Port Harcourt, Nigeria," *African Journal of Reproductive Health*. 4 (2000): 40-47.

Population Reference Bureau, *The World's Youth 2000*. Washington: MEASURE Communications, 2000, 10 -11. www.prb.org/pdf/worldyouths_eng.pdf. Accessed October 31, 2010.

Stein, Nan. *Sexual Harassment in Schools*. Wellesley College Stone Center: National Violence Against Women Prevention Research Center, Wellesley Center for Women, www.musc.ed/vawprevention/research/sexharass.shtml.

Sunday Tribune. 'Health Matters: Vesico Vagina Fistula,' *Sunday Tribune*, Ibadan 9 May, 2010:17.

UNICEF. *Information Sheet – Girls Education*. UNICEF Nigeria Country Office 2007. <Accessed October 3, 2010>

UNICEF. *Information Sheet – Girls Education*. UNICEF Nigeria Country Office, 2007.

United Nations Population Fund, UNFPA Fact Sheet: Young People and Times of Change. Accessed October 3, 2010.

Wolf, Naomi. "The Silent Treatment," *New York Magazine*. New York: Accessed May 7, 2010.

CHAPTER 7

GENDER, SEXUALITY, AND WORK: FEMALE LIVE-IN DOMESTIC WORKERS IN NIGERIA

Zahrah Nesbitt-Ahmed

This chapter, an outcome of previous research on male and female domestic workers in Nigeria, focuses on the perceptions of sexuality of live-in female domestic workers in Lagos.[1] Specifically, it looks at the forms of regulation that employers adopt to control their domestics' sexuality and the reasons for such regulation.[2] Domestic workers are part of the intimate life of the family[3] with the worker usually referred to as "one of the family"[4] or "just like a daughter."[5] Yet, despite this quasi-familial status, domestic workers are treated, often not as family members but as second-class citizens, showing that they are less "members of the family" and more "members of the household."[6]

Bridget Anderson argues that the notion of "being part of the family" works in employers' interests because it seriously weakens employees ability to negotiate terms and conditions.[7] This helps blur the boundaries between paid work and unpaid favors, which in turn often leads to exploitation. This situation is further heightened by the isolation, highly personal nature, and low status of domestic work.[8] As part of their job, domestic workers perform highly personal forms of care such as food preparation or assistance, washing clothes, caring for children or the elderly, and cleaning the bedrooms and bathrooms of their employers' homes.[9] What is particularly interesting is that within a working environment marked by direct, personal relationships, sexuality has not received much attention in the literature.[10] This is surprising because domestic work introduces workers into the intimacy and privacy of a household but they are usually unable to experience intimacy and privacy of their own.

Situating my research in Nigeria involves two major dimensions. First, the existing studies of domestic work in Africa pertain almost exclusively to the southern region, and particularly South Africa.[11] In Nigeria, domestic workers form an integral part of many urban households but due to it not being recognized as a form of employment, minimal research has been performed on this topic thus far. Second, the exploitative working conditions of domestic workers and lack of adequate access to education and any form of information makes it difficult for them to make informed choices and decisions that can enhance their quality of life, which renders them vulnerable to abuse. In the next section, I briefly introduce the terms sex and sexuality and explain their importance in the contemporary labor market before going on to discuss the issue of sexuality in the lives of female domestic workers.

GENDER, SEXUALITY, AND WORK

According to Linda McDowell, for much of the twentieth century, sex was assumed to refer to biological differences between men and women and attributed social differences were considered to be a natural consequence of these biological distinctions.[12] The differentiation of the term (biological) sex from (socially constructed) gender happened in the late 1960s and 1970s during the development of second-wave feminist theory.[13]

With reference to sexuality, McDowell notes that it has a longer and more complex history, emerging in the late nineteenth century, especially in Freudian theory, to capture the diverse patterns of behavior associated with sexual activities and expression. Initially, it used to be seen as "an output of a natural sex drive" but through the works of theorists like Michel Foucault and Judith Butler, sexuality is now seen as a socially constructed set of meanings and behavior.[14] As sexuality is a broader term referring to aspects of social life, such as desires, practices, relationships and identities, this chapter adopts the World Health Organizations' (WHO) definition which states that:

Sexuality is a central aspect of being human throughout life and encompasses sex, gender identities and roles, sexual orientation, eroticism, pleasure, intimacy and reproduction. Sexuality is experienced and expressed in thoughts, fantasies, desires, beliefs, attitudes, values, behaviors, practices, roles and relationships. While sexuality can include all of these dimensions, not all of them are always experienced or expressed. Sexuality is influenced by the interaction of biological, psychological, social, economic, political, cultural, ethical, legal, historical, religious and spiritual factors.[15]

The WHO definition "suggests that social influences around sexuality affect us all."[16] The broader definition of sexuality "from sexual acts *per se* to include representations, everyday interactions and social regulations as well as ideas of fantasy and desire"[17] opens up new areas of research about the economy and, with respect to this chapter, enables research on sexuality and employment to move beyond sexual harassment and consensual sexual relationships in the workplace, and sex work.

Lisa A. Adkins, for example, shows that "sexual relations are key to understanding the power relations between men and women in the workplace."[18] Drawing on research conducted with workers in the hotel, leisure park, pub and catering industries in the United Kingdom, Lisa A. Adkins' shows how women's disadvantages in the labor market are not simply an outcome of the control of their access to jobs and wages, but also that participation in employment for women involves particular forms of sexual and unpaid appropriation of labor—to which men are not subjected. So for women to have access to employment, most have no choice but to occupy the position of sexual subjects.

Recent studies on gender and global industries have begun to examine two patterns of globalized control of sexuality among women workers: first, in regulating the degree of women's sexuality, and second, in regulating the content.[19] These studies show how in some cases, especially in export processing zones, managers often introduce formal or informal rules concerning sexual intimacies and construct particular images of the female factory worker.[20] In some cases, managerial intention is to suppress intimate relations among workers. Aiwha Ong's study of a Japanese company in Malaysia is the classic example where social events were prohibited inside the company and women were required to live in closely monitored dormitories.[21] In other cases, as noted by Winifred R. Poster, sexuality is promoted by production workers and staff.[22] Kevin Yelvington, for example, shows that in Caribbean factories women are encouraged by their male bosses and workers to engage in verbal games like "sweet talk" and sexual bragging, displays of body parts and horseplay.[23] Sexuality is more tightly regulated in the context of domestic work and will be the issue I turn to next.

DOMESTIC WORK IN NIGERIA[24]

To date, there are limited data on the number of persons employed as domestic workers in private households in Nigeria. But there can be little doubt to anyone familiar with Nigeria that domestic work is an important part of the society as there is a culture that supports the practice of having a family or non-family member perform domestic labor.

In colonial Nigeria, for example, British households, as well as a few elite Nigerians and repatriates from Sierra Leone and Cuba, usually employed adult domestics such as stewards, cooks, and drivers, and young domestics known as "small boys" and "baby nurses.[25] Others obtained the assistance of their older and younger relatives, who in exchange for domestic chores and childcare would receive educational or vocational training. This was known as child-fostering and was done mainly through direct contact between the child's parents and employers.[26]

The fostering arrangement is seen as mutually beneficial - the fostering household receives the labor of the foster child while the foster families will help them to pursue diverse educational activities and/or pay monthly sums of money to parents (or children). Unfortunately, employers fail to make the promised education or payments to either the children or their parents. Yet, this trend continues because some parents still believe their children are participating in the traditional and benign fostering arrangement.

Today, due to Nigeria's "dismal performance in education, human development, job creation, human capital development and poverty alleviation" and limited employment opportunities, many low-income people find themselves in affluent homes in cities working as domestic workers to survive.[27] Emmanuel E. Okafor cites poverty as the greatest single force that creates the flow of people into domestic service.[28] Furthermore, those that enter domestic work have little or no education and no alternative form of employment.

On the demand side, the rise in domestic workers' has been linked to increased female labor force participation. The growing entry of women into the labor market has meant that working women have had to shoulder the dual responsibilities of reproduction and production with very little assistance from male, especially adult male, household members.[29] In a traditional Nigerian society, women derived their social status from their roles as a wife and mother but as more women enter the labor market, the pressure and challenge of maintaining cherished traditional values of home keeping, has led to the rise in domestic workers as a substitute labor to assume the woman's role in the household.[30] In this way, the woman-employer is relieved from doing this work herself, and is able to take up paid employment or other activities outside the home.[31]

It should be noted that the living and working conditions of domestic workers have significant implications for their well-being. Domestic workers are faced with uncertain working conditions as a result of domestic work being considered a low status job, by both domestic workers and society. This means that despite the enormous amount of work that domestic workers perform for the families that employ them, they are treated as inferior members of the household. Along with the receipt of little or no pay, findings highlight that female live-in domestic workers have "no clear division between work and private time as working days may run from 5.00 a.m. until 1:00 a.m. and they [are] rarely allowed time off."[32] Some domestic workers can ask for time off, while others only get time off to attend church services on Sundays. Added to this is the fact that live-in domestic workers' rarely have their own private space. Because of the unregulated nature of their work, they have little option to change their situation. Furthermore, they rarely have access to social support networks. This means that regardless of their pay and conditions, domestic workers are committed to work for their employers because they have "few marketable skills, little or no education, and no alternative employment opportunities."[33] Added to this is a complex employer-employee relationship, referred to by Judith Rollins as "maternalism."[34] The "maternalism" dynamic between employers and employees manifests itself in patterned asymmetrical behaviors involving forms of address, space, physical appearance and gift-giving.[35]

In Latin America, studies of domestic workers reveal the persistent use of terms such as *chica, hija* and *muchacha*, all variants on the terms "girl" or "daughter" to address domestic workers regardless of their age, yet they are expected to address their employers as Mrs., Miss, Ms.[36] With respect to space, domestic workers are often confined to particular parts of the house, such as the kitchen, and sometimes they eat separately and often only after their employers have eaten. The wearing of uniforms is another way to maintain social distance between employers and workers, and signifies the inferior status of the employee. Cast-off clothing, discarded appliances and furniture are usually designed to establish the domestic employee's inferiority, especially given that such gifts are often provided in lieu of wage rises and benefits.[37]

"Maternalism" therefore permits employers to exercise a degree of control over lives, personhood, and autonomy of domestic workers considered unthinkable in most public employment situations.[38] Coupled with isolation in the household, abysmal working conditions, and lack of privacy, this can lead to control over domestic workers, and as will be shown in the next section, control over their sexuality. This is possibly one of the most intrinsic elements of the regulation by employers of domestic workers. Unfortunately, research on domestic work rarely discusses the control over domestic workers' sexuality by employers and the impact that this has on the performance of their domestic work.

SEXUALITY AND DOMESTIC WORK

Domestic work is generally seen as lowly, devalued work associated with dirt and disorder.[39] This notion of dirt and domesticity also translates into sexuality:

> ... dirt and sex live in close association, and women who
> clean up things associated with bodies find themselves
> mysteriously deemed sexual and powerful regardless of
> their actual social status.[40]

Previous research highlights that employers have complex emotions about hiring women and girls. Raka Ray argues that this is because the female domestic worker "does not have shame, is not protected, is sexually powerful and immoral, and is therefore a threat to the moral fabric of society."[41] He further notes that in India, "at the forefront of everybody's mind when they hire a young woman is the risk of her potential sexuality, since unprotected women are perceived as sexually dangerous and therefore not respectable."[42] This is echoed by Nicole Constable, where in Hong Kong, the domestic worker is regarded as a potential seductress as one who can both turn a man's attention away from family matters and also deplete his energy for productive and reproductive work.[43] As a result of this "fear," domestic workers are either forbidden by their employers to receive guests, leave the employer's home and pursue intimate relations or even friendships, or they are victims of sexual abuse by males in the household.[44]

SEXUALITY AND DOMESTIC WORK: DISCIPLINE, CONTROL AND VULNERABILITY

The first reason for employer control of domestic workers is their "potential rampant sexuality." Kimberly Chang and Julian McAllister Groves, for example, show how in Hong Kong many local residents and employers presume that the women have an ulterior motive in going abroad "to find a man and obtain financial security." This has led to newspaper headlines such as, "Maids Too Much of a Distraction for Employers" to more startling captions such as "Maid turned to prostitution."[45] In Zambia, fear of female sexuality, together with female employers' lack of trust in their male partners, has led to male dominance in domestic work.[46] Karen T. Hansen, further notes that even when Zambian employers do employ women, they do not let their female domestic workers prepare food because they fear they will mix love potions into the husband's food in order to attract his sexual attention.

Scholars have noted that young "nubile" women in the paid workforce are often represented as bearers of rampant or "uncontained" sexuality.[47] Nicole Constable argues this point out convincingly, in relation to Filipina domestic workers in Hong Kong, where they are constructed as a moral threat to the local community largely because of their status as "unattached" women who, it is further presumed, need to be regulated and controlled.[48]

Prevailing concerns about female domestic workers in Nigeria strike a similar chord. As discovered from interviews with employers, some feel that having female domestic workers "would be like advertising that your husband needs another wife at home."[49] Stories of the easy virtue of female domestic workers in Lagos are also numerous. During one focus group, a participant stated that "Calabar house-girls are truly randy" while a male driver told the story of his "Oga's" former "house-help" who left the house because her attempts to seduce her "Oga" failed.[50] He went on further to state she had a reputation for seducing "Ogas" in the households she worked in so as to improve her working conditions. Whether true or false, the beliefs these stories embody become socially relevant when employers decide to hire female domestic workers.

The second reason, especially when young domestic workers are employed, is to ensure that she "doesn't get herself into trouble." As one woman employer explained, in Constable's study, "even the most well-intentioned domestic workers need a bit of help resisting [sexual temptations]".[51] In this situation, regardless of age, strict forms of discipline are imposed for the workers' own good in case they might be tempted to stay out late, mix with unsavory company, and get into trouble.

Although it is difficult for live-in domestic workers to form sexually intimate and/or conjugal relationships, there is evidence to suggest that, domestics do enter partnerships with men for varying periods of time. The cliché story is one of a married Nigerian man having intimate relations with his "house-girl" as highlighted in the song "Ekaette" by Nigerian singer, Maya Hunt. But this in itself is risky as it is considered reasonable to fire or refuse to employ a domestic worker for "mere suspicion of having sexual relations."[52] Furthermore, if the domestic worker becomes pregnant, the situation becomes more complex, with domestic workers often having to choose between staying pregnant or keeping their jobs. Securing voluntary abortions, even in cases of rape, can be difficult if not impossible in Nigeria where legal abortions are permitted only for specifically defined and medically documented reasons (e.g. to save a woman's life); and so many may turn to illegal and unsafe abortions to keep their jobs.[53]

Employers invariably become owners, not only of their workers' labor but also of their bodies. Sexual ownership by employers may lead to either *denying* their sexuality (i.e. domestic workers are rarely allowed to have intimate social lives or even friendships) or *taking* their sexuality (i.e. domestic workers are seen as sexually available and become vulnerable to sexual violence).

DOMESTIC WORK AND SEXUAL OWNERSHIP: DENYING OR TAKING SEXUALITY

Control that *denies* sexuality ranges from controlling the domestic workers interactions within the home, to minimal movement, contacts and ability to communicate outside.[54] In Peru, Sarah Radcliffe notes that workers can go into the street for brief trips to the market or shops, but often require their employer's permission to do so, and are frequently left in the house when the family goes on an outing. Within the house, employees have access only to specific curtailed spaces- the kitchen, bedroom, and the washing area. Domestic workers are also sometimes denied access to their own family, because of a fear that the family will take back the domestic workers.[55]

While domestic workers are sent on errands, this does not offer opportunities for meeting other people, as these are usually short trips to markets. Furthermore, domestic workers are often not able to use the household phone, and they are discouraged from having visitors, and talking with neighbors or other domestic workers. Although it was noted by Roger Sanjek in a study of domestic maids in Ghana, that employer objections to "sexual encounters" are not only based on the time taken for liaisons and fears that she may become "lackadaisical about her duties while she is thinking about being with her boyfriend".[56] More importantly, employers are also concerned about possibilities of pregnancy and the ensuing responsibilities and costs they might have to assume.[57]

Control that *denies* sexuality makes it difficult for domestic workers to make informed choices and decisions about their personal lives. Furthermore, it dramatically increases the vulnerability of domestic workers to exploitation, intimidation, sexual violence, and harassment.

The tragic irony is that although domestic workers are often viewed as "morally suspect" and a "sexual threat," their weak and subordinate position in the household makes them most vulnerable to sexual mis-treatment. This leads to a situation that I have termed as control that *takes* sexuality.

There are various ways in which sexuality can be taken. For example, in Nigeria, many adolescent boys' first sexual encounters are with their "house-girls." This was highlighted in focus groups conducted with one participant noting that "a lot of Nigerian men messed around with their house help in their teens." This was echoed by another participant who said, "sleeping with house-helps is a way for young guys to practice." This is also common in many parts of Latin America, where Sylvia Chant with Nikki Craske state that "where men wish to 'cut their teeth' without compromising their reputation ... they may have their first sexual experience with prostitutes or live-in maids."[58] Ray Jureidini also echoes this in his study on female domestic workers in Lebanon, where a male respondent "noted how some mothers and fathers in fact encouraged their sons to have sex with the maid to introduce manhood."[59] Control that *takes* sexuality dramatically increases domestic workers vulnerability to intimidation, unsafe sex, pregnancy and STDs. The next section looks at the most extreme case of *taking* sexuality, i.e., sexual abuse.

SEXUAL ABUSE IN THE WORKPLACE

Sexual abuse, while undoubtedly unreported, appears to be shockingly common in domestic work.[60] It may range from grabbing of domestic workers or touching their breasts and buttocks, persistent demands for sex, buying food, money or clothing in return for sex to propositioning them in return for higher wages or more favorable working conditions.[61] There are also cases of rape of live-in domestic workers.[62]

Unwanted sexual approaches and/or demands are not exerted solely by men living in or associated with the household (i.e. female employers' husbands, younger men and adolescent boys in the household, or extended family) but also male domestic workers in the household or the neighborhood. According to a study on adult domestic workers in Uganda, sexual abuse of female domestic workers has been justified "on grounds that some men are enticed by the domestic workers as well as to the youthfulness and beauty of some female domestic workers compared to their wives."[63]

Cases of sexual abuse of domestic workers tend to go unreported because of the unequal power relations that exist in domestic work. The employer may "hire and fire as they please"[64] while the domestic workers' poor socioeconomic status and isolation, as well as threats from the men, makes them unwilling to risk complaining or disobeying their employers for fear of losing their jobs. It should be noted that the extent to which female domestic workers are willing partners in sexual liaisons with members of the employing family is something that is difficult to ascertain because there may be attraction and voluntarism on either side or it may be coerced. While, there is little doubt that domestic workers, especially those who live-in, suffer sexual harassment and rape, as noted by Jureidini "the maid's actions in having sex with the children or with the husband, or just flirting, may be an expression of genuine affection, or a form of assertion of her seductive powers competing with the dominant *madame* of the house."[65]

Also, Tim Meldrum writing on domestic service in 18th century England discusses the unknown number of female domestic servants that travelled to London with the dream of an upwardly mobile marriage to the master's son in the back of their minds. He even goes on to state that affection between master's son and servant, and its sexual expression, clearly flourished in some households.[66] It is also interesting to note that in some parts of the world, girls are attracted to domestic service because it is hoped that, in a wealthier household, they may meet a young man who will wish to marry them.[67] This complicates the notion of sexual control of employers in the workplace.

Despite the sexual abuse that occurs in domestic work, Natalya Dinat and Sally Perberdy have argued that in South Africa, domestic workers isolation may have a protective effect because "it reduces opportunities for starting new relationships" which means that many of these women may not need to use contraceptives or to protect themselves from sexually transmitted infections (STIs) by using condoms because they do not have active sex lives."[68] However, I would like to argue that the isolation and a lack of social support renders domestic workers vulnerable to risky sex, with the accompanying costs of unwanted pregnancies, STDs, and HIV/AIDS.

This is because few domestics receive any health education on sexual and reproductive rights on the job and they tend to have limited access to or use family planning services.[69] In a study on female adolescent domestic workers in Nigeria, Adebanke Akinrimisi highlighted domestic workers lack of knowledge pertaining to HIV/AIDS.[70] She noted that:

> ... over 50 per cent of respondents did not know about STDs even though on average 28 per cent acknowledged being sexually active. Furthermore, majority of domestic workers only knew that 'a victim of AIDS experiences weight loss and then dies'. Finally, while one-third of

respondents knew that they could protect themselves by the use of condoms, some believed that the only solution was praying. Few have accessed family planning services and none have tested for HIV.

In Guinea, the government and several NGOs are providing programs on health education for adolescents, including on HIV/AIDS and reproductive rights. They are trying to reach as many young people as possible through radio programs and audio CDs that are made widely available to local actors.[71] But as most child domestic workers do not have many opportunities to leave the house and participate in education or social events, it is hard to reach this group. Furthermore, as noted by an ILO-IPEC study,[72] in many societies where premarital contact and sex are frowned on and where keeping women and girls at home, including in someone else's home, is seen as a way to protect her from the temptations of association with men and boys, these government interventions could be deliberately ignoring domestic workers because of the belief that being "quasi-daughters" they are safe from sexual abuse as they are being protected by their employers.

So rather than having a "protective effect," isolation may mean that female domestic workers' are not gaining the skills that their peers are more likely to be getting to negotiate safe sex. Furthermore, as noted by Sarah Thomsen, Michael Wainaina, Laura Johnson, Cathy Toroitich-Ruto, and Claire Jagemann, who did a study on domestic workers in Nairobi, "among those few who are sexually active, several are in risky sexual relationships, either because their partner has multiple partners, or because they are not using condoms."[73]

Even if governments and NGOs are able to implement effective health education for domestic workers, such as in the case of Brazil where HIV/AIDS education, prevention and treatment have been integrated into popular locally-produced soap operas and dramas watched by domestic workers, the information may not be taking hold.[74] This is because, as some commentators have noted, approaches which focus on behavioral change are often inadequate as they ignore the context within which people live and have to negotiate behavior change. It is therefore necessary to take into account issues of power, poverty, and gender relations in the social and working lives of domestic workers, so as to better understand how they receive and/or act on information.

CONCLUSION

This chapter provides a brief introduction to the sexualized experiences of female live-in domestic workers. Their perception as dangerous women in the household leads to unusual employer-employee relationships, with the female employer controlling the sexuality of the domestic worker. Employers' discipline and control of domestic workers can be seen as an attempt to exert authority, deprive workers of full social lives, and create an adequately subordinate position for domestic workers within the household.

It is clear from the findings presented here that this control has negative impacts on the sexual and reproductive health of the domestic workers and their ability to have families. Therefore, domestic workers would benefit from knowledge and skills in sexual and reproductive health, as well as opportunities for social interaction. However, there are potential challenges, which may hinder domestic workers' ability to escape the sources of vulnerability that they face. These include the employer's willingness to let their domestic workers learn such information and domestic workers' isolated and sometimes dangerous living and working environment. For this reason, it is necessary to not only focus on individual change but also the broader, structural issues contributing to the invisibility of domestic workers in Nigeria. This needs to involve domestic workers, their employers, and their families.

Notes

1. Information for this chapter is based on data from a study undertaken between June and August 2009 in Lagos, Nigeria with 12 female live-in domestic workers aged 18 to 24, 4 female employers, 2 key informants. A focus group was also conducted using the song "Ekaette." which is about sexual relations with a married man and his female "house-help." It should be noted that due to the small sample size, this study does not claim to be representative of the whole of Nigeria. To complement my findings, the following major studies on sexuality and domestic work were analyzed: Karen T. Hansen (1989, 1990, 1992) on Zambia; Kimberly Chang and Julian Groves (2000) and Nicole Constable (1996, 1997) on Hong Kong; Raka Ray (2000) on India; Ray Jureidini on Lebanon (2006); and Sarah A. Radcliffe (1992) on Peru.

2.   While this paper only focuses on female sexuality in relation to reproduction, immorality and disease, further research looks beyond reproduction and this "essentialist" view of sexuality to how domestic workers
manoeuvre or exert autonomy in their oppressive situations.

3.   Marilyn Thomson, "Workers not maids- organizing household workers
in Mexico," *Gender and Development* 17(2009), 285.

4.   Bridget Anderson, *Doing the Dirty Work? The Global Politics of Domes-
tic Labor* (London: Zed Books, 2000), 122; see also Cynthia Enloe,
*Bananas, Beaches and Bases: Making Feminist Sense of International
Politics*, (University of California Press, 2000); Cecilia Tacoli, "Gender,
Life Course and International Migration: The Case of Filipino Labor
Migrants in Rome" (PhD diss., London School of Economics and
Political Science, 1996), 109; Thomson, "Workers not maids- organizing
household workers in Mexico", 285.

5.   Sarah A. Radcliffe, "Ethnicity, patriarchy, and incorporation into the
nation: female migrants as domestic servants in Peru," *Environment and
Planning D: Society and Space* 8 (1990), 385.

6.   Abigail B. Bakan and Daiva Stasiulis, *Not One of the Family: Foreign
Domestic Workers in Canada* (University of Toronto Press, 1997), 12.

7.   Anderson, *Doing the Dirty Work? The Global Politics of Domestic Labor*,
122.

8.   See also David Katzman, *Seven Days a Week: Women and Domestic
Service in Industrializing America* (New York, 1978), on domestic
service in nineteenth century USA.

9.   See Kimberly Chang and Julian M. Groves, "Neither "Saints" nor "Prostitutes:" Sexual Discourse in the Filipina Domestic Worker Community
in Hong Kong," *Women's Studies International Forum*, 23 (2000), 77.

10. Exceptions to this "absence" of sexuality in the domestic work litera-
ture include the works of Kimberly Chang and Julian M. Groves (2000),
Nicole Constable (1996, 1997), Karen T. Hansen (1989, 1990, 1992), Ray
Jureidini (2006), Raka Ray (2000) and Roger Sanjek (1991).

11. See Jacklyn Cock, *Maids and Madams: Domestic Workers under Apart-
heid* (The Woman's Press Limited, 1989); and Alison King, *Domestic
Service in Post–Apartheid South Africa: Deference and Disdain* (Ashgate
Publishing, 2006).

12. Linda McDowell, "Gender Divisions of Labor: Sex, Gender, Sexuality,
and Embodiment in the Service Sector" in *The Handbook of Service
Industries*, eds. John R. Bryson and Peter W. Daniels (Cheltenham:
Edward Elgar, 2007), 399.

13. Ibid., 399; see also Henrietta Moore, *Feminism and Anthropology*, (Polity, 1988), 10-12.

14. Michel Foucault, *The History of Sexuality: An Introduction*, (New York: Vintage Books, 1990) and Judith Butler, *Gender Trouble*, (London: Routledge, 1990) and *Bodies that Matter* (London: Routledge, 1993).

15. WHO, 2004 cited in Emily Esplen, *Gender and Sexuality: Supporting Resources Collection* (IDS: Sussex, 2009), 3.

16. Paulina Makinwa-Adebusoye and Richmond Tiemoko, "Introduction: Healthy Sexuality in Discourses in East, West, North and Southern Africa," in *Human Sexuality in Africa: Beyond Reproduction*, eds. Eleanor Maticka-Tyndale, Richmond Tiemoko, and Paulina Makinwa-Adebusoye (Action Health Incorporated, 2007), 2.

17. Linda McDowell, "Gender divisions of Labor: Sex, Gender Sexuality and Embodiment in the Service Sector," 400.

18. Lisa A. Adkins, *Gendered Work: Sexuality, Family, and the Labor Market* (GB: Open University Press, 1995), 18.

19. Winifred Poster, "Racialism, Sexuality and Masculinity: Gendering 'Global Ethnography' of the Workplace," *Social Politics*, 2002, 138.

20. Ibid., 138.

21. Aiwha Ong, *Spirits of Resistance and Capitalist Discipline: Factory Women in Japan* (Albany, N.Y: State University of New York Press, 1987).

22. See Poster, "Racialism, Sexuality and Masculinity: Gendering 'Global Ethnography' of the Workplace", *Social Politics*, 2002, 138.

23. Kevin Yelvington, *Producing Power: Ethnicity, Gender and Class in a Caribbean Workplace* (Philadelphia: Temple University Press, 1995), 120-125, 162, 185.

24. Under the ILO's International Standard Classification of Occupations (ISCO), a domestic worker is "someone who carries out household work in private households in return for wages" (ILO, 1990). The current labor law of Nigeria does not define domestic workers. Therefore domestic workers in this chapter are persons who are recruited from outside the employing household and paid by wage, or "in kind", to perform labor in and around the household.

25. Sarah B. Oloko, *Situation analyses of Children in Especially Difficult Circumstances* (UNICEF, 1992), 5; see also Carolyn Brown, "Race and the Construction of Working-Class Masculinity in the Nigerian Coal Industry: The Initial Phase, 1914–1930," *International Labor and Working-Class History*, (2006), 69; Lisa Lindsay, *Working with Gender:*

Wage Labor and Social Change in Southwestern Nigeria (Social History of Africa, 2003).

26. Muhammad Ladan, "The Rights of Child Domestics as Victims of Human Rights Violation and Trafficking in Nigeria," *Paper Presented at a Two-Day Workshop for Judges, Magistrates and Prosecutors*, Abuja, Nigeria, 2005. Ladan defines fostering as the assumption of rights and duties of parenthood by adults who are not the child's natural parents without the latter surrendering their full rights. This practice is common in most West African countries where younger children have often been sent to live with relatives.

27. Emmanuel E. Okafor, "The Use of Adolescents as Domestic Servants in Ibadan, Nigeria," *Journal of Adolescent Research* 24 (2009), 170.

28. Ibid, 189; see also Adebanke Akinrimisi, *Empowerment of Young Persons in Non-Formal Sector: The Case of Female Adolescent Domestic Workers in Municipal Lagos* (Center for Women's Health and Information, 2002), 9.

29. See Naila Kabeer, "Marriage, Motherhood and Masculinity in the Global Economy: Reconfiguration of Personal and Economic Life," *IDS Working Paper 290*, (Brighton: IDS, 2007), 27; and Naila Kabeer, *Mainstreaming Gender in Social Protection for the Informal Economy* (London: Commonwealth Secretariat, 2008), 146-7.

30. Okafor, "The Use of Adolescents as Domestic Servants in Ibadan, Nigeria", 189.

31. Ibid., 189.

32. Zahrah Nesbitt-Ahmed, "Domestic Service in Nigeria: A Gendered Perspective," (MSc diss, London School of Economics and Political Science, 2009), 20.

33. Platform for Labor Action, *Adult Domestic Workers in Uganda: An Analysis of Human Rights and Social Injustice* (Uganda: Fountain Publishers, 2007), 3.

34. "Maternalism" was first suggested by David Katzman (1978) and elaborated by Judith Rollins, *Between Women: Domestics and Their Employers* (Philadelphia: Temple University, 1985), 178. This differs from paternalistic relationships between masters and servants first developed in feudal economies in Europe and later transmitted to developing countries.

35. Rollins, *Between Women: Domestics and Their Employers*, 178; see also Makeda Silvera, *Silenced* (Williams-Wallis Publishers: Toronto, 1983).

36 Rollins, *Between Women: Domestics and Their Employers*, 158-63; see also Sarah Radcliffe, "Ethnicity, patriarchy, and incorporation into the nation: female migrants as domestic servants in Peru," 385; Jacklyn

Cock, *Maids and Madams: Domestic Workers under Apartheid* (The Woman's Press Limited, 1989); Karen T. Hansen, *Distant Companions: Servants and Employers in Zambia, 1900-1985* (Ithaca, NY: Cornell University Press: Ithaca, NY, 1989).

37. Rollins, *Between Women: Domestics and Their Employers*, 189-192.

38. Bakan and Stasiulis, *Not One of the Family: Foreign Domestic Workers in Canada*

39. Shellee Colen and Roger Sanjek, "Introduction: At Work in Homes I: Orientations and At Work in Homes II: Directions," in *At Work in Homes: Household Perspectives, American Ethnological Society Monograph Series 3*, eds. Roger Sanjek and Shellee Colen, (American Anthropological Association: Washington DC, 1990), 5; see also Phyllis Palmer, *Domesticity and Dirt: Housewives and Domestic Servants in the United States, 1920-1945* (Temple University Press: Philadelphia, 1989), 138; Ray Jureidini, "Sexuality and the Servant: An Exploration of Arab Images of the Sexuality of Domestic Maids Living in the Household," in *Sexuality in the Arab World*, eds. Samir Khalaf and John H. Gagnon (Saqi Books: London, 2006), 5.

40. Palmer, *Domesticity and Dirt: Housewives and Domestic Servants in the United States, 1920-1945*, 138.

41. Raka Ray, "Masculinity, Femininity and Servitude: Domestic Workers in Calcutta in the Late Twentieth Century," *Feminist Studies* 26 (2000), 698.

42. Ibid., 698.

43. Nicole Constable, "Sexuality and Discipline among Filpina Domestic Workers in Hong Kong," *American Ethnologist* 24 (1997): 542.

44. On pursuing friendships see Sarah Radcliffe, "Ethnicity, patriarchy, and incorporation into the nation: female migrants as domestic servants in Peru;" on abuse see Makeda Slivera, *Silenced.*

45. Chang and Groves, "Neither "Saints" nor "Prostitutes": Sexual Discourse in the Filipina Domestic Worker Community in Hong Kong," *Women's Studies International Forum* 23 (2000): 74.

46. Karen T. Hansen, "Body Politics: Sexuality, Gender and Domestic Service in Zambia," *Journal of Women's History* 2 (1990): 134-8.

47. See Enloe, *Bananas, Beaches and Bases: Making Feminist Sense of International Politics*; Ong, *Spirits of Resistance and Capitalist Discipline: Factory Women in Japan*

48. Constable, "Sexuality and Discipline among Filipina Domestic Workers in Hong Kong," 540.

49. Zahrah Nesbitt-Ahmed, "Domestic Service in Nigeria: A Gendered Perspective," 18.

50. "Oga" is the term used to refer to male employer.

51. Constable, "Sexuality and Discipline among Filipina Domestic Workers in Hong Kong," 545

52. Chang and Groves, "Neither "Saints" nor "Prostitutes": Sexual Discourse in the Filipina Domestic Worker Community in Hong Kong," 77.

53. The extreme case of such regulation is the compulsory pregnancy and HIV test to which migrant domestic workers in Singapore must submit every six months. Immigration policies in Singapore dictate that any domestic worker found to be pregnant must either voluntarily terminate the pregnancy, or lose her job and face deportation. Immigration policies in Singapore also prohibit migrant domestic workers from marrying or cohabitating with Singaporean citizens or permanent residents. See Human Rights Watch, *Swept Under the Rug: Abuses Against Domestic Workers Around the World* (New York: Human Rights Watch: New York, 2006), 81.

54. Radcliffe, Ethnicity, patriarchy, and incorporation into the nation: female migrants as domestic servants in Peru, 385; see also Human Rights Watch, *Swept Under the Rug: Abuses Against Domestic Workers Around the World*, 73.

55. Ibid., 385.

56. Roger Sanjek, "Maid Servants and Market Women's Apprentices in Adabraka," in *At Work in Homes: Household Perspectives, American Ethnological Society Monograph Series 3*, eds. Roger Sanjek and Shellee Colen (American Anthropological Association, 1990), 44.

57. See also ILO-IPEC, *Helping Hands or Shackled Lives? Understanding Child Domestic Labour and Responses to It* (ILO/IPEC, 2004), 22.

58. Sylvia Chant and Nikki Craske, *Gender in Latin America* (Latin America Bureau, 2003), 146

59. Ray Jureidini, "Sexuality and the Servant: An Exploration of Arab Images of the Sexuality of Domestic Maids Living in the Household", 12.

60. Human Rights Watch, *Swept Under the Rug: Abuses Against Domestic Workers Around the World*, 18

61. See Chang and Groves, "Neither "Saints" nor "Prostitutes": Sexual Discourse in the Filipina Domestic Worker Community in Hong Kong", 77; Platform for Labor Action. *Adult Domestic Workers in Uganda: An Analysis of Human Rights and Social Injustice* (Uganda: Fountain Publishers, 2007), 100.

62. See Human Rights Watch, *Swept Under the Rug: Abuses Against Domestic Workers Around the World* (Human Rights Watch: New York, 2006), 16 and *Bottom of the Ladder: Exploitation and Abuse of Girl Domestic Workers in Guinea*, (Human Rights Watch: New York, 2007), 64-68; ILO-IPEC, *Helping Hands or Shackled Lives? Understanding Child Domestic Labor and Responses to It*, 56; Sarah Thomsen, Michael Wainaina, Laura Johnson, Cathy Toroitich-Ruto, and Claire Jagemann, *Risk of STIs, HIV/ AIDS, and Unintended Pregnancies Among Domestic Workers in Bahati, Nairobi: Results of a Formative Assessment*, (Joint USAIDS, Republic of Kenya and Family Health Incorporated Report, 2007), 23.

63. Platform for Labour Action, *Adult Domestic Workers in Uganda: An Analysis of Human Rights and Social Injustice*, 100.

64. Chang and Groves, "Neither "Saints" nor "Prostitutes": Sexual Discourse in the Filipina Domestic Worker Community in Hong Kong", 77.

65. Jureidini, "Sexuality and the Servant: An Exploration of Arab Images of the Sexuality of Domestic Maids Living in the Household", 12.

66. Tim Meldrum *Domestic Service and Gender 1660-1750: Life and Work in the London Household* (Pearson Education Limited, 2000), 105.

67. ILO-IPEC, *Helping Hands or Shackled Lives? Understanding Child Domestic Labor and Responses to It*, 29.

68. Natalya Dinat and Sally Perberdy "Migration and Domestic Work in South Africa: World of Work, Health and Mobility in Johannesburg", *Migration Policy Series* 40 (2005): 198, 201.

69. Sexual and reproductive health rights (SRHR) is the right for all to make choices regarding their own sexuality and reproduction providing these respect the rights of others to bodily integrity (ELDIS).

70. Adebanke Akinrimisi, *Empowerment of Young Persons in Non-Formal Sector: The Case of Female Adolescent Domestic Workers in Municipal Lagos*, 35-6.

71. Human Rights Watch, *Bottom of the Ladder: Exploitation and Abuse of Girl Domestic Workers in Guinea*, 147.

72. ILO-IPEC, *Helping Hands or Shackled Lives? Understanding Child Domestic Labor and Responses to It*, 22.

73. Thomsen et al., *Risk of STIs, HIV/AIDS, and Unintended Pregnancies Among Domestic Workers in Bahati, Nairobi: Results of a Formative Assessment*, 37.

74. Jacqueline Barsted and Leila Linhares Pitanguy, "Media and Domestic Workers: Modernization of Brazilian society," *Development* 42 (1999): 59-62.

Bibliography

Adkins, Lisa A. *Gendered Work: Sexuality, Family, and The Labor Market.* GB: Open University Press, 1995.

Akinrimisi, Adebanke. *Empowerment of Young Persons in Non-Formal Sector: The Case of Female Adolescent Domestic Workers in Municipal Lagos.* Center for Women's Health and Information (2002), www.cewhin. org/.../Appreciating%20the%20Plight%20of%20**Domestic%20Workers**. doc. (Accessed July 2009).

Anderson, Bridget. *Doing the Dirty Work? The Global Politics of Domestic Labor.* London: Zed Books, 2000.

______. "Just Another Job? Paying for Domestic Work." *Gender and Development* 9 (2001): 25-33.

Bakan, Abigail B. and Stasiulis, Daiva. *Not one of the Family: Foreign Domestic Workers in Canada.* Toronto: University of Toronto Press, 1997.

Barsted, Leila Linhares and Pitanguy, Jacqueline. "Media and Domestic Workers: Modernization of Brazilian Society." *Development* 42 (1999): 59-62.

Brown, Carolyn. "Race and the Construction of Working-Class Masculinity in the Nigerian Coal Industry: The Initial Phase, 1914–1930." *International Labor and Working-Class History* 69 (2006): 35–56.

Butler, Judith. *Gender Trouble.* London: Routledge, 1990.

______. *Bodies that Matter.* London: Routledge, 1993.

Chang, Kimberly and Groves, Julian McAllister. "Neither "Saints" nor "Prostitutes": Sexual Discourse in the Filipina Domestic Worker Community in Hong Kong." *Women's Studies International Forum* 23 (2000): 73-87.

Chant, Sylvia. *Gender, Generation and Poverty: Exploring the "Feminisation of Poverty" in Africa, Asia and Latin America.* Cheltenham: Edward Elgar, 2007.

Chant, Sylvia and Craske, Nikki. *Gender in Latin America.* Latin America Bureau, 2003.

Chant, Sylvia and Mcllwaine, Cathy. *Geographies of Development in the 21st Century.* Cheltenham: Edward Elgar, 2009.

Chant, Sylvia. *The International Handbook of Gender and Poverty.* Cheltenham: Edward Elgar, 2010.

Chen, Martha Alter, Marilyn Carr and Joann Vanek. *Mainstreaming Informal Employment and Gender in Poverty Reduction: A Handbook for Policymakers and Other Stakeholders.* London: Commonwealth Secretariat, 2004.

Chen, Marty. "Informality, Poverty and Gender: Evidence from the Global South." In *The International Handbook of Gender and Poverty*, 463-471. Edited by Sylvia Chant, 463-471. Cheltenham: Edward Elgar, 2010.

Chin, Christine. *In Service and Servitude: Female Foreign Domestic Workers and the Malaysian 'Modernity' Project*. New York: Columbia University Press, 1998.

Cock, Jacklyn. *Maids and Madams: Domestic Workers under Apartheid*. The Woman's Press Limited, 1989.

Colen, Shellee and Sanjek, Roger. "Introduction: At Work in Homes I: Orientations and At Work in Homes II: Directions." In *At Work in Homes: Household Perspectives, American Ethnological Society Monograph Series 3*. Edited by Roger Sanjek and Shellee Colen, 1-13, 176-188. American Anthropological Association: Washington DC, 1990.

Constable, Nicole. *Maid to Order in Hong Kong: Stories of Filipina Workers*. Ithaca: Cornell University Press, 1997.

________. "Sexuality and Discipline among Filipina Domestic Workers in Hong Kong." *American Ethnologist* 24 (1997): 539-558.

Cornwall, Andrea, Susie Jolly, and Sonia Correa. *Development with a Body: Sexuality, Human Rights and Development*. London: Zed, 2008.

Cox, Rosie. *Servant Problem: Domestic Employment in Global Economy*. London: IB Tauris and Co Ltd, 2006.

Cox, Rosie and Narula, Rekha (2003). "Playing Happy Families: rules and relationships in au pair employing households in London, England." *Gender, Place, and Culture* 10 (2003): 333-344.

Dinat, Natalya and Perberdy, Sally. "Migration and Domestic Work in South Africa: World of Work, Health and Mobility in Johannesburg.." *Migration Policy Series* 40 (2005), http://www.queense.ca/samp/sampresources/samppublications/. (Accessed December 2009).

Ehrenreich, Barbara and Hochschild, Arlie Russel. *Global Woman: Nannies, Maids and Sex Workers in the New Economy*. London: Granta, 2003.

Enloe, Cynthia. *Bananas, Beaches and Bases: Making Feminist Sense of International Politics*. University of California Press, 2000.

Esplen, Emily. *Gender and Sexuality: Supporting Resources Collection*. Sussex: IDS, 2009, http:www.bridge.ids.ac.uk/reports/CEP-Sexuality-SRC.pdf. (Accessed March 2009).

Flores-Oebanda, Cecilia. *Addressing Vulnerability and Exploitation of Child Domestic Workers: An Open Challenge to End a Hidden Shame*. Florence: UNICEF Innocenti Research Centre, 2006.

Foucault, Michel. *The History of Sexuality: An Introduction.* New York: Vintage Books, 1990.

Freeman, Carla. *High Tech and High Heels in the Global Economy: Women, Work and Pink Collar Identities in the Caribbean.* Durham, N.C: Duke University Press, 2000.

Hansen, Karen T. "Household Work as a Man's Job: Sex and Gender in Domestic Service in Zambia." *Anthropology Today* 2 (1986): 18-23.

______. *Distant Companions: Servants and Employers in Zambia, 1900-1985.* Ithaca, NY: Cornell University Press, 1989.

______. "Body Politics: Sexuality, Gender and Domestic Service in Zambia." *Journal of Women's History* 2 (1990): 120-138.

Heintz, James. "Women's Employment, Economic Risk and Poverty." In *The International Handbook of Gender and Poverty.* Edited by Sylvia Chant, 434-439. Cheltenham, Edward Elgar, 2010.

Human Rights Watch. "Maid to Order: Ending Abuse against Migrant Domestic Workers in Singapore." *Human Rights Watch* 17, no. 10 (December 2005), http://www.hrw.org/en/reports/2005/12/06/maid-order. (Accessed July 2009).

______. "Swept Under the Rug: Abuses Against Domestic Workers Around the World." *Human Rights Watch* 18, no. 7 (July 2006), http://www.hrw.org/en/reports/2006/07/27/swept-under-rug. (Accessed July 2009).

______. "Bottom of the Ladder: Exploitation and Abuse of Girl Domestic Workers in Guinea." *Human Rights Watch* 19, no. 8 (June 2007), http://www.hrw.org/en/node/10932/section/1. (Accessed July 2009).

International Labor Organisation. *International Standard Classification of Occupations.* Geneva: ILO (1990), http://www.ilo.org/public/english/bureau/stat/isco/index.htm. (Accessed July 2009).

International Labor Organization. *Helping Hands or Shackled Lives? Understanding Child Domestic Labor and Responses to It.* ILO/IPEC (2004), http://www.ilo.org/public/libdoc/ilo/2004/104B09_138_engl.pdf. (Accessed May 2009).

Jolly, Susan and Ilkkaracan, Pinar. "Gender, Sexuality and Sexual Rights: An Overview." *Gender and Development in Brief, Bridge Bulletin* 18 (2007): 1-3.

Jureidini, Ray. "Sexuality and the Servant: An Exploration of Arab Images of the Sexuality of Domestic Maids Living in the Household." In *Sexuality in the Arab World.* Edited by Samir Khalaf and John H. Gagnon, 1-22. London: Saqi Books, 2006.

Kabeer, Naila. "Marriage, Motherhood and Masculinity in the Global Economy: Reconfiguration of Personal and Economic Life." *IDS Working*

Paper 290. Brighton: IDS. (2007), http://www.ids.ac.uk/ids/bookshop/ wp/wp290.pdf. (Accessed December 2009).

________. *Mainstreaming Gender in Social Protection for the Informal Economy.* London: Commonwealth Secretariat, 2008.

Katzman, David. *Seven Days a Week: Women and Domestic Service in Industrializing America,* New York, 1978.

King, Alison. *Domestic Service in Post–Apartheid South Africa: Deference and Disdain.* Ashgate Publishing, 2006.

Ladan, Muhammed T. "The Rights of Child Domestics as Victims of Human Rights Violation and Trafficking in Nigeria." *Paper Presented at a Two-Day Workshop for Judges, Magistrates and Prosecutors, Abuja, Nigeria,* 2005, http://www.dawodu.com/ladan3.htm. (Accessed May 2009).

Lindsay, Lisa A. *Working with Gender: Wage Labor and Social Change in Southwestern Nigeria.* Social History of Africa, 2003.

Makinwa-Adebusoye Paulina and Tiemoko, Richmond. "Introduction: Healthy Sexuality in Discourses in East, West, North and Southern Africa." In *Human Sexuality in Africa: Beyond Reproduction.* Edited by Eleanor Maticka-Tyndale, Richmond Tiemoko, Paulina Makinwa-Adebusoye, 1-18. Action Health Incorporated, 2007.

Meldrum, Tim. *Domestic Service and Gender 1660-1750: Life and Work in the London Household.* Pearson Education Limited, 2000.

McDowell, Linda. "Gender Divisions of Labor: Sex, Gender, Sexuality and Embodiment in the Service Sector." In *The Handbook of Service Industries.* Edited by John R. Bryson and Peter W. Daniels, 395-408. Cheltenham: Edward Elgar, 2007.

Moore, Henrietta L. *Feminism and Anthropology.* Polity, 1988.

Nesbitt-Ahmed, Zahrah. "Domestic Service in Nigeria: A Gendered Perspective." MSc diss., London School of Economics and Political Science, 2009.

Okafor, Emmanuel Emeka. "The Use of Adolescents as Domestic Servants in Ibadan, Nigeria." *Journal of Adolescent Research* 24 (2009): 169-193.

Oloko, Sarah. *Situation Analyses of Children in Especially Difficult Circumstances.* A UNICEF Report in collaboration with J. Shindi, A Olowu, R. A. Mohammed, B., Arikpo and O. Soyombo. UNICEF, 1992.

Ong, Aiwha. *Spirits of Resistance and Capitalist Discipline: Factory Women in Japan.* Albany, N.Y: State University of New York Press, 1987.

Palmer, Phyllis. *Domesticity and Dirt: Housewives and Domestic Servants in the United States, 1920-1945*. Philadelphia: Temple University Press, 1989.

Platform for Labor Action. *Adult Domestic Workers in Uganda: An Analysis of Human Rights and Social Injustice*. Uganda: Fountain Publishers, 2007.

Poster, Winifred. "Racialism, Sexuality and Masculinity: Gendering 'Global Ethnography' of the Workplace." *Social Politics* 9 (2002): 126-158.

Radcliffe, Sarah A. "Ethnicity, patriarchy, and incorporation into the nation: female migrants as domestic servants in Peru." *Environment and Planning D: Society and Space* 8 (1990): 379-393.

Ramirez-Machado, Jose Maria. "Domestic Work, Conditions of Work and Employment: A legal perspective." *Conditions of Work and Employment Series* 7 (2003), http://www.ilo.org/public/english/protection/condtrav/pdf/7cws.pdf. (Accessed May 2009).

Ray, Raka. "Masculinity, Femininity and Servitude: Domestic Workers in Calcutta in the Late Twentieth Century." *Feminist Studies* 26 (2000): 691-718.

Rollins, Judith. *Between Women: Domestics and Their Employers*. Philadelphia: Temple University, 1985.

Salzinger, Leslie. "From High Heels to Swathed Bodies: Gendered Meanings under Production in Mexico's Export Processing Industry." *Feminist Studies* 23(1997): 549-574.

Sanjek, Roger. "Maid Servants and Market Women's Apprentices in Adabraka." In *At Work in Homes: Household Perspectives, American Ethnological Society Monograph Series* 3. Edited by Roger Sanjek and Shellee Colen, 35-62. American Anthropological Association, 1990.

Silvera, Makeda. *Silenced*. Toronto: Williams-Wallis Publishers 1983.

Tacoli, Cecilia. "Gender, Life Course and International Migration: The Case of Filipino Labor Migrants in Rome." PhD diss., London School of Economics and Political Science, 1996.

Tekola, Bethlehem. *Poverty and the Social Context of Sex Work in Addis Ababa: An Anthropological Perspective*. Addis Ababa: Addis Ababa, Forum for Social Studies, 2005.

Thomsen, Sarah, Michael Wainaina, Laura Johnson, Cathy Toroitich-Ruto, and Claire Jagemann Claire. *Risk of STIs, HIV/AIDS, and Unintended Pregnancies Among Domestic Workers in Bahati, Nairobi: Results of a Formative Assessment*. Joint USAIDS, Republic of Kenya and Family Health Incorporated Report, 2007.

Thomson, Marilyn. "Workers not Maids-Organizing Household Workers in Mexico." *Gender and Development* 17 (2009): 281-293.

Yelvington, Kevin A. *Producing Power: Ethnicity, Gender and Class in a Caribbean Workplace*. Philadelphia: Temple University Press, 1995.

Websites

ELDIS: http://www.eldis.org/index.cfm?objectId=2354503B-999A-127E-6DEC2B2E1341E3EA

ILO: http://www.ilo.org/global/lang--en/index.htm

WHO: http://www.who.int/en/

GENDER, VIOLENCE, AND RECONSTRUCTION IN POSTWAR SIERRA LEONE

Peter A. Dumbuya

INTRODUCTION

Colonial and postcolonial leaders have used violence as a tool of statecraft. More specifically, between 1961 and 2002, they used it illiberally to influence the outcome of elections, eliminate or co-opt political opponents, silence critics, effectuate constitutional changes, and keep themselves in power. The Sierra Leonean civil war (1991-2002) focused international attention on the brutal treatment of women and girls in a society that is largely traditional and patriarchal in its conception of sex and gender roles. The use of violence against women and girls in domestic relations was nothing new, but what changed was the degree and intensity to which it was used as a weapon of war; it was systematic, widespread, and destructive. The Revolutionary United Front (RUF), a nonstate actor, initiated the conflict against the government and named it "Operation Liberate the Motherland," to give the impression that it was campaigning to "liberate" a loving, nurturing, and caring nation from rapacious, corrupt, inept, and uncaring politicians. The RUF's invocation of a motherland in peril was seen initially as a celebration of femininity which in Sierra Leone is rooted in the "culture of most communities which support the image of the female as a mother figure existing to reproduce the species and ensure continuity of the community."[1]

However, soon after it began, the conflict degenerated into mass plunder of the country's diamonds and other natural resources, and the RUF was anything but protective of the rights of women and girls who bore the brunt of the decade-long conflict. The Sierra Leone Truth and Reconciliation Commission (TRC), which the enabling law created to pay particular attention to sexual abuses, inter alia, reported that women were the exclusive targets of rape, sexual abuse, and sexual slavery by the RUF and other warring factions, and that the "conflict was essentially self-destructive."[2] The shame, stigma, psychological stress, physical and mental anguish associated with rape and other acts of sexual violence were made much worse by the subsequent discrimination and rejection that women and girls suffered at the hands of relatives, friends, and members of their communities in the post-war era. People who considered rape victims as "dirty," "shameful," and "unworthy" also assumed that they were responsible for the brutal assaults upon their personhood because they either did not resist enough or consented to the sex and cooperated with their tormentors.[3]

According to Amnesty International (AI), more than 250,000 women and girls were subjected to rape, sexual slavery, and other acts of sexual violence.[4] The negative perception of women and girls, engendered by centuries-old traditions and cultural attitudes, manifested itself so powerfully during the conflict that it affected women and girls of all ethnic groups, ages, and socio-economic class. The society's male-domineering ethos, which also contributed to the climate of violence, is institutionalized in the constitution and laws of Sierra Leone. These structural inequalities have in turn entrenched gender bias and discrimination against women. Moreover, in Sierra Leone's patriarchal society, women and girls like those depicted in the writings of travelers and novelists that Edward Said referenced in *Orientalism*, "are usually the creatures of a male power-fantasy. They express unlimited sensuality, they are more or less stupid, and above all they are willing."[5] Sex was and still is regarded as something men do to women and, whether they like or not, women are expected to be submissive and passive.

The chapter begins by locating the unprecedented levels of violence against women and girls in the rough and tumble politics of the postcolonial state. The RUF's initial goal when it invaded the country from neighboring Liberia (where a brutal civil war had erupted in December 1989) was to remove a government which had maintained itself in power by violent means. I argue that gender-based experiences of women and girls during the conflict are rooted in a patriarchal society where violence permeated the political landscape as much as it did the sphere of domestic relations. According to the TRC, domestic violence was often met with a "culture of silence" and impunity that "enabled the armed groups to sexually violate women during the conflict with no thought or fear of accountability."[6] The socio-cultural ethos that existed at the time of the conflict assigned women and girls a very low status, gave them few rights, and generally failed to protect them from domestic violence and sexual violence. This situation, about which the RUF made pious declarations but did nothing to ameliorate, was aggravated by structural and cultural constraints that institutionalized gender-based bias, discrimination, and marginalization of women and girls. Finally, the chapter argues that the remedies that have been proposed or put in place to end violence that specifically targets female sexuality should be seen as part of a comprehensive strategy to empower women and girls through, for example, access to education, economic opportunity, jobs, health care services, and arable land.

VIOLENCE AS STATECRAFT

The downward pressure on the postcolonial state began soon after independence in April 1961 when the country's political leaders began to reinvent the coercive colonial state apparatus.[7] This could be seen in the dismantling of the Westminster parliamentary system of government and the violent political struggles that ensued between Prime Minister Albert Margai (1964-67) and opposition leader of the All People's Congress (APC), Siaka P. Stevens (1968-85). It manifested itself in the disputed elections of March 1967, followed by a military interregnum (1967-68), and the Governor General Sir Henry Lightfoot-Boston's appointment of Stevens as prime minister in April 1968. Up to his retirement in 1985, Stevens, first as prime minister (1968-71) and then as president (1971-85), dealt both with internal and external challenges to his authority with a carrot-and-stick policy. Like Albert Margai before him, Stevens politicized and tribalized the military and police forces by appointing northerners to key command positions,

and by executing senior military officers and political opponents following treason trials in 1971 and 1975.[8] In May 1978, following the
violent suppression of a peaceful student demonstration against his
policies at Fourah Bay College on January 29, 1977, Stevens got the
voters to approve, in a referendum, the one-party constitution.[9]

Stevens continued to solidify his grip on state power by establishing a paramilitary presidential guard, the Internal Security Unit (ISU),
with Cuban assistance, and appointing the heads of the military and
police forces to Parliament under the new one-party constitution. As
part of his strategy to "reimpose political order" on an increasingly
restless and impoverished population, Stevens sought less formal
"accommodations with diamond dealers,"[10] thereby jeopardizing the
return on investments by the British-owned Sierra Leone Selection
Trust (SLST) which, under a 1970 agreement with the government,
retained a 49 percent share in the National Diamond Mining Company
(NDMC).[11] It did not help the diamond mining industry in particular
and the economy in general that systemic and personal corruption
permeated all levels of government and society.[12]

The climax to the new pattern of civil-military relations occurred
in 1985 when Stevens engineered a constitutional coup that ensured
the selection of army Major-General Joseph S. Momoh as his successor
to the APC party and presidency of the state. Momoh's accession to the
presidency (1985-92) raised high but unrealistic hopes and expectations for the country's socio-economic development. Instead, during
his presidency the economy continued its downward spiral, feeding a
groundswell of opposition to the continuation of one-party rule. The
internal opposition pressured Momoh to appoint a Constitutional
Review Commission (CRC) that produced the current 1991 Constitution, while different factions of the external opposition coalesced
around Foday Sankoh and the RUF with the aim of overthrowing
Momoh's government. Speaking of his troops' lack of readiness to confront the RUF, the army commander, Major-General Mohammed S.
Tarawallie, admitted that "we were really caught with our pants down.
The strength of the army was small, a little above the colonial legacy-
and arms and logistics were inadequate, all as a result of the economic
difficulties the country had been going through over the years."[13]

The civil war broke out on March 23, 1991, when the RUF, with
support from Charles Taylor's National Patriotic Front of Liberia

(NPFL), attacked Kailahun District in the Eastern Province of Sierra Leone. The RUF code-named the offensive "Operation Liberate the Motherland." Sankoh, a former army photographer, was found guilty of treason in 1971 and sentenced to a seven-year prison term with a dishonorable discharge from the military. He formed the RUF in 1982 after receiving military training and financial assistance from Libya, Burkina Faso, and Liberia. The former army corporal "nursed an abiding hatred for Joseph Saidu Momoh [the deputy force commander] who succeeded John Bangura as Army Force Commander, and who Sankoh accused of betraying Bangura. With this was also his deep animosity towards the All People's Congress Party (APC), the destruction of which became his consuming ambition."[14] The Liberian civil war and Taylor's objections to the use of Freetown as a staging area for the Economic Community Cease Fire Monitoring Group's (ECOMOG) military operations in his country in part provided cover for Sankoh to launch a military campaign against Momoh's government from areas controlled by the NPFL. The RUF's occupation of Kailahun District and most of the Eastern Province where the APC was unpopular practically denied the government effective control over the region's lucrative diamond mines and agricultural products.[15]

On April 29, 1992, junior army officers from the war front overthrew Momoh's government and established the National Provisional Ruling Council (NPRC) regime with Captain Valentine Strasser as chairman. The loss of two critical pillars of statehood (effective control of the state's territory and the absence of a popularly elected government) was compounded by the RUF's violent campaign against civilians that included rape, sexual abuse, the chopping off of legs and arms, and the abduction of young boys and girls who were then trained as "child soldiers." These terror tactics alienated the people from both the RUF and the NPRC. The military earned notoriety because its soldiers, nicknamed *sobels* (soldiers-cum-rebels), colluded with the RUF instead of fighting it on the battlefield.[16] The 1996 presidential and legislative elections did not end the war nor did they address its root causes. The Sierra Leone People's Party (SLPP) candidate, Ahmad T. Kabbah, won the presidential election, but his government of national unity was top-heavy, comprising twenty ministers, five ministers of state, and thirteen deputy ministers, many of whom served in past governments whose policies and actions precipitated the civil war. The politics of patronage and waste triggered a rash of abortive coups and restlessness in the military that exacerbated tensions and ultimately led to intervention by South African mercenaries, Nigeria, Guinea, ECOWAS, the UN, and Britain.[17]

VIOLENCE AND FOREIGN INTERVENTION

Within the UN system, there is growing recognition that "massive violations of human rights and displacement within a country's borders could constitute a threat"[18] to international peace. This realization eventually led to the organization's decision to intervene in the civil war. This occurred in three phases. The first, the peacemaking phase,[19] began in February 1995 when the Secretary-General appointed a Special Envoy, Berhanu Dinka, to help broker a peace agreement between the government of Sierra Leone (GoSL) and the RUF. In November 1996, Dinka helped negotiate the Abidjan Peace Agreement in Côte d'Ivoire. However, problems of implementation persisted until the overthrow of Kabbah's government in a military coup d'état in May 1997 and the formation of the Armed Forces Revolutionary Council (AFRC) under the leadership of Major Johnny Paul Koroma. The AFRC then invited Sankoh, who was being detained by Nigerian authorities on weapons charges, to join in as deputy leader of the junta.[20]

The second phase, a traditional Chapter VI peacekeeping operation that involved monitoring and legitimizing the Nigerian-led 12,500-member ECOMOG intervention force (authorized by ECOWAS in August 1997 to reverse the coup), followed Kabbah's restoration to power in March 1998. In pursuit of that goal, the UN Security Council established the United Nations Observer Mission in Sierra Leone (UNOMSIL, July 13, 1998-October 22, 1999).[21] The Secretary-General named Francis G. Okelo as his Special Representative to monitor the disarmament and demobilization of former combatants. However, from December 1998-January 1999, the RUF, in collaboration with the AFRC, launched a second offensive against Freetown, following the trial and execution of twenty-four army officers on October 19, 1998, for their role in the May 1997 coup. ECOMOG fought back and recaptured Freetown from the RUF. On July 7, 1999, the GOSL and the RUF signed the Lomé Peace Agreement which, among other things, provided for the establishment of a government of national unity. To ensure the successful implementation of the peace agreement, the UN expanded the role of UNOMSIL and increased the number of military observers to 210 (up from 70 in July 1998).[22]

The third phase, peace-building, which the former UN Secretary-General Boutros Boutros-Ghali defined as "action to identify and support structures which will tend to strengthen and solidify peace in order to avoid a relapse into conflict,"[23] began on October 22, 1999, when the UN Security Council phased out UNOMSIL and established the UN Mission in Sierra Leone (UNAMSIL) to cooperate with the GOSL and RUF in implementing the Lomé Peace agreement.[24] This operation, undertaken pursuant to Chapter VII of the UN Charter, necessitated an increase in UNAMSIL's troop strength from 6,000 military personnel in October 1999 to 17,500 in March, 2001, with an expanded mandate to "monitor progress towards consolidation of State authority throughout the country."[25] On May 1, 2000, the RUF began to kidnap, harass, and terrorize UNAMSIL peacekeepers. By May 15, it had seized over 352 (out of 9,495) UNAMSIL personnel, slowing down the pace of disarmament, demobilization, and reintegration of ex-combatants.[26] The RUF timed these attacks to coincide with the departure of the last contingent of ECOMOG troops from Sierra Leone on May 2, 2000. The near collapse of the UN peacekeeping mission necessitated intervention by Britain on two fronts.

First of all, Prime Minister Tony Blair's Labor government continued to recognize Kabbah's government-in-exile in Guinea following the AFRC coup in May 1997. It relocated its High Commission (headed by Peter Penfold, a Kabbah supporter) there and invited Kabbah to attend the Commonwealth Heads of Government annual meeting in Edinburgh on October 24-27, 1997. However, throughout the period of Kabbah's exile in Conakry, from May 1997-March 1998, Prime Minister Blair resisted calls to intervene militarily in the conflict.[27] Military intervention, as William Fowler has suggested, would have violated the "ethical dimension" of Blair's foreign policy.[28] Instead, Blair looked to the UN and ECOWAS to resolve a civil conflict that did not involve Britain's national or strategic interests.

That the AFRC/RUF junta was not recognized by any government, which denied it legitimacy, was due in part to the condemnation of the coup by Britain which called upon Major Koroma to restore Kabbah's government. In addition to relocating its High Commission to Conakry, Britain also evacuated its nationals as violence escalated and spread throughout Sierra Leone. In concert with the European Union (EU), it suspended development aid to the junta in June, and in July the Commonwealth Ministerial Action Group on the Harare Declaration on the Promotion of Democratic Principles and Fundamental Human Rights recommended that Sierra Leone be suspended from the Commonwealth if the AFRC/RUF junta did not restore Kabbah's government. The International Monetary Fund (IMF) and World Bank (WB) also suspended all fiscal and monetary programs and contacts with the junta despite its decision to continue to honor the structural adjustment program (SAP) instituted under Kabbah's government.

At the UN, the British Ambassador, Sir John Weston, sponsored Resolution 1132 (October 8, 1997) that imposed economic, trade, and travel sanctions against the AFRC/RUF junta. The Security Council established a committee, headed by Swedish Ambassador Hans Dahlgren, to oversee the implementation of the sanctions regime. The Council also authorized ECOWAS "to ensure strict implementation" of the sanctions, and report to Dahlgren's committee on its enforcement activities every thirty days.[29] In July 2000, the Security Council expressed "concern at the role played by the illegal trade in diamonds in fueling the conflict" and broadened the scope of the committee to include monitoring the flow of diamonds from Sierra Leone.[30] The Security Council's decision to impose sanctions against the junta followed an impassioned speech by Kabbah to the UN General Assembly on October 1 in which he asked the international community to save Sierra Leone from the "gulag of horrors" and "systematic genocide" at the hands of the AFRC and its RUF collaborators. The UN Security Council's recognition of the conflict as a threat to international peace and security bolstered ECOWAS's intervention and the sanctions it had imposed on the junta in August 1997.

Secondly, in May 2000, Blair dispatched troops to evacuate about 1,300 British, European Union (EU), and Commonwealth citizens from Freetown ahead of the advancing RUF rebels. Code-named Operation Palliser, British military intervention had a "stiffening" effect upon UNAMSIL which was able to deploy its peacekeepers throughout the country by the end of 2000.[31] Operation Palliser, which ended on June 15, 2000, halted the rebel advance toward Freetown, and a month later, on July 15-16, UNAMSIL, with logistical support from British forces, launched a military operation that freed the remaining peacekeepers being held hostage by the RUF in the eastern town of Kailahun.[32]

On September 10, 2000, British troops rescued the remaining six British and one Sierra Leonean soldier who had been held hostage by the West Side Boys (WSB). A nondescript group of former RUF fighters, ex-AFRC army soldiers, and common criminals, the WSB wanted to "revisit" the Lomé Peace Agreement. Led by so-called Brigadier Foday Kallay, this rag-tag band of thugs claimed to have taken part in the May 1997 coup d'état against Kabbah, but had been excluded from the negotiations leading up to the signing of the Lomé Peace Agreement. On August 25, 2000, the WSB therefore decided to seize eleven British and one Sierra Leonean soldier who were on a routine mission from Benguema, a military camp outside Freetown, to Masiaka. On August 30, the WSB freed five of the British soldiers but held on to the remaining hostages as bargaining chips with the GOSL.

As Fowler has written, "Operation Barras was a political act" and "an exercise in nation-building—a necessarily spectacular endorsement of the rule of law and the elected government in Sierra Leone."[33] In the short term, most Sierra Leoneans viewed the intervention as the decisive element the broke the back of the RUF, forcing it to sign a cease fire agreement in Abuja, Nigeria, in November 2000.[34] Britain's "neo-imperial protection"[35] ultimately allowed UNAMSIL peacekeepers to deploy throughout the war ravaged country. On January 18, 2002, the GOSL officially declared an end to the civil war, followed by the first post-conflict presidential and legislative elections in May.

SOCIO-CULTURAL PERCEPTIONS OF SEX AND GENDER ROLES

The conflict in Sierra Leone exposed women and girls to a latent socio-cultural animus that pro-and-anti-government forces exploited to the fullest by targeting them because of their gender and sexuality. Dyan Mazurana and Khristopher Carlson define gender as the socially constructed identities of men and women, whereas sex roles are biologically determined.[36] Through socialization, they argue, gender roles are assigned to men and women, that such roles do vary from culture to culture, and that they can be affected by other forms of differentiation like race, ethnicity, and class. As examples of gender roles for women in many societies, including Sierra Leone, they cite food preparation and household chores, while child-bearing is a sex or biologically determined role performed exclusively by women.

Olayinka Koso-Thomas has described sexuality as the state of being able to understand oneself as a sexual being and the corresponding ability to develop a successful sexual relationship with another person, presumably of the opposite sex.[37] She posits that one's "maleness" or "femaleness" further depends on one's personal and social gender roles. Personal gender roles are directly related to how individuals regard themselves as sexual beings operating in the society in which they live. In Sierra Leone, for instance, society is patriarchal and dependent upon extended family networks. As a communal society, it defines social gender roles, and has therefore developed a tendency to suppress female sexuality and personal gender roles in favor of social gender roles. One way in which such a society has exerted strong controls over personal gender roles is through "the brutal means of circumcision to curb female sexual desire and response."[38] This practice ensures conduct in conformity with society's expectations of women's sexuality and gender roles which they must perform with docility and obedience; such roles are limited to child-birth/rearing and domestic chores. The UN has described female genital mutilation (FGM) as a traditional practice that is harmful to women's health and lives.[39] It affects 89 percent of Sierra Leonean women, and is sustained by a combination of religious, cultural, and mystical factors that link the practice to female fertility, virginity, good health, prevention of promiscuity, and socio-political cohesion.[40]

In her study of Wunde Chiefdom (Bo District in Sierra Leone), Mariane Femme has examined the institutions, values, and views of self and sociality and how they are often associated with violent practices and strategies of concealment that permeate even domesticity and the wider realm of social relations. She concedes that gender relations are often infused with "a history of violence that is embedded in the very language of intimacy and domestic relations," and that "a Mende marriage must be understood in the context of slavery and in terms of how this institution shaped forms of dependence in the region."[41] Furthermore, she argues that the "tensions and inequalities embedded in the idiom of marriage and kinship" are the result of "conflicting demands placed on wives by their kin."[42] Even the place of abode, the "big house," was a social institution that housed captive farm labor which included female dependents. Among the Kuranko of Koinadugu District, "women of the household occupy the back rooms while the men occupy the front rooms. The backyard is the women's domain, the front verandah (*dandakoro*) and the *luiye* [compound] are the men's domains."[43] This, Michael Jackson contends, makes for socio-spatial distinctions that assign women marginal and subordinate roles to their husbands' households.[44]

The second-order status of women and girls could also be seen in the institution of domestic slavery which, even when abolished in 1926-27, did not erase some wives' perceptions of themselves as "slaves" to draw attention to their plight and to find a way out of their unhappy marriages. Gender inequality continued under new guises such as the practice by husbands to call their former female slaves "cousins."[45] In contemporary Sierra Leonean society, women are also burdened by illiteracy, poverty, and cultural constraints upon their sexuality and gender roles. Women account for 80 percent of the subsistence agricultural labor force that produces 70 percent of the food in Sierra Leone.[46] Despite their centrality to the subsistence and cash crop economies, women's ownership of land is constrained by customary law and tradition that vests ownership in the hands of husbands and male members of the family. Women and girls are also burdened with low levels of education because traditional society favors the education of men and boys. It is estimated that 91.5 percent of women in Sierra Leone are illiterate, with the disparity widening as female students who drop out of school end up in forced or arranged marriages. High rates of illiteracy and lack of opportunity have constrained women's access to the centers of political power. Politically marginalized, poor, and unskilled, women and girls have become economically dependent on their spouses or male members of their families.[47]

The concept "bush wives" or "rebel wives" is akin to the kind of servitude women were subjected to in the 1920s following the abolition of slavery. Then, as during the civil war, they were forced to marry "rebel husbands." Such relationships involved sexual slavery and were maintained by violence. Similarly, since under customary law a woman is a *femme covert*, the presumption is that the husband can use reasonable force against her, and such acceptance of physical violence carried over into relationships forged during the civil war whereby "rebel husbands" were shielded against accusations of rape, sexual slavery, and sexual violence by their "rebel wives"[48] Marital rape did not exist under domestic law until 2007. Prior to that time period, most Sierra Leoneans believed it was the duty of the wife to have sex with her husband even if she did not want to;[49] therefore the husband could not have been guilty of rape unless he had been legally separated from her.[50] The TRC reported that the "abductions and use of young girls and women as bush wives and sex slaves by armed groups during the war could be attributed to the traditional beliefs that governed this issue prior to the war. Some of the armed groups did not consider it an aberration to rape young women or use them as sex slaves."[51] The culture of silence and impunity explain why so little was done to protect them from their abusers.

STRUCTURAL INEQUALITIES

Structural discrimination against women and girls in Sierra Leone is a function of tradition, customary law, statutory law, and the constitution. The current constitution resulted from changed circumstances at home and abroad which led President Joseph S. Momoh (1985-92), on October 11, 1990, to appoint a 35-member National Constitutional Review Commission (NCRC), headed by Peter L. Tucker. The *de jure* one-party system of government, instituted in 1978, had stifled political participation and impoverished the nation. Therefore, at home and abroad, Sierra Leoneans clamored for political change. The NCRC reviewed the one-party constitution of 1978, but instead of finding ways to enlarge the one-party system as the president had wanted, it jettisoned it in favor of a pluralist system. It presented its report to the president on March 28, 1991, five days after the start of the civil war.[52]

The 1991 constitution does not define tradition, but Section 170(3) describes customary law as "the rules of law which by custom are applicable to particular communities in Sierra Leone."[53] It defines statutory law as the law made by Parliament pursuant to the Constitution. Instead of empowering women and girls, the multitude of laws recognized by the 1991 constitution pulled women's rights in different directions. As the TRC reported, "the laws of Sierra Leone are discriminatory against women. While Sierra Leone is governed by a constitution that prohibits the promulgation of discriminatory laws, women are not protected in the areas that affect them most, such as marriage, divorce and inheritance."[54] For instance, customary law treats women as "chattels" to be inherited by their spouses' surviving brothers, and places women generally under the guardianship of male family members.[55] Before 2007, there was no specific law that protected women from domestic violence. The Domestic Violence Act of 2007 (discussed below) subsumes rape (which is a crime under the common law) under harassment (defined as "sexual contact without the consent of the person with whom the contact is made") and sexual abuse (defined as the "forceful engagement of another person in a sexual contact, whether married or not").

Section 27(1) of the 1991 constitution declares that "no law shall make any provision which is discriminatory either of itself or in its effect," whereas Section 27(2) stipulates that "no person shall be treated in a discriminatory manner by any person acting by virtue of any law or in the performance of the functions of any public office or any public authority."[56] Section 27(3) defines discrimination as affording different treatment to different persons because of their sex, *inter alia*, but Section 27(4)(d) claws back key anti-discrimination provisions, adversely impacting women in the areas of marriage, divorce, and property inheritance.[57] In effect, the constitution sanctions and institutionalizes gender and sex-based discrimination with regard to the exemptions it carves out for the application of Section 27 to statutory, customary, Islamic, Christian or the common law in matters of marriage, divorce, and inheritance of property. The framers of these discriminatory provisions did not "seem to take any notice of the developments that have taken place in other countries, or the opinion of the women of Sierra Leone. The reason for this may have been the fear of the Government and Parliament that the application of the non-discriminatory provision of the Constitution to the matters mentioned here would provoke hostile reactions from the male population on cultural and religious grounds. It did not provoke adverse comments from women ten years ago, but today, there is a groundswell of criticism from leaders of civil society and women's movements."[58]

This observation reveals a disquieting constitutional practice in Sierra Leone. First, it suggests that women either condoned discrimination at the time of passage of the 1991 constitution, or did not seem to have registered enough of an opposition to the offending provisions to have them excised from the final bill that reached the president's desk for his signature. Second, the framers of the constitution were not motivated by the numerous international anti-discrimination conventions the country has ratified. These include the Convention on the Elimination of All Forms of Discrimination Against Women (CEDAW), the African Charter on Human Rights, and the African Charter on the Rights and Welfare of the Child. Third, it shows that Sierra Leone is still a patriarchal society in which religious and cultural conformity trump gender equality and human rights. But as discussed below, Parliament has now begun to pass legislation to address some of these overtly discriminatory policies that were written into the 1991 constitution or maintained under tradition and customary law.

WOMEN AS VICTIMS AND PERPETRATORS

Mazurana and Carlson and the TRC have shown that large numbers of women and girls were both victims and forced participants in the military operations of the RUF, civil defense forces (CDFs), and the then Republic of Sierra Leone military forces (RSLMF).[59] Chris Coulter has written that "female informants had played many diverse roles in and had many different experiences of the war. They had perhaps experienced being both victims and perpetrators. Some had been bush wives, others combatants, some by force, some for survival, and others by choice."[60] Some women took on these roles out of personal conviction or simply to survive, and in some instances, it is reasonable to assume that women might have used sex as a way to guarantee their own survival while some romantic liaisons might have developed voluntarily without coercion.[61] In some situations, "bush wives" stayed married to their "bush husbands" when the war ended, while others faced humiliation, rejection, and ostracism by family members for their associations with the rebels.[62]

In addition to military operations that included combat, weapons training, and spying, women and girls were forced to participate in the war as sex slaves, laborers, cooks, porters, care providers, food producers, messengers, diamond miners, and communication technicians. Mazurana and Carlson have argued that these multifarious roles were not fully investigated and appreciated, causing severe underrepresentation of female ex-combatants in disarmament, demobilization, and reintegration (DDR) programs at the war's end in January 2002.[63] They estimated that of the 72,500 former combatants who were demobilized, 4,751 were women (6.5%) and 6,787 were children (9.4%), of whom there were 506 girls.[64] A lack of knowledge of post-traumatic stress disorder among women and girls also hampered their reintegration into society, and for many female survivors, the path to psychological and emotional healing lay in not talking about the war and its attendant atrocities.[65] Table 8.1 shows the relative number of forces for all groups in the conflict, including girl soldiers.

TABLE 8.1: ESTIMATED NUMBER OF FORCES IN CIVIL WAR

FORCE	TOTAL	CHILD SOLDIERS	GIRL SOLDIERS
RUF	45,000	22,500	7,500
AFRC	10,000	5,000	1,667
SLA	14,000	3,500	1,167
CDF	68,865	17,216	1,722
TOTAL	137,865	48,216	12,056

Source: Mazurana and Carlson, "From Combat to Community," 3.

The point of entry into the war for most women and girls was abduction (see Table 8.2) compared to about 12 percent of those who were reported to have joined the RUF voluntarily.[66] Table 8.2 also shows the range of human rights violations that occurred during the war.

TABLE 8.2: TYPES OF HUMAN RIGHTS VIOLATIONS REPORTED TO THE TRC

VIOLATION TYPE	% OF VIOLATIONS	COUNT OF VIOLATIONS	% OF VICTIMS	COUNT OF VICTIMS
Forced Displacement	19.8	7,983	41.6	6,241
Abduction	14.8	5,968	36.4	5,456
Arbitrary Detention	12.0	4,835	29.3	4,401
Killing	11.2	4,514	30.1	4,514
Destruction of Property	8.5	3,404	21.5	3,231
Assault/Beating	8.1	3,246	19.9	2,977
Looting of Goods	7.6	3,044	18.4	2,761
Physical Torture	5.1	2,051	12.8	1,917
Forced Labor	4.6	1,834	11.2	1,675

VIOLATION TYPE	% OF VIOLATIONS	COUNT OF VIOLATIONS	% OF VICTIMS	COUNT OF VICTIMS
Extortion	3.2	1,273	7.7	1,149
Rape	1.6	626	3.9	581
Sexual Abuse	1.2	486	3.2	474
Amputation	0.9	378	2.2	336
Forced Recruitment	0.8	331	2.2	324
Sexual Slavery	0.5	191	1.2	186
Drugging	0.1	59	0.4	57
Forced Cannibalism	0	19	0.1	19
TOTAL		40,242		14,995

Source: TRC Report, Appendix 1:9

Table 8.3 shows that 33.5 percent of the victims who testified before the TRC were female, and Table 8.4 lists the combatant groups responsible for the various atrocities.

TABLE 8.3: VICTIM PROFILE: OF 14,995 VICTIMS REPORTED, AGE AND SEX ARE KNOWN FOR 11,429

GENDER	NO. REPORTED TO TRC	% OF VICTIMS
Female	3,826	33.5
Male	7,603	66.5
TOTAL NO. OF VICTIMS	11,429	100

Source: TRC Report, vol 2, 34

TABLE 8.4: NO. OF HUMAN RIGHTS VIOLATIONS BY WARRING FACTION

YEAR	RUF	SLA	AFRC	CDF
1991	4,055	597	0	29
1992	1,241	222	0	24
1993	758	197	0	9
1994	2,550	368	0	93
1995	3,822	469	0	191
1996	1,231	172	0	180
1997	926	51	325	602

YEAR	RUF	SLA	AFRC	CDF
1998	2,686	0	1,943	473
1999	2,639	0	1,312	352
2000	831	110	0	78

Source: TRC Report, vol 2, 39.

These figures do not represent the actual numbers of victims of the conflict, but only those who reported their wartime experiences to the TRC. It is estimated that 275,000 women and girls were sexually violated by various factions during the conflict.[67] Table 8.4 also shows spikes in violence against civilians in 1991-92, 1994-96, and 1998-99 as the RUF, AFRC, and civil defense forces (CDFs) battled for control of the country. It is interesting to note that the TRC recorded no human rights violations against the SLA from 1998-99 because after the May 1997 coup against Kabbah, the SLA had joined forces with the AFRC/RUF junta.

The RUF's transformation from the promise it made in "Operation Liberate the Motherland" to a violent, sadistic movement lacking ideological coherence remains one of the conundrums of the conflict. Initially, it had promised "to rid Sierra Leone and the rest of Africa out of the evils of black neo-colonialism, fascism, tyranny and dictatorship. ... to liberate, renovate and innovate mother Sierra Leone."[68] Its goal of "providing a personal renewal and the discovery of each person's own potential" as essential to the eradication of "black neo-colonialism, sectarianism, wholesale poverty, tyranny, oppression and dictatorship," and the establishment of a united, self-reliant, free, just, and democratic society"[69] went unfulfilled. In a letter (dated January 6, 1995) sent to the U.S. Ambassador in Accra, Ghana, Alimamy Bakarr Sankoh, the RUF's Foreign Relations Officer, continued to assert that the "The aim of this popular and progressive Operation [Liberate the Motherland] is not only to abolish tyranny, oppression and dictatorship rule, but also to set the pace for political freedom in Sierra Leone." Even as the violence escalated, the RUF continued to present itself as "a traditional, independent, liberation, mass-revolutionary Movement whose Central theme is to build a New Sierra Leone."

Perhaps one can begin to understand the RUF's antipathy towards women and girls by examining its internal structure to which it devoted only one committee, the "Women Concern Committee," to women's issues. At the apex of the structure was the decision-making War Council. It was responsible for training, disciplining, supplying, and equipping the "liberation" fighters. It also enforced the organization's rules, regulations, and standing orders. The War Council consisted of six "wings": the provincial, district, chiefdom, town, section, and village command councils. The Public Relations Office directed the movement's political programs, implemented its decisions, resolutions, and directives, and appointed members of the secretariat.

In addition to the War Council and its six wings, ten committees carried out other responsibilities. Among them was the Administrative and Finance Committee which supervised and coordinated the daily activities of the RUF. To drive home the point that "a revolutionary consciousness as well as an effectively mobilised and properly motivated population is the greatest deterrent to bad governance," the RUF established the Revolutionary Education Committee to educate Sierra Leoneans about their history, development, rights and duties, and what it considered to be the dangers of black neo-colonialism. It also created the Mass Education Committee (to promote mass education as a step toward the liberation of Sierra Leone), a Mass Mobilization Committee (to mobilize all sections of society into the RUF), the Information and Publicity Committee (to gather, analyze, and disseminate information about the RUF), a Human Rights Committee (to promote human rights and fundamental freedoms), a Repatriation Committee (to coordinate the return of refugees and displaced persons), the Relief Service Committee (to provide food, clothing, and health care supplies to the needy), the Agriculture and Food Processing Committee (to acquire and maintain tools and implements), and the Women Concern Committee (to incorporate women into the liberation struggle and forge strong bonds between men and women through revolutionary education).[70]

Outside the RUF's organizing document cited above, little is known or has been written about the Women Concern Committee, but given the atrocities it was reported to have committed, it failed in its efforts to forge strong bonds between men and women through revolutionary education. In fact the RUF's campaign of terror escalated as the theater of war expanded, and rebels and their collaborators used rape as an instrument of control and punishment. Rape is now widely regarded as a form of violence that targets female sexuality, and it has been used in conflict situations to further degrade women and girls socially.[71] The war provided a fertile ground for such abuses to occur as government forces and the RUF directed their attacks against civilians in contravention of Article 3 common to the 1949 Geneva Conventions.[72] Among the Article 3 prohibitions are violence to life and person, including murder, mutilations, torture and cruel treatment, abductions of civilians as hostages, rape, and sexual abuse. The brutality and savagery of the rebel attacks created anxiety and fear among unarmed civilians, thousands of whom fled to the neighboring states.

According to a February 1995 report prepared by the U.S. Committee for Refugees, Liberia and Guinea each had more than 200,000 Sierra Leonean refugees, between 500,000-1,000,000 persons were internally displaced, and more than 10,000 were killed since the beginning of the war in March 1991. By January 1997, the UN reported that 1.6 million of the 4.5 million people in the pre-war years had been uprooted by the war.[73] Anarchy and terror emptied over 300 towns and villages of their inhabitants and rendered the state ungovernable. The most brutal phase of the campaign occurred after the May 1997 coup when the RUF launched "Operation No Living Thing" and "Operation Pay Yourself." During these "operations," RUF rebels, in collaboration with the AFRC, rewarded themselves by abducting and raping women and girls in what the Special Court for Sierra Leone (SCSL) charged as a "criminal enterprise" for which it convicted Issa Hassan Sesay, Morris Kallon, and Augustine Gbao on February 25, 2009.[74]

RETHINKING GENDER AND SEX DISCRIMINATION IN POST-WAR RECONSTRUCTION

The TRC's "imperative" recommendations were those that "ought to be implemented immediately or as soon as possible" by the government.[75] They were aimed at upholding fundamental human rights and the rule of law, and can be implemented by repealing existing laws in whole or in part. The "work towards" recommendations "require in-depth planning and the marshalling of resources in order to ensure their fulfillment in a "reasonable time period," whereas in the "seriously consider" category, the government is not obliged to implement the recommendations.[76] The "work towards" recommendations include the payment of reparations and codification of customary law to conform to the constitution and the country's international law obligations. Gender-specific recommendations appeared in the "seriously consider" category, and they included the provision of micro-credit and skills training for women as well as the creation of a commission to combat gender discrimination. By placing these age-old issues in the second and third tier of recommendations, the TRC might have missed an opportunity to convince the government to sweep away constitutionally-sanctioned sex and gender discrimination in the name of tradition, religion, and custom. Given past institutional and leadership failures that laid the groundwork for the war, a wholesale review and repeal of discriminatory laws must of necessity have been at the front end of the TRC's recommendations.

Nevertheless, three years after the TRC report had been presented to the president, Parliament began to address some of the structural inequalities by passing legislation that left much to be desired. In the *Domestic Violence Act, 2007*,[77] Parliament made it a criminal offense for anyone in a domestic relationship to engage in domestic violence. The law defined ten instances of domestic relationships including one in which the complainant is or has been married to the offender, lives with the offender "in a relationship in the nature of a marriage," is engaged to the offender or in courtship with the offender, and is a house-helper. Proscribed conduct includes economic abuse (unreasonable deprivation of economic or financial resources), harassment (sexual contact without the person's consent and repeated sexual advances), and sexual abuse (forceful engagement of another person in a sexual contact, whether married or not). The law also made mediation or intervention by family members and friends, the traditional in-house means of settling rape and other sexual offenses, not a bar to investigation or prosecution of domestic violence. Punishment could range from a fine of Le 5 million to a two-year prison term or both. Perhaps, the most significant deviation from the past is the inclusion of married and unmarried women as well as house-helpers in the definition of domestic relationships. Fosterage, the practice in which young boys and girls are placed with relatives and friends often in distant cities and towns while they attend school or learn a trade, is often attended by domestic violence (including beatings), rape, and sexual abuse; most, if not all, such offenses go unreported and unpunished. With passage of this law, the hope is that the culture of silence and impunity will begin to disappear, and will be replaced with a culture that respects human rights and human dignity. The *Devolution of Estates*

Act, 2007,[78] applies to persons who die testate or intestate, regardless of their religion or ethnicity. This law empowers women in two critical areas where they were disadvantaged before under tradition and customary law; it allows them to apply for letters of administration to care for the estate of the intestate, and to inherit real and personal property. The testate provisions allow a surviving spouse (included in the definition of a dependant) facing economic hardship to contest a will if the "testator has not made any provision or any reasonable provision for the maintenance of the dependant." One of the limitations of this law is that it exempts family, chieftaincy, or community property held under customary law in which a surviving spouse may have an interest. By providing for the distribution of property to more than one surviving spouse, the law tacitly recognizes and reinforces polygamy which is a key factor in the marginalization of women.

In 2009, Parliament enacted the *Registration of Customary Marriage and Divorce Act, 2009*,[79] which sets a minimum age of 18 years for consenting persons who have co-habited continuously for not less than five years, without performing any customary rites of marriage, to enter into a customary marriage and have that marriage or divorce registered within six months in the local council where they are domiciled. Where either of the prospective spouses is under the statutory age, parental consent or the consent of a guardian or magistrate is needed for the marriage to become valid. The law prohibits persons already married under the Christian Marriage Act, Muslim Marriage Act, or Civil Marriage Act from entering into a customary marriage. If the same persons who are married under customary law then enter a Muslim, Christian, or civil marriage, the customary marriage is deemed to have dissolved by operation of law. More significantly, Section 18 of the law provides that a "wife in a customary marriage shall have the capacity to personally acquire and dispose of properties and to enter into contracts in her own behalf."

Passage of these "women rights bills"[80] was a step in the right direction of empowering women and girls, making it possible for them to end abusive relationships and receive protection under the law, and providing them access to property which in turn will increase their economic independence. However, a lot more needs to be done to end the culture of silence and impunity with regard to domestic violence and sexual abuse. Similarly, women's and girls' socio-economic status can be enhanced through greater access to education, economic opportunities, and real property. Also of importance in ending gender-based legal inequalities is the promotion of a human rights culture by Parliament which has the constitutional duty, along with the president, to incorporate signed international conventions into the country's domestic laws. In the last two decades, the International Criminal Tribunal for the former Yugoslavia (ICTY), the International Criminal Tribunal for Rwanda (ICTR), and the Special Court for Sierra Leone (SCSL), have begun to develop international legal standards to address these offenses, as has the Rome Statute of the International Criminal Court (ICC, July 17, 1998). The SCSL in particular, in a landmark case, *Prosecutor v. Issa Hassan Sesay, Morris Kallon, Augustine Gbao*, Case No. SCSL-04-15-T, February 25, 2009, held that rape, sexual slavery, and forced marriages (other inhumane acts) constituted crimes against humanity, and for which it found the defendants guilty and sentenced them to various prison terms (Issa Hassan Sesay: 20-52 years concurrently; Morris Kallon: 15-40 years concurrently; Augustine Gbao: 6-25 years concurrently).[81] The SCSL also found the defendants guilty of sexual slavery as a war crime pursuant to common Article 3 and Additional Protocol II to the Geneva Conventions of 1949. It found that the defendants, as superiors (leaders and commanders) in the RUF, ordered, instigated, planned, or aided and abetted the commission of these crimes in order to further a joint criminal enterprise which was to seize power (May 1997-April 1998) and control the territory of Sierra Leone.

While the raft of jurisprudential and structural developments, including court cases and the Rome Statute of the ICC, have made a positive contribution toward holding perpetrators to account for crimes committed against women and girls in wartime, a lot more has to be done to remove the kinds of inequalities and vulnerabilities, often in the name of religion, culture, and tradition, that give rise to violence against women and girls in peacetime as well. This calls for, among other things, a thorough review of the 1991 constitution and to amend and/or delete those sections that promote discrimination against women and girls.

CONCLUSION

What I have attempted to do in this chapter is to show how the civil war in Sierra Leone brought the spotlight to bear upon the brutal and violent manner with which individuals in the pro-and-anti-government forces treated women and girls in a society that is largely traditional in its conception of sex and gender roles and human rights. The RUF, a nonstate actor, initiated the civil war and named it "Operation Liberate the Motherland," to convey the impression that its campaign of violence against the government was undertaken to "liberate" a loving, nurturing, and caring country from rapacious, corrupt, and uncaring politicians. The conflict itself degenerated into mass plunder of the country's wealth in diamonds and other natural resources, and was anything but protective of the rights of women and girls. Women and girls bore the brunt of the decade-long conflict. They experienced rape, sexual slavery, and forced marriages which the SCSL has now classified as crimes against humanity and war crimes. The international community, slow at times to respond to conflicts in small, strategically less important states, is beginning to take human rights seriously instead of worrying about state sovereignty.[82]

This chapter has located the etiology of violence in the politico-legal framework and culture that entrenched gender bias and discrimination against women. The constitution, laws, and customs of Sierra Leone offer women and girls very few rights. Violence against women was cloaked in a culture of silence and impunity. The socio-spatial distinctions that existed before the conflict assigned women and girls a low pecking order which every warring faction exploited to the fullest. By highlighting the war's impact on women and girls the expectation is that the remedies that have been proposed or put in place will serve as a first step toward eradicating gender-based bias, discrimination, and violence against women and girls in the postwar era.

Notes

1. Olayinka Koso-Thomas, *The Circumcision of Women: A Strategy for Eradication* (London: Zed Books, 1987), 39.

2. Truth and Reconciliation Commission (TRC) of Sierra Leone, *Report*, vol 3B (Accra: GPL Press, 2004), 85.

3. Amnesty International, "Sierra Leone: Getting Reparations Right for Survivors of Sexual Violence." AFR 51/005/2007, 8.

4. Ibid., 4.

5. Edward W. Said, *Orientalism* (New York: Vintage Books, 1979), 207.

6.   TRC *Report*, vol 3B, 105.

7.   Peter A. Dumbuya, *Reinventing the Colonial State: Constitutionalism, One-Party Rule, and Civil War in Sierra Leone* (Lincoln: iUniverse, 2008).

8.   Thomas S. Cox, *Civil-Military Relations in Sierra Leone: A Case Study of African Soldiers in Politics* (Cambridge: Harvard University Press, 1976).

9.   Dumbuya, *Reinventing the Colonial State*; Abdul K. Koroma, *Sierra Leone: The Agony of a Nation* (Freetown: Andromeda Publications, 1996); Sheikh Batu Daramy, *Constitutional Developments in the Post-Colonial State of Sierra Leone 1961-1984* (Lewiston: Edwin Mellen Press, 1993).

10. William Reno, *Corruption and State Politics in Sierra Leone* (Cambridge: Cambridge University Press, 1995), 104.

11. Alfred Zack-Williams, *Tributors, Supporters and Merchant Capital: Mining and Underdevelopment in Sierra Leone* (Aldershot: Avebury, 1995).

12. Sahr J. Kpundeh, *Politics and Corruption in Africa: A Case Study of Sierra Leone* (Lanham: University Press of America, 1995).

13. *West Africa*, April 3-9, 1995, 499.

14. Koroma, *Sierra Leone*, 143.

15. Paul Richards, "The Political Economy of Internal Conflict in Sierra Leone" (The Hague: Netherlands Institute of International Relations 'Clingendael,' 2003).

16. David Keen, *Conflict and Collusion in Sierra Leone* (New York: Palgrave, 2005).

17. Dumbuya, *Reinventing the Colonial State*.

18. Francis Deng, "Reconciling Sovereignty with Responsibility: A Basis for International Humanitarian Action," in *Africa in World Politics: Reforming Political Order*, 4th ed., eds. John W. Harbeson and Donald Rothchild (Boulder: Westview Press, 2009), 356-57.

19. Boutros Boutros-Ghali, "An Agenda for Peace: Preventive Diplomacy, Peacemaking and Peace-Keeping." Doc. A/47/277-S/24111, June 17, 1992.

20. Dumbuya, "ECOWAS Military Intervention in Sierra Leone: Anglophone-Francophone Bipolarity or Multipolarity?," *Journal of Third World Studies* XXV, No. 2 (2008): 83-102.

21. UN Security Council, *Resolution 1181 (1998)*, Doc. S/RES/1181 (1998). July 13, 1998.

22. UN Security Council, *Resolution 1260 (1999)*, Doc. S/RES/1260 (1999). August 20, 1999.

23. Boutros-Ghali, "An Agenda for Peace," 2.

24. UN Security Council, *Resolution 1270 (1999)*, Doc. S/RES/1270 (1999), October 22, 1999.

25. UN Security Council, *Resolution 1562 (2004)*, Doc. S/RES/1562 (2004), September 17, 2004; UN Security Council, *Resolution 1270 (1999)*.

26. UN Security Council, *Fourth Report of the Secretary-General on the United Nations Mission in Sierra Leone.* Doc. S/2000/455, May 19, 2000.

27. Sir Thomas Legg and Sir Robin Ibbs, *Report of the Sierra Leone Arms Investigation* (London: The Stationery Office, 1998).

28. William Fowler, *Operation Barras: The SAS Rescue Mission: Sierra Leone 2000* (London: Cassell, 2004), 50.

29. UN Security Council, *Resolution 1132 (1997)*, Doc. S/RES/1132 (1997), October 8, 1997.

30. UN Security Council, *Resolution 1306 (2000)*, Doc. S/RES/1306 (2000), July 5, 2000.

31. Norrie Macqueen, *United Nations Peacekeeping in Africa Since 1960* (New York: Longman, 2002).

32. UN Security Council, *Fifth Report of the Secretary-General on the United Nations Mission in Sierra Leone.* Doc. S/2000/751, July 31, 2000.

33. Fowler, *Operation Barras*, 158.

34. Fabrice Weissman, "Sierra Leone: Peace at Any Price," in *In the Shadow of Just Wars: Violence, Politics and Humanitarian Action*, ed. Fabrice Weissman (Ithaca: Cornell University Press, 2004).

35. Jimmy D. Kandeh, *Coups From Below: Armed Subalterns and State Power in West Africa* (New York: Palgrave Macmillan, 2004), 59.

36. Dyan Mazurana and Khristopher Carlson, "From Combat to Community: Women and Girls of Sierra Leone" (Cambridge: Hunt Alternatives Fund, 2004).

37. Koso-Thomas, *The Circumcision of Women*.

38. Ibid., 37.

39. UN Economic and Social Council, "Integration of the Human Rights of Women and the Gender Perspective: Violence Against Women. Report of the Special Rapporteur on Violence Against Women, its Causes and Consequences, Ms. Radhika Coomaraswamy." Mission to Sierra Leone (21-29 August 2001). Doc. E/CN.4/2002/83/Add.2, February 11, 2002.

40. Koso-Thomas, *The Circumcision of Women*.

41. Mariane C. Ferme, *The Underneath of Things: Violence, History, and the Everyday in Sierra Leone* (Berkeley: University of California Press, 2001), 18.

42. Ibid.

43. Michael Jackson, *The Kuranko: Dimensions of Social Reality in a West African Society* (New York: St. Martin's Press, 1977), 40.

44. Ibid.

45. John Grace, *Domestic Slavery in West Africa With Particular Reference to the Sierra Leone Protectorate, 1896-1927* (New York: Barnes & Noble, 1975), 251.

46. Human Rights Watch, "Sierra Leone: "We'll Kill You if You Cry": Sexual Violence in the Sierra Leone Conflict," vol 15, No. 1(A), January 2003.

47. TRC *Report*, vol 3B.

48. Ibid., 105.

49. Ibid.

50. Human Rights Watch, "Sierra Leone."

51. TRC *Report*, vol 3B, 103.

52. Sierra Leone, *Report of the National Constitutional Review Commission Appointed by His Excellency the President Major-General Joseph Saidu Momoh, GCRSL, DCL, to Review the Constitution of Sierra Leone 1978 and the White Paper Thereon*. (Freetown: Sierra Leone Government, March 1991).

53. Sierra Leone, *The Constitution of Sierra Leone 1991*. Supplement to the *Sierra Leone Gazette Extraordinary* CXXII, No. 59 (Freetown: Government Printing Department, 1991).

54. TRC *Report*, vol 3B, 98.

55. TRC *Report*, vol 3B.

56. *The Constitution of Sierra Leone 1991*.

57. Ibid.

58. Peter L. Tucker, *The Sierra Leone Constitution for Laypersons* (Herts: Copyzone, 2003), 20.

59. Mazurana and Carlson, "From Combat to Community;" TRC *Report*, vol 3B.

60. Chris Coulter, *Bush Wives and Girl Soldiers: Women's Lives Through War and Peace in Sierra Leone* (Ithaca: Cornell University Press, 2009), 154.

61. TRC *Report*, vol 3B, 87.

62. Coulter, *Bush Wives and Girl Soldiers*, 3.

63. Mazurana and Carlson, "From Combat to Community."

64. Ibid., 6.

65. Coulter, *Bush Wives and Girl Soldiers*, 174.

66. Macartan Humphreys and Jeremy M. Weinstein, "Who Fights? The Determinants of Participation in Civil War," *American Journal of Political Science* 52, No. 2 (April 2008): 436-455).

67. TRC *Report*, vol 3B, 86.

68. Revolutionary United Front, "Voice of the Masses" (Sierra Leone: Kailahun Town, March 23, 1993), 1.

69. Ibid., 9-10.

70. Revolutionary United Front, "Revolutionary Structure of the R.U.F." (1992).

71. Coulter, *Bush Wives and Girl Soldiers*, 127.

72. Amnesty International, "Country Report: Sierra Leone: Towards a Future Founded on Human Rights." (AFR 51/05/96, September 25, 1996); Amnesty International, "Country Report: Sierra Leone: A Disastrous Set-back for Human Rights." AFR 51/05/97, October 20, 1997.

73. United Nations Security Council, *Report of the Secretary-General on Sierra Leone*. Doc. S/1997/80, January 26, 1997, 6.

74. Special Court for Sierra Leone, *Prosecutor v. Issa Hassan Sesay, Morris Kallon, Augustine Gbao*. Case No. SCSL-04-15-T, February 25, 2009: Judgment Summary.

75. TRC *Report*, 2, 119.

76. Ibid., 120.

77. Sierra Leone, *The Domestic Violence Act, 2007* (Freetown: Government Printing Department, 2007).

78. Sierra Leone, *The Devolution of Estates Act, 2007* (Freetown: Government Printing Department, 2007).

79. Sierra Leone, *The Registration of Customary Marriage and Divorce Act, 2009* (Freetown: Government Printing Department, 2009).

80. Amnesty International, "Getting Reparations Right," 15.

81. Special Court for Sierra Leone, *Prosecutor v. Issa Hassan Sesay, Morris Kallon, Augustine Gbao*. Case No. SCSL-04-15-T, Sentencing Judgment, April 8, 2009.

82. Francis Deng, et al., *Sovereignty as Responsibility: Conflict Management in Africa* (Washington: Brookings Institution, 1996).

Bibliography

Amnesty International (AI). *Country Report: Sierra Leone: Towards a Future Founded on Human Rights.* AFR 51/05/96, September 25, 1996.

______. *Country Report: Sierra Leone: A Disastrous Set-back for Human Rights.* AFR 51/05/97, October 20, 1997.

______. *Sierra Leone: Getting Reparations Right for Survivors of Sexual Violence.* AFR 51/005/2007.

Boutros-Ghali, Boutros. *An Agenda for Peace: Preventive Diplomacy, Peacemaking and Peace-Keeping.* UN Doc. A/47/277-S/24111, January 31, 1992.

Coulter, Chris. *Bush Wives and Girl Soldiers: Women's Lives Through War and Peace in Sierra Leone.* Ithaca: Cornell University Press, 2009.

Cox, Thomas S. *Civil-Military Relations in Sierra Leone: A Case Study of African Soldiers in Politics.* Cambridge: Harvard University Press, 1976.

Daramy, Sheikh Batu. *Constitutional Developments in the Post-Colonial State of Sierra Leone 1961-1984.* Lewiston: Edwin Mellen Press, 1993.

Deng, Francis, Sadikiel Kimaro, Terrence Lyons, Donald Rothchild, and I. William Zartman. *Sovereignty as Responsibility: Conflict Management in Africa.* Washington: Brookings Institution, 1996.

Deng, Francis. "Reconciling Sovereignty with Responsibility: A Basis for International Humanitarian Action." In *Africa in World Politics: Reforming Political Order.* 4th ed. Edited by John W. Harbeson and Donald Rothchild. Boulder: Westview Press, 2009.

Dumbuya, Peter A. "ECOWAS Military Intervention in Sierra Leone: Anglophone-Francophone Bipolarity or Multipolarity?" *Journal of Third World Studies* XXV, No. 2 (2008): 83-102.

______. *Reinventing the Colonial State: Constitutionalism, One-Party Rule, and Civil War in Sierra Leone.* Lincoln: iUniverse, 2008.

Ferme, Mariane C. *The Underneath of Things: Violence, History, and the Everyday in Sierra Leone.* Berkeley: University of California Press, 2001.

Fowler, William. *Operation Barras: The SAS Rescue Mission, Sierra Leone 2000.* London: Cassell, 2004.

Grace, John. *Domestic Slavery in West Africa With Particular Reference to the Sierra Leone Protectorate, 1896-1927.* New York: Barnes & Noble, 1975.

Human Rights Watch. Sierra Leone: "We'll Kill You if You Cry": Sexual Violence in the Sierra Leone Conflict. Vol 15, No. 1(A). January 2003.

Humphreys, Macartan, and Jeremy M. Weinstein. "Who Fights? The Determinants of Participation in Civil War." *American Journal of Political Science* 52, No. 2 (April 2008): 436-455).

Jackson, Michael. *The Kuranko: Dimensions of Social Reality in a west African Society.* New York: St. Martin's Press, 1977.

Kandeh, Jimmy D. *Coups From Below: Armed Subalterns and State Power in West Africa.* New York: Palgrave Macmillan, 2004.

Keen, David. *Conflict and Collusion in Sierra Leone.* New York: Palgrave, 2005.

Koroma, Abdul K. *Sierra Leone: The Agony of a Nation.* Freetown: Andromeda Publications, 1996.

Koso-Thomas, Olayinka. *The Circumcision of Women: A Strategy for Eradication.* London: Zed Books, 1987.

Kpundeh, Sahr J. *Politics and Corruption in Africa: A Case Study of Sierra Leone.* Lanham: University Press of America, 1995. L

egg, Sir Thomas, and Sir Robin Ibbs. *Report of the Sierra Leone Arms Investigation.* London: The Stationery Office, 1998.

Macqueen, Norrie. *United Nations Peacekeeping in Africa Since 1960.* New York: Longman, 2002.

Mazurana, Dyan, and Khristopher Carlson. "From Combat to Community: Women and Girls of Sierra Leone." Cambridge: Hunt Alternatives Fund, 2004.

Reno, William. *Corruption and State Politics in Sierra Leone.* Cambridge: Cambridge University Press, 1995.

Revolutionary United Front. *Revolutionary Structure of the R.U.F., 1992.*

______. *Voice of the Masses.* Kailahun Town, March 23, 1993.

Richards, Paul. "The Political Economy of Internal Conflict in Sierra Leone." The Hague: Netherlands Institute of International Relations 'Clingendael,' 2003.

Said. Edward W. *Orientalism.* New York: Vintage Books, 1979.

Sierra Leone. *Report of the National Constitutional Review Commission Appointed by His* Excellency the President Major-General Joseph Saidu Momoh, GCRSL, DCL, to *Review the Constitution of Sierra Leone 1978 and the White Paper Thereon.* Freetown: Sierra Leone Government, March 1991.

______. *The Constitution of Sierra Leone 1991.* Supplement to the Sierra Leone Gazette Extraordinary CXXII, No. 59. Freetown: Government Printing Department, 1991.

______. *Truth and Reconciliation Commission of Sierra Leone. Report,* vols 1-3B and Appendices. Accra: GPL Press, 2004.

______. *The Domestic Violence Act, 2007.* Freetown: Government Printing Department, 2007.

______. *The Devolution of Estates Act, 2007*. Freetown: Government Printing Department, 2007.

______. *The Registration of Customary Marriage and Divorce Act, 2009*. Freetown: Government Printing Department, 2009. Special Court for Sierra Leone. *Prosecutor v. Issa Hassan Sesay, Morris Kallon, Augustine Gbao*. Case No. SCSL-04-15-T,: Judgment Summary, February 25, 2009.

______. *Prosecutor v. Issa Hassan Sesay, Morris Kallon, Augustine Gbao*. Case No. SCSL-04-15-T, Sentencing Judgment, April 8, 2009.

Tucker, Peter L. *The Sierra Leone Constitution for Laypersons*. Herts: Copyzone, 2003.

United Nations Security Council. *Report of the Secretary-General on Sierra Leone*. Doc. S/1997/80, January 26, 1997.

______. *Resolution 1132 (1997)*. Doc. S/RES/1132 (1997), October 8, 1997.

______. *Resolution 1181 (1998)*. Doc. S/RES/1181 (1998), July 13, 1998.

______. *Resolution 1260 (1999)*. Doc. S/RES/1260 (1999), August 20, 1999.

______. *Resolution 1270 (1999)*, Doc. S/RES/1270 (1999), October 22, 1999.

______. *Fourth Report of the Secretary-General on the United Nations Mission in Sierra Leone*. Doc. S/2000/455, May 19, 2000.

______. *Resolution 1306 (2000)*. Doc. S/RES/1306 (2000), July 5, 2000.

______. *Fifth Report of the Secretary-General on the United Nations Mission in Sierra Leone*. Doc. S/2000/751, July 31, 2000.

______. *Resolution 1562 (2004)*. Doc. S/RES/1562 (2004), September 17, 2004.

UN Economic and Social Council. "Integration of the Human Rights of Women and the Gender Perspective: Violence Against Women". Report of the Special Rapporteur on Violence Against Women, its Causes and Consequences, Ms. Radhika Coomaraswamy." Mission to Sierra Leone (21-29 August 2001). Doc. E/CN.4/2002/83/Add.2, February 11, 2002.

______. 2004. *Resolution 1562 (2004). Doc. S/RES/1562 (2004)* (September 17, 2004).

Weissman, Fabrice. "Sierra Leone: Peace at Any Price." In *In the Shadow of Just Wars: Violence, Politics and Humanitarian Action*. Edited by Fabrice Weissman. Ithaca: Cornell University Press, 2004.

West Africa, April 3-9, 1995.

Zack-Williams, Alfred. *Tributors, Supporters and Merchant Capital: Mining and Underdevelopment in Sierra Leone*. Aldershot: Avebury, 1995.

GENDERED VIOLENCE AND POWER RELATIONS IN THE DRAMA OF TRACIE UTOH-EZEAJUGH

Ameh Dennis Akoh

INTRODUCTION

Feminism and feminist scholarship in Nigeria presents itself as an elastic field of polemics; even, sometimes, musings. This 'tenebrous sense of survival' (to use Homi Bhabha's words) makes it also an unending controversy, which is what also makes the subject defy a single and all-encompassing definition for all cultural milieus. Thus, many feminisms exist within gender discourse in contemporary times, just as there are diverse positions on the subject of gender, gender roles, and gender violence, among others. This chapter provides a brief examination of this controversy as it relates to feminist drama in Nigeria within the last three decades in light of its changing links to feminism(s) and womanism(s). Its focus is on gender-based violence in the drama of Tracie Utoh-Ezeajugh. Utoh-Ezeajugh is herself no longer a 'new' voice in Nigerian drama, having made her debut in 1999 with *Who Owns this Coffin and Other Plays*. Since this time, she has published four other plays, all of which portray the above scenario. This chapter explores the search for progress and utopia in these plays within the power relations that give impetus to feminist deconstruction and theory within post-military, postmodern and postfeminist waves in Nigerian drama. It relates her drama with those of other feminist dramatists in Nigeria with the aim of also delineating what makes the dramatist different in the entire attempt at 'speaking back' to the patriarchal and imperial centre. As the texts used shall demonstrate, in the feminist drama of Utoh-Ezeajugh, violence against women is not only the preserve of men; the 'powerful' women also wield instruments of violence as they utilize it against 'weaker' fellow women as well as men. In such a situation, the women adopt strategies hitherto seen to be manipulated by men alone to oppress fellow women in their bid to acquire power, retain or perpetuate it.

The above will explain why gender may vary between cultures and from time to time. We shall then agree with Liz Stanley that:

> The idea that there is a sharp biological demarcation of males from females with an associated and automatic segregation of behavior patterns has come into question as research has revealed that such boundaries are somewhat less sharp and determinate than has been imagined. Women and men are not always not emphatically distinguished from one another either biologically or psychologically, though social structures may treat people as though they must be distinguished from one another in sharp and discontinuous ways. 'Intersexuality' is a case in point.[1]

Again, this puts to question James Baldwin's position that "any real change implies the breakup of the world as one has always known it, the loss of all that gave one an identity, and the end of safety".[2]

GENDER STUDIES

The field of gender studies in Africa is daily gaining more attention among scholars, policy makers, experts and other concerned individuals. At the core of the early argument in the 1960s in feminist discourse and Africanist studies was the "woman-as-victim" and "woman-as-heroine".[3] The woman-as-victim conceptualization situates African women as powerless and voiceless victims of ever-deepening oppression rooted in layers of male-supremacist "tradition," colonialism, and "development." This representation is polarized by a countervailing set of images that cast African women as "feisty, assertive, self-reliant heroines".[4]

In the 1960s, the earliest feminist publications on Africa depicted African women as strong and resourceful heroines; they argued against the earlier depictions of "oppressed" African women by protagonists of the "civilizing mission" discourses during the colonial era, particularly Christian missionaries and some colonial administrators, as well as by many, generally male, anthropologists. To the feminist activists and scholars of the 1960s and early 1970s, African women in authority presented living examples of a different, more women-empowering, gender regime. Thus, in the pursuit of gender identities, power and construction of selfhood in the literature of the period, traditional research on gender in Africa naturally focused on girls/women, which also consequently engendered the problematizing of boys/men as genderless. This area has created the unconscious exclusion of men from gender studies and limited it to women's studies. This means that in the study of gender there is overemphasis on women as if to say gender means the same thing as women's studies. Again, beyond sidelining men and boys and limiting what we could learn about gender relations (i.e. relations between women and men), it essentialized the allocation of gender roles and lost out on the complexities and dynamics of gender and sexuality constructions within and outside educational settings. Consequently, contemporary evidence-based conceptual and theoretical insights on gender and gender relations have proved insightful on education, particularly on teacher education and pedagogy.[5]

Interestingly, too, since gender studies focus on foregrounding women, feminists have appropriated it for their purpose; more so that feminist theory, as Lisa Turtle puts it, dwells on asking "new questions of old texts" while arguing that the goals of feminist criticism are to develop and uncover a female tradition of writing; interpret symbolism of women's writing so that it will not be lost or ignored by the male point of view; discover old texts; analyze women writers and their writings from a female perspective; resist sexism in literature; and increase awareness of the sexual politics of language and style.[6]

Today, in Nigeria, gender-based drama has sought to achieve all of the above in an anti-intraception that yet poses disparate contradictions in their individual and collective interpretations of sexist conditions and literatures.[7] This is evident in the fact that it is no longer fashionable to delineate the principal culprit of gender-based violence as the man alone; neither will it be an infallible claim to see the major power players as men. Even in the political arena, women have equally proven to be as, dastardly, if not more so than men.[8] Thus, it can be said that both the portrayal in literature and the real life experiences of women have changed over time. Mabel Evwierhoma asserts that this scenario is true since the preoccupation of recent female dramatists with self-actualization and dominant heroines justifies present realities which can be found in the plays written by both male and female dramatists. Accordingly, she asserts further – and this is veritable – that as a member of the society, the female dramatist is at liberty to portray her women characters in line with her authorial goals. This also creates three possibilities, namely the woman as writer, the woman as reader, and the woman as character. It is within this framework that Evwierhoma sees the ideology of power and powerlessness as another choice of the dramatist.[9] Indeed, it is within this realm that one sees clearly on whose side the author resides.

WHAT IS GENDERED VIOLENCE?

The popular opinion on the subject of gendered violence usually refers to it in the context of rape, sexual assault, gang rape, incest, molestation, voyeurism, murder, etc., against women only. All of these are forms of sexualized gender-based violence. It may be added that street harassment, prostitution, sexist jokes, obscene phone calls, sexual harassment, negative portrayals of women in popular culture, pornography and war are all inextricably connected to gendered violence; whether or not they constitute it in and of themselves. There is also the area of violence that is perpetrated on female bodies through the altering and re-shaping of them. Violence that shapes the body takes place in every culture in a variety of forms: foot-binding, birth control devices and methods, female genital mutilation, anorexia and bulimia, widow burning, elective cosmetic surgery, abortion methods, the medicalization of childbirth, and clothing styles are all ways in which the female body is altered/changed/mutilated by cultural practices. In this light, it can be said that *all* violence is gendered.[10]

The term sexualized gender-based violence is sometimes used instead of sexual violence because such violence and subjugation would be interpreted to be a political act, a site of activism and resistance.

Thus, sexual violence implies that rape, sexual assault, and incest are somehow connected to or located in the act of sex. The argument then that is put forward by many feminists and scholars alike that unlike a gun, a knife, or a fist, sex is merely the instrument used to gain and maintain power over another individual or half a population. Consequently, it is believed that it is not women's behavior that needs to be adjusted, but men's. Men are the vast majority of perpetrators of all forms of sexualized gendered violence. The thinking thus is that as a community of scholars, activists, students, practitioners, advocates, professionals, and survivors, the focus must shift from the victims of rape to the perpetrators and the systems that support these acts.

On the other hand, the United Nations Development Fund for Women's (UNIFEM) research considers a more generalized approach, which takes gender violence to mean:

> the individual Man, raising his fist against his wife. It is the gang of boys, cheering on the fight in the middle of a tight circle. It is the young man on a date, acting without regard for the desires of the young woman he is with. It is the man pushed by rage and fear, driving his car to his death. It is the physical or verbal attack, on another man, because of his sexual orientation or religion or skin colour. It is the gangs of men – we call them armies – who have been commanded to view each other as less than human, and to view citizens as something even less. It is violence on the playing field. It is, perhaps metaphorically, perhaps not, our relationship to our natural environment. It is men's violence in a myriad of forms.[11]

As far as it goes, the above scenario still excludes women from being culprits or perpetrators of gender-based violence – only men are i.e., men against women and men against fellow men. Violence against women is an ancient and universal problem occurring in every culture and social group. Power inequalities between women and men and the masculine culture are the major sources of this violence. In 1993, the United Nations offered the first official definition of such violence when the General Assembly adopted the Declaration on the Elimination of Violence Against Women. Article 1 of the declaration defines violence against women as "any act of gender-based violence that results in, or is likely to result in, physical, sexual or psychological harm or suffering to

women, including threats of such acts, coercion or arbitrary depriva-
tions of liberty, whether occurring in public or private life" (Economic
and Social Council 1992). This includes all but are not limited to, what
we have listed earlier. All of these forms of violence are associated with
power inequalities between women and men or between children and
their caregivers, as well as with growing economic inequalities within
and between countries. However, the primary inequality that gives rise
to gender-based violence is the power inequality between women and
men. In 1999, the UN also declared November 25 as the International
day for the elimination of all violence against women. This is an echo
of the Convention on the Elimination of All Forms of Discrimination
against Women (CEDAW) of 1979 which requires that countries party
to the Convention should take all appropriate steps to end violence.
However, it is in the light of this that UNIFEM pools resources together
with countries to gag the continued prevalence of violence against
women and girls. According to the UN Secretary-General's 2006 In-
Depth Study on All Forms of Violence against Women, 89 countries
had some legislation on domestic violence, and a growing number
of countries had instituted national plans of action. The UNIFEM's
approach thus works on several fronts to end the violence and gender
inequality. These efforts are intensified and achieved through advocacy
campaigns and partnerships with governments, civil society and the
UN system. UNIFEM's support for the UN Secretary-General's multi-
year *Unite to End Violence against Women* campaign, launched in 2008
also led to the campaign's regional components in Africa and Latin
America and the Caribbean which was launched in 2009. Earlier on
November 25, 2008, the UNIFEM's *Say NO to Violence against Women*
initiative was meant to advance the objectives of the *Unite* campaign
through social mobilization and it presented more than 5 million sig-
natures to the UN Secretary-General, demonstrating public support to
make ending violence against women a top priority for governments
everywhere.[12]

If gender-based violence is defined as violence involving men
and women, in which the female is usually the victim and which
arises from unequal power relationships between men and women,
then it can be said that a major factor is the politics of power itself.
However, in recent times, it is becoming fashionable to find women's
violence against fellow women, as can also be found in the texts to
be discussed here. This, in a purely Marxist sense, is another dimen-

sion to the general subject of oppression. Violence against women and girls is often referred to as "gender-based violence" because it evolves in part from women's subordinate gender status in society. In most cultures, traditional beliefs, norms and social institutions legitimize and therefore perpetuate violence against women. The use of the term "gender-based violence" provides a new context in which to examine and understand the long-standing phenomenon of violence against women. It shifts the focus from women as victims to gender and the unequal power relationships between women and men created and maintained by gender stereotypes as the basic underlying cause of violence against women.[13]

However, as Nigerian texts demonstrate, the focus should rather include men and women alike. Take for instance, in Julie Okoh's *Edewede*, the violence against the eponymous character, Edewede, is psychological.[14] This psychological torture makes her lose not just her freedom but also self-determination, assertiveness and confidence. Interestingly, as it is common in all of Okoh's plays, the culprits are men while the victims are women. Yet Okoh deemphasizes the voices of the women especially the mother-in-law who assists in the perpetuation of the *status quo*. A contrary scenario is, however, presented in Iyorwuese Hagher's *Lifetimes* where Laide's mother is the one insisting on mutilating her daughter's genitals as a mark of her true womanhood. Indeed, the elderly women in the play insist that the status quo must be upheld, that is, female circumcision as a means of initiating the girls into womanhood.[15] Although the result is fatal, the playwright insists that both men and women are guilty of continuing a retrogressive tradition and calls for a reorientation that is achieved through synergy and selflessness rather than confrontation. This is predicated on the fact that concerted and continued practical advocacy should be promoted to change the attitude of not just men who are seen to be holding the ace to this cultural norm but more importantly the women who insist on the perpetuation of the act. Hagher can thus be seen to be challenging the women to chart a better way of their rites of passage.

It is evident, however, that the espousals above all point to the reality of power relations, namely the 'unequal' power relations between women and men that are created and maintained by gender stereotypes as the basic underlying cause of violence against women. It is also apparent that different perspectives abound as to the understanding of the subject of gendered violence. The Aba (Women's) Riot of 1929 in Nigeria, for instance, was clearly a case of women against the men-controlled colonial government, because even though the "women adopted some aspects of male identity, their rhetoric contained a strong critique of male behavior."[16] This occurred because the power that controlled their existence was dominated, if not completely controlled, by men. The result of the revolt was a reduction in the powers of both the colonial authorities and the local chiefs. The question then arises regarding when the power is principally or wholly wielded by women. Recent Nigerian literary texts have begun to probe into this possibility should it eventually occur. This is why our attention here must shift to the different power relations that exist where women dominated or completely control power. As the plays of our focus shall demonstrate, the different power relations or different types of power in relationships are not between men, but rather women and every woman in the plays are part of the power structures that dwell within the/those walls be it brute force or authority, manipulations or friendship. Thus, in the political terrain, these relationships open up a form of the basic makeup of the struggles of everyday life in that the struggle is not only between men and women, but also between women and women. The women in the plays have both the physical and political power. This variety makes power and its use an interesting duality. It is the subject of power that dominates and drives the actions in the plays of Utoh-Ezeajugh. Olufemi Taiwo puts it more succinctly:

> We perforce confront the question of power. For without power, the market for narratives will feature several in contention, where the buyer will truly be at liberty to purchase the set of narratives that suits her fancy. But power intrudes. It outlaws certain narratives, renders others unattractive, denies voice to yet others, and rules others out of court.[17]

TEXTUAL DISCOURSE

Utoh-Ezeajugh has so far published seven plays, i.e., two collections, entitled *Who Owns this Coffin? and Other Plays, Our Wives Have Gone Mad Again and other Plays*, and *Nneora*.[18] In all of these plays, one is never in doubt as to the direction of the authorial ideology. The dramatist's handling of the issue of violence gravitates between the physical and the psychological as it affects gender and power relations particularly in the Nigerian society. Her emphasis is on the female characters in their bid to 'measure up' with men and even overtake them. In this regard, she exposes the contradictions involved when women are left among themselves in the power game where the powerful women 'assume' masculine roles or roles culturally assigned to men. Thus, the gender war against male dominance always, in the plays of Utoh-Ezeajugh, turn out to be a war among and against themselves. It must thus be made clear that historical conjunction of colonialism and neo-colonialism in which the men of African culture have found themselves up to the present time put them in the unlucky position of vilification in the feminist power game and which thus tends to ignore the women also as their own oppressors or accomplices of their oppressors within this culture or cultures. Oyeronke Oyewumi asserts that just like the African Americans in the United States and blacks in Central or Latin America, the women in Africa experience the need to attach themselves to the same cultural matrix. That will mean also that colonial oppression should be taken in the same light as feminist oppression. This is also misleading as the patterns and operators are different. After all, while it is asserted that colonialism helped to *inferiorize* the females as it did to all natives, and that becoming a woman meant being invisible in the political sphere, the transition to post-independence is also critical to any consideration of power relations.[19] But as the plays discussed here demonstrate, power relations are a product of cultural shifts and societal or socio-political mutations.[20] Again, this varies from culture to culture; thus the veil of culture or tradition or of competition over political power becomes a critical factor in understanding the perspective from which the author draws his or her argument in building characters and situations.

WHO OWNS THIS COFFIN

In *Who Owns this Coffin?*, an organization of women, named the Dynamic Women Dance Group is in session to discuss how their 'rights have been trampled upon' and 'oppressed, suppressed, repressed and humiliated'. Consequently, they resolve not to remain silent to 'such unimaginable actrociousness'. Led by their president, Madam Ekwutosi, the women plan to revolutionize society through their songs, and with which they hope to reach the political and traditional leaders of Nigeria. This first meeting of the women however ends in a fiasco because of the sharp differences among them on their manners of approach to achieving their goals. Mrs. Amtu, for example, does not believe that the issue of corrupt leadership should bother their organization possibly because she herself is a Local Government Chairperson and also guilty of corrupt practices. Others too are concerned because their husbands may be guilty of "wanton acts of marginalization, oppression, suppression, corruption, embezzlement of funds meant for the welfare of women and children."[21] Before the women regroup, we begin already to hear of charges of corrupt practices against Mrs. Amtu. In her conversation with Madam Ekwutosi, the latter advises her to combine the support of powerful men in society and the women's organizations to silence her opponents. Their conversation is interrupted by the entrance of Aima (Madam Ekwutosi's undergraduate daughter), and all attention shifts to her refusal to get married to Colonel Liman, her mother Madam Ekwutosi's boyfriend. Madam Ekwutosi hopes to curb Colonel Liman's desire for many young girls by encouraging him to marry Aima even though the latter refuses. Aima's refusal is a major source of her mother's present worry. If Aima will agree to marry him instead of the 'poor' prospective university lecturer Teddy, Madam Ekwutosi thinks that it will make Colonel Liman feel committed to helping her political career, especially now that she is facing corruption charges for failing to execute a contract awarded to her some years earlier when she was a member of the National Constitutional Conference. This relationship is, to her, critical to her becoming a member of the National Assembly in the next elections. However, as opposition mounts on the two powerful but corrupt women (Ekwutosi and Amtu), they employ every available means to wriggle out of the impending shame. Mrs. Sijuade, an influential woman and national vice president of the National Council for Women Societies becomes their last resort. But they are disappointed when, instead of helping them, she chronicles their misdeeds and promises to join in bringing them to book, because "in this war with the men, we must never imitate those obnoxious vices which have eaten deep into their system."[22] This is because they embezzle public funds, use their political office to intimidate, oppress and extort money from people. The guilty women (Ekwutosi, Amtu) together with Hajia Binta, another corrupt women who as principal of a secondary school is accused of diverting funds into her personal purse, all resolve therefore to fight 'rough' and eliminate Mrs. Sijuade and others on their way to political ascendancy. As the play ends, the secret plan to eliminate the latter is exposed. This weakens the resolve of the women. The Narrator at the end summarizes the playwright's call for caution in the bid to acquiring political power and change:

> The road to change is not as smooth as many of us would prefer. The highway is strewn with pitfalls, detours and stop-signs...Remember your African values...Put down all weapons aimed at each other, it is an abomination to the Earth. Take up arms against all corrupt practices for then you will be fighting a just war. Reject all corrupt and morally debasing attributes for they desecrate the land... Purge yourselves of inherent vices for these contradict the very ideals you must tenaciously uphold.[23]

In *Who Owns this Coffin?* Utoh-Ezeajugh thus confronts the feminist argument that the women are always the victim of men's (gender) violence. Her voice here is different from the norm. In this all-female character play, the playwright exposes the hypocrisy, hidden motives, intrigues, betrayal, and fraud that exists when women are also engaged in seeking power or when they are already in power. She seems to be saying that gender does not determine the direction of power play; it is largely a question of the individual person who wields it. Unlike many of her female counterparts who always vilify men for all oppression against women and society, she chooses to be unrepentantly different and castigates the women represented by the Dynamic Women Dance Group for hijacking the feminist movement for personal aggrandizement. Her target therefore in this play is women who have not only set out to make a career out of feminism but have become overtly violent in their *modus operandi* to achieving their goals, as they gag genuine dissident voices and go to any length to even completely exterminate the real heroes (or heroines) of genuine (feminist) liberation struggles.

For Madam Ekwutosi, a single mother, former member of the Federal Constitutional Conference and President of the Group, the organization is only a means to attaining a more lucrative political end. To fortify her political and financial position in the Group and the ambition of winning a seat in the House of Representatives or alternatively, a ministerial appointment, she warms the bed of any willing male campaign donor and sacrifices her daughter to a senior army officer as wife, even against the girl's wish. Mrs. Sijuade aptly and rhetorically reveals Ekwutosi's adventures in the following way:

> Must you play the whore to every man for his favours?
> Your reputation is increasingly becoming embarrassing
> ... rubbing off on all women! ...You have gone to bed with
> every army officer you have had access to ...You have des-
> ecrated womanhood.[24]

Her life generally is a track record of immorality and fraud. She sees her conduct and methods as the most proactive avenues to power and wealth. This is the legacy she wishes to pass to her female children, especially Aima. Thus, she pursues her ambition in all earnestness with her daughters as test models and uses strategies of political thuggery and 'elimination' as a last resort. She sends her daughter, Aima, to school to achieve this goal as a willing sacrifice of the sexual violence of a mother who is now a beneficiary of power and in whose mind the means justify the ends in power play. Aima has no choice of her own in this regard even though she tries to do so but she is unsuccessful. She helplessly becomes her mother's commodity of exchange for her political elevation. Thus, Aima's "identity and sexuality are controlled and exploited by individual men, as well as by a patriarchal society, but this control is compounded by the cooperation of her own mother." [25] This oppression or violence takes place outside of the authority of the father because Madam Ekwutosi had the girl outside of marriage.

To justify the argument that perceptions of masculinity and femininity are formed in early childhood, the playwright chronicles the activities of the women in the play as is evident in the actions of Ekwutosi and others in their relationship with their underage children. A critical factor here is that as Aima is forced to lead a life of commoditizing her sexuality as is her younger sister Nkoli, who is still in the primary school. According to UNIFEM research, the argument being made here is that as early as two years of age, children understand their gender identity. From about three years of age, children begin to avoid actions and activities they believe to be inappropriate for their sex simply because it is appropriate for the other. It is therefore important to address the issue of gender equity at an early stage in children's lives in order to address emerging gender inequalities. This is why some may argue that to end violence against girls and women and promote their human rights, we need to educate boys and girls to honor both the "masculine" and "feminine" values that are within themselves and society. Research suggests that when fathers and other male family members offer a positive role, boys develop a more flexible vision of manhood and are more respectful in their relationships with women. All members of the family have important roles in raising boys, including fathers and grandfathers. In many cultures, fathers have played a limited role in the upbringing of their children, particularly during infancy. Fortunately, this is changing with modernization and the increasing dominance of the nuclear family. Mothers often reinforce traditional ideas about manhood by showing that they do not expect sons to do household chores or express their emotions.[26] But, again, the scenario presented in the play shows a situation where the children are not given the opportunity for guidance and guardianship from both parents since the women are either domineering at home, in a state of marital crises, or are single mothers like Madam Ekwutosi who only teaches her daughters on 'short-cuts' to success.

The rabid search for power by the women gives birth to a myriad of challenges as the anti-corruption searchlight beams on them. Thus, apart from the internal wrangling within the Group, their purported ideals hit the rocks when, besides Madam Ekwutosi, two other influential members, i.e., Hajia Binta, a school principal and Treasurer of the Group, and Mrs. Amtu, a local government chairperson, face demotion and removal respectively for their general impropriety. This is especially detrimental to the latter's ambition of running for Senate in the next elections. All three seek help from Chief (Mrs.) Sijuade, a rich widow, business woman, philanthropist, and vice-president of the National Council of Women Societies, whose influence had earned them their vantage positions and who has been of immense assistance to the Group's objectives which she had thought to be genuine. Unfortunately for them, Mrs. Sijuade has been receiving privileged information lately on all their indecent and shady activities. While she struggles to sustain the legacy of her late husband in helping the less privileged in her community, she channels her donations through the Group, but these items are often misappropriated by the president and her executive council.

> My husband had beautiful dreams for his community. I
> have tried to realise those dreams. But thanks to people
> like you, I get frustrated time and time again. When I give
> things to be distributed to the poor, widows and orphans,
> you and your cohorts appropriate everything for your-
> selves.[27]

Mrs. Sijuade castigates them as traitors and saboteurs of the women's movement and leaves them to face the consequences of their misdeeds. Unrepentant in their blinkered quest to shield and sustain their ambition, the women plot the death of Mrs. Sijuade, and, while on her sick bed, they prepare a coffin and place it at a crossroads with her name boldly inscribed as a symbol of their determination to elimi-nate her. They are convinced that a woman like Mrs. Sijuade would not only frown at their conduct but also expose them for punishment. This plot is however exposed by Mrs. Tansi, a member of the Group. The play is thus a satiric exposé of women's folly and general cants in their bid for liberation. The form of violence on Mrs. Sijuade even while still on her sickbed by her fellow women is enough torture to send her to an early grave, and it places the 'new' political women in positions hitherto occupied by men. However, it shows the extent to which women, also, can go in their rabid search to upstage the status quo. But, again, the playwright (herself a fellow woman) does not spare this group of power-seeking, wealth-crazy women as she reveals their excesses and foibles.

OUR WIVES HAVE GONE MAD AGAIN

Our Wives have Gone Mad Again presents a group of women who are political power seekers. In their first gathering in the house of Inyang Mpang where the wife, Ene Abah-Mpang, is actually the head of the family, the women including Ene, Funmi Anifowose-Sabio, Mairo Bello-Ikemefuna, and Ifeoma Eze-Longpole discuss their take in the next general election. Top on their agenda is how to ensure the success of the women's sole presidential candidate, Chief (Mrs.) Irene Okpiribe-Sabio, at the polls. Beyond being in control of their homes, they adopt various ways of silencing their husbands further in order gain full political stronghold of their families and country. Ifeoma, for example, gets a strategy from Ene in the following words:

> Next time your husband picks a quarrel with you, make
> [sure] you teach him a lesson. Keep a weapon handy. You
> can put the weapon in a corner of the house where you
> can easily reach it. That big pestle your house girl uses
> to pound yam can serve the purpose. When he makes a
> move towards you, draw him towards your weapon. Take
> the weapon and deal him a deadly blow at the back of the
> head. If hit him hard enough, he will pass out.[28]

To strengthen their plans, the women move to a supposedly safe
drinking bar in town, where unknown to them, their husbands are also
having fun 'away' from home. Both sides are disappointed that their different aims have been exposed and temporarily defeated. Undaunted,
the women relocate to the home of the Mpang's for further planning.
Irene assures them: "We have covered a lot of political ground. The
smell of success is wafting closer."[29] One of such grounds is that Irene
has divorced her husband and married another man, Gambo, described
as a 'delectable twenty-five year old, Ibadan-educated Ph.D. holder'.
The women applaud this decision since the young man's credentials
will boost Irene's chances at the polls. Also, even with a Ph.D., the man
is also seen to be a docile person who will not argue with his wife on
any matter. The next ground the women have covered is the hiring of
some young beautiful girls who are assigned the special duty to 'track
down' their political opponents, 'seduce them and get them into compromising positions'.[30] While they discuss this plan, Ifeoma rushes in
to announce that she has just killed her husband, thanks to the strategy
earlier given to her by Ene. The police run after her into the women's
meeting, but as it has become a practice with the Nigerian police, the
police officer takes a bribe of one hundred thousand naira and rather
helps the women to cover up the crime. All the while, Inyang, who has
been hiding in the house, appears on the scene ready to quit his marriage to Ene for fear of being the next victim of the women's violence.
Ene's attempt to track him down with a weapon fails and he escapes.
The women however trudge on with their electioneering campaigns
amidst violence, blackmail, mudslinging, and the like. The play ends
on a note of hope for the women's candidate as they appear to have
silenced all voices of dissent.

In *Our Wives Have Gone Mad Again* (which is the title play for
the second collection), Utoh revisits the subject matter of gender and

power that she had raised in *Who Owns this Coffin?* two years earlier. The play is a kind of revision of Ola Rotimi's *Our Husband Has Gone Mad Again*, and thus the dramatist again presents an unusually different position from the general feminist representation of man as the only oppressor. Consequently, it is not only 'our husband' (men) that can go mad in politics, but rather, 'our wives' (women) do much more, if given the opportunity. Women in this play have become oppressors themselves, perpetrating all kinds of violence both at home and on the political scene against not only their fellow women as in *Who owns this Coffin?* but also against men, especially those with dissenting voices. The men, consequently, become workers at home and serve as a means of achieving their wives' political and social ends; this is similar to Iyorwuese Hagher's *Mulkin Mata* where, after a bloody revolution occurs, the women organize themselves into a coterie of power brokers, power wielders, and oppressors in a three-pronged decree of role-reversal, by which the Women's Government enact three decrees that give roles hitherto performed by men to women and vice versa, namely, banning of all men from holding both political offices and leadership of the family for a century; men are to take over all chores hitherto undertaken by women, like cooking of meals, baby-sitting, cleaning of houses, and tending to clothes and the farm, act as telephone operators, receptionists, stewardesses and petty traders, and thirdly, sex prohibition which is aimed at giving the women the freedom and more opportunity to work without distraction from their husbands (nay, 'wives'!).[31]

Thus, in *Our Wives*, the playwright satirizes the women in their obsessive drive for political power and the indecent and dehumanizing approaches they utilize such as participation in thuggery, bribery and corruption, assassination, and unlawful arrests, etc., which men hitherto were accused of. These have become strategies used by the 'new' women in politics and power. Besides, they choose and drop male partners at will, most particularly when such relationships are anathema to their political ascendancy. A typical example is the case of Chief Irene, presidential flag bearer of the Liberation Peoples Party (LPP) who unceremoniously dropped her legal husband for a new and more dynamic one for reasons of political expediency. Ifeoma also violently murders husband Zeus and covers it with the assistance of her fellow political women, while Ene's attempted murder of her husband Inyang fails. However, Irene is at the forefront of the political maneuvers. In her new position as party flag bearer, she unfolds her dreams for the nation and men in particular in a comic role reversal:

> Oh I have great plan. I will create a ministry for men affairs under which he [her husband] can run such programmes as Better Life for Rural Men, Husband Support Programme and many other lucrative...sorry, I mean expedient programmes.[32]

Thus, like Madam Ekwutosi, Chief Irene pursues this rabid ambition in a reign of folly and terror, assassination of political opponents, etc. This is evident in the swift and mysterious death or disappearance of her political opponents or fellow contestants. Again, in quick succession, those who raise their voice in protest are violently manhandled:

> 7th MAN: (shouting) It is a lie. Bitch, you killed my brother!
>   (the thugs descend on him, beat and drag him out).
> BOY: You blackmailed my father!
> OLD MAN: I will expose you! You assassinated my son!
>   (The thugs are busy, beating and dragging people away.
>   Confusion reigns in the gathering).[33]

This is what characterizes Irene's campaign period until she eliminates all voices of dissent, including the police. But it is interesting to note that just like men in politics, the women also know how to 'clean up' their misdeeds as in the case of the murder of Ifeoma's husband and at the last political rally when policemen come to arrest Irene for murder:

> GAMBO: (intervening) Excuse me sergeant, may I have
>   a word with you privately...Money will also be shared
>   at the end (The crowd start yelling in ecstasy. Gambo
>   and 3rd policeman confer by the corner. Gambo brings
>   out a parcel and gives 3rd policeman. They smile and
>   shake hands).
> MAIRO: (Shouting) Yes! After all, what a man can do, a
>   woman can do even better.[34]

The obvious merit of *Our Wives* is in its ideological twist from the norm, a twist which stands as a foil to the almost infallible picture of the 'new' woman presented by some feminist writers in their bid to overthrow patriarchy that ignores the intricacies of time, environment, and individual experiences. This is in spite of the report in UNIFEM that seems to canvass for the recognition of the various pressures placed upon men that may result in violent reactions, as well as the need for men to take responsibility for their actions. Again, it is as a result of the thinking that, predominantly, gender power relations have left a legacy whereby women are more likely to be disadvantaged relative to men, have less access to resources, benefits, information and decision-making, and to have fewer rights both within the household and in the public sphere because, "in the past, these concerns and the struggle for gender equality have often been narrowly perceived as "women's issues," and gender programs have been designed to focus only on women."[35] However, in her plays, Utoh-Ezeajugh puts it clearly that when given the same opportunity, women are not different from men.

CONCLUSION

Utoh-Ezeajugh's plays are simple and executed without the usual political cants prevalent in the plays of her fellow 'new' feminist voices in Nigeria, like Julie Okoh and Irene Salami. These playwrights' aesthetics of ambivalence makes them rely overmuch on ideological politicizing that diminishes their plays to mere political campaigns. What has privileged our dramatist above this group is partly her intrepid spirit in venturing into an alternative artistic path, which, while recognizing the place of the women, still takes an unambiguous post-feminist stance; a privilege which she appropriates, bringing her close in ideo-aesthetics to the latest artistic career of Tess Onwueme.[36] It is also obvious that Utoh-Ezeajugh's 'tenor of temperance' shifts towards a humanist perspective rather than feminist agitation, "which aims at re-channeling literary emphasis to more debilitating phenomena in contemporary society other than the re-inscription of gendered disputations."[37] This is also evident in her shorter plays like *Cauldron of Death*.

It is obvious that few feminist writers in Nigeria are now coming to terms with these realities, namely the fact that the roles hitherto created by men and which were seen as jaundiced are now been recreated by the former as a form of self-reflection of these realities. This suggests that even when revolutions are involved, they are not the hitherto facile feminist or sexual hullabaloo of upstaging patriarchal canons that gravitate in the end towards creating a sexist society that it may have originally sought to eliminate. Again, this is part of the whole set of contradictions that the plays of our present dramatist seek to undermine. The plays demonstrate the dynamism of men (women) and power, which can be wielded by any of the sexes, and its direction can only be determined by the individual wielder.

Notes

1. Liz Stanley, "Should 'Sex' really be 'Gender'– Or 'Gender really be 'Sex'? in *Gender: A Sociological Reader*, eds., Stevi Jackson, and Sue Scott (London: Routledge, 2002), 34.

2. See James Baldwin's quote from http://www-rohan.sdsu.edu/~gwick/GV.html.

3. For detailed analysis on this, see Andrea Cornwall, *Readings in Gender in Africa* (Bloomington: Indiana University Press, 2002).

4. Ibid.

5. Fatuma Chege, *Young People Constructing Gendered and Sexual Identities: Implications for HIV/Aids in African Contexts* (Cice: Hiroshima UniversityO1-02-2006) home.hiroshima-u.ac.jp/cice/forum/73pp.pdf.

6. Lisa Tuttle, *Encyclopedia of Feminism* (Harlow: Longman, 1986), 184.

7. David Ingram, *Critical Theory and Philosophy* (St. Paul, Minnesota: Paragon, 1990), 75.

8. This is evident in power play, thuggery, corruption, etc., and women especially in politics have equally been found to be guilty of the same evil. Consider, for instance, Patricia Etteh, Iyabo Obasanjo-Bello, the Ibori women (recently convicted along with their benefactor for fraud), Turai Yar'Adua, etc. in Nigeria and their activities in the political sphere, and it becomes apparent where the 'new' woman is heading.

9. Mabel Evwierhoma, *Female Empowerment and Dramatic Creativity in Nigeria* (Ibadan: Caltop Publications, 2002), 1-28.

10. See the United Nations Development Fund for Women (UNIFEM) Gender Fact Sheet No.5 www.**unifem**-usnc.org/files/MDG%20**Fact**%20**Sheet**.pdf for details on this.

11. Michael Kaufman, founder White Ribbon Campaign quoted in UNIFEM, 1.

12. UNIFEM, 2. The recent advocacy is drawn from the Convention of all Forms of Discrimination against Women, New York, 18 December, 1979. See http://www2.ohchr.org/english/law/cedaw.htm. This can also be found on

http://www.unifem.org/gender_issues/violence_against_women/ and http://www.un.org/ga/search/view_doc.asp?symbol=A/61/122/Add .1&referer=/english/&Lang=E.

13. Ibid.

14. Julie Okoh, *Edewede* (Owerri: Totan Publishers, 2000).

15. Iyorwuese Hagher, *Lifetimes* (Kaduna: JVC Press, 1999).

16. Toyin Falola, *Colonialism and Violence in Nigeria* (Bloomington: Indiana University Press, 2009), 120. The Aba Women's Riot of 1929 took place in the present Abia State of Nigeria and it was a protest against the tax regime of the then colonial government in the area.

17. Olufemi Taiwo, *How Colonialism Preempted Modernity in Africa* (Bloomington: Indiana University Press, 2010), 239.

18. The name that appears on the two published collection of plays is Utoh but has since changed to Utoh-Ezeajugh as can be seen in *Nneora: An African Doll's House* (Awka: Valid Publishing Company, 2005). The other plays are: *Our Wives Have Gone Mad Again and Other Plays* (Awka: Valid Publishing Company, 2001), which contains *Our Wives Have Gone Mad Again, Everyday is for the Thief*, and *Cauldron of Death* and *Who Owns This Coffin? And Other Plays* (Jos: Sweetop Publications, 1999), with *Who Owns this Coffin, The Night of a Thousand Truths*, and *Forest of Palm Trees*. The discourse shall however dwell more on the two title plays.

19. Oyeronke Oyewumi, "Colonizing Bodies and Minds: Gender and Colonialism" in *Postcolonialisms: Anthology of Cultural Theory and Criticism*, eds., Gaurav Desai & Supriya Nair (Oxford: Berg, 2005), 355.

20. I have appropriated and twisted Fanon's position to our advantage here, especially on the reciprocal bases of national culture and the fight for freedom. See especially pages 166-199 of Frantz Fanon, *The Wretched of the Earth*, (Harmondsworth: Penguin, 1967). See also Leila Ahmed's "The Discourse of the Veil" in *Postcolonialisms*, 315-338 which discusses needed reforms especially in Islamic countries.

21. Utoh-Ezeajugh, *Coffin*, 32

22. Ibid, 61.

23. Ibid, 74.

24. Ibid, 63-64.

25. Juliana Makuchi Nfah-Abbenyi, "Toward a Lesbian Continuum? Or Rethinking the Erotic" in *African Literature: An Anthology of Criticism and Theory*, eds., Tejumola Olaniyan & Ato Quayson (Malden, MA: Blackwell, 2007), 746.

26. UNIFEM, 5.

27. Utoh-Ezeajugh, *Coffin*, 65.

28. Utoh-Ezeajugh, *Our Wives*, 31-32.

29. Ibid, 60.

30. Ibid, 62.

31. Iyorwuese Hagher, *Mulkin Mata* (Ibadan: Heinemann, 1991).

32. Utoh-Ezeajugh, *Our Wives*, 77. This is apparently a parody of the Better Life for Rural Women program and the excesses of the women led by First Lady Mrs Maryam Babangida (1985-1993) in Nigeria. The program turned out to be a wasteful ventured as it merely revealed the ostentation of the major actors rather than bettering the lives of the rural women it purported to assist.

33. Ibid, 78.

34. Ibid, 81-84.

35. UNIFEM, 3.

36. See Ameh Dennis Akoh, "Travelling Theory: The Feminism and Womanism of Tess Onwueme," *The Creative Artist: Journal of Theatre and Media Studies* 2, no.1 (2008): 52-67, which explains in details this paradigm shift.

37. Izuu E. Nwankwo, "Tenor of Humanism: Re-Reading Femininity in the Drama of Tracie Utoh-Ezeajugh," *The Creative Artist* 2, no.1 (2008): 170-184. The play exposes further the consequences of parental neglect or overindulgence of children.

Bibliography

Ahmed, Leila. "The Discourse of the Veil." In *Postcolonialisms: An Anthology of Cultural Theory and Criticism*. Edited by Guarav Desai, and Supriya Nair, 315-338. Oxford: Berg, 2005.

Akoh, Ameh Dennis. "Travelling Theory: The Feminism and Womanism of Tess Onwueme." *The Creative Artist: Journal of Theatre and Media Studies* 2, no.1 (2008): 52-67.

Chege, Fatuma. *Young People Constructing Gendered and Sexual Identities: Implications for HIV/Aids in African Contexts*. Cice: Hiroshima University, 2006. Accessed 10 January, 2010. home.hiroshima-u.ac.jp/cice/forum/73pp.pdf.

Convention on the Elimination of All Forms of Discrimination against Women New York, 18 December 1979. Accessed 1 December, 2010. http://www2.ohchr.org/english/law/cedaw.htm.

Cornwall, Andrea. *Readings in Gender in Africa*. Bloomington: Indiana University Press, 2002.

Evwierhoma, Mabel. *Female Empowerment and Dramatic Creativity in Nigeria*. Ibadan: Caltop Publictions, 2002.

Falola, Toyin. *Colonialism and Violence in Nigeria*. Bloomington: Indiana University Press, 2009.

Fanon, Frantz. *The Wretched of the Earth*. Harmondsworth: Penguin, 1967.

Hagher, Iyorwuese. *Mulkin Mata*. Ibadan: Heinemann, 1991.

_______. *Lifetimes*. Kaduna: JVC Press, 1999.

Ingram, David. *Critical Theory and Philosophy*. St. Paul, Minnesota: Paragon, 1990.

"Masculinity and Gender-Based Violence." United Nations Development Fund for Women (UNIFEM) Gender Fact Sheet No.5. Accessed 13 January, 2010. www.unifem-usnc.org/files/MDG%20Fact%20Sheet.pdf.

Nfah-Abbenyi, Juliana Makuchi. "Toward a Lesbian Continuum? Or Rethinking the Erotic." In *African Literature: An Anthology of Criticism and Theory*. Edited by Tejumola Olaniyan, and Ato Quayson, 746-752. Malden, MA: Blackwell, 2007.

Nwankwo, Izuu E. "Tenor of Humanism: Re-Reading Femininity in the Drama of Tracie Utoh-Ezeajugh" *The Creative Artist* 2, no.1 (2008): 170-184. Okoh, Julie. *Edewede*. Owerri: Totan Publishers, 2000.

Oyewumi, Oyeronke. "Colonizing Bodies and Minds: Gender and Colonialism." In *Postcolonialisms: Anthology of Cultural Theory and Criticism*. Edited by Gaurav Desai, and Supriya Nair, 339-361. Oxford: Berg, 2005.

Stanley, Liz. "Should 'Sex' really be 'Gender'– Or 'Gender really be 'Sex'?" In *Gender: A Sociological Reader*. Edited by Stevi Jackson, and Sue Scott, 31-41. London: Routledge, 2002.

Taiwo, Olufemi. *How Colonialism Preempted Modernity in Africa*. Bloomington: Indiana University Press, 2010.

Tuttle, Lisa. *Encyclopedia of Feminism*. Harlow: Longman, 1986.

"UNIFEM takes Action." Accessed 1 December. 2010. http://www.unifem.org/gender_issues/violence_against_women/

Utoh-Ezeajugh, Tracie. *Nneora: An African Doll's House*. Awka: Valid Publishing Company, 2005.

_______. *Our Wives Have Gone Mad Again and Other Plays*. Awka: Valid Publishing Company, 2001.

_______. *Who Owns This Coffin? And Other Plays*. Jos: Sweetop Publications, 1999.

CHAPTER 10

MAURICE AMUTABI'S *BECAUSE OF HONOR:* GENDER RELATIONS AND SOCIAL UPHEAVAL IN EAST AFRICA

Eliza Mary Johannes

Because of Honor by Maurice Nyamanga Amutabi published in 2009 is a fictional novel set in an imaginary village, Chelani, on the coast of East Africa. It focuses on Amina, a young Muslim girl. While it is nonetheless recognizable, there are tensions between the religions of the book, Christianity and Islam on one hand, and on the other hand, the African indigenous belief systems. The author underscores how religion has supported patriarchy and facilitated the constraining of women's lives through social and physical violence. Evidently, they are oblivious of the changes that modern Western education has introduced in society as a way to eradicate some of the violence committed on women in their patriarchal societies. The female characters in the book inhabit complicated but composite social spaces and sites. Women are powerless and are generally marginalized, largely represented against a backdrop of a structured social and cultural terrain, dominated by long-term religious and cultural patriarchies. They are constantly vulnerable to marginalization, compelling them to be in a permanent process of negotiating with the men in their societies. The women appear to lose in their efforts to seek redress. They are in precarious spaces, similar to what Homi has described as "in-between spaces, not moving forward or going back."[1] The perceived "in-between" spaces or points of permanent transition "provide the terrain for elaborating strategies of selfhood, singular or communal" which are represented by the mother-daughter characters of Chiku Babu and Amina Babu in very surreal and tragic ways.

The purpose of this chapter is to interrogate the metaphor of 'honor' and explain how this phenomenon is used to justify violence against women in African societies. I use the characters in the novel such as Bela, Amina, Chiku, and Turudi, to show how the role of these characters dramatically intersect with gender, class, patriarchy, and sexuality in in everyday life and history. In "Because of Honor," the women who disobey or defy 'society' suffer violent and far-reaching consequences which often include death. Such women are frowned upon, secluded, and regarded as social pariahs. In the novel, the male characters like Isa Babu and his son Jumbe use violence to control women's sexuality through socially-sanctioned practices such as female circumcision, vagina-sewing, and forced marriages. The older males impose themselves as guardians of the females as well as younger men in the society. They use rituals and practices that are certainly violent to control the women's bodies and the general physical space they inhabit. They use female circumcision, the veiling system and the restriction of their movement to define and control women's sexuality.

The veil is generally used to conceal the face of the woman from males that are not familiar with the particular female. The essence of this is that women do not have the choice to choose their partners in life. Instead, it is the male relatives who choose husbands for them through marriage arrangement deals that accompany the custom. As for the confinement, the woman is restricted to particular residences, meaning that it is the males who are the chief bread winners of the family that control the physical and psychological spaces which women inhabit. In other words, women's places in society are socially constructed through the use of subtle violence.

Amutabi uses the story of the heroine of the novel, Amina, to provide an escape from the hopeless life she finds herself in while living in the eponymous village of Chelani. He uses Amina to demonstrate the dislocation and relocation from the margin with the objective of facilitating a renegotiation of religious (Islam) and cultural (Swahili) sensitivity of male actions in African societies. Is such an escape possible in reality? Are the acquisition of an education and involvement in political action the only ways through which women can have equal footing with their male counterparts in African societies? In what ways can female agency be enhanced in Africa? How can masculinity be tapped for the good of society without doing violence to women? Is it possible for societies to renegotiate cultural and religious values in order to escape violent relationships? These are some of the questions that this chapter addresses.

The fate of African women is affected by culture, traditions, religion, and family obligations. African women are born into societies in which they are often powerless to change their own realities. They sometimes have no political, social, and economic representation and are often regarded as a burden on family resources when they are unmarried. The African girl child thus is owned from birth until her death. She is a daughter, a sister, and a wife. The cycle is a never ending one as it is passed on from mother to daughter. As such, *Because of Honor* encompasses the Chelani of Kenyan society's inability to protect the girl child from a crime committed by her family against her. In the African male- dominated culture and society, women are often the product of violence. Bela, Turudi, and Amina Babu are a prime example of women in communities that are closed- minded and are not receptive to change even when the change may be for the good of the community at large. In the imaginary Chelani, the body of Bela lay in the center of her parents' compound. Alongside her body was a rope and her father, the speaker of the house, insisted that his daughter "committed suicide" even though the injuries on her body, as Amutabi writes, were inconsistent with the suicide claim. His family and those who came to pay their respects to Bela were unconvinced of the story, yet no one dared to challenge him. Bela was a murder victim, killed by her father and brother, in order to preserve what was perceived to be the maintenance of the family's honor. Bela's fate it seemed had been sealed when she refused to marry a man chosen by her father, belying the fact that masculine control is prevalent. In Chelani, girls who refused to be married off by their parents often were regarded as rebels, girls of shame, and 'spoiled.' She was the first to die of violence of this manner in her community as most families poisoned their daughters who refused to marry the chosen husbands. Bela was rebellious against Chelani norms and as such, was another mouth to feed in her father's house.

Be that as it may, the cultural norms that favor males over females, and economic hardships faced by many African families all contribute to the marginalization of rural African women. The demands of subsistence economies in Africa place enormous burdens on every member of the family, including children. In this regard, African children are often viewed simply as extra hands for herding, farming, and domestic chores. With limited assistance for parents to keep up with domestic and farm responsibilities, mothers and fathers often choose which gender in the family should receive education, and in most cases, the girl child gets deprived of having educational opportunities, remaining at home to assist with domestic chores while the male child enjoys the privileges that modern education has to offer. This is captured very well in *Because of Honor*, when Amina with her mother's help, plans to escape from her rural home in Chelani to Mombasa, stemming from the murder of Bela for not preserving the family honor. It is important to mention that modern western and indigenous value systems work hand in hand to perpetuate the marginalization of the girl child by favoring the boys for educational opportunities.[2]

The relevance of *Because of Honor* to the ongoing gender discrimination is that it calls our attention to it. In addition, parents and teachers also play important roles in determining the beneficiaries of education for empowerment. There is little doubt that they treat females differently from the males. Female students are frequently expected to perform at a lower academic level than their male peers; hence, they are often discouraged from achieving higher levels of academic development. Furthermore, early marriages often take precedence over education. Even when it concerns the choice of courses, the African girl child is often herded towards the softer options, as society utilizes negative stereotypes about them. They are discouraged from taking such courses as math and science on the basis that they will not perform well. However, perhaps the most effective discouragement is the belief that female students will never use such academic skills because they will be married off before completing their primary or secondary school education.[3] Equally the same, society does not expect them to acquire jobs that require such skills. As results girls end in low paying jobs, often do not earn enough to make ends meet. Apart from economic considerations, other factors constrain female participation and success in schools. These conditions include parental attitudes against what a majority of rural families refer to as "the second colonial influence" on their daughters, i.e., is, wanting a life of their own and postponing marriage. Emphasis is placed on having numerous children, as this will provide economic stability for their parents. The amount of time spent in initiation rites and the longing for girls to acquire traditional skills also contributes to the tendency to neglect education.[4] It is with these conditions in mind that Amina thought of escaping from her rural community and the masculine culture that defined rural Chelani.

Putting these questions in a broader context, it is important to note that a girl's education is irrelevant to her extended family because it does not bring wealth to the household, particularly to her father. Paradoxically, for Amina's father, this education was not perceived in such a minimalist context. Similar to the situation of the common families in the region, the dowry that was offered in exchange for a daughter's marriage, was seen to bring immediate wealth to the girl's family, and made her feel valuable to her new community. Girls that are between the ages of 15-25 and are unmarried are considered a burden in their families and communities. They are often regarded solely as another mouth to feed in their father's house. The male child is considered a good investment when equipped with education, because if he succeeds, he is able to assist his parents economically. In reality, it is the male child who drains the family's assets as he requires them in order to create his own family. In this regard, the girl children in Babu's family were also expected to bring in the wealth, yet investing in their education was viewed as a waste of resources.

Most indigenous African communities hold the view that the male child is more helpful than the female. This is what Richard[5] and William[16] summarize as the concept of "culture lag," or "socio-cultural lag," suggesting that a community can develop differentially both socially and culturally. A culture lag takes place when the material part of a culture moves rapidly in advance of the non-material part. This process can also be reversed, whereby the non-material culture is able to move ahead of the material culture. Brinkman and Ogburn provide the example of different groups with certain forms of jobs adequate for women. According to the authors, factors influencing changes in social attitudes can be adjusted as time passes. Cultures change when changes are provided to the recipients, a process that Africans have come to accept. Yet, certain aspects of the culture have changed and consequently, have enhanced the status of both men and women in African societies. The notion that we choose what part of change to embrace is detrimental to our political stability because economic development and social gain require equal participation of all individuals. However, the level of development, i.e., social, political or economic, all require various types of support. As such, education for rural women in Africa requires sustainability from the policy-maker's point of view and the international communities' involvement.

THE ROLE OF RELIGIOUS BELIEFS IN OPPRESSING WOMEN IN KENYA

In Because *of Honor*, the idea of "free woman" conjures negative images as is evident in Babu's family. The women in Chelani have been brought up to believe that a woman should always have a suzerain, that she should be owned by a man, be he her father, uncle, brother or husband. An un-owned woman spells disaster. A woman who is unmarried and goes against the father's will is presumed to be available for the pleasure of all males and is treated as such. The successful single woman who manages her affairs without a man is an affront to patriarchy and a direct challenge to masculinity of men who deem to 'possess' her as Amutabi demonstrates in the case of Amina at the university. Amina is abducted by Islamic fundamentalists with the view of punishing her for adhering to dogmatic Islam. Indeed, a majority of African women are struggling to be free from this requirement/ compulsory attachment to men. Women want the right to be fully human, whether or not they choose to be attached to men. Therefore, liberation for women must occur in the realm of culture and religion. African patriarchal systems often forbid questions of this nature and women who dare to raise such questions are disrespectful to the prevailing social order.

In such heightened debates surrounding the role of women, some Africans are puzzled when Christian women say that it is the will of Christ, if not the church, that women should be free to respond to the fullness that God expects of all human beings. What constitutes this fullness and who determines its dimensions? Women want to search for the truth about human life and how to live it. They want to decide for themselves of what constitutes a liberating life.[7]

Most African women feel that their livelihood is limited to their biological condition while their sons and daughters continue to climb onto "slave ships" leaving the women desolate in an arrangement that uses them as tools. *Because of Honor* recognizes the fact that the situation has continued, rendering the African woman as an onlooker, a peacekeeper, and a subservient human being. Amina's brothers were provided education while the girls remained at home to work for the family. Indeed, the African daughter is expected to be supportive and hide from outsiders their festering wounds. They are supposed to be custodians of all the ancient healing arts and keepers of the secrets that numb pains inflicted by internal aggressors. Women are to pray, sing, and carry the loads. They are expected to tend the wounds from battles which they are not allowed to fight in. Women are only permitted to look on from a distance for their own good. So we stand, shaking loosened wrists in desperation, as we are powerless when watching our brother's flounder. All this is captured adequately in the different chapters of the book.

The book brings to mind the mindless discussions of fruitless five year development plans and multi-party elections that continue to take place, as with quiet desperation the African daughter tries to apply ancient remedies to heal the wounds of the society. The African daughter, standing at the fork in the road, must determine which direction to take as is exemplified by Mama Musa when she tells her during her escape that she divorced her first husband because of ill treatment. And because Mama Musa had not been given sufficient education, she decided to study privately for exams that opened the door for her to apply to a teacher training college. She ended up becoming a primary school teacher. This example gave Amina the assurance that she too could succeed.

THE NEW WOMAN IN AFRICA

One can no longer argue the fact that a majority of Africans are very religious and that few months go by without religious feasts and festivals that cannot be divorced from religious symbols. Any African bonded to culture is a regular visitor to church and religious rituals and priests. Equally, poverty is driving more populations who normally adhered to traditional religion such as pastoral populations to join the church in return for food. As mentioned previously, three religions claim the allegiance of Africans: traditional African religions, Christianity, and Islam. Traditional religion continues to be recognized and remains a major source of meaning as a living religion, but it seems that it is recognized most often when modern religion fails or criticizes the culture in which our brothers are so imbedded. In other words, traditional African religion is often called upon when modernism critiques what benefits the African male. There is no doubt that all three religions form the backbone of African religious life.

In most African countries, the close relationship of religion and culture is visible in educational institutions. Studies in religion are offered in all different levels of education and often are supported by national budgets. Religion has come to be recognized as part of African cultures and religion is included in the humanities curriculum. For the African, God is involved in all aspects of life, including politics and economics and is present in the lives of people from birth to death. If being religious is attested to by an individual's persistent presence in church, the argument cannot be made against the African woman as she is often more religious than the African male.

The role of religion in the life of the African woman gives rise to many unanswered questions. Does a woman's modern role as a church-founder give her an entry into political power? What is the effect of her exclusion from certain types of religious enclaves? What is the relationship between religion and psychology for an African woman? Perhaps it is my bi-national living experience rather than dual citizenship, as well as the intellectual nature of my studies in women and gender studies that point me to these missing questions.

Religion in Africa as elsewhere has a variety of manifestations. World religious like Christianity and Islam claim many adherents and by in large, they have become dominant religious factors in African people's lives. But it must never be forgotten that indigenous culture and religion are so significant within African life that neither Muslim nor Christian in Africa can be totally free of the values that emanate from the traditional African religions. There are, and this too must not be overlooked, large and critically influential sectors of African communities that remain faithful adherents to the religion of their ancestors. Often these persons operate entirely outside western parameters and usually ignore the attempted standardization of national laws. A good example of such communities include the Turkana of Kenya.

The African woman must be viewed as being under the pervasive value system of these three religions: African, Christian, and Islamic and the (male) adherents of one or the other. Few persons in Africa whether male or female, declare themselves free thinkers, agnostics, or atheists. As such, we are dealing with the experiences of women living in communities that take religion seriously, women who admit the influence of religion on their world view and consequently on their ways of life.

It is often argued that traditional African religions and cultures afford adequate and requisite participation for women. This ignores the fact that women's common experience in Africa is that by the time a woman has spent her energies struggling to be heard, she has barely the energy left to say what she wanted in the first place. It is true that women close to royal thrones were formidable powers and may still be. However, one also ought to hear the women who warn us against basking in the glory of "old shells," retained to govern social relationships when the material causes that gave rise to those structures are no more or are fast fading. The "our women are not oppressed" statement is ideological and emanates from Africa. It seeks to render feminism a non-issue to Africa.

WOMEN'S BONDAGE TO RELIGION AND CULTURE

In many societies in Africa, women often pay for follies of their African brothers. It seems that women in male-domineering societies are left with few alternatives in their relationships with men. In order for women to defeat men in a non-physical way, it would entail utilizing the power of magic or witchcraft. When African women are not allowed to use physical means to challenge men's oppression, men often live with the fear that women will use mystical powers to avenge themselves. Men kill, beat, rape and enslave women, yet it is women's silence that bothers then most, leading them to fear imaginary, female aggressiveness. On the continent, the more silent a woman is, the more her society accuses her of witchcraft. There is an East African saying that women should be feared, a slogan often found on public transportation; this speaks to a psychological conflict between the African woman and the male. Resistance to violence— rape, beating, and other forms of abuse – by a woman often confirms to her society that she is abnormal, that is, a witch.

CONCLUSION

African women have started to question the mystery of the African male's secret society. No African should close his/her eyes and lips in the 21st century. Denouncing injustice is a necessary action that would lead to the healing of the whole community which we are designed to be in charge of, for which women are the caretakers of the generations. Women have to mediate the sense of urgency to share the power and mysteries of life without resorting to violence. If they do not do so, they lose their important roles as the communicators of life. African women need to challenge the traditions that exclude them from the art of foretelling and from economic, political and social representation, if indeed they abide by African traditions, folktales, and myths. Their readings of the lives of gods and goddesses would allow them to participate in all public life and seek wisdom according to their ability and inculcation. The African myths that emphasize reciprocity between women and men recall efforts to transform the relationships between women and men. Reciprocity in hospitality, for example, challenges the assumption that men have no service to render to women. Indeed, with each action, men or women remain whole and the relationship is one of interaction for mutual benefit. There must be positive relationships between African men and women, a relationship Africa has yet to recognize and achieve.

If we do not know where we are going, at least we know where we are coming from. Our past provides examples of ways in which women can be supported and positively affirmed. Traditional society worked for African women through networking of friends, wives, women selling similar commodities, or through the exchange of skills such as pottery, weaving, and beadwork. The African women carried on their work, in addition to having children, assuming their marital roles, and attending funerals. Women supported each other across different regions and worked for the common good of all. The question today is whether it is possible to adapt these traditions today in the modern era? Amutabi's *Because of Honor* seems to suggest that this process of collaboration among women for security from their own communities is impossible because loyalty to traditions is too embedded in their history and culture.

Notes

1. H. K. Bhabha, *The Location of Culture* (London: Routledge, 1994).
2. See Sifuna and Chege. *Girls' and Women's Education in Kenya: Gender Perspectives and Trends*. Nairobi : Unesco, 2006.
3. In her book, *Women's agency and educational policy: the experiences of the women of Kilome-Kenya, Ndunda* discuss how chaos and dowry limit the education a girl receives. (Ottawa: National Library of Canada, 1996).
4. While Ndunda discusses the limits of access to education for the girl child, Hyde argues that rituals and traditions play a role in parents neglect to aid further a daughter's education (Washington, DC: Education and Employment Division, 1989).
5. R.L. Brinkman, "Cultural Lag: Conception and Theory," *International Journal of Social Economics* 24(6): 609-627.
6. W.F. Ogburn, *On Culture and Social Change*, edited by O.D. Duncan (Chicago: University of Chicago press, 1957).
7. See Sharon Welch's discussion of liberation theology and the politics of truth in chapter 2 of her book, *Communities of Resistance and Solidarity: A Feminist Theology of of Liberation* (Maryknoll: Orbis Books, 1985).

Bibliography

Karin A. L Hyde. *Improving Women's Education in Sub-Saharan Africa: A Review of The Literature.* Washington, DC: Education and Employment Division, 1989.

Becher, Jeanne. *Women, Religion, and Sexuality: Studies on the Impact of Religious Teachings on Women.* Philadelphia: Trinity Press International, 1991.

Mercy, O. *Daughters of Anowa: African Women and Patriarchy.* New York: Orbis Books, 2005.

Kiluva-Ndunda, Mutindi Mumbua. *Women's agency and educational policy: the experiences of the women of Kilome, Kenya.* Albany: State University of New York Press, 2001.

Sharon, W. *Communities of Resistance and Solidarity: A Feminist Theology of Liberation.* Maryknoll: Orbis Book, 1985.

Sifuna, Daniel N. and Fatuma, N. *Girls' and Women's Education in Kenya: Gender Perspectives and Trends.* Nairobi: UNESCO, 2006.

Part Three

GENDER, LAW, SEXUALITY, AND RELIGION

GENDER EQUALITY AND CUSTOMARY LAW IN SOUTH AFRICA

Celumusa Zungu

INTRODUCTION

The right to participate in the cultural life of one's choice is guaranteed in the 1996 constitution of the Republic of South Africa.[1] As the right to culture is embodied in the Republic of South Africa's supreme law of the country, the state is obliged to respect, protect, and promote that right.[2] The entrenchment of the right to culture, the recognition of customary laws, and recognition of certain customary institutions and traditional leadership in the post-1994 constitution of the Republic of South Africa has resulted in questions being raised about South Africa's commitment to gender equality in customary law.[3] This is because customary law has been viewed as being "systematically discriminatory" against women.[4]

At the time of constitutional negotiations that gave birth to the new constitutional order founded on amongst other things, human dignity, equality, and the advancement of human rights and freedoms, women under customary law in South Africa had no contractual capacity.

They were subjected to guardianship of their fathers that passed on to their husbands once they got married.[5] They could not own or inherit property. Neither could they be appointed as chiefs. This is viewed as being the cause of the double jeopardy that South African women faced. They were not only treated as inferior, but these practices also contributed to women's loss of economic power. The baggage carried by customary laws and some cultural values and practices appears to contradict South Africa's national agenda for the creation of a non-racist and non-sexist society.

South Africa has signed some international instruments aimed at promoting gender equality. It is a party to a Convention on the Elimination of All Forms of Discrimination Against Women.[6] Therefore it must, in terms of the Convention, eliminate gender based discrimination.[7] South Africa is also a signatory to the Protocol to the African Charter on the Rights of Women in Africa which requires states to modify the social and cultural patterns of conduct of women and men, with a view of achieving the elimination of harmful cultural and traditional practices.[8]

The traditional leaders in South Africa appear to have been aware of the problematic situation of placing competing interests between customary laws and the right to culture in the constitution advocating gender equality. At the time of negotiating the content of the Bill of Rights before the provisions of the constitution were documented, traditional leaders tried in vain to have customary laws and the right to culture exempted from the application of equality clause contained in the constitution.[9]

This chapter, therefore, aims to evaluate the approach adopted by South African courts when dealing with the clash between discriminatory customary laws and the right to gender equality. This is done through an analysis of judicial reasoning as it appears in case law. An argument by some writers that customary law can be effectively transformed through evolutionary processes rather than through judicial interference and promulgation of rigid laws will be examined in the light of the extent to which litigation has succeeded in transforming customs and making them compatible with democratic values of gender equality. Finally, it will be argued that South Africa is still far from achieving gender equality in the sphere of customary law.

THE BILL OF RIGHTS, CUSTOMARY LAW, AND THE CONSTITUTION

Right to equality is highly valued in South Africa.[10] It is, like the right to culture, contained in the Bill of Rights that is the cornerstone of democracy in South Africa.[11] Its significance in the post- apartheid era in South Africa is evidenced in the preamble of the constitution itself and also that of the Equality Act.[12] Even though the right to culture is not as detailed as the right to equality is, right to culture is also important in South Africa.[13] It is also universally recognized. Article 27 of the International Covenant on Civil and Political Rights provides that:

> In those states in which ethnic, religious or linguistic minority exist, persons belonging to such minorities shall not be denied the right, in the community with the other members of their group, to enjoy their own culture, to profess and practice their own religion, or to use their own language.

Article 17 of the African Charter on Human and Peoples Rights provides that every individual may freely take part in the cultural life of his/her community. It further states that the promotion and protection of moral and traditional values recognized by the community shall be the duty of the state. Article 22 further expands this idea and states:

> All people have the right to their economic, social and cultural development with due regard to their freedom and identity and in equal enjoyment of the common heritage of mankind.

The Universal Declaration of Human Rights also recognizes the importance of a right to culture.[14] Besides the international instruments, the constitution of the Republic of South Africa is committed to the protection and development of culture as section 185 of the constitution established The Commission for the Promotion and Protection of Rights of Cultural, Religious and Linguistic Communities which is aimed at promoting respect for cultural rights.

Right to culture and the right to equality are like all other rights, not absolute. They may be infringed only in a constitutionally permissible manner. Application of customary law may also be limited by the constitution as it must only be applied if it is not offending the provisions of the constitution. The conflict between the customary laws, cultural values, and gender equality has resulted in litigation wherein appropriate relief or declaration of rights has been sought from competent courts who are then tasked with deciding on the rights that need to prevail.[15]

THE COURTS, THE LIMITATION OF CONSTITUTIONAL RIGHTS AND CASE LAW

The judicial authority of the Republic of South Africa is vested in the courts and when interpreting the Bill of Rights, the courts must promote the object and the spirit of the constitution.[16] The courts also need to consider the provisions of section 36 of the constitution when deciding whether a customary law provision impacting negatively on women constitutes a justifiable limitation to the right to gender equality. This section provides that a fundamental right may be limited in terms of general application to the extent that the limitation is reasonable and justifiable in an open and democratic society based on human dignity, equality and freedom, taking into account all relevant factors including the nature of the right, the importance of the purpose of the limitation, the nature and extent of the limitation, the relation between the limitation and the purpose and less restrictive means to achieve the purpose.

A number of the landmark judgments have emerged in the constitutional court in South Africa where the court had to ascertain if discriminatory cultural practices and customary laws can, in terms of section 36 of the constitution, limit the right to gender equality. These cases deal with a variety of discriminatory customary laws and practices which include proprietary consequences of the divorce under customary law versus the right to gender equality; the right to inherit under customary law versus the right to equality; the right to be appointed as an executor versus the equality clause and the right to be appointed as chief under customary law in the light of the constitution.

PROPRIETARY CONSEQUENCES OF A DIVORCE UNDER CUSTOMARY LAW: *Gumede versus the President of South Africa*[17]

Under customary law, the husband has sole control over family property.[18] Consequently, if the marriage is dissolved, the wife is not entitled to any property. This is contrary to the right to equality as embedded in the constitution of the Republic of South Africa. The first post-1994 court case brought to court to test the constitutionality of a customary law provision relating to the proprietary consequences of the dissolution of a customary marriage (divorce) was that of *Gumede versus The President of the Republic of South Africa*. This case also brought under spotlight the issues of ownership of property as well as control over family property even during the subsistence of a customary marriage.

The facts of the case are that Mrs. Gumede entered into a customary marriage with her husband in 1968. Since the inception of that customary marriage, she was never employed. Her husband forbade her from seeking employment. She remained a primary care giver to their children. After more than 30 years of marriage, her husband instituted divorce proceedings, wanting to terminate the customary marriage. At the time, she was an old aged pensioner living on government pension as her husband had stopped supporting her. Because she had been married in terms of the customary law, the proprietary consequences of their divorce was subjected to customary law stipulating amongst other things that a man is the head of the family and also the owner of all property in the family home. This meant that Mrs. Gumede was to receive nothing at the time of the divorce as her husband was, in terms of the customary law, entitled to all property. Before a divorce was granted, she approached the High Court seeking an order declaring the proprietary consequences of her divorce as being unfairly discriminatory to women married under customary law.

In approaching the case, the court firstly ascertained if indeed there was discrimination. The answer was in affirmative. As this discrimination was based on gender, it was presumed to be automatically unfair. The government had to seek justification for the existence of that law. The court found that there was no justification for the customary law. It held that the customary law provisions under attack "strikes at the very heart of the protection of equality and dignity our constitution affords to all and to women in particular."[19] It was further held that that the marital property system under customary law in question "renders women extremely vulnerable by not only denuding them of their dignity but also rendering them poor and dependent."[20] The court proceeded and declared invalid the following legislative provisions that regulated the proprietary consequences of a customary marriage: Section 7(1) of the Recognition of Customary Marriages Act. This Act provided that proprietary consequences of a customary marriage entered into before the commencement of the Recognition of Act continue to be governed by the customary law.

- Section 20 of the Natal Code of the Zulu Law provides that the head of the family is the owner of and has control over property in the family home.
- Section 22 of the Natal Code of Zulu law provides that the members of the family are under the control of and owe obedience to the head of the family, who at all times were men.

It was further declared that all women married under monogamous customary marriage entered into before the recognition of Customary Marriages Act came into operation were deemed to be in community of property, except those terminated by death or divorce prior to the judgment in this case. The Judge remarked that "the case underlines the stubborn persistence of patriarchy and conversely, the vulnerability of women during and upon termination of customary marriage. At another level, the case poses intricate questions about the relative space occupied by pluralist legal systems under the umbrella of one supreme law, which lays down a common normative platform."[21] Even though this may be considered as a victory for women married under customary law, those that are married in polygamous, customary marriage are not protected as their marriages are not deemed to be automatically in community of property.

THE RIGHT TO OCCUPY PUBLIC OFFICE UNDER CUSTOMARY LAW: *Shilubana versus Nwamitwa*[22]

This case tested the constitutionality of customs or practices used to decide on the issue of ascending to traditional leadership in some traditional communities in South Africa.

In terms of the customary law, a women may not hold a political office.[23] Only men can be appointed as chiefs. This gender-based discrimination, competing with the constitutionally entrenched right to equality was under scrutiny in the case of *Nwamitwa versus Shilubane* brought to the Constitutional Court in the post-1994 constitutional reform period in South Africa. In this case, Ms. Shilubane's father who was a chief passed away in 1968. As a female, custom did not allow Ms. Shilubane to take over the chieftainship. The brother of her deceased father, Richard, then took over the throne as Ms. Shilubane's father, who was deceased by then, had no male heir. When Richard passed away, his son, Sidweel Nwanita, wanted to succeed to the throne and become a chief. Ms. Shilubane then approached the court for relief as she wanted to get the chieftainship that was not given to her in 1968 when her father passed away. In court, a representative from the Xitsonga traditional leadership testified that it was a taboo for a woman to be a Chief and moreover, that Ms. Tinyiko Shilubane, maintained she was married to the Shilubane clan and if she were made a Chief, the succession would be difficult because her children are Shilubane and not Nwamitwa.

The constitutional court ruled in Ms Shilubane's favor, stating inter alia that any custom that discriminates against women is contrary to the right to equality enshrined in the constitution. The right to culture, the court held, must conform to the spirit of the constitution. The court further stated that the customary law must be developed so that it can conform to the spirit of the constitution. However, the court stated that the ruling in this case did not indicate that all women previously denied ascendancy to the throne were then automatically entitled to traditional leadership.

THE RIGHT TO INHERITANCE UNDER CUSTOMARY LAW: *Bhe and Others Versus the Magistrate, Khayelitsha*[24]

This case dealt with the issue of the constitutionality of the law that governed the administration of the estate of Black people that had died interstate. The Intestate Succession Act dealt with estates from other population groups other than Blacks. The Black Administration Act 38 of 1927 encoded customary law of succession. It thus dealt with estates of black people except those married under civil law. In terms of the Act, women were excluded from inheriting property under customary law. The advent of the constitutional democracy committed to promotion of gender equality in 1994, clashed with the customary law of primogeniture regarding intestate succession. The cases of *Bhe and others versus the Magistrate Khayelitsha* was the test case that challenged the constitutionality of intestate succession under customary law governed by the Provisions Black Administration Act, 32 of 1927.

In the Bhe Case, the Applicant Bhe, who was the mother of two daughters of her deceased husband. Prior to his death, she was staying with the deceased and their children. After her husband died, Ms. Bhe and her children were not appointed as heirs to the estate of the deceased. The reason was that they were females. The property in the estate of the deceased included informal housing and building material for the house. Ms Bhe had bought the material before the death of her husband. The father of the deceased was then appointed as the only heir to the estate which included the house occupied by Bhe. When he wanted to sell the property, Bhe approached the court regarding the exclusion of her daughters from inheriting the estate of their father. She argued that her exclusion was unconstitutional as it was gender-based. She wanted her daughters to be appointed as heirs.

The court ruled in her favour, arguing that the practice or custom providing that only male heirs can inherit was contrary to the right to equality under the constitution of the Republic of South Africa. This case was consolidated with the case of *Shibe v Sthole and Others*[25] which also came before the court, attacking the customary law prohibiting women from inheriting. Ms. Shibe's brother had died intestate. Ms. Shibe was the only surviving sibling of her deceased brother who was not married and did not have children. The Black Administration Act prohibited her from inheriting. The reason for exclusion was that she was a woman. The estate was, therefore, to be inherited by her male cousins in terms of the customary law. She approached the court, contending the customary rule was unfairly discriminatory and denied the right to equality. The court ruled in her favor.

In reaching its decision, the court scrutinized the rationale behind the existence of the custom and described it as a set of rules:

> designed to preserve the cohesion and stability of the extended family unit and ultimately the entire community....The heir did not merely succeed to the assets of the deceased; succession was not primary concerned with the distribution of the estate of the deceased, but the preservation and perpetuation of the family unit. Property was collectively owned and the family head was the nominal owner of the property, administered it for the benefit of the family unit as a whole. The heir stepped into the shoes

of the family head and acquired all the rights and became subjected to all the obligations of the family head.[26]

Therefore, it was observed that circumstances of today do not always make it possible for the people of the same household to live together and share the same property. Therefore, the customary law had not been adapted to the conditions of the society in the new era.

From the foregoing case, South African courts have been proactive in striking down customary laws that offend gender equality. Constitutional law jurisprudence so far does indicates than in all cases dealing with the clash between customary law and gender equality, the equality clause has prevailed. However, there is a view that the constitutional guaranteeing of equal rights alone will not emancipate women from oppression. Zethembe Mpungose argues that oppression of women is sustained by certain social institutions such as marriage, motherhood etc.[27] Writing on customary law in South Africa, Thomas Bennet also maintains that patriarchal societies are still remarkably common. Zethembe Mpungose further states some cultures ensure that women as early as childhood grow up with a subordinate mentality.[28] An argument that women's own mentality is also a cause for not vigorously attacking some customs holds water more especially when observance of some customs signifying the patriarchal nature is considered.

WOMEN AND CULTURAL PRACTICES

Some cultural values and practices impacting on women are discussed briefly below:

Ukungena custom

Ukungena is defined as a process wherein a man inherits his brother's wife.[29] On a report submitted to the Minister of Justice in South Africa on April 2004, Madam Justice Yvonne Mokgoro defines ukungena as a union with a widow undertaken on behalf of her deceased husband by male relatives to raise a male heir or to increase the nominal offspring of a deceased.[30] The definition manifests a view that in terms of the custom, a woman is like a property that can be transferred from one person to another without a woman's consent. Twenty rural women affected by this custom appear to have accepted it because of fear that no one within their families will provide for them after the death of their husbands.[31]

More than half of the women interviewed held that the custom of ukungena is useful to them as men provide some form of security and support if there are disputes. They made a particular example of the functioning of traditional courts wherein a women must be represented by a man. They feel that men that listen to disputes take seriously the concerns raised by women.

Ukuhlola Custom

The Ukuhlola custom is commonly known as the virginity-testing custom. Virginity tests are performed by old women. The testing is done by inspecting the genitals of girls to ascertain if they have had sexual encounters.[32] In South Africa, the prevalence of this custom is in the areas of Msinga and Pietermaritzburg. Lobola cattle or money paid to the parents of a bride prior to onset of a customary marriage being solemnized in traditional way, is said to have been the reasoning behind the existence of this custom. More lobola was paid if a girl was a virgin. If a girl is found not to be a virgin after marriage, the husband is entitled to claim back part of lobola. [33]This is a form of gender inequality as it is only women who are subjected to this testing. Some women are of the view that the ukuhlola custom must be maintained. Nomagugu Ngobese who is a sex educator has trained a large number of women to perform the testing. In her opinion, the custom must be retained. She states: "Human Rights are individual rights, which is not the way for us."[34]

The Ukuthwala Custom

This custom forces a girl to become somebody's wife whether she likes it or not. With only three months into the year 2009 alone, 89 young girls had to run away from home after being forced to marry old men in Kwa Cele in Lusikisiki, Pondoland South Africa.[35]

The Head master of Zwelibongile High school gave information that a 14 year old girl from his school was abducted by 5 men who wanted her to marry another man.

The proponents of the custom are of the view that they are merely following their forefather's actions. Some of young girls subjected to the ukuthwala custom are as young as 12 years of age. They are forced to leave schools and marry old men. This is contrary to section 29 of the constitution which provides that everyone has a right to basic education. According to the newspaper article, some of the men that marry young girls are believed to be HIV positive. This is allegedly done in some parts of the Eastern Cape Province, South Africa, and is done under ukuthwala custom.[36] The view is that this custom still perpetuates gender inequality and treatment of women as objects. Although the ukungena and ukuthwala customs are contrary to the right to gender equality, currently there is no case law showing that these customs have previously been tested in a court of law for their constitutionality under current dispensation.

REPUBLIC OF SOUTH AFRICA AND GENDER EQUALITY

In spite of some customary laws seriously hindering progress towards realization of gender equality, the provisions of the constitution have resulted in some progress being made. In her Report during a discussion with Napalese government on drafting a gender sensitive constitution and transitional justice process in Pretoria on November 28, The Minister of the Presidency revealed that South Africa was ranked 7th worldwide in terms of representation of women in the legislature. On October 27, 2009 The World Economic Forum's Global Gender Gap ranked South Africa number 6 on the rankings of the countries where women face the least discrimination. Almost half of Cabinet Ministers in the Parliament in South Africa are women. This was not the position in the past.

CONCLUSION

Case law jurisprudence from the South African constitutional court case reveals that the right to gender equality usually prevails when it competes with discriminatory customary laws. However, the fact that customs like ukutwala, ukungena, and ukuhlola have not been eliminated and are still practiced shows that there is still a lot that must be done to achieve gender equality in the rural areas. Therefore, eradicating discriminatory practices in the rural areas is still a challenge, particularly if women are not complaining. The legal system and courts can often be powerless in these circumstances. Illiteracy and poor socio-economic conditions continue to be the contributing factors towards women's subservice, leading to the violation of their rights. Educating women and making them more independent may contribute to the elimination of inequalities. Catherine Albertyn maintains that the use of the constitution as a means to affect social change has been limited to individual organizations and alliances only.[37] Nomthandazo Ntlama is of the similar view as she states that women living in traditional and tribal systems have a limited ability to participate in social change litigation. They are unable to exercise their legal rights. Complicated court processes also perpetuate the problems of the illiterate citizens and those who live under poor socio- economic conditions.[38]

Notes

1.   Section 30 of the constitution of the Republic of South Africa, Act 108 of 1996 provides that everyone has the right to the use of the language and to participate in the cultural life of their choice, but no one exercising these rights may do so in a manner inconsistent with any provision of the Bill of Rights.

2.   Section 2 and section 7 of the constitution.

3.   Section 211 of the constitution of the Republic of South Africa recognizes the institution, status, and the role of traditional leadership according to the customary law and the courts are, under subsection 3, obliged to apply customary law when that Law is applicable but subject to the constitution.

4.   Victoria Bronstein, "Reconceptualising the customary law debate in South Africa; (1998) *South African Journal of Human Rights* 388, p. 392.

5.   Ibid, 390.

6.   The convention prohibits all forms of gender based discrimination.

7.   Adopted 18 December 1979,G.A.Res,34/180,U.N. GAOR,34th Session., Supp.NO.46, U.N.Doc.A/34/46 (1980).

8.   It was signed by South Africa on January 2000 and is available on www.africa-union.org.

9.   Felicity Kaganas and Christinah Murray, "The Contest Between Culture and Gender Equality under South Africa's Interim Constitution"(1994) 21FSL 409.

10. It is a founding value in the constitution and shows a change from the apartheid era wherein discrimination was legalized. Section 1 of the constitution states that The Republic of South Africa is a democratic state founded on human dignity, achievement of equality and advancement of human rights and freedoms, non-racist and non-sexist.

11. Section 7 of the constitution.

12. The preamble to the constitution which is on page 1 indicates that the injustices of the past are recognized and the constitution is adopted to heal such divisions and lay a foundation for the development of a democratic and open society in which the government is based on the will of people and every citizen is equally protected by the law. Promotion of Equality and The Prevention of Unfair Discrimination Act 4 of 2004 also acknowledges the past inequalities and its objective is to give effect to the rights to equality.

13. It is guaranteed in the constitution and as a constitutional right, the obligations it imposes must be fulfilled in accordance with section 2 of the constitution.

14. Article 22 of the Universal Declaration of Human Rights provides that "Everyone, as a member of society ... is entitled to realization of the economic and, social and cultural rights indispensable for his/her dignity and the free development of the personality."

15. Sections 167 to 170 of the constitution.

16. Section 39 of the constitution.

17. Gumede versus The President of the Republic of South Africa and Others 2009 (2) BCLR 243(CC). Judgment delivered by the constitutional court on December 11, 2008.

18. Thomas Bennett, *Customary Law in South Africa* (Juta and Company Ltd, Lansdowne 2007), 263.

19. Gumede versus President of the Republic of South Africa and Others 2009 (3) BCLR 243 paragraph 36.

20. Ibid paragraph 36.

21. Ibid paragraph 1.

22. Shilubana versus Nwamwitwa 2009 (2) SA 66 (CC).

23. Thomas Bennett, *Customary Law in South Africa* (Juta and Company ltd Lansdowne, 2007), 121.

24. Bhe and Others versus Magistrate, Khayelitsha 2005(1) BCLR 1 (CC).

25. *Ibid.* Judgement delivered by the Constitutional Court on October 15, 2004.

26. *Ibid* at paragraph 1.

27. Zethembe Mpungose, *"Perceived Gender Inequality Reflected in Zulu Proverbs: A Feminism Approach:"* 21 (Faculty of Humanities, Development and Social Sciences, University of Kwa Zulu Natal, February 2010) 21. Also available at *http://researchspace.ukzn.ac.za*.or *http://hdl.handle.net/10413/1515* posted on October 28, 2010.

28. *Ibid at page 23.*

29. Daily dispatch online journal dated February 09, 2010, "Old values protect the weak"http//www.dispatch .co.za/article.aspx?id=379052.

30. South African law reform commission project 90 Report submitted in terms of section 7(1) of Act 19 of 1973).

31. All of the women interviewed are from Msinga area which is a rural area in Kwa Zulu Natal Province, South Africa. Twelve of them are illiterate. The remaining 8 -left school prior to reaching grade 6.

32. Medical News Today September 30, 2008: *Virginity Testing Puts South African Gorvernment,at odds.* available on www.medicalnewstoday.com.articles/123522.

33. Charles, Dlamini *"A Juridical Analysis and Critical Evaluation of Ilobolo in a changing Zulu Society"* at page 231 1983 unpublished LLD thesis University of Zululand,Empangeni.

34. Medical News Today September 30, 2008 available on www.medicalnewstoday.com.articles/123522.

35. *Daily Sun Newspaper,* March 2009.

36. Khan Ndjamena, "Schoolgirls being forced into early marriage in Transkei," *The Herald Newspaper,* December 02, 2009.

37. Catherine Albertyn, *"Defending and Securing Rights through Law: Feminism, Law and Courts in South Africa "* Politikon, (November 2005): 219.

38. Nomthandazo Ntlama, " *Equality: A Tool for Social Change in Promoting Gender Equality,"* a paper presented at the Conference of the Law Society of the Northern Provinces. *Available online www.saifac.org.za.*

Bibliography

Albertyn, Catherine, "Defending and Securing Rights through Law: Feminism, Law and Courts in South Africa," *Politokon* (November 2005): 219.

Bennett, Thomas. *Customary Law in South Africa.* Juta and Company: Lansdowne.

Bhe and Others versus The Magistrate, Khayelitsha 2005 (1) BCLR I (CC);

Bronstein, Victoria Bronstein, "Reconceptualising the Customary Law Debate in South Africa." South African Journal of Human Rights (1988):388.

Daily Dispatch On line Journal February 09,2010 " Old Values Protect the Weak". www.Dispatch.co.za/Article.aspx?id=37052

Daily Sun, March 2009.

Dlamini, Charles. "A Juridical Analysis and Critical Evaluation of Ilobolo in a Changing Zulu Society 1983. Unpublished LLD Thesis," University of Zululand Empangeni.

Gumede versus The President of the Republic of South Africa and Others 2009 (3) BCLR 243 (CC), Case number 50/08.

Kaganas, Felicity and Christinah Murray, "The Contest between Culture and Gender equality under South Africa's Interim Constitution" (1994): 21 FSL 409.

Medical News Today, September 2008.Available on http://www.medicalnewstoday.com.articles /123522.

Ntlama Nomthandazo, "Equality: A Tool for Social Change in Promoting Gender," a paper presented at the Conference of the Law Society of the Northern Provinces. *Available online www.saifac.org.za*

Nwamitwa versus Shilubane 2009(2) SA 66;

Shibe Versus Sthole and Others 2005(1) BCLR 1 (CC).

The Constitution of the Republic of South Africa Act No 108 of 1996

The Herald Newspaper December 02, 2009.

The Promotion of Equality and Prevention of Unfair Discrimination Act No 4 of 2000.

The Recognition of Customary Marriages Act No 120 of 1998.

The Black Administration Act 38 of 1927.

The Kwa Zulu Natal Code of Zulu Law.

The Intestate Succession Act No. 81 of 1987.

The Convention on The Elimination of Discrimination Against Women.

The Protocol to the African Charter on the Rights of Women in Africa.

The African Charter on Human and People's Rights.

The International Covenant on Civil and Political Rights.

The Universal Declaration of Human Rights.

POLITICS AND SEXUALITY IN NORTHERN NIGERIA IN THE SECOND HALF OF THE TWENTIETH CENTURY

J.M. Ayuba

INTRODUCTION

The re-introduction of *shari'a* law in 1999 in some parts of northern Nigeria, has forcefully brought the issue of gender and sexuality in the region to international attention. *'yan daudu"* (Hausa homosexuals) are considered to be a social problem and their activities sinful and evil by some Muslims in the region. Conservative religious and political leaders periodically condemn them as purveyors of sexual immorality and tacitly encourage their abusive treatment, including arrest, extortion and physical violence by government-backed vigilantes and law enforcement agents. The aim of this chapter is to contribute to the debate on gender and sexuality in northern Nigeria. It will be argued that the introduction of *Shar'ia* law in some parts of northern Nigeria has had a negative impact on the social and economic survival of homosexuals in the region. This chapter does not attempt to present a comprehensive overview of sexuality in northern Nigeria. Instead, it will analyze how the issue of sexuality emerged from obscurity to become a prominent issue in the late nineteenth and early twentieth centuries in northern Nigeria and will therefore bridge the gap that exists in the historiography of *'yan daudu"* in the region. This chapter will also highlight some of the challenges and stigmitization that homosexuals experience in northern Nigeria under the *Shar'ia* law.

AN OVERVIEW OF NORTHERN NIGERIA

Until recently, northern Nigeria was considered to be the heartland of Hausaland with culturally homogeneous groups that are politically conservative and devoted to Islamic tradition that dictates appropriate gender roles and sexual morality. Although the Hausa language is spoken widely in the region and the local people share similar cultural practices, there are some groups, especially in the north-central area of the region for whom the influence of Islam is limited. Since the sixteenth century, the Hausa states have been decisive factors in the cultural, economic and political history of central West Africa. For centuries, the Hausa-speaking city-states were engaged in the Trans-Saharan trade beyond West Africa, stretching to North Africa and the Middle East. Thus, the Hausa city states emerged as southern terminals of the Tran-Saharan caravan trade. With the increase in trade relationships over time, Muslim traders began to settle along some of the trading routes and gradually began to influence the local people. Thus, by the ninth century A.D. Islam began to make an inroad into Hausa land. An increasing numbers of Hausa-speakers themselves began to be converted to Islam. It would be safe to assert that the trade probably influenced political and religious development as ideas from the Middle East and North Africa made their way south to the cities. The Hausa city states emerged out of a number of small communities, typically surrounded by stockades, enclosing not only houses but also agricultural lands. Kano became the largest and most prosperous of the city states by the late fourteenth and early fifteenth centuries and Arab and Berber traders resided in the city along with local merchants. It also became the leading centre for Islamic culture in the region. Eventually these various communities coalesced to form larger groups, which in turn acquired the size and status of city-states.[1] The process of conversion of the local people to Islam, as noted earlier, gradually progressed to the royal courts and Islam was adopted as the official state religion by the *masun sarauta* (ruling classes). Despite the adoption of Islam as a state religion by the Hausa ruling classes, local religions like the *bori* spirit possession movement continued to be a part of religious lives of the people. In other words, before the jihad in the nineteenth century, the number of individuals who accepted Islam was small, and those who did, usually practiced it along with traditional Hausa religious beliefs. As Stephen Pearce observed, "Muslim rulers negotiated a metaphysical minefield, depending on legitimation from and the protection of indigenous gods even while also maintaining allegiance to a religion for which such accommodation was anathema."[2] The religious syncretism in Hausaland led to a reform movement that began in Gobir in 1804 under the leadership of Usman Dan Fodio. The origin of the Sokoto jihad has been sufficiently dealt with by scholars and only needs mentioning here briefly.[3] Central to the emergence of the reform movement were the political, economic, religious, and social conditions in Hausaland in the eighteenth and early nineteenth centuries. There was a general dissatisfaction with the Hausa governments of the day as corruption and oppression were common. Although various grievances were political and economic in nature, they were articulated in religious terms. For example, the *jangali* (cattle tax) and other levies on the Fulani herdsmen and their political marginalization were some of the political and economic reasons that contributed to the outbreak of the jihad. The jihad led to the formation of the Sokoto Caliphate, which was a loose confederation of emirates that recognised the leadership of Usman Dan Fodio as "Commander of the Faithful." By the mid-nineteenth century, there were about 30 emirates and sub-emirates linked to Sokoto. One of the immediate consequences of the jihad was the change in the rulers' title from *Sarki* (king), to emir, signalling the dawn of a new Islamic era. In other words, the rule of emirs replaced the secular Hausa regimes. The jihad also led to the introduction of an orthodox form of Islam, which was hostile to women's presence in public life and against local religions like the *bori* cult. It is important to mention that before the jihad, women played an important role in the history of the northern parts of Nigeria and there were instances of some of them being appointed to important public roles. For example, Queen Amina who ruled Zaria in the sixteenth century extended the frontiers of her kingdom and subdued some of the Hausa states. However, the role of women after the jihad in some parts of Hausaland began to wane and their public roles, titles and offices disappeared or were transferred to or assumed by men. Although after the jihad in Zazzau, for example, women's titles such as *sarauniya, magajiya* and *mardanni* were bestowed upon the daughters of the first emir, they were subsequently removed from women and either retired or assumed by men, or retained at a wholly formal level.[4] Despite the success of the jihad, syncretic religious practices like the *bori* cult continued in the caliphate.

The British conquest of northern Nigeria in the early twentieth century gave the emirs more powers by extending their jurisdiction which enabled them to rule more areas than they did in the pre-colonial period, especially in the "pagan" areas in central Nigeria. After the military subjugation of the region, the main problem faced by the British was how to make colonial rule function in areas without any central authority. The system of indirect rule was introduced in part to alleviate the shortage of European staff in northern Nigeria. Local emirs were therefore allowed to rule under the supervision of the British. Beyond the economic and political transformation experienced by the peoples of northern Nigeria during the colonial period, the legacy of British rule left behind a cultural mind set and system of values which profoundly altered the pre-existing ones. The spread of Victorian and Christian values to local people was demonstrated in their changing attitude towards the issue of sexuality and same-sex relationships, about which local people had previously been largely unaware or tolerable. In the next section, I focus on the changing attitudes towards sexuality as a result of colonial contact.

'YAN DAUDU': HAUSA HOMOSEXUALS, TRANSVESTITES, OR PIMPS?

Views on sexuality in Africa can vary dramatically from culture to culture over time and even within cultures at specific times. Before the colonisation of Africa in the late nineteenth and early twentieth centuries, some African cultures have tolerated same-sex relations. For example, warriors among the Azande in the Central African Republic taught boys to act as their wives. The Azande warriors routinely took on young male lovers between the ages of twelve and twenty, who helped with household tasks and participated in sexual relationships with their older husbands.[5] According to Evans-Pritchard

> Homosexuality is indigenous. Azande do not regard it as
> at all improper, indeed as very sensible for a man to sleep

> with boys when women are not available or are taboo... In
> the past this was a regular practice at court. Some princes
> may even have preferred boys to women, when both were
> available. This is not a question I can enter into further
> here beyond saying I was told that some princes sleep with
> boys before consulting poison oracles, women being then
> taboo, and also that they sometimes do so on other occa-
> sions, just because they like them.[6]

Among the Hausa people, *'yan daudu'* are variously described as homosexuals, transvestites, or pimps. However, the *'yan daudu'* as a social category offers a challenge to the simple division of male-female gender identities. The Hausa example shows that these categories rarely coincide with those of other cultures and are uniquely different from the Western construction of being gay. Assigning a sexual identity to *'yan daudu'* highlights some of the problems of assuming that same sex acts are homosexual or gay. Although some *'yan daudu'* do engage in sexual relations with other men, the practice of *daudu* is culturally understood in terms of gender rather than sexuality.[7] *Dan daudu* (singular) performs women's work and considers himself 'womanlike' but does not normally cross-dress and is still addressed and treated as male by other members of the community and thus, cannot be regarded as a transvestite. Also, some of the *'yan daudu'* cannot be described as bi-sexual as they do not see homosexuality as incompatible with heterosexual marriage or parenthood. For Hausa males, marriage is not a matter of emotional attachment, love, or even choice; it is a fundamental moral and social obligation to the family and the wider community. It is against this background that the *'yan daudu'* can be understood. Due to their close association with *karuwai* (prostitutes) *'yan daudu'* are sometimes regarded as *'yan kawali* (pimps) because of the tips received from men that they assist in meeting a *karuwa*. However, *'yan daudu'*'s close association to *karuwai* attracts other gay men and permits them to meet without blowing their cover.[8]

There is limited research on *'yan daudu'* as a social category and some of these studies refer to them in relation to *karuwanci* (prostitution) or the *bori* cult or both. However, Rudolf Pell Gaudio performed an excellent study on *'yan daudu'* as sexual outlaws in the city of Kano which was published in 2009.[9] He describes *'yan daudu'* as 'feminine men' whose social life differs in important ways from gay men in the

West.[10] It is difficult, if not impossible to reconstruct the history of *'yan daudu'* as a social category or *daudu* as a social activity before the nineteenth century. This is because historical records about *'yan daudu'* are scanty and only began to be written during the colonial period in the early twentieth century. These records are mostly written by people who had little first- hand acquaintance with *'yan daudu'*. Colonial and post- colonial records are silent about *'yan daudu'* and they are treated as merely others or as noted earlier, referred to in relation to prostitution or the *bori* cult of possession. However, as Gaudio has noted, in the late twentieth century, "'*yan daudu* had come to be identified in many people's eyes as sexual outlaws – people whose gender and sexual practices made them unfit for membership in northern Nigerian society."[11] Why did *'yan daudu'* emerge from obscurity to the limelight in the late nineteenth and early twentieth century? It is this question that the next section aims to analyze.

FROM OBSCURITY TO LIMELIGHT: A HISTORY OF *YAN DAUDU*, 1900s TO 1950s

There is a problem in reconstructing the history of homosexuality in Africa before the nineteenth century in general. Besides the scanty nature of information that exists, sources from the nineteenth century are mostly written by European travellers, missionaries, and colonial administrators and thus, the records were expressions of how they perceived the local people and, as such, have to be considered with care. In other words, most of the documents were not written for local people, but were aimed at readers in Europe. This trend continued even after colonial rule and the emerging African elites accepted the Western understanding of homosexuality. According to William Naphy, "many modern African leaders are determined to deny past events which they see as casting 'slur' on their ancestors. Effectively, both colonial and post-colonial leaders accept Western Christian understanding of homosexuality as 'sinful' and 'evil.'"[12] For example, the late President Daniel Arap Moi of Kenya maintained that the word homosexuality does not exist in African languages while President Robert Mugabe of Zimbabwe compared homosexuals to dogs and pigs.[13] With the exception of China, where the Yellow Emperor is credited with introducing homosexuality, other cultures tend to see it as the vice of other people; the British blame the Norman conquerors for introducing homosexuality to Britain while the French point the finger at the Italians, Bulgarians, or North Africans and, on their part, the Italians shift the blame onto Bulgaria and North Africa.[14] In northern Nigeria, the Arabs are blamed for introducing homosexuality into the region during the period of the Trans Saharan Trade.[15] However, Murray and Roscoe argue that when scholars state that homosexuality is not an African phenomenon it has real social consequences since "they stigmatise those who engage in homosexual behavior and those who are grappling with gay identities."[16]

As already mentioned, the spread of the Western view of homosexuality to Africa in the nineteenth century was due to the social, political, economic, and cultural dominance of the British. Thus, in order to fully understand the changing nature of local views towards sexuality in northern Nigeria in the late nineteenth and early twentieth centuries, it is important to look at the European notion of sexuality in the nineteenth century. One of the consequences of the French Revolution and the subsequent Napoleonic wars across Europe was the emergence of extreme conservatism. As Naphy has argued, "many rulers and elites in Europe looked back on the excesses and violence of the years surrounding the French Revolution and concluded that liberalism was the problem."[17] Thus, the European nations that entered the nineteenth century, expanding into other areas of the globe "were not driven by the ideology of *liberte, egalite, fraternite,* [but]... were rather reacting against Enlightenment and Revolutionary ideologies and becoming increasingly conservative, moralistic, supremacist and bourgeois as the century progressed."[18]

Victorian Britain in the nineteenth century was dominated by the belief that an individual's sex and sexuality forms their identity. In other words, the Victorians chose sexuality as the basis for delineating their identity from the aristocracy, peasants, and emergent working classes. According to Michel Foucault,

> Toward the beginning of the eighteenth century, there emerged a political, economic, and technical excitement to talk about sex...This need to take sex 'into account,' to pronounce a discourse on sex that would not derive from morality alone but from rationality as well, was sufficiently new that at first it wondered at itself and sought apolo-

gies for its own existence. How could a discourse based on reason speak like that?[19]

The term "homosexuals" was a nineteenth century invention when the "world of perversion" was discovered. Before this, till the end of the eighteenth century, sexuality was controlled by three major codes; canonical law, civil law and the Christian pastoral. They all defined what was "normal" and approved and what was condemned. The norm was the sexual relation of a husband and wife, everything else such as adultery, rape and sodomy were considered as equally condemned. Thus the same sex relations were seen as a category of forbidden acts. They were "against the nature," but more importantly, against the law. When the category "unnatural" was discovered, the "homosexuality" was taken apart as its own category and "homosexuals" were considered as a sub-race. The members of this special category were viewed sexually peripheral, deviant and even sick. The sexual orientation of "homosexual" was always present and it was the cause to all his actions. He became "a personage, a past, a case history, and a childhood, in addition to being a type of life, a life form, and a morphology, with an indiscreet anatomy and possibly a mysterious physiology". The categorisation of homosexuality was also constituted in psychiatry, psychology and medicine that confirmed the view of homosexuality as something permanent, a quality of a person, contrary to previous comprehension of sodomy which was totally a temporary aberration.[20]

The Victorians were obsessed with sexuality and the role of the sexes in a family. They considered prostitutes and homosexuals as the greatest danger posed to heterosexual reproduction and morality. The Victorian dictum was that women belonged in the home, nurturing their family while the husband became the central reference point for discussions concerning sexuality. Despite these strong Victorian views on sexuality, morality and family, homosexuality was widespread in Britain in the nineteenth century. It was so widespread that in 1808, the *Times* reported how the Home Secretary, Lord Liverpool ordered Hyde and James' Parks to be closed at night to "prevent these scandalous practices." The British response to the widespread activities of homosexuals was to make laws and punishments harsher and more frequent. In the period 1800-34, eighty men were hanged in England for Sodomy. In 1828, the burden of proof was lessened by Peel's bill to make conviction easier and as a result, in the period 1836-56, a further 200 men were hanged for sodomy.[21]

The beginning of British rule in northern Nigeria in the early twentieth century brought with it Victorian values and views on sexuality. The colonial service was a male institution in all its aspects: its 'masculine' ideology, its military organisation and processes, its rituals of power and hierarchy, and its strong boundaries between the sexes. Thus, this perception was brought to Nigeria by colonial officials and missionaries and they internalized a set of values and attitudes about what they considered to be the natural and proper role of the sexes, ignoring what was pre-existing in some Nigerian societies.[22]

POLITICS, MORALITY AND '*YAN DAUDU*' IN THE POLITICS OF DECOLONIZATION IN THE 1950s

The destruction of the *Dar al-Islam* by the British during the conquest of northern Nigeria came as a shock to the majority of Muslims in the region. Some members of the *Dar al-Islam* were to leave for Mecca and most of them ended up in Sudan while others stayed behind.[23] The politics of decolonization regenerated the Muslim identity in the north and many Muslims began to accept the humiliation they suffered during Christian colonization as a matter for the past. Although there were still few alive who remembered the humiliation, many more memories thrived in the Sudan, among children of the emigrants who failed to reach Mecca. Thus, the excitement of impending independence and the re-establishment of a better kind of *Dar al-Islam*, if not a complete *Dar al-Islam*, now seemed a real possibility for the future. Politically, the notion of *Dar al-Islam* "retains a powerful appeal to all those still troubled by the shame of colonialism and the pervasive cultural changes labelled 'modernity' (*zamani*) with non-Muslim trappings."[24]

Islam became a major factor in the politics in northern Nigeria and the achievement of independence in 1960 ushered in an era of religious politics in the region. The Northern People's Congress (NPC) dominated the government and was controlled by Muslims and it was expected to provide for the spiritual well-being of all Muslims under their control. Thus, the role of the party in offering religious services to the local people became evident as politicians used government funds to embark on extensive mosque building projects in the Muslim community in order to secure local support.[25] Also, conversion campaigns represented an extensive expansion and reinterpretation of the role of the Regional Government in the provision of religious services to the region's Muslim community. The NPC was in firm control of northern Nigeria and it spent more than a decade constructing an image of the North that stressed the continuity of a religious and political tradition that traced its origin back to Usman Dan Fodio, with the Premier of the Northern Region, Sardauna, being the inheritor of that long heritage. Sardauna supported the establishment of the Jama'at Nasr al-Islam (JNI) in 1962, which was designed to improve Islamic education and also serve as a platform for the promotion of the political and religious aims in northern Nigeria. The political aim of the association was to canvass support for the NPC (a Muslim dominated party), which would in turn help in the spread of Islam in northern Nigeria. At the same time, Bello attempted to establish in 1962/63 a new religious movement under the name of *Usumaniyya* as an effort to unite the north not only politically, but also religiously. In 1962, he published a *silsila* which depicted him as a descendant of Usman Dan Fodio and the Prophet Mohammed. The *Usmaniyya* was intended to cultivate the legacy of the leaders of the jihad and to unite all Muslims in northern Nigeria under one umbrella.[26]

During the politics of decolonization, there was a desire by Muslims to protect northern Nigeria as a Muslim land. This development led to a re-emergence of religious reform movements, which tried to find answers to the numerous challenges of the new era. The competition between the movements and their respective networks led to not only the religious but also the political mobilization of Muslims in northern Nigeria. Since the 1950s, the religious scholars together with their supporters had taken an active part in politics and became sought after partners for the political parties. In order to prepare for the re-establishment of a *Dar al-Islam*, there were local campaigns against un-Islamic practices like prostitution and the activities of '*yan daudu*'. Conservative religious and political leaders periodically, apart from condemning '*yan daudu*' as agents of sexual immorality, considered them as a social problem and their activities ungodly. According to *malam* Ishiaka, "Allah unequivocally refers to acts of homosexuality and sexual impropriety as lewd and sinful."[27] In quoting the Qur'an, he argued that Islam sanctions only heterosexual relationships: "And of His Signs is that He has created wives for you from among yourselves that you may find peace of mind in them, and He has put love and tenderness between you. In that, surely, are Signs for a people who reflect."[28] The commonly quoted Qur'anic verse that shows God's displeasure with homosexuality is the destruction of Sodom, "You approach men with lust instead of women. Nay, you are a people who exceed all bounds."[29]

Some of the newspaper columns and articles written during that period indicate that there was a general feeling amongst some Muslims in the region of the need to address the menace of the activities of prostitutes and *'yan daudu'*. On July 16, 1959, the *Northern Star* published a letter from *malam* Kumbo asking the emir of Kano and his council to help solve a number of ills, including "the stupid behavior of *'yan daudu'*." He maintained that as a true Muslim, he would not want this kind of immorality to take place in a *kasashen Musulmi* (Muslim land). Also in July 1959, Muhammadu Korau wrote to the editor of *Daily Comet* that *yan daudu* "are the ones who are spreading the obscenity... along with other things that it would not be appropriate for me to say in this upstanding newspaper." While some considered both *karuwai* and *'yan daudu'* as a fundamental social problem, others directed their attacks only on *'yan daudu'* as they were considered to be doing more harm than the *karuwai*. In a letter to the editor of the *Daily comet* in 1957, Namadi wrote that the activities of *'yan daudu'* have transgressed the limits set by God and their acts are damaging to the status of northern Nigeria as a Muslim land.[30]

As already mentioned, there is a close association between *'yan daudu'* and *karuwai*. The anti-prostitution campaigns in northern Nigeria during the 1950s were aimed at restoring morality and putting an end to their sinful activities. However, during such campaigns, the NPC controlled law enforcement agents took the opportunity to intimidate and harass prostitutes who were sympathetic to NEPU. It is important to note that NEPU involved women in its party activities and it was the first political party in northern Nigeria to establish its women's wing in Kano in 1953.[31] Thus, the clampdown on *karuwai* was associated with their support for NEPU. Although the leadership of NEPU supported the idea of anti-prostitution campaigns, they complained that only prostitutes supporting their party were often arrested. In a letter to editor of the Kano based *Daily Comet,* in July 1959, a NEPU supporter wrote, "today there are more than 100 NPC women in this city whose houses have not even been entered, while NEPU women have been arrested."[32]

POLITICIZING *SHARI'A*?: POLITICS, RELIGION AND MORALITY, 1999-2006

After Nigeria achieved political independence in 1960, political and ideological conflicts within northern Nigeria became the order of the day as Muslims became frustrated by the continued moral decay and widening gap between the elites and *talakawa*. Looking at the report card of the region since independence and decades of military dictatorship, the people of northern Nigeria continued to feel short-changed as they failed to realise the promises of independence. The irony is that the political landscape of Nigeria has been dominated by people of northern extraction, but the region has remained underdeveloped and the majority of the people live in abject poverty with high levels of unemployment and illiteracy. Although there is a high level of poverty in Nigeria, it is most widespread in the northern parts of the country. Thus, the high and persisting level of poverty in Nigeria is a northern phenomenon. In some of these states, there is a near total collapse of the infrastructure, a virtual absence of new investments, while practically all the states depend essentially on revenues accruing from the Federation Account. There is no state in the north with less than a 60 per cent poverty level, alongside the north-west geopolitical zone having some states with a 90 per cent poverty level. In a study conducted by the Ministry of Finance with the World Bank in 2008, its findings revealed that northern Nigeria has the highest number of children not going to school in the world. This depressing situation has made many Muslims take solace in religion and their unshaken belief that only Islamic rule can create a society based on justice and equity. Thus, *shari'a* cannot be totally dissociated from political demands by local people which was capitalized on by politicians for political gains.

The clamour for the implementation of *shar'ia* was motivated by the people's ardent desire to do away with injustices, corruption, impunity, immorality and other social vices bedevilling the region. For example, during the run up to the 1999 election, in order to gain local support in the gubernatorial elections in Zamfara State, Ahmad Sani adopted *shari'a* as a vote winning tactic in his campaign which won him an election that he would otherwise have lost.[33] After he was sworn into office, Ahmad Sani reintroduced *shari'a* based on the 1960 Penal Code that was still in force. He introduced a new method of *shari'a* enforcement that affects the everyday lives of the local people.

Homosexuals and prostitutes became one of the obvious targets as they continued to be blamed for the woes suffered in northern Nigeria because of their sinful activities. In January 2000, Zamfara became the first state in northern Nigeria to enact the *shari'a* Penal Code and this example was followed in May by Niger State, where the government, like that in Zamfara, fully supported the adoption of that legal system. Other northern states, prompted by popular pressure, followed suit. By 2001, eleven northern states had re-introduced *shari'a* into their legal systems. Seven of them introduced *shari'a* Penal Codes; one amended the existing 1960 Penal Code with provisions of *shari'a* criminal law, and three others enacted *shari'a* Penal Codes. These Penal Codes have adopted most of the provisions of the 1960 Penal Code, and added new provisions on Qur'anic offences (*hudud* offences) like theft, unlawful sexual intercourse, robbery, defamation and drinking alcohol. The fixed punishment for *zina* is to be stoned to death for persons who are currently married or have ever contracted a valid marriage. For those who have never contracted a marriage, the punishment is one hundred lashes and, in addition, banishment for men. Sodomy (defined as intercourse by penetration in the rectum of a man or woman) is regarded as *zina* and punished in the same way.

In principle, the expansion of *shari'a* could have included many areas in economic and social development, such as provisions for the collection and distribution of *zakat* (the charity tithe, which is one of the five pillars of Islam), or the implementation of regulations prohibiting charging interest on loans by banks. In practice, however, it did not go much beyond elaborating punishments for offences like theft, *zina*, prostitution and alcohol consumption. The dangerous aspects of politicising *shari'a* law in northern Nigeria is not just the serious shortcomings in the drafting, content and implementation, but the claims that the new *shari'a* acts of 1999-2002 incorporate perfectly a universal God-given code, and that to raise any issues of possible defects is unIslamic and anti-*shari'a*. The first *shari'a* Penal Code enacted in Zamfara shows every sign of hasty drafting: incorrect cross-referencing, incorrect and defective wording, omissions, and contradictions.

Thus, religion and politics combined to degrade and also to an extent, persecute homosexuals and same-sex activities. Religious leaders in northern Nigeria together with their supporters have taken an active part in politics and become sought after partners for political parties. They use their position to influence not only the opinion of their members, but also that of politicians. The religious influence on politics is not only reflected in the pronouncements of politicians but also in the way that homosexuals are treated by law. Although federal law in Nigeria has made homosexuality illegal and punishable by fourteen years in prison; with the reintroduction of Islamic law in some parts of northern Nigeria, punishment went beyond federal law on homosexuality and as far as legitimising their stoning to death. Therefore it would seem that neither Christianity nor Islam in northern Nigeria disseminate wholesale tolerance of sexual orientation, however they differ in how it should be legally viewed and punished. Discrimination on the basis of sexual orientation is a violation of human rights and 'yan daudu' because of their sexuality have been denied what Gaudio described as "cultural citizenship" in northern Nigeria. Cultural citizenship, according to him, emphasises the hierarchical nature of social constructions of identity and the negotiations and conflicts that inevitably take place over who can do what, where, when, with whom, and with what resources.[34] Because 'yan daudu' are highly stigmatized, they are wary of outsiders asking after their affairs. However, some that were willing to be interviewed maintained that their conditions were better before the introduction of the *Shari'a* law. According to Saleh, "we used to sale our food at the parks without the fear of being molested, but at the moment, the means of our livelihood has been taken away."[35]

An attempt in 2006 by Federal Legislators to deny 'yan daudu' and other sexual minorities of their rights was greeted with both local and international condemnation. The legislation was first introduced in January 2006 by the then Minister of Justice, Bayo Ojo. The controversial bill, entitled the "Same Sex Marriage (Prohibition) Act," would imprison anyone who spoke out or formed a group supporting lesbian and gay people's rights, and would silence virtually any public discussion or visibility around lesbian and gay lives in Nigeria. Human Rights Watch (HRW) issued a strongly-worded protest against the "sweepingly homophobic bill." According to HRW "this law strikes a blow not just at the rights of lesbian and gay people, but at the civil and political freedoms of all Nigerians. If the National Assembly can strip one group of its freedoms, then the liberties of all Nigerians are at risk."[36] On their part, a panel of United Nations (UN) human rights experts maintained that Nigerian lawmakers would counter their country's international commitments by approving the bill. The human rights experts issued a statement in February 2007 expressing "deep concern" about the draft. "Provisions of the draft bill discriminate against a section of society, are an absolutely unjustified intrusion of an individual's right to privacy and contravene Article 1 of the Universal Declaration of Human Rights."[37] They concluded that the proposed law will make persons engaging in, or perceived to be engaging in, same sex relationships in Nigeria more susceptible to arbitrary arrests, detention, torture and ill-treatment and expose them even more to violence and attacks on their dignity.[38]

Although the bill was not signed into law because of both local and international pressure, it led to increased homophobic attacks, intimidation and threats. Thus, 'yan daudu' in northern Nigeria have a well-founded fear of being ill-treated, not by the authorities, but from the local community and society at large. The International Gay and Lesbian Human Rights Commission (IGLHRC) received reports of an increase in arbitrary arrests and detentions of alleged 'yan daudu'.[39] Several 'yan daudu' in northern Nigeria have been convicted and sentenced to death for engaging in homosexual activity, however, there is no evidence that a death penalty has yet been carried out for this crime.[40] A decade after the re-introduction of *shari'a* law (1999-2009), the fervour has fizzled out while disillusionment about its patchy application is becoming more strident. According to Alhaji Garba, "People are disillusioned with the insincerity, deception and hypocrisy which characterize the implementation of *shari'a*."[41] Since the introduction of *shari'a*, politicians have hijacked the return to Islamic law to advance their own political agendas. Ten years after its implementation, there is little to show that *shari'a* law has had a positive impact in a region still battling graft, moral decay, and searing poverty.

CONCLUSION

The re-introduction of *shari'a* law should have checked vices and moral decay across northern Nigeria. Purifying the region by getting rid of 'yan daudu' and *karuwai* would have created the social conditions necessary for the full implementation of *shari'a* and thus, improved public morality along Islamic lines, leading to justice and prosperity for all. However aspirations for a just and decent society were dashed by self-seeking politicians who hid under the implementation of *shari'a* to promote their personal political interests, using 'yan daudu' as a target to achieve their political aims. The threat by the enforcers of the Islamic law in northern Nigeria coupled with the increasing intolerance of *'yan daudu'* has made them dinosaurs of the modern age and thus, endangered. Many of the *'yan daudu'* have gone underground and some of them have abandoned their businesses especially selling luxury foods such as fried chicken at ceremonies and at motor parks in parts of northern Nigeria.

Notes

1. Ikime, O. *Groundwork of Nigerian History* (Ibadan: Heinemann Educational Books, 1980), 5.

2. Pearce, Stephen "Identity, Performance and Secrecy: Gendered life and the "modern" in Northern Nigeria," *Feminist Studies*, 2007.

3. A.M. Kani, *The Intellectual Origin of the Sokoto Jihad in Nigeria* (London: Al-Hoda 1988); M. Bello, *Infakul Maisuri*, translated and paraphrased by E.J. Arnett, as *The Rise of the Sokoto Fulani* (Kano: Government Printers 1922); Last, *Sokoto Caliphate* (London: Longman Press); R.A. Adeleye, *Power and Diplomacy in Northern Nigeria: The Sokoto Caliphate and its Enemies, 1804-1905* (Second Edition: London: Longman Press 1977); J.P. Smaldone, *Warfare in the Sokoto Caliphate: Historical and Sociological Perspectives* (Cambridge: Cambridge University Press 1977)..

4. M.G. Smith, *Government in Zazzua* (London: Oxford University Press 1960), 131.

5. Evans-Pritchard, E.E, (1970) Sexual Inversion among the Azande, *American Anthropologist*, 72 (6), 1428-1434.

6. Evans-Pritchard 1971, 183.

7. Rudolf Gaudio, "Male Lesbians and Other Queer Notions in Hausa" in Stephen Murray and Will Roscoe (eds), *Boy-Wives and Female Husbands: Studies of African Homosexualities* (New York: St. Martin's Press 2003), 119.

8. *Ibid.*

9. Rudolf Pell Gaudio, *Allah Made Us: Sexual Outlaws in Islamic African City* (Sussex: Blackwell, 2009).

10. *Ibid,*10.

11. *Ibid,* 31.

12. William Naphy, *Born to Be Gay: A History of Homosexuality* (Gloucestershire, 2006).

13. Gaudio, *Allah Made Us*, 180.

14. Stephen O. Murray, *Homosexuality in "Traditional" Sub-Saharan Africa and Contemporary South Africa: An overview.*

15. Personal communication with Mohammed Rabiu in Lafia, 20 January 2010.

16. Stephen Murray and Will Roscoe (eds), *Boy-Wives and Female Husbands: Studies of African Homosexualities* (New York: St. Martin's Press 2003), XXII.

17. William Naphy, *Born to Be Gay*, 235.

18. *Ibid.* It should be noted that one of the one of the first acts of the French Revolutionary Parliament was the decriminalization of sodomy..

19. Foucault, M, *The History of Sexuality*, Vol.1, (London: Penguin Books, 1976), 25.

20. Ibid., 40, 43.

21. William Naphy, *Born to Be Gay*, 241.

22. See H. Callaway, *Gender, Culture and Empire: European Women in Colonial Nigeria* (Oxford: Oxford University Press1987), 4.

23. Personal communication with Professor Murray Last, 22 December 2009 in London. See also Murray Last, "The Search for Security in Muslim Northern Nigeria," *Africa*, 78 (1) 2008, 49.

24. *Ibid.*

25. For detail discussion on religion and politics during the decolonization period, see Jonathan Reynolds, *The Times of Politics (Zamanin Siyasa); Islam and the Politics of Legitimacy in Northern Nigeria, 1950-1966* (London: International Scholars Publications, 1999).

26. Roman Loimeier, *Islamic Reform and Political Change in Northern Nigeria* (Illinois : Northwestern University Press,), 113.

27. Interview with *malam* Ishiaka at Andaha, 13 January 2010.

28. Qur'an 30:22.

29. Qur'an 7:88.

30. *Daily comet* in 1957.

31. Sklar, *Nigerian Political Parties*, 419.

32. See *Daily Comet*, 16 July, 1959, "Any Politics in Raid of Kano Prostitutes?" *Daily Comet* 17 July, 1959, "N.A. Police and prostitutes."

33. It should be noted that in Islamic tradition, in every century, a reformer (*mujaddid*) will appear among local Muslims and transform or renew

it. Ahmad Sani was thus, referred to by some ordinary Muslims as a *mujaddid* when he reintroduced the *shar'ia* law in Zamfara.

34.   *Ibid*, 7-8.

35.   Interview with Saleh Usman at Lafia, 4 February 2010.

36.   See Human Rights Watch (HRW). September 2004. "Political Shari'a'? Human Rights and Islamic Law in Northern Nigeria." And also HRW 2007 "Christian Leaders in US Condemn Nigeria's Anti-Gay Bill."

37.   United Nations (UN). 23 February 2007. Office of the UN High Commissioner for Human Rights (OHCHR). "Independent UN Experts Express Serious Concern over Draft Nigerian Bill Outlawing Same-Sex Relationships."

38.   *Ibid*.

39.   The International Gay and Lesbian Human Rights Commission (IGLHRC) 15 July 2005.

40.   *Ibid*.

41.   Personal communication with Alhaji Garba, 14 January 2010.

Bibliography

Adeleye, R.A. *Power and Diplomacy in Northern Nigeria.* London: Longman, 1971).

Callaway, B.J. *Muslim Hausa Women in Nigeria.* New York: Syracuse, 1987.

Callaway, H. *Gender, Culture and Empire* Urbana: University of Illinois Press, 1987).

Douglas and Kaberry, P. (eds.) *Man in Africa.* London: Anchor Books, 1971).

Dudley, B.J. "The Northern Peoples' Congress" in J.P. Macintosh (ed) *Nigerian Government and Politics.* Evanston, 1966.

Foucault, M, *The History of Sexuality,* Vol.1. London, 1976, 25, Penguin Books.

Kani, A.M. *The Intellectual Origin of the Sokoto Jihad in Nigeria.* London: Al-Hoda, 1988).

Last, M.D. *The Sokoto Caliphate.* London: Longman, 1967.

Mahdi, A. *The Hausa Factor in West African History.* Zaria: ABU Press, 1978.

Paden, J. *Ahmadu Bello, Sardauna of Sokoto: Values and Leadership in Nigeria.* Zaria: Hudahuda, 1986.

Reynolds, J.T. *The Times of Politics (Zamanin Siyasa): Islam and the Politics of Legitimacy in Northern Nigeria, 1950-1966.* London: International Scholars Publications, 1999.

Roman Loimeier, *Islamic Reform and Political Change in Northern Nigeria*. Illinois: Northwestern University Press, 2003.

Roscoe (eds), *Boy-Wives and Female Husbands: Studies of African Homosexualities*. New York: St. Martin's Press 2003.

Rudolf Pell Gaudio, *Allah Made Us: Sexual Outlaws in Islamic African City*. Sussex, 2009.

Smaldone, J.P. *Warfare in the Sokoto Caliphate: Historical and Sociological Perspectives*. Cambridge: Cambridge University Press, 1977.

Smith, M.F. *Baba of Karo: A Woman of the Muslim Hausa*. London: Oxford Pres, 1952.

Smith, M.G. *Government in Zazzau*. London: Oxford University Press, 1960.

______. *The Economy of Hausa Communities of Zaria*. London: HMSO, 1955.

Whitaker, C.S. *The Politics of Tradition, Continuity, and Change in Northern Nigeria*. Princeton: Princeton University Press, 1970.

William, Naphy, *Born to Be Gay: A History of Homosexuality*. Gloucestershire, 2006.

Yahaya, A.D. *The Native Authority System in Northern Nigeria 1950-1970*. Zaria: ABU Press, 1980.

Yakubu, M. *An Aristocracy in Political Crisis*. Aldershot: Avebury, 1996.

SEXUALITY, RELIGION AND SPIRITUALITY

A. A. Lawal

INTRODUCTION

Since the last quarter of the 20th century, contemporary publications, through the print and electronic media, have established the fact that women in patriarchal societies have suffered various degrees of discrimination, segregation, inequality, oppression and marginalization. Indeed male dominated societies have adopted the instrumentalist application of sexuality, gender, sexism, etc. to truncate the aspirations of women in economic, political, educational and religious spheres.[1] The chapter restricts its focus to the sphere of religion and examines how women were denied equality with men under the Christian, Islamic and African traditional religious belief systems.

As expected African women, under the positive impact of modernization, globalization and the information highway, organized various subtle forms of protests, resistance and condemnation of the patriarchal monopoly of rights and freedoms. African women, like their counterparts in Europe and North America, engaged in activism and publications on feminist hermeneutics, feminist theologies, theologies of liberation, and Mariology.[2] The questions addressed in this chapter are as follows: Are men considered to be more spiritual than women in Christianity, Islam and African traditional religions? Is there any normative standard set for spirituality in the three belief systems? The chapter argues that different degrees of spirituality exist in situational sexualities since spiritual power, nature, knowledge and experience are not static but dynamic as a believer in any religion observes both the ebb and flow of spiritual contact with the divine. Hence, spiritual experiences of these sexualities vary: men, women, heterosexuals, homosexuals, hermits, hermaphrodites, henotheists, transvestites, bi-sexuals, and the transsexuals in the three belief systems under consideration.

The paper is divided into three parts. The first part critically examines the diverse sexualities and spiritualities in Christianity, Islam (in Africa), and African religion. The second part explores the forms of marginalization of women in the three belief systems while the third section is devoted to the factors that facilitated the successful protests of liberation movements and female activists in the drastic reduction of marginalization of women in Christianity and African religions except Islam with some obvious reasons.

SEXUALITY AND RELIGION IN AFRICA

Sexuality has many definitional perspectives in different cultural environments and religious orientations. Thus, space constraint does not permit a disquisition of sexuality in specific culture areas of Africa. But a general and definitional perspective of sexuality in Christian theology will be emphasized.

To understand sexuality, there is a need to clarify the difference between sex and gender. Sex refers to female and male physiology and their respective sex organs, while gender refers to the roles attributed by society to women and men. These roles are described as feminine and masculine. Despite the indisputable polarity of role distinction, there is an unending interaction between the biological and social traits, hence women can be masculine and men can be effeminate in behavior, attitude and social values. This is why both masculine and feminine behaviors are perceived in different ways in various cultural environments. Thus, sex is a biological aspect of human behavior and the social meaning we attach to people's experience of sex and gender.[3]

Sex also is about the physical 'sex act', penetration and such sexual practices as anal and oral sex. But sexuality, which involves sexual activity, embraces more experiences and behavior in the life of everybody in the society. Sexuality encompasses a set of ideas, meanings and social practices such as sexual behavior like monogamy, polygamy, polyandry, etc.; sexual identity such as heterosexual, homosexual, bi-sexual, trans-sexual; sexual desire, sexual relations, sexual politics etc. Indeed, we have many commonly ingrained ideas and attitudes about female and male sexuality and stereotypes about what is sexually acceptable for women and for men in patriarchal societies.[4]

In Christian theology, sexuality involves a symbol system that is socially and historically relative, and is also fundamental to human beings. It has to do with our identity, personality and daily existence. It affects the structure of our brains, the way to relate to persons, the way we understand and explain our world, how we organize our lives, occupations, our choice of sexual activity and social status. Biblical injunctions emphasize a strict control and regulation of sexuality by purity laws and moral agents. Sex must be by mutual consent and 'good sex' does not connote sexual abuses, hostility and domination but rather equality and an equitable share of ecstatic sexual pleasure. Hence Jesus enjoined mutual agreement, love and respect between a husband and a wife and forbade divorce. During a periodic fast, a couple must by a common agreement, abstain from sex and thereafter resume sex relations.[5]

Thus far, we have various forms of sexuality in the various religions in and outside Africa, whether imported, indigenous or syncretic. And despite the dichotomy between men and women's sexuality, there are social-cultural interactions that blur the boundary between them, hence the universal prevalence of homosexuality, trans-sexuality, heterosexuality, bi-sexuality, celibacy and transvestism.

SPIRITUALITY AND RELIGION IN AFRICA

There has been an unending debate on the difference between spirituality and religion. While a school of thought upholds the value and benefits of spirituality and condemns religion as useless, another school articulates a closer relationship between the two. It claims, by experiential knowledge, that religion is a stepping stone to spiritual growth.[6] However there are spiritualities in terms of diverse spiritual experiences in Christianity, Islam and African religions involving the active participation of men and women. Hence the spiritual experience and orientation is profound, diverse, and infinite. It is personal and private. It cannot be played back or subject to a critical review. It will therefore be erroneous to claim that a man is more spiritual than a woman in the same religion.

What then is spirituality? An indispensable and pervasive aspect of our existence is our conscious experience of the spiritual. Every normal human being has this conscious experience that includes the "inner experience." By this is meant conscious thoughts, mental images, dreams and visions, trances, as well as the "outer experience" or sensory experience that is connected with ordinary conscious perception of things beyond our minds or brains." Worthy of consideration is the level, content and intensity of the conscious spiritual experience of any man or woman in any religion or without any religion.[7]

Continuity of spiritual consciousness can be affected by radical change in time and place in terms of its ebb and flow. High spiritual experience can be re-invigorated by discipline, fasting, praying, meditation, abstinence from sex and wine and reading the scriptures.

However, the biblical spirituality, which is quite peculiar, is worth considering to enrich our understanding. There is a difference between the spirit and the Holy Spirit, just as God is different from the gods. The spirit is an animating force within living personal beings. It is the breath of life. It is the life center of every human being and synonymous with the soul, the real inner person in each of us. After death, the spirit leaves the body. Hence, the body is lifeless. But after a righteous person's death, his or her spirit lives in heaven. The spirit is the immaterial part of the human personality; it is the seat of our insight, emotions and will. It knows our thoughts and understands our state. Christians are enjoined to cleanse themselves from all defilement of flesh and spirit and to be holy both in body and spirit.[8]

To Christians, God is Spirit and those who worship Him must do so in Spirit and in truth. God regenerates a sinful man/woman and transforms him or her into a holy and righteous being. Thus God makes it possible for a sinner to attain true spirituality. "It is the Spirit that gives life, the flesh (the material component of our being) profits nothing." God gives to the believer His divine nature, character and attributes, spiritual understanding and a spiritual vocabulary to articulate divine truths in a spiritual manner. A genuine spiritual Christian is one who is mature in cultivating the fruit of the Spirit and living a Spirit-filled life. On the contrary, the carnal Christian is one who remains immature, jealous, quarrelsome, proud, impure and corrupt in life. All marks of true spirituality include walking by the Spirit to be filled with the Spirit to possess His power, to own and exercise His gifts.[9]

As Christians believe, through the new birth, our spirit is made alive to God and sensitive to the inner voice of the Holy Spirit. Constant renewal of the Spirit in us keeps the attitudes of our mind under His control and enables our spirit to think along spiritual lines in agreement with the mind of Christ. "Thus the regenerated human spirit when humbly submitted to Christ is capable of meekness and gentleness toward others." Yet there are diverse spiritualities among male and female Christians in the various denominations like the Anglicans, Methodists, Baptists, Lutherans, Catholics, the Apostolic Faith, the apostolic Church, the Pentecostals and the Aladura or the White Garment Churches. The various sects in Islam and African religious also uphold diverse spiritualities.

WOMEN'S SEXUALITY AND SPIRITUALITY IN MALE-DOMINATED AFRICAN CHURCHES

Prior to the emergence of contemporary feminist historiography, little or nothing is known about pre-colonial women's world, their sexual beliefs and practices and spirituality in male dominated churches. The missionaries, especially the Catholics defined their image negatively as satanic agents of sexual temptation of men. Even novels by colonial administrators misrepresented women as inferior and impure. It was the belated anthropological research and publications that disproved the erroneous judgments and stereotypes of the missionaries. We need to note that the imported European Christianity did not deviate from male domination and the subordination and marginalization of women.[10]

Notwithstanding, women in the various denominations in the pre-colonial and colonial period were known for their spiritual powers, signs and wonders. In the 18th century, Beatrice of the Congo and Fumaria were charismatic female leaders in the church. The later was believed to have seen the Virgin Mary and exercised some spectacular gifts in detecting and punishing sin. In the 19th century South Africa the Xhosa medium Nonquase, while serving under her uncle Mhlakaza who was a prophet, interpreted the visions of the prophet. In 1856, the medium in alliance with another young prophetess Nonkosi, instigated many other female diviners to consult with the ancestral spirits for the panacea against British colonial penetration and conquest. Their large followership embarrassed the British. The two leaders were arrested and imprisoned. But Nongquase was released later to return to her home in the eastern province of the Cape where she died between 1898 and 1905.[11]

In 20th century Zimbabwe, some inspired women who communicated with the ancestral spirits established their own churches and had a large followership. Indeed, Mai (mother) Chaza of Methodist background was a charismatic leader known for her remarkable healing power in Zimbabwe. She was believed to have died and been resurrected, and received divine instructions to abstain from alcohol and sex. She combined Christian spiritual gifts with herbal medicine for healing women of sterility and blindness. By 1950s she had about 70,000 worshipers in the neighborhood of Harare and Bulawayo. After her death a man took over and used her name in working signs and wonders.

Alice Lenshina Mulenga, who had Scots Presbyterian training, founded her church in Northern Rhodesia (present day Zambia) following a vision in 1953. She started anti-witchcraft purification movement and promised a better life if her followers abandoned their pagan practice. She died and rose again and between 1957 and 1963 her followers increased from 50,000 to 100,000. Similar Christian movements led by charismatic women were replicated in Cote d'Ivoire, in 1913, Tanzania in 1963 and Kenya by 1970 for the eradication of witchcraft, illness and evil spirits.[12]

These few examples illustrate the early natural reactions of women to their subordination and marginalization in the male dominated churches. They demonstrated that spirituality is not the exclusive reserve of men hence their individual initiative to establish their churches that attracted large numbers of male and female worshippers.

WOMEN'S SEXUALITY AND SPIRITUALITY IN ISLAM

A diligent perusal, digest and critical analysis of the image of a woman in the Qur'an, the Hadith, the writings of the jurists and the opinions of modern Muslim scholars and authors will definitely cause one to endorse a declaration that her sexuality, and spirituality have been circumscribed by many injunctions that are enforced by the husband and other moral agents in the brotherhood.

Although the Qur'an recognizes her as a biological and social being and a believer who will be admitted to heaven provided she fulfills all the religious requirements by faith, she is subject to her husband's control according to God's plan. She is the object of sexual pleasure and gratification without any bargain or compromise, hence the prevalent inherent inequality of women to men in Islam.

The Qur'an gives a detailed outline of a woman's status vis-à-vis that of a man in marriage, divorce, witnessing, inheritance, veiledness and concubinage. As always, the emphasis is on inequality and the rights of man over the woman to restrict her to the private space.[13]

Islam endows man with right to keep concubines along with his wife or wives to fulfil his sexual needs although incest and sodomy are taboo. Both the Qur'an and the Hadith permit the man to beat his wife whenever she is rebellious, (disobedient, stubborn, uncooperative, disrespectful, self-opinionated, rude, arrogant and adulterous). Beating is a form of discipline for refusal for sex, for going out without permission and for neglecting her religious duties.[14]

Although the veil is obligatory, it is compulsory for women in the Islamic states to guard their private parts and cover their adornments and charms in the pubic space. But in the privacy of their marital homes they are free to unveil in their interactions with their siblings. Male servants who stay with them at home must not have sexual desires or they are castrated. Islam strongly forbids homo-sexism and transvestism in any form. No wonder women are seriously enjoined to adhere to the stipulated dress codes. Basically, apart from using the veil, they are to avoid any flamboyant ornamentation of the face to display their charms in the public otherwise they could seduce or tempt men. While walking along the street they are to avoid twisting their waists and titling their heads otherwise they will end up in hell, because they temp the hearts of men.[15]

If a woman attends a mosque for prayer in a scented or perfumed dress, she is regarded as a prostitute and God does not accept her prayers until she goes home to wash herself. Women who violate the dress codes are cursed by the Qur'an ...on the logic of its conception of women as the source of temptation and evil which make man the victim. The essence of the veil and other dress codes is to prevent temptation, preserve society, protect the women's chastity, virtue and honor.

Islam also justifies the circumcision of girls and boys on the ground that the tradition facilitates the removal from the male organ a lot of excrements that can cause cancer, while it preserves the honor for women and makes them more enjoyable. Indeed, circumcision is believed to diminish women's lust or tone down their sexual desire by removing the clitoris.[16]

A woman is subordinated to her husband in religious rites although Islam equalizes the faith and religious responsibilities of men and women to merit admission to heaven or hell due to negligence. They must observe the five pillars of Islam but men only call for prayers and lead worship in the mosque where the women sit in a separate section. Women's religion and spirituality are perceived by men to be deficient and no premium is placed on their fasting and prayer unless their husbands permit them to perform certain rites. The women need the permission of their husbands to fast and attend the mosque for the Jumat on Fridays. If they are not allowed, they pray at home. The denial of permission for women to fast is predicated on the men's right to enjoy the women sexually at all times. On no account should any religious obligation rob the men of sexual enjoyment except by mutual agreement, otherwise they provoke God's anger as recorded is the Qur'an.[17]

Notwithstanding the restrictions on women on the exercise of their sexuality and spirituality in orthodox Islam, the impact of modernization, globalization and the information highway has caused conflicts over equality of men and women in religion and religious institutions in contemporary times all over the world. The United Nations has committed all member states to enforce the fundamental human rights of their citizens and aliens. Indeed the proliferation of both local and international Non-Governmental Organizations (NGOS) and the activism of women with the free legal assistance have to a large extent effected some drastic improvements in the social, political and economic lives of women in Muslim countries in Africa and the world.

WOMEN'S SEXUALITY AND SPIRITUALITY IN AFRICAN RELIGIONS

It is in African religions that women enjoy their sexuality and spirituality in both male dominated and female dominated religious institutions. Contemporary spiritualities of women regard the body and sexuality as the sources of knowledge of the divine. Their bodily experience especially, childbirth and menstruation, offers them opportunities within the self and nature, with which they live daily.

No wonder eco-feminism convinces us that women are closer to the natural environment than men in their use of flowers around the house and offices.[18]

A noticeable aspect of women's spirituality is the use of female images for the divine for an allegedly genderless god or goddesses. In their use of metaphors for these deities, the spirituality of women emphasize motherhood on the assumption the god or goddess is like the mother of humanity and nature. How this women's spirituality diffused throughout Africa and the world is yet to be investigated, because contemporary women's spiritualities share similar ritual practices like worshipping in circles, dancing, singing, clapping their hands, building altars, following guided meditations, invoking spiritual powers and female images and employing ritual elements that appeal to the senses of touch, taste and smell. In other words the female worshippers use dance, physical contact, incense and candles, food and fruits in the shrines and the white garment churches.[19]

In pre-colonial matriarchal societies in West Africa, there emerged men and women of remarkable supernatural powers that were deployed for protecting their societies from external invasion and natural disasters. After their death, they were deified and worshipped; hence the proliferation of male and female deities in contemporary times with whom the votaries communicate for solutions to challenging societal problems.

The Owan of Edo State in Nigeria worship such goddesses as Oron, Ekeva, Omouwa, Ome, Ovbiagbede and Ozalla in their respective shrines with elaborate periodic ceremonies which commemorate their spectacular contributions to the society. These were married woman who were deified after they died. Owan was the goddess of death and life. Ekeva turned into a stream upon her death and became the goddess of protection and mother of the people. Omouwa, a married woman, died childless. As her buried corpse decayed, it turned into a river which later flowed into the Owan River. The villagers forbade the eating of any fish from the river and Omouwa spirit in Owan River has been invoked several times to solve myriads of societal problems successfully. Ovbiagbede fought for human rights throughout her lifetime because she defended justice and equity among the Afuze people. After her death, she was deified and a monument was erected for her worship as a fertility goddess. All the shrines of the goddesses were taken care of by women except those of Emeora and Vokha by men.[20]

Comparative African religious studies demonstrate the replication of similar spiritual phenomena in other parts of Africa emphasizing that those later deified were associated with witchcraft, magic and herbal medicines which were employed for the welfare of people in their respective societies.[21] Even in Yorubaland, the male dominated Ogboni fraternity has an important and indispensable female member titled the Erelu or Iya Abiye who carried out specific assignments. During the annual Osun and Obalufon festivals, a virgin young lady called Arugba features prominently and she is believed to have the supernatural power to communicate with the deities and transmit their messages to the society. In Egungun and Oro cults which are male dominated, and which forbid women to move near their groves/ shrines and impose curfew on women respectively, an old and power- ful woman called Ìyá Àgan is involved in the decisions at Igbo Igbale on the annual festivals. Women are the usual poets and praise singers of the divinity called Sango and while men and women dance to Bata music in a circle, the spirit can arrest any man or woman. Instantly the medium is worshipped as the physical representative of the deity. The writer has witnessed how very old men and women paid obeisance to a young female Shango medium in Ila-Orangun, Osun state of Nigeria.[22]

There are goddesses in Sierra Leone, Ghana and the Cameroons that are worshipped and are believed by the people to improve the soil fertility, and grant bumper harvests once fertility rituals are correctly performed. Their devotees can conjure rain during any draught. Apart from female dubia among the Igbo and the sangoma of South Africa who are endowed with supernatural healing powers, there are women as bold as lions with the use of witchcraft and charms to lead male warriors in times of civil crises or wars in contemporary Africa. One remembers some interesting anecdotes of the exploits of female war- riors recently in the Ife-Modakeke war, which is reminiscent of the his- toric bravery of the Amazons of Dahomey in the 19th century and the Bete of Cote d'Ivoire. The latter female warriors often defeated male warriors from other villages through their use of adultery, witchcraft and hypnotism.[23]

The palace women under the Alafin of Oyo in the 19th century were not marginalized for their sexuality and spirituality, instead they were honored and respected on account of their loyalty and the functional utility of their services. The Alafin recruited women with cosmic powers from diverse geographical areas to constitute the female Ilaris. Recruitment was based on some criteria which included powers of witchcraft, herbalism and divination by which the gods were consulted daily. They prophesied to the king about any impending political or environmental crises and suggested the relevant preventive measures like rituals, sacrifices and the purification of the ancestral shrines and sacred forests.[24]

The women were the "ears" and the "eyes" of the Alafin, upholding him spiritually, physically, politically, and militarily. In other words they were the powers behind his longevity, health, successful rule and military victories. The women, otherwise called the Iya Abiye, Iya mi Osoronga, the Eleye or Alaye supported and still support the crowned Obas in Benin (Edo State) and Yoruba land. The women "with sixteen eye balls" were spies who could read the minds and motives of the chiefs who frequented the palace daily and confided in the Alafin whom they identified as potential traitors. If they could not counsel the Alafin publicly, some senior chiefs conveyed their warnings, advice and suggestions to the Alafin on specific state policies and implementation.[25]

The women in their designated offices, bore chiefly titles and wore specific identification symbols on their hair and dresses and skin scarification which commanded respect in the public space. Each of them performed a categorical ritual in her shrine to commune with the gods and transmit the divine message to the Alafin through the royal messengers. At times the most sensitive and secret messages were coded for the Alafin to decipher. If he could not, some specialists in Oyo folklore, who were always in the palace, were called upon to help the Alafin interpret the coded messages.[26]

THE CONTEMPORARY DEVELOPMENTS THAT ADDRESSED WOMEN'S MARGINALIZATION

Many social changes in Europe and North America since the last quarter of the 20th century had significant spillover effects on Africa and other parts of the world as regards the sexuality and spirituality of African women and their marginalization in Christianity, Islam and African religions. As mentioned above, modernization, globalization and the information highway improved the rate at which any events occurring anywhere in the world were beamed by satellite transmission. Thus, the telephone, handsets, the computer, newspapers, magazines, books, journals and the television sets enabled and still enable people to know what happens in different parts of the world. The improvement of international and intercontinental air travel and shipping also facilitated the migrations of peoples for various reasons.[27]

Thus, the foregoing factors enabled women of the various religious institutions in Africa to learn about the landmark achievements of the women liberation movements, liberation theologies, gender and feminist studies in Europe and North America. Indeed, many African men and women who were abroad and witnessed and enjoyed the benefits of the changes, were eager to effect similar changes in Africa; hence the emergence of groups of women activists especially in the universities in the 1970s and 1980s. At several fora such as the local, national, regional, continental and inter-continental conferences, seminars, symposia and workshops, the problems of women were brought to the front burner. Such problems included discrimination, repression, oppression, exploitation, deprivation, inequality, sexual abuse and harassment etc.[28]

Even the United Nations and its organs organized similar for public awareness, and declared the decade and year of women liberation. African nations joined others in implementing the resolutions of the United Nations on fundamental human rights with particular attention to gender balance and gender equality in appointments, promotions, political, social and economic spheres.

Today, women are actively involved in religious services as prophets, reverends, pastors, teachers, pastors and evangelists in the Pentecostal churches. They appear on television screens preaching the gospel and exercising the gifts of healing and deliverance. Women now found their churches and serve as general overseers. Indeed, widows of founders of churches have successfully taken over the administration and management of such institutions. Christians, female and male are now free to change from one denomination to another without any sanction, just as Muslims get converted into Christianity and vice versa. Similarly many witches, wizards, and diviners now freely change their faith by becoming Christians or Muslims. The change also facilitates marriage between men and women from various belief systems as exemplified by Christian wives and unbelieving husbands who convey the children and their wives to church on Sundays.

Although women are not turbaned as imams in Islam, and are not allowed to call for prayers, many of the orthodox restrictions are now relaxed and some programs similar to those in Christian churches are now introduced to curb the rate at which young ladies and women drift into Christianity. Even in North Africa and other nations in Sub-Saharan Africa, the number of liberated or emancipated Muslim women is increasing. They do not wear the veil and appear in the public space, as politicians, activists and spokespersons.

CONCLUSION

The global post-cold war changes have impacted positively on the spirituality of women in all religions whether male-dominated or female-dominated. Women have carved out a niche for themselves in all religious institutions and have commanded men's respect for their sexuality and spirituality. They have maintained their identities and catered for themselves without compromising their faith, sexuality, and honor while seeking advanced spiritual knowledge and experience. But they are yet to overcome some sexual and spiritual bias and stereotypes in the Catholic and the Apostolic Faith, Islam, and some African religions. In particular, they are not ordained as cardinals or bishops in the Catholic Church and neither are they permitted to join with the congregational prayers of the Apostolic Faith during menstruation. Even in Islam, women's menses automatically nullifies the prayers of any Muslim in contact with them. Women are still compelled to cover their heads while praying otherwise they absorb heaps of curses from spirit – beings called 'maleka'.[29] Men and women are still forbidden to stand side by side in the mosque to pray. Women cannot call for prayers or preach in the mosque. They are not appointed as imams and neither can they officiate at wedding, naming and funeral ceremonies, dedication of mosques, buildings, institutions, conferment of titles, installations of emirs, shehus and turbaning of dignitaries.[30]

In African religions, and herbal medicine, contact with menstrual blood and menstrual pad is usually avoided to guarantee divine acceptance of sacrifices and the efficacy of herbal therapies. Seasoned herbal medicine practitioners patronize herbal vendors who are menopausal women or virgins to buy herbs that are efficacious. Herbs sold by menstruating women are believed to lose their potency.[31] Indeed some charms will fail to work if men put them on and have sex with women. Rather rings, leather, belts and wrist bands are to be removed when sleeping with women otherwise they either disappear or become powerless. The mystery of contact with women or menstrual blood is yet to be scientifically investigated and analysed.[32]

Notes

1. Chris Barker, *Cultural Studies* (London, Sage Publications, 2003, 279), 280-89, 290-3). Beryl Madoc-Jones and Jennifer Coats, ed., *An Introduction to Women's Studies* (Oxford, U.K. Blackwell Publishers Ltd., 1996).

2. Letty M. Russell and J. Shannoa Clarkson, eds., *Dictionary of Feminist Theologies* (Louisville, Kentucky, John Knox Press, 1996).

3. Melanie Mauthner, "Understanding Sexuality" in Beryl Madoc-Jones and Jennifer Coats, ed. *An Introduction to Women's Studies* (Oxford, U.K. Blackwell Publishers Ltd., 1996), 134.

4. Ibid., 135.

5. Carol S. Robb, "Sexuality" in Letty M. Russell and J. Shannon Clarkson, eds. *Dictionary of Feminist Theologies*, 258.

6. For details see Lisa C. Deluca, "Spirituality Vs. Religion", http://spiritualgrowth. Suite 101.com.article,cfm/spiritualityvs religion, 3/4/2010 ; « Religion and Spirituality » in about.com Newsletters, http://atheism. about.com/od.religionnonreligion/a/spirituality.htm,3/4/2010.

7. Peter Unger, *Identity, Consciousness and Value* (New York, Oxford University Press, 1990), 39, 40-41, 53.

8. Charles F. Pfeiffer, Howard F. Vos. John Rea eds; *Wycliffe Bible Dictionary* (Peabody, Massachusetts, Hendrickson Publishers Inc., 1999, 1618).

9. Charles, F. Pfeiffer et. Al. *Wycliffe Bible Dictionary*, 1619.

10. Catherine Coquery – Vidrovitch, *African Women: A Modern History* (trans. By Beth Gillian Raps). (Boulder, Colorado, Westview Press, 1997), 46.

11. Ibid., 47.

12. Ibid., 48.

13. Hamdun Dagher, *The Position of Women in Islam* (Vilich, Austria, Light of Life, 1995), 7-8.

14. Ibid., 95-99, 101.

15. Ibid., 113-17. Islam forbids pornography, beauty contest, fashion parade, strip dance, prostitution etc.

16. Ibid., 119, 121.

17. Ibid., 126 – 128.

18. Cynthia Eller "Women's Spirituality" in *Dictionary of Feminist Theologies,* eds., Letty M. Russell, et. al, 276.

19. Ibid., 277.

20. Onaiwu W. Ogbomo, *When Men and Women Mattered: A History of Gender Relations Among the Owan of Nigeria* (Rochester, New York, University of Rochester Press, 1997), 66-69, 70, 72-76.

21. For details see, Newell S. Booth, Jr. ed., *African Religions: A Symposium* (New York, Nok Publishers Ltd.), 1977; E. Bolaji Idowu, *African Traditional Religion* (London, SCM Press Ltd.), 1978; T. O. Ranger and Isaria Kimambo, eds., *The Historical Study of African Religion* (London, Heinemann Educational Books Ltd.), 1972; E. A. Adegbola ed. *Traditional Religion in West Africa* (Ibadan, Daystar Press), 1983.

22. Oral communication with Dr. Caleb Orimogunje, Senior Lecturer, Department of Linguistics, African and Asian Studies, University of Lagos, Yaba, Nigeria, January 1, 2010.

23. Catherine Coquery, *African Women* ... 46 see also Justus Nzemeke, "Position of Women in Pre-colonial Africa" in Eno Blankson Ikpe ed., *Women and Power in Africa* (Lagos, Fragrance Communications Publishers, 2009), 27-58.

24. Oral communication with Dr. Tunde Akinwumi, Associate Professor, Department of Art History, University of Agriculture, Abeokuta, September 16, 2009.

25. Mojubaolu O. OKome "African Women and Power: Labor, Gender and Feminism in the Age of Globalization" in Eno Ikpe ed. *Women and Power in Africa* ..., 130, 131.

26. Oral communication with Dr. Tunde Akinwumi ... September 16, 2009.

27. For details on globalization, global economic flows, global cultural flows and new social movements, see Chris Baker, *Cultural Studies,* 167-169, 170-79, 180-184.

28. Mercy Amba Oduyoye, "African Feminist Theology" in Letty M. Russell et. Al. *Dictionary of Feminist Theologies,* 112 -114; Joyce Ann Mercer, "Liberation" in Letty M. Russell et. al. *Dictionary of Feminist Theologies,* 168.

29. Oral Communication with Mr. Omolade, a contractor to the University of Lagos, Yaba. October 9, 2009.

30. Oral communication with Mr. Junaid, Senior Lecturer, Department of History and Strategic Studies, University of Lagos, Yaba. October 9, 2009.

31. Oral Communication with Jimoh Abimbola, Herbal Medicine Practitioner, Lagos, October 9, 2009.

32. Oral Communication with Dr. Caleb Orimogunje, Senior Lecturer, Department of Linguistics, African and Asian Studies, University of Lagos, Yaba. October 9, 2009.

Bibliography

Adegbola, E.A., *Traditional Religion in West Africa*. Ibadan: Daystar Press, 1983.

Baker, Christ. *Cultural Studies*, London, Sage Publications, 2003, 279, 280-89, 290-3.

Beryl Madoc-Jones and Jennifer Coats, ed., *An Introduction to Women's Studies*, Oxford, U.K. Blackwell Publishers Ltd., 1996.

Booth, Newell S. Jr., ed, *African Religions: A Symposium*. New York: Nok Publishers Ltd., 1977.

Coquery-Vidrovitch, Catherine. *African Women: A Modern History*, translated by Beth Gillian Raps. Boulder, Colorado: Westview Press, 1997.

Dagher, Hamdun. *The Position of Women in Islam*. Vilich, Austria, Light of Life, 1995.

Deluca, Lisa C. "Spirituality Vs. Religion", http://spiritual-growth. Suite 101. com.article,cfm/spirituality vs religion, 3/4/2010, "Religion and Spirituality" in about.com Newsletters,

Eller, Cynthia. "Women's Spirituality" in *Dictionary of Feminist Theologies*, eds., Letty M. Russell.

Idowu, E. Bolaji, *African Traditional Religion. London: SCM Press Ltd, 1978.*

Mauthner, Melanie. "Understanding Sexuality" in Beryl Madoc-Jones and Jennifer Coats, ed. *An Introduction to Women's Studies*. Oxford, U.K. Blackwell Publishers Ltd., 1996, 134.

Oduyoye, Mercy Amba. "Africanist Feminist Theology" in *Dictionary of Feminist Theologies*, edited by Letty M. Russell et. al.

Ogbomo, Onaiwu W., *When Men and Women Mattered: A History of Gender Relations Among the Owan of Nigeria*. Rochester, New York: University of Rochester Press, 1997.

Okome, Mojubaolu O. "African Women and Power: Labor, Gender, and Feminism in the Age of Globalization" in *Women and Power in Africa,* edited by Eno Ikpe.

Pfeiffer, Charles F., Howard F. Vos, and John Rea, eds., *Wycliffe Bible Dictionary,* Peabody, Massachusetts, Hendrickson Publishers, Inc., 1999.

Ranger, T.O and Isaria Kimambo, eds., *The Historical Study of African Religion.* London: Heinemann Educational Books Ltd., 1972.

Robb, Carol S. "Sexuality" in Letty M. Russell and J. Shannon Clarkson, eds; *Dictionary of Feminist Theologies,* 258.

Russell, Letty M. and J. Shannoa Clarkson, eds., *Dictionary of Feminist Theologies.* Louisville, Kentucky, Westminster John Knox Press, 1996.

Unger, Peter. *Identity, Consciousness, and Value.* New York: Oxford University Press, 1990.

AFRICAN RELIGION AND THE SEXUAL EXPLOITATION OF WOMEN

Adepeju Olufemi Johnson-Bashua

INTRODUCTION

Nigeria remains a traditional society despite many new changes and external impact. This adherence to traditions has greatly affected the attitudes towards women's rights and social stance especially in rural societies. Religion teaches us that sexuality is a gift from God; it is a profound endowment which should be acknowledged as a characteristic of our humanity and a potent tool to facilitate human growth in all ramifications. Unfortunately, religion like many other institutions put in place by man to maintain his co-existence, has become a double-edged sword especially when the role of nation-building is taken into consideration. For example, it has been used for the subordination of women in the society, particularly within the African communities.

Discussions of religion as a form of social control may create an assumption that religion is only a negative force in women's lives. Over the years, it has played a prominent role in reconstructing the status of women by providing them with the opportunity for spiritual leadership in certain positions, both within the African society and religion. It has also become an important source for the feminist movement and other social and political movements for human liberation and resistance to oppression.

In many parts of the world including Nigeria, it is evident that women have become active in the struggle to overcome a strong cultural pattern of male domination. In the Nigerian context, women's sexuality is infringed upon, denied, and abused in many dimensions, from the family; and in economic, social, and political domains. This is because women in Nigeria, like other African countries, have been greatly subjected to all forms of discrimination and violence based on the belief that men are far superior to women. This gives men the license to abuse women with the assurance they would never be penalized, thereby reducing the male-female relationship to purely sexual and prevents women from regarding their husbands as co-builders and partners in development.

This chapter attempts to examine the role of women generally in Nigeria by explicating the ways in which they have been sexually exploited, the implication of this sexual exploitation, and the role that religion can play in curbing this problem.

WOMEN IN NIGERIA

Nigerian women a have played important roles in the development of their immediate environment. For example, women like Mrs. Olufunmilayo Ransome-Kuti, Queen Amina of Zaria, Mrs. Margaret Ekpo, and Mrs. Dora Akunyili have exerted strong political and economic influence in Nigerian history which has made them role models for other women thereby proving that women are not the weaker sex. Socially, the struggle of women such as Mrs. Amba Oduyoye has also given rise to the feminist movement and gender studies in the universities and other liberation movements.

The place of women in the contemporary Nigerian society is similar to the status of women in African traditional society. In highlighting the role of Nigerian women in development, three periods i.e., the pre-colonial, colonial, and postcolonial, will be briefly examined. During the pre-colonial era, opportunities existed for women to take leadership roles in politics, religion, social, and economic life.[1] This is because under the pre-colonial customary laws in most Nigerian societies, women were considered to be free adults but they were still subordinant to men. The pre-colonial Nigerian economy was basically at a subsistence level and Nigerian women participated effectively in this economy by contributing to the sustenance of the kin groups. A woman who was without a craft or trade, or who was totally dependent on her husband, was not only rare, but was regarded with disrespect by other women. According to Gloria Chuku "in pre-colonial times, Igbo women had their own land, separate from their husbands. They determined how and when to use the proceeds accrued from their farming and processing activities."[2]

The primary responsibility of women was to take care of the home and they also contributed substantially to the production and distribution of goods and services. They participated extensively in agriculture and trade both locally and with other communities in the procurement and sale of various food items and related commodities. They were fully involved in farming and food processing, for example, fish drying, garri processing, salt production, etc. Most often, these women supplied the means of sustenance for entire households. Based on the significant position that women played as farmers and food processors, Chuku suggests that, "women held their families' bowls or stomachs."[3]

The role of women was also highly visible in spiritual matters and this is probably based on the belief that women are considered to be more spiritual and more naturally prone to religious observance and piety than men. This can be classified into two aspects: first, by providing music, songs and dances required during religious activities and second, they officiated as priestesses, diviners, healers, traditional birth attendants, and often times as custodians of sanctuaries for gods and goddesses.[4]

In the political realm, amongst the Yoruba, the Oba ruled with the assistance of a number of women headed by the Iyalode.[5] Their main responsibility was to participate in the decision-making processes as they helped to settle disputes in their wards and compounds. Thus, women assisted in the maintenance of law and order and, in traditional Yoruba society. The Oba's wives (Aya, Oba, or Olori) were also influential in state affairs and there were occasions when women were employed to monitor and influence foreign policy decisions in some Yoruba States. The case of Moremi who revealed the secret of Igbo power to Ife is a good example.[6]

The colonial period marked the beginning of the fall of the Nigerian women. Colonial policies and statutes were clearly sexist and biased against women. Economically, it seriously undermined the prestige of the traditional occupations of Nigerian women because the colonial economy was an export-oriented one. Many of the smaller markets hitherto dominated by women gradually disintegrated as a result of the emergence of expatriate firms such as United African Company (U AC.) This was further compounded by the denial of access to medium and large scale loans to women and lack of adequate finance was a crucial hindrance to effective female participation in economic policies.[7]

Politically, colonialism affected Nigerian women adversely as they were denied the franchise and very few of them were offered any political or administrative appointments; this means that the women's wing of political parties possessed very little functional relevance. It was only during the 1950s that three women were appointed into the House of Chiefs, namely Chief (Mrs.) Olufunmilayo Ransome-Kuti (appointed into the Western Nigeria House of Chiefs); Chiefs (Mrs.) Margaret Ekpo and Mrs. Janet Mokelu (both appointed into the Eastern Nigeria House of Chiefs).[8]

In Nigeria today, the position of women has improved considerably despite the fact that most of the discriminating laws against women have not been abolished.[9] The efforts of the women's organizations to mobilize and revitalize their participation especially politically, are desirable and encouraging. There is an increase in the number of women political appointees as councilors, chairpersons of local government councils, commissioners, and ministers. In other areas, women are not lagging behind; they have experienced some success as academics, engineers, medical doctors, surveyors etc. and there are also women serving in the police departments, army, customs offices, and the navy and divisions of road safety. In the religious sphere, women also service as church founders, leaders, and pastors.

NIGERIAN WOMEN AND SEXUAL EXPLOITATION

Sexuality is a fundamental aspect of human existence; it is a part of everyday life. It defines the very essence of one's humanity; and characterizes the entire structure of the human being whether an individual is a man or as a woman. It is an integral part of personal self-expression and self commitment to others.[10] According to the World Health Organization (WHO), the term sexuality is a central aspect of being human and encompasses sex, gender identities and roles, sexual orientation, eroticism, pleasure, intimacy, and reproduction. Sexuality is experienced and expressed in thoughts, fantasies, desires, beliefs, attitudes, values, behaviors, practices, roles and relationships. While sexuality can include these dimensions, not all of them are always experienced or expressed.[11]

Religiously, sexuality is not just an isolated biological or physical phenomenon that is accidental to human beings, but rather it is a profound endowment from God which affects the behavior of the individual including his mental attitudes and processes. Sexuality orients a person towards other human beings and since its complete actualization involves a partner, it affects the social life of a community. The term sexual exploitation could mean the misuse, abuse, mistreatment, taking advantage, and manipulation of women and children.[12] This has been done in different communities in Nigeria in the following ways.

Sexual Discrimination

A significant portion of women in Nigerian society are culturally submissive. Despite recent urbanization processes, many traditional social norms remain intact and even well-educated women can still be marginalized. Women cannot inherit property even when they are the only surviving member of the family.[13] Thus, women are trapped in a rigid hierarchy were the will of men is to be respected. This makes them extremely vulnerable to the manipulation and influence of the men. Thus, varying forms of marginalization and discrimination against women based on the believe that men are superior to women is what Amba Oduyoye aptly describes as sexism.[14] This is a situation where society sees women as fragile and frail and women are sometimes not allowed to assume "the so-called male roles". Men are regularly held up as the norm of humanity; and women are usually otherwise restricted to participating in the biological process of procreation. Oduyoye observed that sexism at its most blatant degree makes women subservient to men and brings about the disdainful and violent ways in which some men treat women.[15]

Sexiism reduce male-female relationships to that of the sexual, the familial. Because of this the system, gender inequality still affects sexual relationships because it imposes distinct disadvantages on women and girls in their ability to negotiate safe sexual practices in their relationships. For example, a woman cannot dictate to her husband how she wants to be made love to, or that the husband should use condoms during sexual intercourse. Nor can she deny allowing her husband to have sexual intercourse when he is in the mood for it, even if she is unwilling to do so.[16]

Spousal abuse, especially wife beating, is common in the Nigerian society. Such violence is an active male strategy to subdue women into accepting their domination. Fear of beating and rape keeps many women from questioning their husbands' sexual escapades. For unmarried girls, the situation is worse. For example, if a rape is reported, it is the girl who suffers the shame and chances of her getting married in the future are significantly diminished. Under such circumstances, women's ability to protect themselves is minimal. "Unfortunately, sexual and domestic violence also appears to be accepted by the community and is seldom reported to the constituted authority for necessary disciplinary actions. Most times violence is reinterpreted by women as a sign of their partner's love."[17]

Cheap Labor

The Nigerian society is structured in a way that encourages male domination of women.[18] There are clearly defined sex roles while various taboos ensure conformity within these roles.[19] For instance, it is traditionally believed that men should not participate in domestic work including child rearing because such tasks are considered to be the exclusive domain of women. Consequently, domestic work is becoming more tedious especially for the rural women and this is partly due to the fact that women have to combine agricultural activities with domestic chores which leaves them little or no time to engage in the sustained effort needed to achieve their personal goals.[20] Consequently, women work very long hours, are poorly fed and clothed, and are often deprived of emotional and physical care.[21] This has consequently led to the increase in child labor. This is a situation where children are procured from impoverished rural families by middlemen, driven only by commercial motives and transported long distances to work in urban households. These children are worked very hard and are forced to o undergo dehumanizing treatment from their employers. The worst aspect of this is that the girls are vulnerable to sexual harassment and exploitation not only from employers, but often from older male workers.[22]

Poverty

Despite huge incomes derived from oil wealth, the scope of poverty has become a national embarrassment despite the fact that since the mid-1970's, every government in Nigeria has made attempts to tackle it. The quest for economical improvement by the Nigerian government seems to be a failure which deals a serious blow upon the citizens,-especially the women. The situation is worse for the women who are mostly affected by the current economic recession because they constitute the majority of the unemployed, the poor (52 percent of the rural poor), and the socially disadvantaged.[23] The recent worsening economic situation has forced women to become more dependent on men; whether as husbands or boyfriends for economic support.[24]

In homes where women are the bread winners, the economic pressure of dependent children and inadequate financial support from their husbands, makes them vulnerable to extra-marital affairs in order to sustain their families.[25] The case becomes more problematic when there are young girls within the household. They are left with no other alternative to improve their lives especially in terms of education or career improvement rather than participating in prostitution and other means of survival. In this new context, women's personal resources, including their sexuality, have new-found economic potential. Pre-and extra-marital sexual encounters increasingly involve the transfer of material resources, such as money and gifts from a man to his female partner.[26]

Prostitution

Despite the fact that many Nigerian women are familiar with the culturally-accepted norms of the society concerning sexual relations, there are still many women who live the precarious and dangerous life of the sex worker. The prime reason is a pressure that is even greater than culture and religion which is poverty.[27] Prostitution is the practice of commercializing sex, a situation whereby a woman permits a man to have sex with her in return for money or other favors. This practice is increasing in many Nigerian societies and has been the major means by which the HIV/AIDS disease has spread alarmingly. Women who engage in prostitution are usually between the ages of 25 to 30 years and practice their trade in varying proportions in hotels, bars, brothels on the streets, etc. Olatunji Orubuloye and colleagues[28] observed that about 60% of these women are either single, unmarried, separated, or divorced. Half of them become mothers before embarking on the trade and are financially responsible for their children who in most cases are looked after by their grandmothers in their hometowns. Teenage girls are being forced into prostitution due to the Nigerian economic crisis.

SEXUAL EXPLOITATION OF WOMEN: IMPLICATIONS FOR NIGERIAN SOCIETY

The prevalence of sexual exploitation of women obviously has some impact on the Nigerian society generally. Some these implications include the following.

Impact on health and well-being

While it is true that men are increasingly involved in prostitution, girls and women still comprise the majority of actors. Gender discrimination is one of the major factors that place women at greater risk of sexual exploitation. Sexual exploitation of women can result in short-term and long-term harm, resulting in psychological, emotional, physical, and social distress. It can also result in mental health issues, which can include substance abuse, eating disorders, personality disorders, depression, and conflict in romantic or interpersonal relations.[29] Women also suffer from sexual diseases (including HIV), violence, abuse, drug addiction, unwanted pregnancies, forced abortion, malnutrition, and social rejection.[30]

Psychologically, sexually-exploited women remain prisoners of their damaged psyche despite undergoing rehabilitation.[31] The longer a woman stays in the sex industry, the harder it is to overcome the trauma of the violence they have been exposed to. Women's physical and mental well-being is further harmed by the isolation and marginalization they suffer from their families and communities.

Impact on the Family and Child

According to Faulkner,[32] sexually-abused children report feelings that something is wrong with them, that the abuse is their own fault, and that they should blame themselves for the abuse. Consequently, victims may feel inadequate, embarrassed, isolated, guilty, shameful, and powerless.[33] For these reasons, many people suppress what they perceive as a shameful secret until later in life. David Finkelhor and Angela Browne[34] found the long-term effects of maltreatment include poor self-esteem, difficulty trusting others, anxiety, feelings of isolation and stigma, depression, self-destructive tendencies, sexual maladjustment, and substance abuse. The negative effects of incest, the most common form of sexual abuse, can be compounded by the reactions of parents, siblings, and other important people in the child's life. For example, in some cases, the siblings of the survivor blame the abused child rather the perpetrator of the abuse, either because they believe the perpetrator's denials or simply because of the explanation provided by the abuser. When a child wonders if her mother knew about the abuse but did nothing to stop it, she can lose trust in both parents.[35] The fathers, uncles, and other family members who sexually abuse children are also affected by the abuse, too. Most of them live double lives, i.e., an upstanding family man on one hand versus being an obsessed, self-loathing sex criminal on the other hand.

Furthermore, due to the disparity between men and women, a wide gap is left in spousal relationships, most particularly in the area of taking concrete decisions which can improve the family. The woman's opinion and suggestions are seldom consulted. Social norms regarding male power in sexual and reproductive decision-making are contrasted with restrictions on female sexuality.[36] Generally speaking, women are under more pressure to remain monogamous and are often unable to ask for sex, determine family size, or suggest the use of condoms with husbands. These norms of female behavior were traditionally imparted into the women from their youth by their elders, who cautioned against premarital sex and pregnancy and instructed girls on how to fulfill the roles of a good wife and mother.[37] Sexual activity is often seen as a private matter, making communities reluctant to act and intervene in cases of sexual exploitation.

Exposure to HIV/AIDS

The AIDS epidemic has exposed the barbaric treatment to which Nigerian women are subjected. Their special vulnerability also exposes men and children to the deadly disease. The catchphrase of the war against HIV/AIDS has been 'Say No to Unsafe Sex.' It is unclear how realistic is this for women in Nigeria. It should be apparent from the discussion above that their power to say 'No' is indeed limited. Decisions on safe sex are left with men. Women are rarely in a position to insist on the use of a condom if their partners do not want it. Nor can they protect themselves by using a female condom without their husbands' permission or they may be accused of having extra-marital affairs.[38] Campaigns for safe sex do not take into account the conditions in which the majority of Nigerian women live.

The secrecy attached to women's sexual experiences through religious-cultural norms contributes in no small measure to women's vulnerability to HIV/AIDS. "This has led to the growing concern on the disparity in HIV infection levels between men and women in many parts of Africa, especially in adolescent age groups where many more girls are infected than young males. Secrecy and stigmatization also explain to a large extent why potential victims of HIV/AIDS often refused to be tested. Most women are therefore not aware that they are infected."[39]

The prevalent sexual exploitation of women exposes them to risky sexual behaviors which contribute to the growing trend of poor reproductive and sexual health outcomes, including unwanted pregnancy, abortion, violence, and infection from STDs and HIV/AIDS.[40] The rise in prostitution has increased the spread of AIDS, coupled with the fact that contraceptive costs have gone up due to the currency collapse which has forced the Nigerian government to cut down on the heavily subsidized distribution programs.

THE ROLE OF RELIGION IN CURBING SEXUAL EXPLOITATION IN NIGERIA

Religion is an intrinsic aspect of every human life in Nigeria and it forms the essential bed-rock upon which peoples' moral and social obligations are based. The importance of religion today cannot be overemphasized. It has helped in no small measure to instill order in the society as well as to control vices in public and private affairs. Religion has brought different races and people together to interact and share ideas on matters of common interest. It has protected the weak and catered for the poor and has contributed to the improvement and enhancement of life through enlightenment, education, health and social services.

The tenet of the various religions in Nigeria is vehemently opposed to promiscuity, manipulation, irresponsibility, and sexual exploitation. After all these religions teach us that sexuality is a profound gift from God. It should be accepted as a characteristic of our humanity and used to facilitate human growth towards identity and maturity. Religion can be either a resource or a roadblock for battered women. As a resource, it encourages women to resist mistreatment. As a roadblock, its misinterpretation can contribute to the victim's self-blame and suffering and to the abuser's rationalizations. Abused women often say, "I can't leave this relationship the society and African religion says it is wrong to do so."[41]

Whatever the various religions and religious institutions in Nigeria have done to date to combat sexual exploitation of women, it must be conceded that in this cause they have been a sleeping giant. Nevertheless, there is hope in its untapped potential to demand justice and to offer compassion because religion is uniquely qualified and responsible to address the evil of sexual slavery for several important reasons. First, it is the first resource to which most Africans find solace. Secondly, it has inherent strength and divine purposes which empower it to provide aftercare to those who have been sexually exploited.[42]

In the last few years, religious bodies in Nigeria have taken concrete steps to combat sexual exploitation of women and girls. Most of these religious bodies work with NGO's to assist victims by apprehending and making sure that those who perpetuate this act are prosecuted. Victims are also assisted with rehabilitation processes and reintegration with their families. For example, the Catholic Church is one of the churches that have responded constructively to the abuse of women by stating through the council of Bishops that "As pastors of the Catholic Church in the United States, we state as clearly and strongly as we can that violence against women, inside or outside the home, is *never* justified. Violence in any form"—physical, sexual, psychological, or verbal"—is sinful; often, it is a crime as well. We have called for a moral revolution to replace a culture of violence. We acknowledge that violence has many forms, many causes, and many victims—men as well as women."[43] Such a response by the church can help break this cycle. Many abused women seek help first from the Church because they see it as a safe place.

Furthermore, the church has helped to launch catholic organizations against trafficking in women (COATNET), which in December, 2002 helped spurn a broader coalition, including non-Catholics: Christian Action and Networking Against Trafficking in Women (CAT)[44] The catholic effort will encourage more churches and other religious bodies to become actively involved in combating sexual exploitation of women. It is imperative for Christians to come to terms with the abominable assault on the given dignity of every woman. Christians east and west, must decide how best to pray and to put feet to prayer, how best to comfort the afflicted, and how best to combat those who ignore the most basic of human rights.[45]

CONCLUSION

Nigerians must let go of traditional notions of male dominance. As Martin Foreman, Director of the AIDS Program of the Panos Institute, London, has said: "...the AIDS epidemic cannot be contained until men are persuaded to reassess their traditional concepts of masculinity. Without men, there would be no AIDS disease."[46] Women must be empowered to make decisions about their own bodies. They must be encouraged to resist religious, cultural, and economic pressures to engage in unwanted sexual relationships. They must be in a position to avoid unprotected sex. An enabling atmosphere should be promoted by the Nigerian government, including sponsored seminars and conferences.

Finally, this should not be a problem of concern to Nigerians alone. Humanist groups all over the world should show their support in eradicating the social, cultural, and economic conditions which have allowed sexual exploitation to thrive. It is time to wage war against these conditions and waging war means talking openly about sexual issues. It calls for breaking the silence. Men irrespective of their socio-economic status need re-orientation. There is the need for gender education, enlightenment, awareness and consciousness- raising among men which must target all age groups irrespective of social class. Re-orientation of men's mind set via gender education could greatly enhance women's empowerment. This could be achieved through organized seminars, training, and workshops for men as well as the introduction of gender studies into the primary, secondary and tertiary institutions.

Notes

1. Bolanle Awe, *Nigerian Women in Historical Perspectives* (Madison: University of Wisconsin, 1989), 42.

2. Gloria Chuku, Igbo Women and Economic Transformation in Southeastern Nigeria, 1900-1960 (New York: Routledge, 2005), 22..

3. Ibid.

4. Mojubaola Olufunke Okome, "African Women and Power: Reflections on the Perils of Unwarranted Cosmopolitanism," *Jenda: Journal of African Culture and Women Studies,* (2001): 47-65.

5. Bolanle Awe, The Iyalode in the Traditional Yoruba Political System" in *Sexual Stratification: A Cross-Cultural View,* edited by Alice Schlegel (New York: Columbia University Press, 1977), 144-160.

6. Samuel Johnson, *History of the Yorubas.* (Lagos, C.M.S. Bookshops, 1921), Repr. 1956, 125.

7. Chuku, "Igbo Women and Political Participation in Nigeria 1800s-2005," 81-103.

8. Benjamin Obi Nwabueze, *Constitutional History of Nigeria.* (London: Longman Press, 1982), 20-21.

9. Obafemi Awolowo, *Thoughts on Nigerian Constitution* (Ibadan: Oxford University Press, 1966), 42.

10. Victor Igbum, *Contemporary Sex Education in the Light of Christianity* (Markudi: Aboki Publishers Ltd, 2003), 12.

11. World Health Organization, *Report of a Technical Consultation on Sexual Health.* (Geneva: 2002), 1-30.

12. M. Amba Oduyoye, "Violence against Women: Challenges to Christian Theology," *Journal of Inculturation Theology* (Enugu: Snap Press Ltd, 1994), 39.

13. Edwin, I. Nwogugu, *Family Law in Nigeria* (Nigeria: Heinemann Educational Books, 1990), 397.

14. Oduyoye, *"Violence Against Women: Challenges to Christian Theology," Journal of Inculturation Theology,* 44.

15. Ibid.

16. Wanbui Wa Karanja, "Outside Wives" and "Inside Wives" in *Nigeria: A Study of Changing Perceptions of Marriage in Transformation of African Marriage,* edited by David Parkins and David Nyamwaya (Manchester: Manchester University Press, 1987), 257.

17. Catherine Macphail, "Condom Use Among Adolescents and Young People in a Southern Africa Township, *Social Science and Medicine* 52 (2001):1613-1627.

18. Jackie Stacey, "Untangling Feminist Theory" in *Introducing Women's Studies: Feminist Theory and practice,* edited by Diane Richardson and Victoria Robinson (London: Macmillan Press, 1991), 49-73.

19. Olabisi Aina, "Women, Culture, and Society" in *Nigerian Women in Society and Development,* edited by Amadu Sesay and Odebiyi Adetanwa (Ibadan: Dokun Publishing House, 1998), 6.

20. Bolanle Adetoun, "Men, Women, and Violence: Conceptualization and Perspectives," Lecture series delivered at the Gender Institute of the Council for the Development of Social Science Research in Africa (CODESRIA), Dakar, Senegal, June 12-19, 1997, 12.

21. Gita Sen, Adrienne Germain, and Lincoln Chen, eds., *Population Policies Reconsidered: Health Empowerment, and Rights* (Cambridge M.A.: Harvard University Press, 1995), 117-92.

22. James Garbarino et al, *The Psychologically Battered Child: Strategies for Identification, Assessment and Intervention* (San Francisco, CA.: Jossey-Bass, 1986), 68.

23. Gruskin et al., *Population Policies Reconsidered: Health Empowerment. and Rights,* 122.

24. John Caldwell and Pat Caldwell, "Women's Position and Child Mortality and Morbidity in Less Developed Countries" in *Women's Position and Demographic Change* edited by Nora Federici, Karen Oppenheim Mason, and Solvi Sogner (Oxford: Clarendon Press, 1993), 220.

25. Caldwell et al., "Women's Position and Child Mortality and Morbidity in Less Developed Countries," 222.

26. Carmel Dinan, "Sugar Daddies and Gold-Diggers: The White-Collar Single Women" in *Female and Male in West Africa,* edited by Christine Oppong (London: George Allen & Unwin, 1983), 21.

27. Alemika Emmanuel, "Sexual Crimes: Legal and Social Responses" in *Reforms and Review of Gender-Based Sexual Offences Laws in Nigeria,* edited by O. Briggs, et. al. (Lagos: Nayee Pub. Company Ltd, 2003), 112-124.

28. Oruboloye Olatunji, et al., "Commercial Sex Workers in the Shadow of AIDS" In *Sexual Networking and AIDS in Sub-Saharan Africa: Behavioural Reaserch and the Social Context, Health Transmission Centre,* edited by Olatunji Orubuloye (Canberra: The Australian National University, 1994), 210.

29. Bolanle, "Men, Women and Violence: Conceptualization and Perspectives," 12-22..

30. Esta Soler. "Domestic Violence is a Crime: A Case Study - San Francisco Family Violence Project" In *Domestic Violence on Trial: Psychological and Legal Dimensions of Family Violence*, edited by Daniel Sonkin. (New York: Springer Publications, 1987), 215.

31. Bessell A. Van der Kolk, *Psychological Trauma* (Washington, DC: American Psychiatric Press, 1987), 52.

32. Nancy Faulkner, "Pandora's Box: The Secrecy of Child Sexual Abuse," *Sexual Counseling Digest*, 18th September, 1996, 1-3.

33. Faulkner, "Pandora's Box: The Secrecy of Child Sexual Abuse," 2.

34. David Finkelhor and Angela Browne. "Impact of Child Sexual Abuse: A Review of the Research," *Psychological Bulletin, 99* (1986): 66-77

35. M. Sheinberg and P. Fraenkel, "Loyalty Divided: Ambivalence Haunts the Victims of Sexual Abuse," *Family Therapy Networker, 23*(3) (1998): 63-78.

36. Christine Obbo, "Gender, Age and Class: Discourses on HIV transmission and Control in Uganda" In *Culture and Sexual Risk*, edited by Han Ten Brummelhuis and Gilbert Herdt (Australia: Gordon and Breach Publishers, 1995), 79-95.

37. Christine Oppong,"Traditional Family Systems in Rural Settings in Africa" In *Family Systems and Cultural Change*, edited by Elza Berquo and Peter Xenos (Oxford: Clarendon Press, 1992), 70..

38. Chika Nnorom, "Unmet Need for Contraception: Health Implications for Mothers and Children in Ehime Mbano, Imo State, Nigeria," *Journal of Society Development and Public Health.* (2005):48-64.

39. Olatunji Orubuloye, "Commercial Sex Workers in the Shadow of AIDS," 210.

40. Simon Gregson et al, "Sexual Mixing Patterns and Sex-Differentials in Teenage Exposure to HIV infection in Rural Zimbabwe," *The Lancet.* 359(2002):1896-1903.

41. Bolanle Awe, "Men, Women and Violence: Conceptualization and Perspectives," 12-22.

42. Joy Bussert, *Battered Women: From A Theology of Suffering to an Ethic of Empowerment* (Minneapolis, MN: Division in North America, Lutheran Church in America, 1986), 65.

43. United States Conference of Catholic Bishops. *Confronting a Culture of Violence: A Catholic Framework for Action. A Pastoral Message of the U.S. Catholic Bishops* (Washington, D.C.: USCCB Publishing, 1994), 21.

44. CAT, *Christian Action and Networking Trafficking Against Women: An Oriented Guide* (Brussels: 2003), 23-24.

45. United States Conference of Catholic Bishops. *Confronting a Culture of Violence: A Catholic Framework for Action, A Pastoral Message of the U.S. Catholic Bishopsm,* 29.

46. Martin Foreman, *AIDS and Men: Taking Risk or Taking Responsibility?* (London: the Panos Institute and Zed books Ltd, 1999), 1-240.

Bibliography

Baron Jonathan, *Against Bioethics.* London: The MIT Press Cambridge, Massachusetts, 2006.

Beauchamp Tom and Childress James, *Principles of Biomedical Ethics.* New York: Oxford University Press, 2009.

Cohen-Keltenis, Peggy and Pfafflin Friedemann. *Transgenderism and Intersexuality in Childhood and Adolescence, Making Choices.* Thousands Oaks and London: Sage Publication, 2003.

Elliot Carl. *Better Than Well.* New York, NY: W.W. Norton & Co., 2003.

Feinberg Leslie, *Transgender Warriors,* Boston: Beacon Press. 1996.

Finnis John, *Natural Law and Natural Rights,* Oxford: Clarendon, 1980.

Green, Simon Richard, "A Typical Psychosexual Development" in *Child and Adolescent Psychiatry,* ed. Michael Rutter, and Eric Taylor. London: Blackwell Scientific, 1994.

Jones, William, *Hippocrates,* Vol. 1. Cambridge, MA: Harvard University Press, 1923.

Transgender, Transsexual, Gender Identity Disorder, *http:/www.web4health. info/en/answers/sex-gender-what.htm.*

Ulrichs, Karl Heinrich, Forschungen über das Räthsel der mannmännlichen Liebe. Trans. Michael, Lombardi-Nash as *The Riddle of "Man-Manly" Love: The Pioneering Work on Male Homosexuality,* Buffalo, N.Y.: Prometheus, 1994.

Zucker, Kenneth. and Bradley, Susan Jane, 1995. *Gender Identity and Psychosexual Problems in Children and adolescents.* New York and London, The Guilford Press.

AMEH DENNIS AKOH is Associate Professor of theatre theory and criticism at the Osun State University, Nigeria. He attended universities of Jos and Ibadan, Nigeria where he also taught for some years. He has recently been Sub-Dean of the Faculty of Arts and Humanities at the Kogi State University, Anyagba, Nigeria. His areas of research interest include Dramatic Theory and Criticism, Sociology of Literature, and Cultural Studies. He has over 30 publications in refereed local and international journals and books including *The Literary Criterion, Journal of Global Initiatives, African Journal of Arts and Cultural Studies, Nigerian Theatre Journal* and *Lagos Notes and Records*. He is the Editor of the *Nigerian Journal of Indigenous Knowledge and Development*. He is currently working on a collection of essays on postcolonialism, community, and space.

JONATHAN M. AYUBA studied for his Ph.D. at the School of Oriental and African Studies, University of London and he is currently a Senior Lecturer at the Nasarawa State University, Keffi Nigeria. His research interests includes the nature of the relationship between the centralised and the decentralised societies in the West African savannah, focussing on the relationship between the Sokoto caliphate and the "pagan" communities in what would later become northern Nigeria in the nineteenth and early twentieth centuries. He is also interested in British colonial rule in West Africa and the social and political history of Nigeria and Sino-African relations after the cold war. He has published in peer reviewed journals, edited books, and presented papers in both national and international conferences on some of these themes.

Adepuju Johnson Bashua is a lecturer in the Department of Religion at Lagos State University, Nigeria. Her scholarly works have appeared in local and international journals.

Bola Dauda had his first degree in social sciences at the University of Ife in 1974, worked as a teacher and a civil servant in Nigeria between 1974 and 1983, and obtained his masters and doctorate degrees in public administration from the University of Liverpool in 1985 and 1988 respectively. He has held academic positions at the Universities of Liverpool, Leicester, and Edge Hill University College of Lancaster, and is a life member of the UK Coaching Academy and an honorary fellow of the University of Leicester. He is a published novelist and commentator on the human condition and author of half a dozen books, including *The American Way, Why Am I Here?* and *Living a Life of Abundance*. He has contributed extensively and effectively to academic discourses in public policy and his works have been translated to French, Spanish, and Chinese. He recently returned to live in Nigeria with his wife, Omobola, and now spends his spare time in freelance academic research and writing, public speaking, coaching and mentoring, traveling, and writing his memoirs for parents, guardians, and his godchildren.

Peter A. Dumbuya is professor of history at Fort Valley State University in Georgia and attorney at law in the state of Alabama. He is the author of *Reinventing the Colonial State: Constitutionalism, One-Party Rule, and Civil War in Sierra Leone* (2008), and co-author of *Assessing George W. Bush's Africa Policy and Suggestions for Barack Obama and African Leaders* (2009). His current research focuses on elections, party politics, and postwar reconstruction in Sierra Leone, south-south relations between Brazil and Africa, and United States relations with Africa.

Toyin Falola is the Frances Higginbotham Nalle Centennial Professor of History and Distinguished Teaching Professor at the University of Texas at Austin. He is the Nelson Mandela Professor of African Studies at Large, the Julius Nyerere Chair in Modern African Studies at Benue State University in Nigeria, and the Ibn Khaldun Distinguished Research Professor. He is the author/editor of more than 114 books, numerous journal articles, and book chapters. He has received numerous teaching awards, including the 2000 Jean Holloway Award for Teaching Excellence, the 2001 Texas Excellence Teaching Award, the 2003 Chancellor's Council Outstanding Teaching Award, and the 2004 Academy of Distinguished Teachers Award. He is the recipient of numerous awards through the years including the 2008 Quintessence Award, the 2007 Distinguished Africana Award, the 2007 Amistad Award for Academic Excellence in Historical Scholarship on Africa and the African Diaspora, the 2007 SIRAS Award for Outstanding Contribution to African Studies, and the Africana Studies Distinguished Global Scholar Lifetime Achievement Award from Indiana University Purdue University Indianapolis.

BESSIE HOUSE-SOREMEKUN is the Public Scholar in African American Studies, Civic Engagement, and Entrepreneurship, Professor of Political Science, and Professor of Africana Studies at Indiana University Purdue University Indianapolis. She is also the Founding Executive Director of the Center for Global Entrepreneurship and Sustainable Development at IUPUI. She has published five books, numerous journal articles, and book chapters. Over the past fifteen years, she also created four other entrepreneurial centers, including the National Center for Entrepreneurship, Inc., the Center for the Study and Development of Minority Business at Kent State University, the Entrepreneurial Academy of the Cleveland Empowerment Zone, and the Youngstown Entrepreneurial Academy, in collaboration with a host of community partners. These centers have helped to create many new businesses and contributed to economic development processes in the United States. She has written and received twenty-one grant awards and other funding support totaling more than $1.2 million from federal, state, and local agencies/foundations, as well as several universities to conduct research on globalization and entrepreneurship and to develop business training programs to create jobs, enhance economic development, and promote economic self-sufficiency.

ELIZA MARY JOHANNES received her B.A from the Evergreen State College, M.A in African Studies and a Ph..D . in Policy Studies from the University of Illinois at Urbana-Champaign. She is currently teaching courses in African American History and Black women in the Diaspora. In addition, she is an adjunct professor at Parkland College in Champaign Illinois.

ALEXANDER KURE lectures in the Department of English and Drama of the Kaduna State University, Kaduna where he is also the Director of General Studies. His major research interest is in Comparative Literature as he interrogates gender, conflict, and environmental issues. He is a member of the Linguistics Association of Nigeria (LAN), Nigerian English Studies Association (NESA), and English Language Teachers Association of Nigeria (ELTAN).

ADEBAYO AYINLA LAWAL is Professor of History, University of Lagos. A recipient of the Fulbright and Rockefeller Fellowships, a co-editor of Fundamentals of Economic History, (Lagos, 2003), an international contributing editor and member of Organization of American Historians, he has authored over fifty chapters in books and articles in leading journals. Professor Lawal is a former head, Department of History and Strategic Studies and former sub-dean, Faculty of Arts, University of Lagos. He has just returned from his sabbatical at the Department of History and International Studies, University of Benin, Benin City. His research areas include African economic history, demographic history, corruption, African traditional medicine, the African diaspora, environmental history, and Chinese studies. He has conducted research and attended conferences in North America, Europe, Asia and Sub- Saharan Africa.

ZAHRAH NESBITT-AHMED is a doctoral researcher in the Department of Geography and Environment at the London School of Economics. She obtained a BSc in Geography from the University of Reading and an MSc in urbanization and development from the LSE. She has worked for Christian Aid, UNICEF UK and Penguin Books. Her areas of interest include the Urban Informal Economy, Gender and Sexualities, and Men, Masculinities and the Gender Division Labor. She works at the British Journal of Sociology and is currently researching on the private lives of domestic workers in Nigeria, investigating the reasons how and why they challenge or comply with the restrictions imposed upon them.

OLADUNNI O. OBILADE is a Medical House Officer at the Obafemi Awolowo University Teaching Hospitals Complex, Ile- Ife, Nigeria. She obtained her MB Ch.B at the Obafemi Awolowo University in 2009. Her current area of research interest is the interplay of poverty and power on women's reproductive health. She is a Women's Right activist and has been a volunteer member of the NGO, Women against Rape, Sexual Harassment and Sexual Exploitation (WARSHE, Nigeria) for the past ten years.

OLUYEMISI O. OBILADE is a Reader (Associate Professor) in the Department of Continuing Education, Obafemi Awolowo University, Ile-Ife,Nigeria. She obtained her Ph.D. from the same university in 1992. She holds the 2006 Executive Business Education Certificates of both the Harvard Univ. Business School (USA) and the Cambridge Univ. Judge Business School (UK). In the 2005/2006 academic session, she was an International Women's Federation (IWF) Leadership Foundation Fellow as well as the HERS-SA Grant Fellow. In 2008, she was a grant Fellow of the African Women's Development Fund (AWDF). Her research interest is in the tripartite area of adult education, gender, and development with focus on a contextual critical appreciation of the interface of different matrices of domination with gender in development within patriarchal culture. She is an active founding member of an NGO, Women against Rape, Sexual Harassment and Sexual Exploitation (WARSHE, Nigeria).

CECILIA ABIODUN OLAREWAJU is a lecturer in the Department of Home Economics, Adeyemi College of Education, Ondo. She is also a Ph.D. student in the Department of Nutrition and Dietetics, University of Agriculture, Abeokuta. She obtained her first and second degrees from Obafemi Awolowo University, Ile-Ife. She has published in local and international journals. Her research interest is the role of one's diet in the treatment of common ailments. Her Ph.D. research work is on Prevalence Rate of Non Communicable Diseases and Nutrition Evaluation of the Elderly in Ondo State.

HARMONY O'ROURKE earned her Ph.D. in African History from Harvard University and is currently Assistant Professor of History at Pitzer College in Claremont, California. Her dissertation, "Diaspora, Gender, and Identity: Remaining Hausa in the Cameroon Grassfields, c.1890 to Recent Times," is based on research funded by a Fulbright-Hays Doctoral Dissertation Research Award and the Frederick K. Sheldon Research Fellowship from Harvard University. Her dissertation is the first major study to address the history of Hausa diasporic communities in the Cameroon Grassfields. Both a social and legal history of this largely Muslim population, it focuses on the ways in which geographic dispersal and complex hierarchies of gender, religion, ethnicity, and race have shaped people's capacity to define themselves and their communities as Hausa. Grounded in rich material from Islamic court cases and oral interviews, as well as research conducted in colonial, missionary, and government archives in Cameroon, Britain, Switzerland, and France, her work illustrates the myriad ways that people of diverse social statuses and cultural backgrounds established, challenged, and exploited various forms of power and authority in order to exert anew their understanding of Hausa identity in the diaspora.

INIOBONG I. UKO is an Associate Professor of English in the Department of English, University of Uyo, Uyo. Her major area of research is African women's writing, specifically, a cross-cultural study of African and Diasporic women's writings. She has published extensively in journals and books in Nigeria, Ghana, the United States of America, and Germany. She is the author of the seminal book *Gender and Identity in the Works of Osonye Tess Onwueme.*

CELEMUSA DELISILE ZUNGU holds Master of Laws Degree from the University of KwaZulu Natal, Durban, South Africa. She is a Magistrate and also a Presiding Officer in Pietermaritzburg Equality Court, Kwa Zulu Natal province, South Africa. Prior to her appointment as a Magistrate, she was a practicing attorney, having practiced from 1997 up to 2003. She is a Vice Chairperson of Black Lawyers Association, Pietermaritzburg branch.

Zaynab Alkali 25
Zimbabwe 133, 256, 276
zina 263
Zungu 235
Zwelibongile High School 244